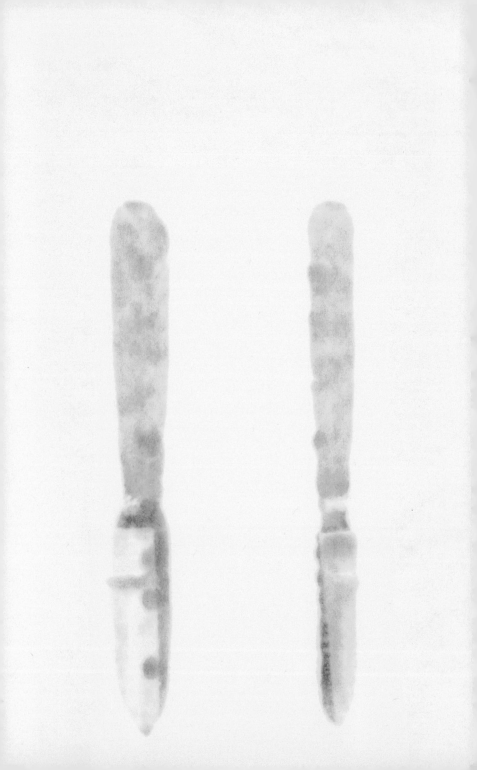

Plot Outlines of 100 Famous Plays

PLOT OUTLINES OF 100 FAMOUS PLAYS

Edited by
VAN H. CARTMELL

GLOUCESTER, MASS.

PETER SMITH

1975

63-32197 7.22.76 2-15-77

ISBN: 0-8446-0539-5

Introduction

That any two people making a selection of one hundred particularly famous plays from the world's storehouse would turn up with identical lists is almost unthinkable. That any reader of this book, with any knowledge of the drama whatever, will concur completely with the present choice is most unlikely. But at least two-thirds of the titles here presented would, I think, be included in nine out of every ten compilations of a similar nature.

The selection of these particular plays has been necessarily arbitrary, but I have tried to restrain prejudice and keep always in mind the one restriction indicated in the title—the word "famous." To qualify as such, the play need not be great, nor even good, and certainly not the latter in a moral sense, for in this category even an infamous play may yet be a famous one.

Over and above a certain indication of longevity, I have sought for plays representative of a people and an era, but even in this there are pitfalls for the anthologists. For that which is popular is not necessarily representative: the plays of Shakespeare would, in the main, present a most inaccurate picture of Elizabethan England to any but the most tutored reader. Another difficulty is one of interpretation. A play famous in the country of its origin may be virtually unknown in other lands, whereas a less prominent one may have considerable foreign vogue. It is therefore most probable that in the selection of the plays of other nations I have been guilty of many omissions. I can only plead that those chosen are, I believe, those most familiar to American readers. That all of them have at one time or another been famous is, I trust, beyond dispute.

One hundred is itself an arbitrary figure. To distinguish between the merits of the ninety-ninth selection and those of what might have been the one hundred and first is obviously splitting hairs. And although a hundred seems to be a liberal number, it still proves somewhat cramping when one considers the obvious desirability of including nearly all of Shakespeare. It is rather difficult to defend the inclusion of "Abie's Irish Rose" at the expense of "Othello," but six plays by a single author seemed a reasonable maximum, considering the limitations imposed. The six of Shakespeare actually selected were the result of a very considerable amount of balloting among acquaintances of varying degrees of mental attainment which showed an astonishing degree of unanimity. At least five of those chosen were on almost every list. "The Tempest" and "The Taming of the Shrew" ran "Julius Caesar" a close race for the sixth place.

The sequence of the plays is roughly chronological in reverse order. In each group the most recent play is given first. This is due to a purely personal belief that such an arrangement makes for greater readability, and those chiefly interested in the development of the drama in a given country may find variety in working upstream.

One further word of explanation may be necessary. The omission of any plays from the Far East is due to the fact that the technique of Oriental drama is so different from that of the Western World—and its application so remote from what the modern reader thinks of as the theater—that it seemed justifiable to limit this collection as we have.

Needless to say, these outlines are necessarily barren fodder compared with the rich nutriment to be found in the great majority of the plays themselves. It is my earnest hope that the reader will not only find this volume useful as a reference book, but will go further and sample the delights afforded by a greater familiarity with the complete texts of the original plays themselves.

V.H.C.

New York,
June, 1945

Acknowledgments

Grateful acknowledgment is made to the following individuals and organizations for their kind cooperation in giving permission to include plot outlines of plays copyrighted and published by them:

American Play Company, for *Rain*, by John B. Colton and Clemence Randolph, based on a story, *Miss Thompson*, by W. Somerset Maugham; *The Witching Hour*, by Augustus Thomas.

Walter H. Baker Company, Inc., for *The Second Mrs. Tanqueray* and *Trelawney of the Wells*, by Arthur Wing Pinero; *The Old Homestead*, by Denman Thompson.

The Bobbs-Merrill Company, for *The Yellow Jacket*, by George C. Hazelton and J. H. Benrimo, with the permission of Mrs. Hazelton and Mrs. Benrimo.

Coward-McCann, Inc., Publishers, for *Journey's End*, by Robert Cedric Sherriff, Copyright, 1929, by R. C. Sherriff.

Curtis Brown, Ltd., for *Grand Hotel*, by Vicki Baum.

Dodd, Mead & Company, A. P. Watt & Sons, Miss Rowena Jerome, for *The Passing of the Third Floor Back*, by Jerome K. Jerome; for *Pelléas and Mélisande*, by Maurice Maeterlinck.

Doubleday & Company, Inc., for *Sherlock Holmes*, by William Gillette; *Monsieur Beaucaire*, by Booth Tarkington; *Design for Living*, by Noel Coward; *R.U.R.*, by Karel Capek.

E. P. Dutton & Company, Inc., for *Six Characters in Search of an Author*, by Luigi Pirandello.

Duell, Sloan & Pearce, Inc., for *Tobacco Road*, by Erskine Caldwell.

Farrar & Rinehart, Inc., for *Lysistrata*, by Aristophanes; *The Green Pastures*, by Marc Connelly.

Richard W. Fitch, for *The City*, by Clyde Fitch, published by Little, Brown & Company.

Samuel French, Inc., for *Lightnin'*, by Winchell Smith and Frank Bacon, Copyright, 1918, by Winchell Smith, John Golden and Frank Bacon; *He Who Gets Slapped*, by Leonid Andreyev, Copyright, 1922, by Brentano's, Copyright, 1921, by The Dial Publishing Co.; *Outward Bound*, by Sutton Vane, Copyright, 1923, by Sutton Vane, Copyright, 1924, by Boni and Liveright; *The Liars*, by Henry Arthur Jones, Copyright, 1909, by Henry Arthur Jones, Copyright, 1936 (in renewal), by Dorinda Thorne; *If I Were King*, by Justin Huntly McCarthy, Copyright, 1901 (in Novel form), by R. H. Russell, Copyright, 1922, by Justin Huntly McCarthy; *The Easiest Way*, by Eugene Walter, Copyright by Eugene Walter; *Abie's Irish Rose*, by Anne Nichols (the Play), Copyright, 1924, by Anne Nichols, Copyright, 1927 (Novel), by Anne Nichols, Copyright, 1937 (Acting Edition), by Anne Nichols; *They Knew What They Wanted*, by Sidney Howard, Copyright, 1925, by Sidney Howard. All Rights Reserved.

Harcourt, Brace and Company, Inc., for *What Price Glory?*, by Maxwell Anderson and Laurence Stallings, from "Three American Plays," Copyright, 1926, by Maxwell Anderson and Laurence Stallings.

Brian Hooker, for *Cyrano de Bergerac*, by Edmond Rostand.

George S. Kaufman, for *You Can't Take It with You*, by George S. Kaufman.

Charles Rann Kennedy, for *The Servant in the House*, by Charles Rann Kennedy, published by Harper and Brothers, and in the Collected Edition of Mr. Kennedy's plays by The University of Chicago Press.

Alfred A. Knopf, Inc., and Russel Crouse and Howard Lindsay, for *Life with Father*, by Russel Crouse and Howard Lindsay.

Little, Brown & Company, for *The Barretts of Wimpole Street*, by Rudolf Besier.

Liveright Publishing Corporation, for *The Guardsman*, by Ferenc Molnár; *The Dybbuk*, by S. Ansky.

The Macmillan Company, Publishers, for *Juno and the Paycock,* by Sean O'Casey.

Dr. Edmond Pauker, Plays, for *Liliom,* by Ferenc Molnár, published by The Garden City Publishing Company, Inc.

Random House, Inc., for *Anatol,* by Arthur Schnitzler; *The Emperor Jones,* by Eugene O'Neill; *Riders to the Sea,* by John M. Synge.

Charles Scribner's Sons, for *The Petrified Forest,* by Robert E. Sherwood; *Justice* and *Strife,* by John Galsworthy; *The Bonds of Interest,* by Jacinto Benavente; *The Father,* by August Strindberg, *The Admirable Crichton* and *Peter Pan,* by James M. Barrie.

The Viking Press, Inc., New York, for *The Weavers,* by Gerhardt Hauptmann, translated by Ludwig Lewisohn, Copyright, 1912, 1940.

V. H. C.

Contents

xii CONTENTS

IRISH PLAYS

FRENCH PLAYS

BELGIAN PLAYS

ITALIAN PLAYS

SPANISH PLAYS

GERMAN AND AUSTRIAN PLAYS

Plot Outlines of 100 Famous Plays

AMERICAN PLAYS

Life with Father

BY HOWARD LINDSAY AND RUSSEL CROUSE

HOWARD LINDSAY *was born in Waterford, New York, March 29, 1899. Educated at Boston Latin School and Harvard, he subsequently appeared in silent pictures, vaudeville and burlesque. Joined Margaret Anglin in 1913, and remained with her company for five years. He has collaborated with other playwrights in adapting many stories to the stage—notably with Russel Crouse in "Life with Father," based on stories by Clarence Day.*

RUSSEL CROUSE *was born in Findlay, Ohio, February 20, 1893. Educated in the schools of Toledo, and began his career as a reporter on Cincinnati and Kansas City papers. Came to New York and was a columnist on the* Evening Post *when he wrote his first play in 1931. Thereafter, he collaborated with Corey Ford and others, mostly in writing musicals. His first collaboration with Lindsay resulted in "Anything Goes." He has also adapted plays for the screen and is the author of several books.*

It is a morning calling for even more than her usual diplomacy as Vinnie Day, wife of the forthright and somewhat irascible Mr. Clarence Day, marshals her family to breakfast in their substantial home on Madison Avenue, New York City, in the 1880's.

First, there is Annie, the new maid (one of a long procession of "new maids" in the Day household), to be introduced to Mr. Day. Annie is upset at the prospect, although Mrs. Day hopefully reassures her, "Don't be nervous. You'll get used to him." Then, visitors are arriving that day, and Father is always difficult to reconcile to such disturbances of the domestic routine. In addition, Father will not be pleased to hear that Clarence, Jr. needs a new suit. And there are a number of other sundry items which must be brought to his attention.

Mr. Day, an attractive man in his forties who fairly exudes vitality, soon appears, and his sons stand respectfully at attention as he comes down the stairway. Beside Clarence, Jr., the oldest, there are John, about fifteen; Whitney, thirteen; and Harlan, six. All the Days have red hair.

Father crisply and decisively disposes of the initial problems as his wife presents them: Clarence, Jr. shall have no new suit until he enters Yale; until then, he will wear Father's black suit, cut down. (Why can't they have a maid who knows how to serve? And now why is Annie sniffling? He hasn't said a word to her, was talking to Vinnie.) At his home there will be no musicale for the missionary fund at which, so Vinnie has planned, a lovely girl is to whistle sixteen different musical selections, all for the price of twenty-five dollars. Mr. Day will most certainly not pay twenty-five dollars for any human "pea-nut stand."

There are a few more matters to be adjudged. Father, whose conscientious auditing of Vinnie's accounts is a monthly ordeal, authorizes trial charge accounts at Lewis & Conger's and McCreery's, hoping that this will somehow simplify his task; rebukes the cook for the coffee; loudly harangues Tammany Hall as he reads the morning paper to himself. Breakfast finished, he dons his square derby, gathers up his stick and gloves, and, with dignity, marches off to his office. His departure is accompanied by the sound of crashing dishes—Annie has fallen downstairs. On being questioned, she explains that Father has threatened to put her in jail.

The visitors—Cora, an attractive cousin, about thirty,

and Mary Skinner, a pretty girl of sixteen—arrive. Clarence and Mary immediately become infatuated with each other. Later in the afternoon, Father returns and greets the guests cordially; but after they have gone upstairs he sternly rebukes Vinnie for having invited them to stay with the Days. "Damn gypsies!" he scolds. ". . . I bought this home for my own comfort. . . . Send 'em to a hotel."

Father is restored to at least temporary amiableness when he himself precipitates a real commotion. He happens to mention casually to Mary that he has never been baptized—his parents were free-thinkers. On hearing this, Vinnie is really shocked. Something must be done at once! Father must be baptized! But Father scornfully declares that he is a damn good Christian anyway, and that he certainly will not have any such folderol as a baptism performed at this late date. He goes to dress for dinner, leaving Vinnie to ponder his remarks. She realizes, all at once, that the unbaptized Father has no name in the sight of the church—they may not even be married! She gasps as her eyes fall on her children. She resolves that Father shall be baptized.

The following Sunday, Cora and Mary have finished their visit and are about to leave. Clarence, still unhappily clad in his father's made-over suit, suffers acute embarrassment when Mary comes to bid him a fond farewell. Things would be different if only he had a suit of his own! Father Day, observing their unusually agitated parting, says to Clarence, "There are things about women I think you ought to know!"

He solemnly closes the doors to the room, sits beside his son, hesitates, and then advises him that women aren't the angels he might think them; men have to run the world, a woman doesn't think at all—she gets stirred up. He adds that if a man knows how to handle women he will be all right, and that Clarence now knows all about women. Clarence, however, eagerly questions further, and Father realizes, with something of a jolt, that he is expected to be more specific. He closes the conversation abruptly: "There are some things gentlemen don't discuss! I've told you all you need to know. The thing to remember is—be firm!" He then proceeds to audit the household accounts with Vinnie. Soon she is weeping mildly, and he signs the checks in resignation. Clarence, too, has decided to be firm and not write to Mary until she has written to him. But as she leaves the house he grabs a piece of note paper and begins: "Dear Mary——"

Two days later, Vinnie is feeling a bit ill, but the boys are in a state of elation. John has come home with jobs for Clarence and himself. They are to have the sales agency for "Bartlett's Beneficent Balm—A Boon to Mankind," and are to be paid a commission of twenty-five cents on every bottle sold. Feeling that it might add greatly to the value of their sales talk if they are able to say that the Balm is used in their own home, the boys put some—quite a lot, in fact—in Mother's tea.

Three hours later, the doctor has come, the minister has been sent for, and Father arrives home in a cab. The doctor is worried—it seems almost as if Vinnie has been poisoned. But Father knows what the matter is. He tells the minister, the Reverend Dr. Lloyd, that it is something on Vinnie's mind which is making her ill, and he urges Dr. Lloyd to tell her that for him to be baptized would be just a lot of damn nonsense. The latter suggests prayer, and begins an appeal for "this miserable sinner," Vinnie. Then Father takes over in direct address to the Deity: "Oh, God! You know Vinnie's not a miserable sinner. She's a damn fine woman! She shouldn't be made to suffer. It's got to stop, I tell You, it's got to stop! Have mercy, I say, have mercy, damn it!"

Vinnie has heard her husband's voice, and, from long and faithful habit, comes to the stairway in her nightgown to see if he needs her. Father, deeply touched, blurts: "Vinnie—I know how much I need you. Get well, Vinnie, I'll be baptized. I promise . . . I'll do anything! We'll go to Europe . . . you won't have to worry about the accounts——" Vinnie faints. Father lifts her in his arms, and Dr. Lloyd, beaming with satisfaction, reminds him that he has promised to be baptized. Father, aghast, cries, "Did I? Oh, God!"

A month later, John gleefully reports earnings of sixteen dollars apiece for himself and Clarence from sales of "Bartlett's Beneficent Balm." But the boys have been paid off in bottles of the Balm, an unhappy fact which almost stuns Clarence. It seems that, on going to McCreery's to pick up a china dog his mother had ordered, he arranged for the purchase of a fifteen-dollar suit. Father refuses to be interested either in the suit or in Vinnie's new plan for having him baptized in a quiet ceremony out of town, but he definitely is interested in the china dog which he commands to be taken out of the house immediately, adding, as an afterthought, that he never will be baptized while this eyesore remains on his property. His remarks inspire Clarence with an idea: if the fifteen-dollar dog is returned to McCreery's, the Days will be credited with the exact amount to pay for his suit. Vinnie agrees that the suit won't cost Father a cent. She tells young Clarence to be sure to engage a cab to take them to the baptism next day.

In the morning at breakfast, Father suffers several aggravations: he is baffled by the china dog-and-suit transaction, irritated when Cora and Mary arrive in an extravagant cab, and incensed by the news that a neighbor's dog has died from the effects of the "Beneficent Balm." He commands the boys to return the purchase price of the Balm to every buyer—at a total cost (including the dog) of one hundred and thirty-eight dollars. This sum, Father makes clear, is to come out of John's allowance, beggaring him until he reaches the age of twenty-one!

In the midst of all this, Vinnie announces the arrival of the cab to take them to the baptism. After a final struggle —in which the true facts connected with the poisoning of Vinnie with the "Beneficent Balm" are revealed—Father weakens in recollection of his wife's narrow escape from death. He stalks out to the cab with a valedictory: "Damn! Damnation! Amen!" Clarence, in his own suit at last, is able to kneel at Mary's feet.

You Can't Take It with You

BY GEORGE S. KAUFMAN AND MOSS HART

GEORGE S. KAUFMAN *was born in Pittsburgh, November 16, 1889. He worked as a reporter on various newspapers and in 1914 became a member of the dramatic staff of the New York* Tribune, *and then of the New York* Times. *His first success was "Dulcy," written with Marc Connelly in 1921. This was followed by an extensive list of comedies, farces, and satires, written in collaboration with many distinguished writers. Among his more famous works were "Beggar on Horseback" (written with Marc Connelly), "The Royal Family" (written with Edna Ferber), "June Moon" (written with Ring Lardner), "Of Thee I Sing" (the Pulitzer Prize musical comedy written with Morris Ryskind and with a score by George Gershwin), and "Once in a Lifetime" and "The Man Who Came to Dinner" (both written with Moss Hart). Two of his later successes were his adaptation of J. P. Marquand's novel, "The Late George Apley," and "The Solid Gold Cadillac," the latter written with Howard Teichmann. Kaufman died in 1961.*

MOSS HART *was born in New York, October 24, 1904. He went to work at the age of seventeen as an office boy in a play producer's office. While there he wrote his first play— a failure. Later, Hart became associated with the Little Theater movement, directing various groups in Newark and Brooklyn. In 1929, he began work on "Once in a Lifetime." Sam Harris agreed to produce it if Hart would consent to changes in the play made, at Harris' suggestion, by George Kaufman. Thus began the collaboration between Hart and Kaufman which resulted in so many notable successes. Together they won the Pulitzer Prize in 1937 with "You Can't Take It with You." Moss Hart, alone, wrote the book for the musical play, "Lady in the Dark," and the American Air Force play, "Winged Victory." Hart achieved success as a writer of prose with "Act One," a volume of autobiography, and climaxed a successful career as a theatrical director by staging the record-breaking musical comedy, "My Fair Lady." He died December 20, 1961.*

Life is pleasantly daft at the roomy uptown New York City home of Grandpa Vanderhof, a lively little man of seventy-five who, for the last thirty-five years, has been determinedly "relaxing" and having fun—collecting snakes and attending commencement exercises. He has a small income from a rented house and an interesting family who, like Grandpa, do just as they please.

Penelope Vanderhof Sycamore, or Penny, his daughter, a gentle and plump little woman of fifty, is writing her eleventh play; playwriting suggested itself to her eight years ago when a typewriter was delivered to the house by mistake. Essie, her pixie daughter, about twenty-nine years old, a dance enthusiast, wears ballet slippers almost all the time, but as a vocation she makes Love Dream Candies which her husband, Ed Carmichael, a devotee of the xylophone, sells. Paul Sycamore, Penelope's husband, manufactures fireworks in the cellar, with the assistance of Mr. DePinna who came to the house to deliver the ice eight years ago and has remained ever since. Granddaughter Alice is a lovely, quiet and conventional girl of twenty-two. Rheba, the cook, and Donald, her friend and helper, complete the household, but a semi-official member is Mr. Kolenkhov, a Russian dancer who gives Essie dancing lessons.

Essie, while dancing dreamily to Ed's xylophone, has just remembered to inform Grandpa that there have been a few letters for him within the last couple of weeks from the United States Government (nobody remembers just what became of them). Alice comes home from work and

creates mild excitement when she announces that the boss's
son, Tony Kirby, is calling for her later to go to a theater.
Alice loves and understands her family, but she begs them
to be on their best behavior when Tony arrives.

While Alice is dressing, a young man comes to the
door and Penny greets him effusively, thinking he is Kirby.
But he turns out to be Mr. Henderson, a revenue agent,
whose letters to Grandpa have gone unanswered. He wishes
to collect twenty-two years' back income taxes from him.
Grandpa questions him pointedly as to just what he would
get for his money, and Mr. Henderson leaves with threats.
On the way out he bumps into pet snakes, hears a test
salute of bombs from the cellar, and abandons his Panama
hat which, by coincidence, just fits Grandpa.

Mr. Kirby, a nice young man not long out of Yale, arrives soon after and meets the beaming family. Before
Alice can hurry down, the friendly Grandpa has offered
him a tomato, Penny has passed the candy from a plaster-
skull ashtray, and Mr. DePinna thinks he remembers having read that Tony's father was recently indicted. Alice
and Kirby leave for the theater.

When they return later in the evening, the living room
is in darkness, but the strains of Donald's accordion can
be heard upstairs, and there comes an occasional loud
bang from the fireworks-makers in the cellar below. Donald comes down in his nightshirt for some candy, and
Penny, in a bathrobe, makes a brief appearance to get her
manuscript, "Sex Takes a Holiday." Essie and Ed return
from a movie and casually discuss Grandpa's approval of
their having a baby. Tony eventually seizes an opportunity
to tell Alice that he loves her. She confesses her love for
him, but declares that her family is of a different world
from his—"it just wouldn't work." Tony convinces her, however, that they can't live apart.

A week later, there is much activity—and worry for
Alice—in planning a get-acquainted dinner for Tony's parents who are invited for the following night. A visitor of
the day is Gay Wellington, an actress whom Penny has
met on a bus and has induced to read her play. Miss

Wellington, an enthusiastic drinker, now quite subdued by gin and the effect of seeing Grandpa's snakes, has passed out on a couch.

Details of the epochal party have been settled by evening, and Penny, in a smock and rakish tam-o'-shanter, is finishing a painting of a discus thrower—Mr. DePinna, in Roman costume, posing as model. Miss Wellington, still prone on the couch, opens her eyes, sees Mr. DePinna, and passes out again. Grandpa has found some feathered darts and is throwing them at targets, giving an occasional regretful glance at Miss Wellington's adequate posterior. The huge and hairy Mr. Kolenkhov, shirtless on this hot night, is teaching Essie, who is in full ballet costume, some new dance turns. Ed is playing the xylophone. The doorbell rings, and into this setting come the three Kirbys, in full evening dress. Tony, it seems, has confused the date of the party and they have arrived a day early.

The Kirbys are greatly embarrassed and start to withdraw, but Grandpa insists that they come in. Penny seconds him with the assurance that the Sycamores were "just spending a quiet evening at home." The snakes removed to quiet Mrs. Kirby, Penny sends Donald to the A. and P. for frankfurters (Mr. Kirby suffers from indigestion), canned corn and soup.

For Alice, who comes home just then, the evening is a nightmare. First, Miss Wellington snorts back to consciousness and weaves out of the room, pausing to call "Hello, Cutie!" to Mr. Kirby and to coyly muss his hair. After dinner, Mr. Kolenkhov, discussing wrestling, suddenly hurls Mr. Kirby to the floor and sits triumphantly upon him. Later, at Penny's insistence, they all play a word game which develops hints of some discord between the elder Kirbys.

Alice gives up when Mrs. Kirby suggests that it is time to go. She tells Tony that their romance is impossible. The elder Kirbys leave, but soon return—bundled in by Department of Justice agents who have become suspicious of the random messages (such as "Dynamite the Capitol!") which Ed, who just likes to print, has been enclosing in his candy boxes. The G-men find the explosives in the cellar and order everybody under arrest. They refuse to permit Mr. DePinna to return to the cellar for his pipe and, as the party is marshaled for the trip to a police station, a year's supply of firecrackers, pinwheels and assorted fireworks explodes and shakes the house.

The following day, the Sycamores are somewhat subdued by the collapse of Alice's romance, although they cheer up a bit when they recall that Mrs. Kirby was put in the same cell with Rheba and a strip-teaser, and that Mr. Kirby was discomfited when ordered to share his bath with Donald. All, after a night in jail, have received suspended sentences for making fireworks without a license. Mr. Kirby refused to explain why he was on the premises at all.

Tony has come on a fruitless errand to see Alice. Kolenkhov is there and asks if he may invite the Grand Duchess, Olga Katrina, who has the day off from her duties as a waitress at Childs, to dinner. The Sycamores are delighted, and the Grand Duchess—every inch the Grand Duchess, despite an ancient dinner gown and a moth-eaten fur—sweeps in. Soon she has taken charge of the kitchen to make blintzes.

Mr. Kirby comes to fetch Tony (who is now ready to go, after repeated rebuffs by Alice), but he is halted by Grandpa's challenge that Tony is too nice a boy "to wake up twenty years from now . . . mixed up and unhappy" the way his father is. The outraged Mr. Kirby shouts that he is not unhappy. He views as un-American Grandpa's argument that money-chasing isn't everything—you can't take it with you. Tony bolsters Grandpa's argument for the happy life, reminding Mr. Kirby that he still secretly cherishes a forbidden boyhood saxophone in the back of his clothes closet. Tony confesses that he purposely confused the date of the dinner party so that his people could see a really happy family. He declares that he is through forever with his father's office which he hates.

Mr. Kirby is looking at his son with new interest when the Grand Duchess appears to ask how many there will be for dinner. "The Czar always said to me, 'Olga, do not be stingy with the blintzes,'" she tells them. Grandpa presents the awed Mr. Kirby, who agrees that he would like very much to stay to dinner with Tony who is now embracing the happy Alice. Penny interrupts to recall that another letter from the government is in the icebox. But this letter apologizes to Grandpa who, the government has discovered, is dead and doesn't owe a cent. It seems that, eight years ago, the Sycamores had casually buried Charlie, the milkman who had stayed with them for five years, under Grandpa's name, since no one knew his own name, and now Grandpa has simply told the government that he is Martin Vanderhof, Jr.

Dinner is served, and Mr. Kirby reluctantly defers his intensive study of Ed's xylophone to go to the table. Penny warns him that he must be careful of his indigestion, but he answers, "Nonsense! I haven't any indigestion," as the blintzes are borne in.

Tobacco Road

BY ERSKINE CALDWELL

Born in White Oak, Georgia, December 17, 1902. After a public school education, he attended Erskine College, South Carolina, the University of Virginia and the University of Pennsylvania. Following his graduation he became a stagehand, professional football player, newspaper writer, lecturer and editor. In 1933 he received the Yale Review award for fiction. A few of his many works are, "God's Little Acre," "Journeyman," "The Bastard," "You Have Seen Their Faces," and "North of the Danube"—the latter two in collaboration with his former wife, Margaret Bourke-White. "Tobacco Road," which was written in 1932, ran for seven and a half years, and broke all records for number of performances on the stage.

In a squalid shack in Georgia's back country, some thirty
miles from Augusta, lives the remnant of the Lester family,
last of many generations of "crackers" who once prospered
in the raising of tobacco and cotton. But the soil is exhausted now, and utter poverty, helplessness and degener-
acy are pressing the starved, ignorant survivors of once
proud pioneers toward inevitable extinction.

In the decaying Lester hovel, hard by an old tobacco
road, live Jeeter Lester, an aging, incredibly dirty and lazy
reprobate whose obsession is to remain on the land that
his forefathers and himself have tilled; Ada, his pellagra-
ridden wife, gaunt and feeble, whose only concerns are
food, snuff and the welfare of her now-married daughter
Pearl, about fourteen years old; daughter Ellie May, a
coltish girl of eighteen, cursed with a disfiguring split lip;
and son Dude, a scrawny, stupid, impudent boy of sixteen. There were some fifteen other children, but they are
either dead or gone from the home—the Lesters are hazy
now even as to their names. Jeeter's mother, a silent and
ignored old crone, completes the household.

Jeeter's grandfather had lost the farm, but a benevolent
landlord, Captain John, after granting too much food and
seed credit, failed to make the farm pay and left the
community, giving Jeeter permission to live on there, free
of rent. Shiftless and without credit, Jeeter has had no crop
in seven years, with the exception of some trifling garden
produce. He is always intending to plant a crop or cut and
sell a load of wood, "one o' these days," but passes the
time, chiefly, in dozing on the porch—between raids on his
neighbors' gardens and cellars—and piously waiting for God
to provide.

Jeeter now is unsuccessfully trying to patch the ragged
inner tube for his wreck of a car, his last possession, but
one so worthless that even the sheriff has scorned it. Dude
is amusing himself by bouncing a ball off the battered wall,
amiably calling his father a dirty old liar and driving the
terrorized Grandma under the porch by threats to hit her
in the head with the ball. Ada appears, and Dude enter-
tains himself further by predicting that she will be buried

in the ragged dress she wears, not the "stylish" one for which she is constantly longing, and that Jeeter's body will be left in the empty corncrib for the rats.

They are interrupted by the arrival of Lov Bensey, Pearl's husband, a huge, shambling "cracker" who earns a dollar a day at the railroad coal chute. Lov, carrying a sack of turnips which he guards carefully, has come to Jeeter with a protest. It seems that Pearl refuses even to talk to him, runs into the bushes when he appears, won't do any cooking and, worse, "She don't sleep in the bed with me, that's what." He has given Jeeter seven dollars in consideration of the wedding, and is both bewildered and outraged.

Jeeter is vainly trying to bargain with Lov for some of the turnips in exchange for a paternal order to Pearl to mend her ways, when Dude calls attention to the fact that Ellie May, long smitten with Lov, is "horsing"—wriggling on the ground and squealing in primitive passion. The neglected Lov sits beside her, but as he begins to fondle her, Jeeter makes a lunge for the turnips and scuttles off into the brush. Ellie May, aided by Grandma and Ada, who are armed with sticks, succeeds in delaying Lov's pursuit of Jeeter, and he finally goes gloomily home.

Another visitor to the barren yard is Sister Bessie Rice, a portly woman preacher of about forty, loud and hearty. Jeeter appears at a run, pursued by Dude who seizes him at the gate and extracts more turnips from Jeeter's pockets, then throws his father to the ground. Sister Bessie joins the family in eating the turnips, obliges with individual prayers for all, reserving the last for Dude whom she forces down beside her in the praying circle, holding his legs in her arms. Dude finds this not unpleasant, and Sister Bessie fondly intimates that she is considering him as her next husband. Peabody, a neighbor (Jeeter boasts that he is the sire of roughly half of Peabody's children), interrupts them with the news that old Captain John is dead and his son, Captain Tim, is returning. Jeeter, hope renewed, excitedly prepares to burn off his fields, expecting credit and benevolence once again.

The next morning at dawn, Sister Bessie returns. The

Lord has told her to marry Dude, and she finally corners
the bashful youth. He agrees to the wedding when she
promises to buy a new automobile (with a loud horn) with
the eight hundred dollars' insurance left by her late husband, and also to set him up as a preacher. They go for
the license. Then Lov reappears with the news that Pearl
has run away. When Lov has gone, Jeeter leaves for the
fields, but he returns, dragging Pearl who has been hiding
in the brush. She rushes into her mother's arms. Jeeter
thoughtfully fingers her dress to note the new maturity of
her figure. He orders that she go back to Lov, but Ada
informs Jeeter that he isn't her father; Pearl was the issue
of a passer-by when Jeeter was absent borrowing a mule.

While Jeeter and Ada have gone to steal some corn
meal, Lov makes a pitiful plea to Pearl to return, but Ada
returns and routs him with a stick. Jeeter urges that Lov
take Ellie May, but he goes somberly off and the scorned
Ellie May falls upon her pretty sister in a jealous rage.
The sound of an automobile horn breaks in, and Dude and
Bessie return triumphantly in a new car; it lacks a fender,
however, since Dude had driven into a wagon, probably
killing its Negro occupant. Bessie proceeds to marry herself
to Dude, then promptly pulls him into the house. All
the Lesters are peering through the windows with interest
when Captain Tim and Payne, a banker, arrive.

They bring the shocking news that the bank now owns
the property—Jeeter must either leave or pay a rent of a
hundred dollars a year. He is offered work in the mills at
Augusta, but will not leave his land. Jeeter is suddenly inspired with the thought that Tom, his most prosperous son
who lives not far away, undoubtedly will provide the hundred dollars. He hurriedly sends Dude and Bessie off in the
car to Tom to get the money.

The next morning, Jeeter, who has slept on the porch in a
vain wait for Dude and Bessie, learns that Grandma has
disappeared. He reflects complacently that she probably
has been burned to death in the fields. Says he, "I'll go out
and look around one of these days." Lov appears with a
gift of precious salt pork; he has "just got to have Pearl

back." He finally offers Jeeter two dollars a week if Pearl will return to him, but again Ada sends him away. Ada begs Jeeter to use the money from Tom to take the family to Augusta where the women will support him by working in the mills, but Jeeter refuses.

Dude and Bessie return (minus a headlight from another collision) to tell Jeeter that son Tom suggested that his father go to hell; he also casually observed that Sister Bessie "used to be a two-bit slut when he knowed her." Jeeter desperately tries to borrow Bessie's car so that he may sell a load of wood, but they find that a wheel is bent and that they have been driving without oil—besides, Bessie won't let him have the car anyway. Jeeter calls Bessie an old bitch, and she is replying that he and all the Lesters are of parallel ancestry, when Jeeter, suddenly seeing Pearl, recalls Lov's offer. Here is his salvation.

Jeeter grabs the girl, intending to return her to Lov, and fights off Ada while he sends Dude and Bessie for Bensey. Ada helplessly runs after them, and, as the car is started with a proud blast of the horn, she gives a shriek of agony. Ada drags herself back on hands and knees—the wheels of the car have passed over her. Jeeter, still holding Pearl's arm, relents enough to let her embrace Ada, but he won't grant his dying wife's appeal to free Pearl. Suddenly Ada bites Jeeter's hand, and Pearl flashes down the road with a cry, "Good-bye, Ma." Ada laughs bitterly once, then dies.

Lov has appeared, and Jeeter tells him and Dude to dig a deep hole in the fields and to bury Ada there. "Ada would like that," he says. He asks a prayer from Sister Bessie, then sends Ellie May off to Lov's home. "Be nice to him, and maybe he'll let you stay. He'll be wanting a woman pretty bad right now," he tells her.

He looks down at Ada's body and says: "You shouldn't have done that, Ada. One way and another it didn't do anybody much good, except maybe Pearl." He sits on the porch, leaning against an upright, hat tilted over his eyes as when he dozes, and abstractedly pinches a bit of soil to dust between his fingers. Then movement ceases, and a rotten shingle falls from the sagging porch.

The Petrified Forest

BY ROBERT E. SHERWOOD

ROBERT SHERWOOD, *three times winner of the Pulitzer Prize, was born in New Rochelle, New York, in 1896. He wrote his first play, "Barnum Was Right," for the Hasty Pudding Club at Harvard. Sherwood's education was interrupted when, during World War I, he enlisted in the Canadian Black Guard, serving in France. After many months in a hospital, as a result of a wound received in battle, Sherwood returned to America an ardent pacifist. He modified his philosophy only when, at the time of World War II, he came to feel that, in this instance, war was the only answer. Sherwood's literary career began when he became associated with Robert Benchley and Dorothy Parker on* Vanity Fair. *Upon his resignation from that magazine, Sherwood was an editor of* Life, *covered motion pictures for the New York* Herald, *was literary editor of* Scribner's. *"The Road To Rome," his first produced play, was an outstanding success. Sherwood then devoted his entire time to playwriting, and created such outstanding dramas as "Idiot's Delight," "Abe Lincoln in Illinois," and "There Shall Be No Night." He carried his plays around in his head and wrote them with unbelievable speed. Alfred Lunt and Lynn Fontanne have been starred in many Sherwood plays. Some of Sherwood's critics accused him of writing "hokum," but the consensus of opinion is that he was a master of American comedy, as well as a serious dramatist who grew in stature in his later years. His last productions were concerned with serious themes of timely and universal significance. He died in 1955.*

In the Black Mesa Bar-B-Q lunch room in Arizona, late one autumn afternoon, Gabby Maple, young, pretty and resentful, listens to Bozo Herlitzlinger's amorous proposals with skepticism and little interest. She doubts that Bozo, an ex-football player and erstwhile gas station attendant, can prove a satisfactory substitute for her long-cherished desire to visit France. Gabby and her father, Jason Maple, were deserted when Jason's bride of the first World War returned to her native France, unable to bear the lonely Arizona desert any longer. Gabby, instead of resenting her mother's abandonment, longs to follow her. Jason, too, has his dream of leaving the crossroad lunch room to own a big gas station in Los Angeles. However, his father, Gramp Maple, a veteran of pioneer days, insists that the desert offers enough challenge for anyone, and refuses to sell the lunch room or to allow his son and granddaughter to use any of the twenty thousand dollars he has invested in Liberty Bonds. Everything will be theirs someday, but his money is not for corner sites in Los Angeles or wild trips to France.

In the lunch room, Bozo has surprised Gabby reading the poems of François Villon, which, in his own vernacular, are "pretty hot pash," and he assumes Gabby to be ready for love. Bozo's ideas of romance are largely physical—indeed, most of Bozo runs to brawn. He kisses her. "You're going to love me, Gabby," he tells her.

Alan Squier, a thin, vague stranger, with an air of having seen better days, comes in. Bozo, who is confident of success with Gabby, leaves her to attend to this customer. Gramp appears. He brings news that Duke Mantee, a notorious gunman, and his gang have just shot up a near-by town and are reported to be escaping along the highway that runs past the lunch room. Gramp, a hearty admirer of the two-gun school, boasts to Alan that Billy the Kid had once shot at him. Jason, a defender of law and order, stops in at the lunch room to tell Gabby that he is on his way to a Legion meeting, called to make plans for waylaying the bandits. Gabby is more interested in Alan than in the gun-men when she learns that Alan is a writer. Here is a flesh-and-blood specimen from the world she longs to know.

Gabby tells Alan of her mother and of her longing to visit her in France. Alan looks at Gabby's book.

"You share your mother's opinion of the desert . . . but you'll find solace in the poems of François Villon," he assures her. He tells Gabby of his own life; of the stark novel he had written at twenty-two; how his publisher's wife divorced her husband to marry Alan, supporting him in temporary luxury until he failed to prove a celebrity and to thus fulfill the promise of her ambitious dreams. She then divorced him. Gabby wonders what Alan wants now. "I suppose I've been looking for something to believe in," he tells her.

"What have you found?" Gabby wonders.

"Nothing so interesting as an old man who was missed by Billy the Kid and a fair young lady who reads Villon," Alan answers.

Gabby shows Alan some paintings she has done. He is impressed with her potential ability. When she says she must be free to develop her talent, Alan points out that she had been thoroughly engrossed with Bozo a few moments before. Gabby dismisses Bozo's efforts briefly. "Where are you going now?" she asks Alan.

Alan will go wherever the road leads. This road, Gabby tells him, goes to the Petrified Forest, a place of dead stumps and trees.

"A suitable haven for me," Alan observes. "Perhaps that's what I'm destined for—to make an interesting fossil for future study."

Gabby suggests that they both go to France. Alan can have Bozo's job until Gramp's money is hers. He won't have to marry her. Alan is touched with her offer, but he refuses it. Bozo, returning, is angered when he finds Alan kissing Gabby farewell. He is further disgusted when he finds that Alan cannot pay for the meal he has just eaten. Motorists, Mrs. Chisholm, a chic, world-weary woman, and her husband, a pillar of capitalism, enter. Gabby now suggests that the Chisholms give Alan a lift in their car. She slips him a dollar. After he has gone, Gabby, realizing the small possibility of escape from this life, turns to Bozo. But

Bozo's triumph is brief, for Alan returns. The Chisholm car has been captured by the gunmen, and the robbers, led by Duke Mantee, are on the way to the Black Mesa. Gramp is delighted when the outlaws appear. While the gangsters eat, Alan has several drinks and becomes voluble. "All evening I've had a feeling of Destiny closing in——" he murmurs.

Duke, the bandit, finishes his meal. Now he must wait for his girl who escaped in a second car. They have arranged to meet here. Gramp, the happy host, wants to know if they intend to spend the night. "Can't say, Pop," Duke tells him, carelessly. "Maybe we'll decide to get buried here."

"You'd better come with me, Duke," Alan suggests. "I'm planning to be buried in the Petrified Forest. . . . It's the graveyard of the civilization that's been shot from under us. That's where I belong—and so do you, Duke. For you're the last great apostle of rugged individualism——" Alan has spoken with the bitter realization of his failure in a world peopled by such men as Chisholm, with his go-get-it tactics; Gramp, living in the past, suspicious of change; Jason, with his calm acceptance of things as they are. He has recognized that his own passive resistance is akin to Duke's more spectacular rebellion.

Bozo decides to attempt to capture the gangsters. Just then, the Chisholms return. They distract Bozo and a gangster shoots him in the hand. Mr. Chisholm offers Duke two hundred dollars to let him and Mrs. Chisholm leave, but Duke, pocketing the money, refuses.

Gabby now tells Alan that she loves him. However, he is too obsessed with his own failure to respond emotionally, and tries to persuade Gramp to give her the money to be free. When Gramp refuses, Alan makes his five-thousand-dollar insurance policy payable to Gabby, then asks Duke to shoot him—taking care, of course, that Gabby knows nothing of his plan. Duke agrees. Gramp thinks no woman is worth five thousand dollars, but Alan calls him a forgetful old fool. "Any woman is worth everything any man has to give," he tells Gramp. As for Gabby, he says, "She's the renewal of vitality and courage—and aspiration—all the strength that has gone out of you. Hell—I can't say what she is—but she's essential to me, and the whole damned country and the whole miserable world."

Mrs. Chisholm, oddly enough, seems to understand. "You're in love with her, aren't you?" she says to him. "Yes, —yes, I suppose I am," Alan answers. "I want to show her that I believe in her . . ." Mrs. Chisholm wonders if Alan means all that he says about a woman's value. He assures her that he does, then points to Duke as another man who feels the same way. Duke would be bound for Mexico and safety this moment—had he not decided to wait for a girl.

Gabby, unaware of Alan's intention, begins to doubt her own vision. Alan tries desperately to renew her faith in herself. She must have the courage and strength he has lacked, he insists. Mrs. Chisholm tries to help Alan. When Mr. Chisholm tries to stop her interference, she turns on her husband in a rage. What does he know of her? He has filed her soul away as he has everything else he touches, she scoffs. They are headed for a sensational quarrel when Alan diverts their attention by asking Duke what sort of a life he has had. "A hell of a life," Duke answers.

"I don't believe it," Mrs. Chisholm tells him. "You've had the one supreme satisfaction of knowing you're a real man."

Alan, knowing that Duke will soon carry out his promise of the bullet, tells Gabby that he loves her. "You'll find a line in that verse of Villon's that fits—something about 'Thus in your field my seed of harvestry will thrive.' I've proven barren soil for that seed—but you'll give it fertility and growth and fruition," he assures her. Gabby interprets his professed love as something they will share—they will be happy together, she believes. Alan agrees that they'll be happy—in a funny sort of way—for he has found what he wanted.

Jason now returns, accompanied by two Legionnaires, with the news that a posse is headed for the Black Mesa. Duke's "moll" has been captured—and she has talked. Duke hastily prepares to escape, using the Chisholms, their chauffeur and the Legionnaires as shields aboard the Chisholm car. He has forgotten Alan.

"Duke!" Alan calls.

"Do you still want it?" answers Duke.

"It's no matter whether I want it or not. You've got to——"

"O.K., Pal," Duke says. He shoots him.

While the gangster escapes, with the posse in hot pursuit, Alan lies dying. Gabby refuses to believe that he will die. "It's all right," she tells him. She insists that she can make him live.

"I had to come all this way to find a reason," Alan breathes. "Oh, if people only had guts enough, they'd always find . . . The Duke . . . understood what it was I wanted. . . . I hope you'll——"

Gabby, holding Alan's body, says, almost to herself, " 'Thus in your field my seed of harvestry will thrive—For the fruit is like me that I set. . . .' "

The Green Pastures

BY MARC CONNELLY

Born in McKeesport, Pennsylvania, December 13, 1890, his full name being Marcus Cook Connelly. Was educated in Washington, Pennsylvania. Became a reporter on the Pittsburgh Dispatch *and wrote a humorous column for the* Gazette Times. *He later contributed verses and articles to magazines, but is best known for his lyrics written for many musical comedies. Collaborated on "Dulcy," "To the Ladies," and "Merton of the Movies." Among his other successful plays are: "Beggar on Horseback," "The Farmer Takes a Wife," "Helen of Troy, New York." "The Green Pastures," written in 1930, received the Pulitzer Prize award.*

In a Negro Sunday school in Louisiana, Mr. Deshee, the preacher, is picturing for the wide-eyed children the miracle of Creation and the glories of Heaven as he envisions them.

Just before the Creation, the angels—all Negroes—are having a gay old-fashioned fish fry. Men Angels, Mammy Angels and the little Cherubs are all in their Sunday best of spotless robes and fluttering wings, the children in stiffly starched suits and dresses, the girls with ribbons in their hair and on their wing tips. A chorus of spirituals is hushed as the Angel Gabriel raises his hand and shouts: "Gangway! Gangway for de Lawd God Jehovah!" God, a tall, benign old Negro in black Prince Albert coat, black trousers, white shirt and bow tie, enters.

After a brief ritual, the picnic goes on, God playing happily with the children—until he samples the custard. He says: "Dis custa-d don't seem seasoned jest right. It needs jest a little bit mo' firmament in it . . . I'll jest r'ar back an' pass a miracle. Let it be some firmament! I don't want jest a little bitty dab of it. Let it be a whole mess of firmament!"

In the darkness, a Mammy Angel complains that there is too much firmament, the Cherubs are getting wet and may catch cold, so God passes another miracle. "Let dere be a place to dreen off dis firmament! As a matter of fac', let dere be de earth! An' let dere be de sun, an' let it come out an' dry my Cherubs' wings!"

The sunlight comes, and the angels peer over a railing, exclaiming at the sight below. God doesn't have to look to see it. He says: "It's a good Earth. I ought to have somebody to enjoy it. I'm goin' down dere . . . an' pass out one of de most impo'tant miracles of all: Let dere be man!"

So Adam and Eve are created, but they eat the Forbidden Fruit, and soon Cain, a stalwart young Negro, has killed his brother. God tells Cain that he had better "git." When Cain enters into a shoddy flirtation with a flashy young girl in the Parish of Nod, God reflects: "Bad business. I don't like de way things is goin' at all."

God walks over the Earth on Sunday, but finds only jazz in place of hymns, wickedness and derision all around him. He asks the flowers how they are getting on, and they reply: "We O.K., Lawd!" But a kneeling group of humans whom he thought to be at prayer turn out to be dice players, and he learns more of human sin. He is about to "wipe 'em all off de face o' de Earth" when Noah, dressed as a rural preacher, mistakes him for a fellow-minister and takes him home to dinner.

Here he reveals himself, and advises Noah to build himself an Ark to escape the coming Flood. He orders Noah to save two of every animal in the world. Noah hopefully suggests two kegs of liquor, but, at his continued insistence, there is a loud thunderclap and Noah agrees: "Yes, Lawd. One keg." Noah builds the Ark. When the Flood is over, he exclaims at the beauty of the washed Earth. God answers: "I sort o' like it myself . . . I'm gonter start all over again . . . I only hope it's gonter work out all right."

But from his office in Heaven, where two Scrubwomen Angels are busy at their cleaning, he sees again his humans "squirmin' an' fightin' an' bearin' false witness," and he decides to find a new place for his children—in Canaan. He consults Abraham, Isaac and Jacob about a leader, and agrees that "dey don' come no better" than Moses. He accosts Moses in the burning bush, makes him "de best tricker in de whole world," and sends him off to free his people from Pharaoh.

Moses' magic before Pharaoh is triumphant; he leads his people within sight of the Promised Land. But God appears and, because Moses has broken the Tablets of the law, tells him: ". . . You got to be punished. You can't go in wid your people, but you gonter have a Promised Land jest de same . . . Come, ol' man," and he leads Moses gently to Heaven.

But again the children of Israel displease the Lord with their conduct in Babylon. Here, at a night club, where the King of the Babylonians and the High Priest of the Hebrews are enjoying a floor show, a prophet reproaches them for their frivolity and is shot at the order of the King. The frightened High Priest attempts to placate the Lord; but now, wholly aroused, he enters the night club in a clap of thunder and announces: "Dat's about enough. I've stood about all I kin from you . . . yo' Lawd is tired. I'm tired of de struggle to make you worthy of de breath I gave you. So I renounce you. I repent of dese people I made and I will deliver dem no more."

He goes back to his private office, incensed against all mankind. Abraham, Isaac, Moses and Jacob plead in vain for his continued intercession for his children. Only when Jerusalem is threatened by the Romans does he weaken and return to Earth to see, especially, Hezdrel, a soldier who has attracted his attention. He finds Hezdrel guarding a temple, and identifies himself as "jest an ol' preacher from de hills" who "wanted to see how things was goin' here."

Hezdrel tells him that the defenders are not afraid to die because they have faith in God. But he abandoned you, the Lord protests. Not the God of Hosea, Hezdrel answers. "Ain't he de same Jehovah dat was de God of Moses?" asks the Lord. And Hezdrel replies: "Dat ol' God of wrath an' vengeance? Oh, no. We got annudder God now—de God o' Hosea, de God of mercy." To the Lord's query if it isn't the same God, Hezdrel doesn't know, but says that they found him in the only way, through suffering.

The Lord, leaving, asks Hezdrel if he wants him to bear any message, and Hezdrel says: "Tell de people in de hills dey don't have to be afraid if dey only trust in de God o' Hosea." The Lord replies: "I will. If dey kill you, Hezdrel, I'll bet dat God of Hosea'll be waitin' for you."

Back in his armchair, God is looking pensively at his angels, and Gabriel asks: ". . . Lawd, is it somethin' serious?" God answers: "Very serious, Gabriel. I'm jest thinkin' about somethin' new dey found out. . . . Mercy . . . through sufferin'. . . . It's awful important. . . . Did he mean dat even God must suffer?"

A voice from below pierces the silence of Heaven: "Dey goin' to make him carry it up dat high hill! Dey goin' to nail him to it! Oh, dat's a terrible burden for one man to carry!"

God rises with a sad smile and murmurs, "Yes!" as the angels chorus, "Hallelujah, King Jesus!"

They Knew What They Wanted

BY SIDNEY HOWARD

SIDNEY COE HOWARD, *a Californian, was a product of the George Pierce Baker Workshop at Harvard, the school which influenced such men as Eugene O'Neill, Robert Sherwood and Thomas Wolfe. His literary career was interrupted by service in the American Ambulance Corps and Aviation Corps during the first World War. After his return from overseas, he worked as special investigator and feature writer for the* New Republic *and* Hearst's International. *"Swords," his first play, which opened in New York in 1921, starred Clare Eames, whom Howard later married. "They Knew What They Wanted," a character play which was awarded the Pulitzer Prize, was produced in 1924, starring Pauline Lord and Richard Bennett. Among Howard's later plays are, "The Silver Cord," "Half Gods," and "The Late Christopher Bean." His plays evidence a keen sense of characterization and expert craftsmanship. At the time of his death in 1939, Howard was working on a dramatization of Carl Van Doren's biography, "Benjamin Franklin," which was to have been the concluding production for the second season of the Playwrights' Company, in which Howard's associates were Robert Sherwood, Maxwell Anderson, S. N. Behrman and Elmer Rice.*

Father McKee peers 'round Tony Patucci's living room where Joe, the handsome young migratory worker who helps manage Tony's vineyards, is making festive preparations for his employer's wedding, now only a few hours away. Tony, a middle-aged Italian, magnificent in his Sunday best, is delighted to have an audience with the priest. Father McKee must hear how sweet and plump and pretty his fiancée, Amy, is—how he saw her at an Italian restaurant in San Francisco where she was a waitress, fell in love with her, and, on returning to California's Napa Valley, had Joe write for him innumerable letters, describing to Amy his comfortable home, the Ford, the vineyards; how, after sending Amy a photograph, she had agreed to come to Napa Valley to marry Tony. Father McKee fears that Tony is making a mistake. He suggests that he would do better to choose a girl from their small parish. But Tony feels sure that his bride will not be any of the dire things Father McKee suspects her to be. "She like a rose, all wilt'. You puttin' water on her an' she come out most beautiful," he tells the padre.

Tony has been celebrating his good fortune all morning with wine and he is far from steady, but he insists on starting off to meet his bride who is due at the railroad station. However, Amy arrives alone, hurt and displeased because her prospective husband has not met her train. Father McKee and Joe console her, and she soon becomes absorbed in admiration of the house, happily reflecting that she has escaped the city where she had been forced to find work. "When I come in here and seen all you done, fixing things up for the wedding and all . . . and smelt that wind, I said to myself, 'Amy, old kid, you're in the gravy,'" she enthuses. "You're dead right," Joe agrees. "That's just what I said when I came here . . . I only intended to stay a few days. I'm that way, see? I been here goin' on five months now."

When Father McKee leaves them alone for a few moments, Joe and Amy find that they can talk easily and naturally. He tells her of his Communistic ideas, of his work in San Francisco as a labor organizer for the I.W.W. While Amy understands few of his theories, she listens interestedly until Father McKee's return.

While Amy unpacks her small trunk, the priest asks, "Joe, do you think she . . . ?" Joe unhesitatingly vouches for Amy's virtue, for he has sensed in her a naïve shyness, an embarrassment at the thought of marrying a stranger—though she has tried to hide her discomfort by talking with an over-degree of self-confidence.

Father McKee leaves to attend to his duties until time to return for the wedding in the afternoon. Then Joe discovers that Amy is under the impression that he is Tony. Before he can clear up this misconception, Father McKee returns, carrying Tony. He has found him on the road under the wreckage of the Ford. The doctor comes, for news of the accident has traveled swiftly in this small Italian community. His examination shows that Tony has broken both legs; his recovery will take at least six months. Tony calls continually for the astonished Amy, insisting that the marriage be performed this afternoon, in spite of his injury. The doctor finally agrees, with the proviso that he be allowed to stay and see that the bridegroom does not kill himself with excitement and wine.

Amy now tells Joe that she will not go through with the ceremony. It is revealed that Tony, in his anxiety to have her come to him, sent Amy a picture of Joe with his proposal, pretending that the photograph was one of himself. Joe makes Amy see that Tony has not maliciously deceived her. When Amy thinks of going back to her old job—and the other waitresses' cutting remarks and curious questions—she relents, agreeing to marry Tony.

The doctor is amazed that Tony is able to survive his accident, to take part in the wedding and the fiesta that follows, without suffering any ill effects. Before leaving that night, he assures Tony that he has only to take care of himself to be well and strong again. The neighbors, after drinking quantities of Tony's wine and exhibiting their innumerable children for his approval and envy, say good night.

Amy sits alone in the living room, tiredly removing the diamond earrings that are Tony's bridal gift. Joe, who has been settling Tony for the night, finds her there. He congratulates her on her conduct. "Some girls would have been sorer'n you was over what old Tony done to get you here. But you're a real sport . . . a great girl an' I'm all for you," he tells her, admiringly.

"Oh, for God's sake, leave me alone, can't you?" Amy retorts. "I wish I was dead." Joe tries to comfort her. She breaks into hysterical sobs, but does not move away when Joe puts his arms around her. Tony calls from the adjoining room. Amy suddenly remembers that Tony, not Joe, is her husband. She tries to go to him, but Joe bars her way into the bedroom. Amy runs out of the house. Joe hesitates only a moment before following her.

Three months later, Tony has almost recovered, for Amy has been an excellent nurse. Joe has seen that the vineyards are well cared for. Amy and Joe have not forgotten their brief affair on Tony's wedding night, but they have chosen to ignore it by mutual agreement. Amy has begun to love Tony for his kindness and generosity, and Joe is beginning to be anxious to get back to San Francisco and his union activities. Then the doctor tells Joe that Amy is going to have a child. She had come to him a week before, and he had lied to her. "I didn't have the heart . . . (to) tell her what the trouble was . . . Tony isn't the father . . . he couldn't be," he says to Joe.

Amy is terrified when Joe confirms her fears. She is grieved at the thought of hurting Tony, and is disgusted with her weakness of three months before. Joe persuades her that she must come with him to San Francisco. He promises to take care of her, even though there is no pretense of love between them. "Somebody's got to help me out," she tells him. "There ain't nobody but you. . . . Poor Tony . . . how good he's been to me. . . . And all the time he was so crazy for a kid. I can't stick around here now."

While Joe is packing his clothes, Tony, who has been sunning himself in the arbor, wheels himself into the living room where Amy is staring into space. She rouses when she sees Tony. She tells him how happy she has been here —how grateful to him she is—then confesses the whole story, insisting that he blame not Joe, but herself. "I was crazy," she says.

"You been Joe's woman!" Tony answers, incredulously. Amy tells him that she has never loved Joe—nor has she been alone with him since the night she married Tony. When Joe comes to take Amy away, Tony raises himself from his wheel chair to reach for the gun hanging on the wall. He tries to shoot the younger man. Joe manages to get the gun away from Tony, who falls to the floor. Amy hurries to get her bag, for they must go away before Tony injures himself or Joe. While she is gone, Joe promises Tony that he will take care of her, but Tony is not satisfied. When Amy returns, Tony grasps her skirt. She must stay here with him and have her baby. Joe is no good for looking after her. "You goin' listen, Amy. You don' love Joe. You love Tony," he pleads. Amy reminds her husband that everyone will know the truth if she stays—he'd regret his decision later. However, Tony overrules her protests. He has the house—all his money—and no one to leave it to. He is probably too old to hope for his own children; he will take her child instead. "What you done was mistake in da head, not in da heart. . . . Mistake in da head is no matter," Tony insists.

Joe, alone, leaves for San Francisco, the same swaggering, footloose vagabond. Amy has the security of a home. And Tony reflects, happily, "We tellin' evrabody he's Tony's baby. Den evrabody say Tony is so goddam young an' strong he's break both his leg and havin' baby just da same! Ees good, eh?"

The Emperor Jones

BY EUGENE O'NEILL

Born in New York, October 16, 1888, the son of one of America's most successful actors, James O'Neill. His full name is Eugene Gladstone O'Neill. He went to Princeton for a year, but was not a student and did not return.

*He picked up small jobs where he could find them—was
a gold digger in Honduras, a reporter and a railway conductor. For two years he went to sea; his experiences in
Central and South America furnished background and
material for his later writings. He studied playwriting at
Harvard under Professor George P. Baker. In 1918 he became associated with the Provincetown Players which presented a number of his one-act plays. "The Moon of the
Caribbees, and Other Plays of the Sea" (1919) was his
first publication. "The Emperor Jones," which expressed
with compelling power a man's reversion to primitive fear
in an African jungle, was produced in 1921. "Beyond the
Horizon" won for O'Neill his first of four Pulitzer Prizes.
Among his other plays are "Anna Christie," "The Hairy
Ape," "Marco Millions," "Desire Under the Elms," "The
Great God Brown," "Strange Interlude," "Mourning Becomes Electra," "Ah! Wilderness," and "The Iceman Cometh." "Long Day's Journey Into Night" was produced in
1956. O'Neill died in 1953.*

Rebellion has come at last to end the reign of the Emperor
Jones—formerly Pullman porter Brutus Jones in the States,
twice a murderer there, and now a contemptuous monarch
looting the blacks to whose obscure West Indies island he
had come two years ago as a stowaway fugitive from a
Southern chain gang.

Awakened in late afternoon by Smithers, his Cockney
overseer, Jones, a tall and powerfully formed Negro of
middle age, strides into his throne room in a blue uniform
coat sprayed with brass and gold, pants of bright red, and
brass-spurred patent leather boots. A pearl-handled revolver is at his belt.

In spite of Smithers' news that the blacks have taken to
the hills to cast their spells upon him, the Emperor main-
tains his swaggering confidence. Throughout his rule, an
eminence achieved largely through a legend that he could
be killed only by a silver bullet, he has craftily "loaded
de dice" for just such a day. Says he: "I ain't no fool. I

knows dis Emperor's time is sho't. What good is money if you stays back in dis raggedy country? When I sees dese niggers gettin' up dere nerve to turn me out and I'se got all de money in sight, I beats it quick."

His chuckle of confidence becomes a little forced when Smithers adds that the horses have been stolen, that it is a twelve-hour struggle through the great forest to the coast, "an' these blacks can sniff a trail in the dark like 'ounds." But Jones boasts: "Dawn tomorrow I be on de coast. Dat French gunboat takes me to Martinique, and dere I is safe wid a mighty big bank roll in my jeans."

From the hills comes the first faint, measured thumping of a tom-tom. For a moment, apprehension creeps into the Emperor's face, but still he will not admit fear. "Dose fool niggers don't known when dey's dealin' wid a man who's been a member in good standin' of de Baptist Church," he says.

So, with five lead bullets "fo' common bush niggers," and a silver one for himself should he be caught, he saunters out through the front door of the palace ("de Emperor leaves de way he comes"), and across the plain with a casual, "So long, white man."

But nightfall at the edge of the great black forest finds Jones shaken and exhausted as he throws himself on the ground to rest. The beat of the tom-tom seems louder and nearer. He gropes under the stones for the food he has hidden; he can find none. He lights a match but frantically extinguishes it as the beat of the drum seems to heighten. The trees become bewilderingly unfamiliar, and glittering eyes appear in the forest gloom.

Jones quavers: "Who dar? What's you? Git away f'om me befo' I shoots yo' up!" He fires into the darkness. With the shot, the tom-tom booms faster; the Emperor, hungry and now in terror, plunges into the forest, faced with hours of struggling through the brush to the relentless cadence of the pursuing drum.

At length, his hat lost and his uniform torn, he reels into a small clearing and stops to rest. Suddenly he hears a clicking noise and turns toward the sound. In the moonlight he sees the dim, crouching figure of a Negro, endlessly shaking dice. Jones joyfully rushes toward him with hand outstretched.

"Is dat yo', Jeff? I'se sho' mighty glad to see yo'! Dey tol' me yo' done died f'om dat razor cut I gives yo'. . . ." Then, in panic: "Ain't yo' gwine look up? Cain't yo' speak? Is yo' . . . a ha'nt?" He jerks out his gun and shoots. The figure disappears, but the tom-tom takes on a faster tempo and Jones plunges blindly away through the trees, running now.

At eleven o'clock, his spurs and sweat-soaked coat discarded, he sees a misty road, with a gang of shackled Negro convicts at work. A white guard motions Jones to take his place in line, striking him with his whip. When the guard's back is turned, Jones springs to crash a shovel upon his skull, but his upraised hands are empty. "Ghost or debbil, I kill yo' again!" he bawls and fires at the guard's back. The road and the figures disappear, and Jones leaps off in even wilder flight.

He comes to another clearing and sinks in his rags before a stump to pray for forgiveness, for safety from the blacks, for an end to "dat drum soundin' in my ears." The clearing silently fills with Southern planters and belles in costumes of the 1850's, and he realizes that he is being offered at a slave auction. In delirious rage, he fires two shots at the auctioneer, then races on. He falls at last, utterly spent, but now a chorus of black men, swaying in ghostly unison, appears around him. He finds himself singing with them in aching sorrow and desolation, then staggers on, his moaning voice trailing after him to a more insistent, triumphant pulsation of the tom-tom.

Like a sleepwalker now, he comes to an altar-like structure of rock by a river and kneels before it. A witch doctor, body dyed red, with horns upon his headdress, prances from the trees and begins a chant of sacrifice. Jones suddenly knows that it is he who must offer himself. The priest summons from the river a gigantic crocodile, but Jones fires his last bullet of silver and his tormentors disappear. The Emperor lies with his face to the ground, whimpering in ultimate misery.

At dawn, at the edge of the forest exactly where Jones had entered it, are waiting Lem, ape-faced leader of the blacks, a few of his soldiers, and Smithers. The overseer is protesting scornfully that spending the night merely in beating the drum and "castin' silly spells" is a waste of time, that the blacks should press on into the forest in their pursuit; but Lem says only: "We cotch him. You see."

Suddenly there is a snapping of twigs in the underbrush and the soldiers, at Lem's gesture, cock their rifles and glide among the trees. Shots are heard, accompanied by exultant yells. The beat of the tom-tom ceases. Says Lem: "I took um money, make um silver bullet. Make um strong charm, too." The soldiers reappear, carrying the body of Emperor Jones.

What Price Glory?

BY MAXWELL ANDERSON AND
LAURENCE STALLINGS

MAXWELL ANDERSON *was born in Atlantic, Pennsylvania, December 15, 1888. He began his career as a teacher in North Dakota and California; later went into journalism and wrote editorials for the* New Republic *and for the* New York Globe *and* World. *In 1924 his play,* "What Price Glory?," *inspired by the first World War and written in collaboration with Laurence Stallings, was the outstanding dramatic event of the season. Four years later, his play,* "Gods of the Lightning," *written in collaboration with Harold Hickerson, dealt with the Sacco-Vanzetti case. His other plays include:* "Elizabeth the Queen," "Mary of Scotland," "Key Largo," "High Tor," "Winterset," *and*

*"The Eve of St. Mark." He also wrote a number of imagi-
native radio plays. Anderson died February 28, 1959.*

LAURENCE STALLINGS *was born in Macon, Georgia, November 25, 1894. He was seriously wounded in the first
World War, returning to this country to become a dramatic
critic and literary editor of the New York* World. *With
Maxwell Anderson, a fellow staff member on the* World,
*he wrote the realistic and sensationally successful play,
"What Price Glory?." Other successful works based on his
war experiences are a novel, "Plumes" (1924), and the
scenario for the moving picture, "The Big Parade" (1925).
In 1935–36 he was leader of the Movietone Ethiopian
Expedition in connection with the Ethiopian War.*

The paths of two hard-boiled soldiers, unscrupulous rivals
in a hundred ribald romances over the globe, cross again
in 1918 when into a French farmhouse, used as headquarters by the United States Marines, there strides a
brawny, truculent sergeant who demands to see the company commander. He announces that he is First Sergeant
Quirt, new top sergeant in "this lousy outfit." He saltily
delivers other unfavorable opinions of the headquarters and
the underlings in it, and, learning that Captain Flagg is
absent, goes out to find him.

Flagg, equally as belligerent and uninhibited a personality as Quirt, arrives by another path. Enraged that his new
top sergeant has disdained to wait for him, he sends men to
fetch him. Before they return, the kittenish Charmaine,
daughter of the innkeeper, Cognac Pete, comes in, and
Flagg has to assure her that her fear that he is deserting
her is groundless; he is only going to Paris on leave—and
of course he loves her.

Charmaine has gone when Quirt returns. Flagg, without
looking up from his papers, asks him if he can handle a
company of Marines. Quirt replies, with characteristic contempt for the formalities, "Cut the comedy; you ought to
know me." Flagg whirls in profane recognition of his new

sergeant, suffering the painful recollection that Quirt has been "poison" to him wherever they have soldiered together. But he admits that Sergeant Quirt is "the best damned soldier there is," and soon the two men are reminiscing amiably about old times.

As usual, they fall to quarreling over the strategy and moral aspects of old romantic campaigns, but when the platoon leaders arrive to meet the new sergeant, Flagg tells them that Quirt is to be boss in his absence, over his second in command, Lieutenant Aldrich. Later, he orders Aldrich to lock Quirt up promptly whenever he starts drinking seriously.

Even a world war, however, is inadequate to prevent a renewal of the Flagg-Quirt philandering contest. Quirt, alone when Charmaine reënters in search of the Captain, loses no time in making overtures to her, in spite of her protest that she is Flagg's girl. An interruption, in which Quirt with a single punch quiets a disorderly soldier, quite impresses Charmaine, and she hugs him appreciatively. Quirt suggests that she may forget Flagg, now that a man of his caliber has arrived.

Flagg's revenge appears at hand eight days later when he returns from his leave. He has hardly benefited by his trip: he never reached Paris, having been jailed for fighting with a military policeman, and now has been retrieved, still somewhat drunk, from a nearby bar by Quirt. A caller is Cognac Pete who, through an interpreter, complains to the Captain that a Marine has seduced his daughter, and that the miscreant must marry Charmaine and pay him five hundred francs as balm for his outraged fatherhood.

Flagg, assuming with excellent grounds that he himself is guilty, begins to bargain, suggesting, for a start, a compromise of three hundred francs. But Cognac Pete is going to General Headquarters with his story if he is denied full reparation here. Quirt helpfully murmurs, "Think fast, Captain," and Flagg, his memories of similar treacheries aroused, suspiciously demands to know what Quirt has to say about the affair. The Sergeant is blandly ignorant, but when Flagg tells Pete to identify the seducer, Pete points with conviction to Quirt. The triumphant Captain orders Quirt to marry the girl at once, and to sign over two-thirds of his pay to her or face court-martial.

A clean-cut victory for Flagg appears certain when a runner brings word that the company is to move up, and a general enters to order capture of a German officer for questioning. Quirt dolefully returns with Charmaine and a chaplain, but recovers his wits when the general orders that they be quick about the wedding, revealing that the order is to move on in twenty minutes. Quirt calls the wedding off, convincing Flagg that he is now too much needed to permit of such diversions as weddings. He hurries out, leaving Flagg to solace Charmaine. Flagg, the sportsman, tells her that she had better just forget the episode, that they may never come back and, besides, life is chiefly designed for fun anyway. He kisses her good-bye. The company sets out for battle.

The tragedy of war intrudes later when, in a wine cellar in disputed territory, Flagg appears, almost crazed by lack of sleep and battle strain, carrying Aldrich whose arm has been shot off. Flagg puts him in a bunk, orders morphine, and sags to rest a moment upon his own bunk. Moore, another lieutenant, staggers in, crying that his men are driving him mad with their pleas for rest.

He turns on Flagg and shouts hysterically: "And since six o'clock there's been a wounded sniper in the tree by that orchard angle, crying: 'Kamerad! Kamerad!' just like a big crippled whip-poor-will. What price glory now? Why in God's name can't we all go home? Who gives a damn for this lousy, stinking little town but the poor French bastards who live here? You talk of courage, and all night long you hear a man who's bleeding to death on a tree calling you 'Kamerad' and asking you to save him. . . . Flagg, I tell you, you can shoot me, but I won't stand for it! I'll take 'em out tonight and kill you if you get in my way! . . ."

The tough Flagg leaps up in fury, then puts an arm around Moore, leads him to a bunk and gently tells him to rest. He returns to his own bunk. Quirt, after giving Moore his chocolate, asks permission to "prowl around."

As he leaves, two new lieutenants arrive. Flagg greets them with a sneer for their crisp uniforms, and suggests that perhaps two such bright young men will capture the prisoner whom the general wants so badly that he will grant leave to the entire company which effects the capture.

Quirt stumbles in, wounded in the leg. Flagg snarls that Quirt has sought a wound so he can go to Charmaine. Quirt chortles over his luck, and Flagg roars: "In ten minutes, I'm going to be wounded or bumped off, or have that God-damned prisoner!"

"Try to get killed, will you?" Quirt calls in farewell, but Flagg takes one of the new lieutenants and soon drags back the prisoner. The capture of the German means rest for his men.

Back in Cognac Pete's tavern, Flagg and Quirt meet again—Quirt, drunk, wearing a major's stolen coat over his hospital pajamas, and Flagg bleary with exhaustion and wine. They fight over Charmaine, then deal a pack of cards, the winner to get the girl and a pistol, the loser only a chance to race a bullet to the door. Flagg deals; Quirt, the loser, upsets the table bearing the candle and pistol, then runs. Flagg's shot misses him in the darkness.

The Captain has just returned to Charmaine when a runner brings orders that the company must return to the line at once. Flagg first tells the runner to report him missing, kisses Charmaine, then pulls his tired body erect. He says: "I may be drunk, but I know I'll go——" and reels out.

Quirt comes down the stair from his hiding place and asks Charmaine if she loves "Papa." She says she does, but he answers, "Then you better kiss him good-bye." He limps to the door and calls: "Hey, Flagg! Wait for Baby!"

Abie's Irish Rose

BY ANNE NICHOLS

Born in Dale's Mills, Georgia. At sixteen she went to New York because of her ambition to become an actress. She finally got small parts in "The Shepherd King," and acted in vaudeville. Soon she began writing plays herself, some of of the best-known being "Heart's Desire," "Linger Longer Lettie," and "Just Married" (in collaboration with Adelaide Matthews). Several of her plays had been Broadway successes when "Abie's Irish Rose" opened for its record-breaking run of 2,532 performances.

Abie Levy, an admirable young man in business with his wealthy father, Solomon Levy, has just been secretly married by a Methodist minister to pretty Rose Mary Murphy, an Irish girl and proud of it. Abie, wounded in the first World War, had met Rose overseas where she had gone as a singer to entertain the soldiers. They had decided to marry when she came to New York on a visit from her West Coast home.

But the newlyweds are badly frightened at the prospect of telling their fathers of the marriage, for Solomon has bitterly opposed Abie's union with any but a Jewish girl; and Rose's father, Patrick Murphy, inordinately proud of his Irish blood, is equally determined that Rose shall marry an Irishman. The mothers of both the young people are dead. Abie, fearing that his father will discharge him from his job and disinherit him, brings his bride home merely as a girl friend, hoping that his father, once he meets Rose, will accept her in spite of her nationality.

Indeed, Solomon is suspicious and hostile at their meeting, but he melts into warm hospitality when Abie, in a

panic, says that Rose's father is Solomon Murpheski. The
elder Levy promptly hails her as Jewish Rosie Murpheski,
and begins a campaign to make her his daughter-in-law.
He insists that she bring her trunk from her hotel at once,
and urges her to stay at the Levy home where she will
be assured of good Kosher food.

Supper passes without disaster, although Rose thought-
lessly uses the word blarney, infuriating Solomon. He tells
her: "I once had dealings with a fellow named Murphy,
and what he didn't do to me! Every time I hear dot void
blarney it reminds me of dot Irisher." Solomon surprises
the couple in a kiss, and delightedly announces that they
are to be married next week by a rabbi.

On the day of the wedding, a week later, Solomon has
turned the house into a veritable bower of oranges, both to
remind Rose of her California home and to provide ample
fruit for refreshment as well as decoration. But Rose is in
terror; her father is on his way East to the wedding, and
she is praying that the Jewish ceremony will be over by
the time his train, now an hour late, can arrive.

Rosie and Abie insist that the wedding take place at the
appointed time, Abie believing that his father is sure to
be won over by their observance of his religious rites. The
ceremony is underway—complete with music and brides-
maids—when the doorbell rings, and big, brawny and belligerent Patrick Murphy, a prosperous contractor in California, walks in with Father Whalen, his home priest
whom he has brought with him to perform the marriage.
Patrick at once spots the oranges, "the color of the damned
A.P.A.'s," and, fearing she is marrying a Protestant, calls
loudly for Rose.

Solomon tiptoes in to quiet the intruders, and, guessing
that Patrick may be Rose's father, asks if he is Solomon
Murpheski. Patrick blurts out his real name and says he
is looking for the home of Michael Magee, the name Abie
and Rose have fancifully given to Solomon. Further talk
discloses the truth, and Solomon rushes in to stop the wedding. But it is too late—Rabbi Samuels has tied the knot.

Solomon, in an agony, realizes that his son has married

"a little Irish A.P.A.," (he has heard Patrick contemptu-
ously use the initials), and declares that he shall die from
shame. Patrick chases him out in a rage, and Father
Whalen and Rabbi Samuels, discussing what they can do
to bring peace, discover that they once met overseas during the war when "Catholics, Hebrews and Protestants
alike . . . came to realize that all faiths and creeds have
about the same destination after all." They become friends
at once.

The fathers decide that, since Rose was married by a
rabbi under an assumed name, the wedding isn't legal; then
Abie discloses their earlier marriage by the Methodist minister. Patrick declares this to be of no account, and Solomon
goes to call his lawyer. The priest and Rabbi Samuels conspire, and, in the absence of the parents, Father Whalen
hurriedly marries them in the Catholic faith while Rabbi
Samuels valiantly guards the service from interruption.
The fathers reënter—to learn that their children again are
married, this time beyond any question.

A year later, on Christmas Eve, Abie and Rose are living
happily in a modest apartment, although they have been
forsaken by their fathers, and Abie has had to find new
work at small pay. Rose is singing an Irish lullaby to a
tiny baby in her arms, and Abie is kneeling contentedly at
her side. They put the baby to bed in an adjoining room
and return together to trim the Christmas tree. Then Rose
leaves to heat the baby's milk, and Abie, humming the
lullaby, admits two callers, Mr. and Mrs. Cohen, old family friends.

The Cohens reveal that the elder Levy is evidently lonely
and unhappy; he has said that he is going to leave his
money, not to Jewish children alone, but "to all kin's of
childrens; can children help it vhen dhere parents are
voolish?" Then Father Whalen appears, and reports that
Patrick, who has not even written to his daughter, is well
but has sent no message to her. Rose goes into the kitchen,
where the Cohens are gingerly minding a cooking ham,
and Father Whalen opens the door to admit Patrick. Patrick is bearing armloads of girls' toys, for he has never

even considered that his grandchild might be a boy. Father Whalen induces Abie to keep the others in the kitchen, and Rabbi Samuels enters as Patrick goes downstairs to fetch another load of toys. He is not disposed to forgive Rose. He has only come to see if his granddaughter looks Irish, he says; if she does, he will leave his money to her.

Rabbi Samuels has just told the priest that Solomon is sure the baby is a boy, when Solomon himself enters furtively, loaded with boys' toys. Patrick returns, and the two grandfathers, bristling at each other, ostentatiously place their toys under the tree, each deriding the other's assumption of the sex of the child. They come near to blows several times, in spite of the efforts of the priest and the rabbi to end their intolerance. Then Rabbi Samuels puts in the delighted Patrick's arms a baby boy—Patrick Joseph Levy. Then to the crestfallen Solomon he brings a baby girl, Rebecca Levy. Abie and Rose have been blessed with twins!

The joyous grandfathers, their enmity forgotten in admiration of their grandchildren, swap them—the girl to Patrick and the boy to Solomon—and give forth a fine discord of Irish and Jewish lullabys. Solomon finally expresses to Patrick the wish that the girl will someday marry "a good Irishman, like yourself," and Patrick suggests that the boy be renamed Solomon Levy and the girl Rose Mary.

Abie and Rose run to their fathers for a happy reunion and mutual forgiveness, and the Cohens come in bearing the ham. Says Patrick to Solomon: " 'Tis Christmas. Merry Christmas, Sol!" And Solomon replies warmly: "Goot Yonteff, Patrick!"

Lightnin'

BY WINCHELL SMITH AND FRANK BACON

WINCHELL SMITH *was born April 5, 1871. Was educated in the Hartford public schools and later studied at the Lyceum Theatre school of acting in New York. He did not become prominent until he produced in New York (with Arnold Daly) a series of plays by George Bernard Shaw —the first, "Candida," starting the Shaw vogue in America. Thereafter, he gave up acting and became entirely a dramatist and director, collaborating at times with other playwrights. Died June 10, 1933.*

FRANK BACON *was born in Marysville, California, January 16, 1864. He left school at fourteen and became, successively, sheepherder, photographer, newspaper writer and candidate for the California legislature. Joined a California stock company in 1890, acting over six hundred roles in the next few years. He organized a stock company in Oregon, then came to New York in vaudeville. Collaborated with Winchell Smith in writing "Lightnin'" which began a run of 153 weeks in New York in August, 1918. Died suddenly in Chicago, where he was playing, on November 19, 1922.*

Old Bill Jones, called Lightnin' because of his serene laziness, is an amiable, gentle liar, braggart and tippler, theoretically the host at his wife's Calivada Hotel, a small building directly on the California-Nevada state line at Lake Tahoe. Lightnin' claims to have been a distinguished figure in almost any vocation mentioned—lawyer, soldier, civil engineer, and promoter—but he has always "been cheated out of my share."

It was Lightnin's wife's idea to turn their home into a summer hotel (Lightnin' always takes the credit), and it now is a fairly prosperous mecca for divorce-seeking wives who wish to establish legal residence in Nevada, yet to also have the advantage of a California address. Mrs. Jones runs the place with the help of an adopted daughter, Mildred Buckley.

One of Lightnin's friends is young John Marvin, a neighbor who has hoped to make a home for his mother on some property nearby. She fell ill, however, and he took her to a hospital in San Francisco. There she died, but not before she sold the property to a lawyer, Raymond Thomas, with whom John was temporarily studying law. Mrs. Marvin was paid in worthless stock. Thomas re-sold the property to the railroad, and John is now being threatened with arrest for having removed the timber, previously sold. Lightnin' promises John that, should there be a lawsuit, he will appear to testify for him.

Thomas comes to the hotel to further a scheme for buying the hotel property from the gullible Mrs. Jones. He wants it because it contains a valuable water-power site. He is industriously pressing his project on Mrs. Jones and Mildred, who once had been employed in his San Francisco office. He is going to pay them in stock which, he says, will make them all rich.

Among the new arrivals at the hotel are Hammond, Thomas' confederate in his frauds; lanky Sheriff Blodgett, who has come to arrest Marvin; Lem Townsend, who is running for district judge; Margaret Davis, a vaudeville dancer who is seeking a divorce and at once takes the eye of Townsend; and Marvin, who has completed the clearing of the lumber on his former tract. Marvin again meets Mildred whom he has admired in Thomas' office.

Marvin learns that Thomas is employing his familiar tactics to defraud the Joneses, and he warns Lightnin' not to sign the deed until he has investigated. Mrs. Jones, who would like to see Mildred married to Thomas, promptly takes a dislike to Marvin, and Thomas strengthens her disapproval by telling her that Marvin is a timber thief. She is about to complete the deal, however, when Marvin and Lightnin' interfere, declaring Thomas and Hammond thieves. The Sheriff attempts to arrest Marvin with a Nevada warrant—but Marvin, after a scuffle, stands on the California side of the lobby and the Nevada warrant is worthless.

Mrs. Jones and Mildred are convinced that Marvin is only a mistaken busybody. Mildred declares that she detests him, but she saves him again from the Sheriff. Hammond tries to get the tipsy Lightnin' to sign the deed—but learns only that Lightnin' taught Buffalo Bill all he knew and, when in the bee business, had driven a swarm of bees across the plains in dead of winter without losing a bee!

Hammond, announcing that he has taken over management of the hotel, threatens to throw Lightnin' out unless he signs. Mrs. Jones also issues an ultimatum: the promoters are taking her and Mildred to San Francisco tomorrow, and unless Lightnin' signs he must shift for himself, she will be through with him. Lightnin', loyal to his promise to refuse his signature until Marvin approves, declines to do so, and disappears.

The conflict between Marvin and Thomas reaches the courtroom of Townsend (now elected judge) in Reno, when the railroad sues to recover for the timber. Also before the court is the case of Jones vs. Jones. Thomas, to get Mrs. Jones' signature, has induced her to sue Lightnin' for divorce, arguing that she will be better able to find and provide for her missing husband when the hotel is sold and she has ample funds. Marvin enters through a window in order to outwit the waiting Sheriff.

The gallant Townsend puts Mrs. Davis' divorce case ahead, however, and promptly dismisses her plea when Thomas substitutes for her own lawyer who is ill. The Judge himself takes over her re-examination and as promptly grants her suit, for he intends to marry her later in the day.

The missing Lightnin' now enters timidly, wearing a G.A.R. uniform, and tells Marvin that he is keeping his promise to appear to testify in his timber suit. He has been in a Soldiers' Home, has sent his wife six dollars of his pension, but has had no reply. He is thunderstruck to learn that she is trying to divorce him on grounds of non-support, cruelty and drunkenness.

Marvin defends Lightnin' and is able to bring out, in examination, much of the villainy of Thomas and Hammond. He succeeds, as well, in disproving most of their charges against old Lightnin'. But when it is revealed that Marvin is not yet an accredited lawyer, the record is erased. Marvin informs Lightnin' that he is privileged to defend himself; and Lightnin', prompted by Marvin, does an equally good job of exposing the schemers. Townsend postpones the action in order to learn more about the conspiracy, and Lightnin' offers to give his wife the divorce if she wants it and to go back to the Soldiers' Home. Mrs. Jones, however, decides that Lightnin' is right, withdraws her suit and begs his forgiveness.

Later, back at the hotel, Townsend, bringing his bride for a honeymoon, discloses that Thomas and Hammond have confessed. Marvin has won his case and the Joneses have recovered their hotel, plus a considerable sum for rental of the power rights. Lightnin' fires Hammond's hotel manager, then re-hires him as bartender, and Mrs. Jones contendedly goes back to her kitchen.

Lightnin', as a final stroke of manipulation, tells Marvin that Mildred is sorry for her mistrust and really loves him. He then gives Mildred a ring which he says, with some exaggeration, has been sent by Marvin. The lovers are reconciled and Lightnin' obligingly drinks to their happiness.

The Yellow Jacket

BY GEORGE COCHRANE HAZELTON
AND J. HARRY BENRIMO

GEORGE COCHRANE HAZELTON *was born January 20, 1868, at Boscobel, Wisconsin. Was educated in Washington where his father was a Congressman. Decided to become a dramatist, and acted in various roles with Edwin Booth's company. He later studied law at George Washington University. Practiced law for many years in New York and Philadelphia, but subsequently returned to the dramatic field. In 1912 he collaborated with J. Harry Benrimo in writing "The Yellow Jacket," his most successful play. Died June 24, 1921.*

J. HARRY BENRIMO *was born in San Francisco June 21, 1874, his full name being Joseph Henry McAlpin Benrimo. His first appearance as an actor was in that city in 1892. In 1897 he made his New York debut in "The First Born." Appeared in the same part in London later that year. For many years he acted in New York and London, and from 1912 to 1917 was co-author of various plays— notably "The Yellow Jacket" (with George C. Hazelton), "Taking Chances" (with Agnes Morgan), and "The Willow Tree" (with Harrison Rhodes). He was also the producer of many plays. Died March 26, 1942.*

Wu Sin Yin, ruler of a province in China, is unhappy despite his riches and august position in the world. He is tired of his first wife, Chee Moo, and her baby son, Wu Hoo Git, and plans a "secret and courteous" murder so that he may devote himself wholly to his second wife, Due

Jung Fah. He has tried poisoning Chee Moo's flowers, but
that killed only the birds and bees.

He summons the father of his second wife, Tai Fah
Min, who advises that Chee Moo may be discreetly dis-
patched by the farmer, Lee Sin, who "will gently plough
a furrow in Chee Moo's neck and the gods will smile on
such husbandry." The plan meets the approval of Due
Jung Fah and her scheming maid, Tso, and Lee Sin is
summoned.

The honest farmer at first refuses, since Chee Moo is
the mistress of his wife, Suey Sin Fah; but he capitulates
when told that his failure to produce the head of Chee
Moo will mean the death of his own wife. Suey Sin Fah,
who does not wholly like Tso, advises, however, that he
kill the maid instead, and alter her head to simulate that
of Chee Moo. Tso, who has overheard the original plot for
Chee Moo's death, is gloating over the prospect when Lee
Sin duly clips off her own head with his sword.

Chee Moo, meanwhile, has been warned of her peril by
a dream sent by Ling Won, the spirit of Wu Hoo Git's
great-grandfather, and is fleeing to the mountains. Ling
Won appears to her, forecasts that the baby will become
ruler if he journeys alone, and summons her to death. She
writes the child's name and a prayer on his garment in her
own blood, and then dies. Lee Sin and his wife find the
child, read the message, and take him to their home.

Twenty years later, Wu Hoo Git is grown to young manhood in ignorance of his noble birth, and Due Jung Fah's
son, the Daffodil, is on the throne. Wu Hoo Git complains
that he feels the blood of eagles in his veins, and demands
to know of his true parents. He sets out in the world to
find them when Lee Sin and his wife, fearing for his life,
still refuse to tell him the secret.

Word of his journey, however, reaches the effeminate
and crafty Daffodil, who declares that he would contend
with Wu Hoo Git "man to Daffodil," except that "it might
break my fingernails and establish a bad precedent." He
summons the humpbacked Yin Suey Gong, a dealer in
girls, to tempt the young Wu Hoo Git to destruction.

The youth appears, inquiring for his ancestors, and Yin Suey Gong, with flattery and the counsel that only wine and women matter, takes his purse of gold in exchange for the maid, Chow Wan. They leave in a flower boat "to float among lotus plants upon a silvery river of love," but before Chow Wan agrees to teach him of women, she sends him home for more gold. When he returns with a second purse, Yin Suey Gong has re-sold Chow Wan for more money to an emperor, and the enraged Wu Hoo Git cuts off his hump. Chow Wan returns, but repulses the youth for killing the source of her gold, and he restores Yin Suey Gong's hump which revives him.

But Wu Hoo Git is truly loved by Moy Fah Loy, daughter of Tai Char Soong. They meet at the tomb of her mother, Plum Blossom, where Moy Fah Loy has gone to pray for escape from her arranged marriage to another. Wu Hoo Git has knelt because the name on the tomb has captured his fancy—he has adopted the dead Plum Blossom in lieu of his own unknown mother. The two confess their love for each other, but Moy Fah Loy's nurse takes her away. The disconsolate Wu Hoo Git tries to hang himself, but is rescued by Git Hok Gar, a philosopher sent by the spirit of Chee Moo.

The philosopher assures the youth that all is not lost because he has no ancestors, and accompanies him back to the home of Lee Sin to "make himself great in right living" so that his ancestors may find him. The father of Moy Fah Loy arrives with her to revenge himself upon Wu Hoo Git for the disgrace of speaking to the maid at the tomb, and at his taunt that the youth is without ancestors and unworthy of her, Suey Sin Fah reveals the secret of his birth.

Tai Char Soong agrees that if Wu Hoo Git proves his boast to achieve his heritage, he may wed Moy Fah Loy. Bearing the sword of Lee Sin, his baby jacket and a slipper of Moy Fah Loy as his charms—his love has promised to come to his aid whenever he shall shake the slipper—he sets out with Git Hok Gar to claim his rightful place.

But the Daffodil knows of his second coming, and from

his palace conjures a series of obstacles to foil his rival. He interposes a mountain and a stream; but, armed with the courage of his sword and guided by the pattern of his mother's blood upon the baby jacket, Wu Hoo Git passes safely. Then Daffodil sends Loy Gong, the awesome God of Thunder, but Wu Hoo Git routs him, telling him: "I fear you not. My wisdom buds with courage, impregnable to gods and man, and teaches me that every word—might or heavenly power has one still higher before whom it quails— called love."

The Daffodil calls upon Kom Loi, a spider, to enmesh the youth, but he shakes the slipper of Moy Fah Loy and her disembodied spirit comes to rescue him. He desires to embrace her, but is disappointed that only her spirit has come. He chides her: "It was an august oversight. You should have brought your impressive body with you." The philosopher comments that "experience and years only can know spirit love," and they continue on their peril-strewn path.

The spirit of Tai Fah Min, the grandfather of the Daffodil, comes now to frustrate Wu Hoo Git; he confronts him in the guise of a tiger, then of a fox, but the youth cuts off his tail and slays him. The Daffodil conjures another mountain peak and a violent snowstorm, and Git Hok Gar lies down to die after giving Wu Hoo Git his coat. The youth tries to scale the mountain of progress, and is saved from freezing by the spirit of Chee Moo. He comes at last to the palace where the fearful Daffodil is waiting to pelt him with tiles.

Wu Hoo Git enters the throne room, sword in hand, and orders the Daffodil from the throne. The latter, glad to escape with his head, gives him the Yellow Jacket, symbol of rule, and chooses as his prison-to-be "a garden filled with smiling flowers."

Wu Hoo Git, declaring that his first act shall be one of mercy, grants the Daffodil's plea, and triumphantly ascends the throne of his ancestors. He shakes the slipper to summon Moy Fah Loy, and, assured when she appears that she has brought her impressive body with her, seats her at his side. Above, the spirit of Chee Moo declares, "The world and wisdom are his."

The Easiest Way

BY EUGENE WALTER

Born in Cleveland, Ohio, November 27, 1874. Did his first writing as a reporter on a Cleveland newspaper, and later on the New York Sun. He served in the U. S. Cavalry, and subsequently became advance agent for various theatrical companies. His first play was "Paid in Full" (1908). His second and most successful play, "The Easiest Way," was written in 1909. He also wrote scenarios for film plays. He died in September, 1941.

Laura Murdock, a young actress who has been playing in a Denver stock company for the season, is visited unexpectedly at a woman friend's ranch by Willard Brockton, a New York broker with whom she has been living for two years. Brockton has arranged a part for her in a show, soon to open in New York, and has come to accompany her back to the East Coast.

But Laura tells Brockton that, for the first time, she is really in love—with John Madison, a penniless young newspaperman, and that they are planning to work hard for a year or two and then be married. She has told Madison of her whole life: how she entered the theater as a girl, had scarcely been virtuous, later married and had a child, her husband finally dying a drunken suicide. Madison has confessed his own shortcomings, and has accepted her happily.

Brockton tells Laura that he will not stand in her way if she "can start out now and be a good girl." He warns her, nevertheless, that she is used to luxury and that it won't be easy for her to struggle alone again for a living. Later, he cautions Madison of the danger, promising that, should Laura ever come back to him, he will see that Madison is told. Brockton and Laura return to New York separately, and Madison remains at work in Denver, hoping to earn enough money to go to her soon.

Six months later, Laura has come to the end of her resources and her courage. She has not told Madison of her plight, but she is living in a shabby room, has pawned everything of value, and has haunted the theater district for work. But there she is virtually blacklisted—due to the influence of Brockton, she suspects.

To her room comes Elfie St. Clair, an old friend who is cared for by a wealthy man. Elfie reproaches Laura for wasting her time, telling her that the man she loves will only jilt her when her beauty has faded in waiting. "I want you to be square with yourself," Elfie explodes. "You've lost all that precious virtue women gab about. When you've got the name, I say get the game."

Laura orders her out, but a note from her landlady demanding the rent compels her to ask help. Elfie sneers a refusal and Laura breaks down. She cries: "I've stood this just as long as I can! Every day is a living horror!" Elfie induces her to see Brockton, who is waiting outside in his car. Laura puts Madison's pictures under her pillow and awaits Brockton.

When the broker comes in, she tells him simply: "Will, I'm ready to come back." He is delighted, but he insists that she make good his promise to Madison by sending him a good-bye note which Brockton dictates. The note ends: "What I am doing is voluntary . . . I do not love you." Brockton gives her money and leaves. Laura, sending for her pawned clothes, gives the maid a ten-dollar tip and hands her the letter to post. But, at the last minute, she snatches the envelope back and burns it. She throws herself across the bed, staring into space.

Two months later, Brockton and Laura, at breakfast, are reading the newspapers, and Brockton casually asks if she ever had an answer to her letter dismissing Madison. Laura says "No," but just then she receives a telegram which startles her. She is evasive as to its sender, and Brockton tells her that his newspaper reports the arrival of Madison in Chicago—that he is the discoverer of a rich Nevada mine. Brockton demands that she give him the telegram, and reads Madison's message: "I will be in New York before noon. I'm coming to marry you, and I'm coming with a bankroll. I wanted to keep it a secret, but I can't hold it any longer. . . ."

Then Laura confesses that the letter to Madison was not mailed, and that she has been corresponding with him. "I— I simply couldn't help it," she says. Brockton rages: "I feel as though I could wring your neck! Don't you know that I gave Madison my word that if you came back to me I'd let him know? You've made me out a liar—you've made me lie to a man—a man—you understand." Laura pleads for his silence so that she may go away with Madison, but Brockton refuses, granting her only the opportunity to tell John, alone, of her return to Brockton. While she is waiting for him, Elfie calls and advises her to tell Madison nothing, but to marry him quickly. Then Brockton, she says, will keep silent.

The happy Madison arrives. He demands that Laura leave with him in a few hours to be married and take a train for the West. Laura agrees to pack at once while Madison sees some newspapermen. He goes, and soon Brockton slips in with his passkey. Convinced that she has told Madison nothing, he sits down to wait for him. To Laura's hysterical pleas, he replies: "Do you think I'm going to let a woman make a liar out of me? . . . I like that boy, and I'm not going to let you put him to the bad." However, after she tempestuously lays her guilt before him and cries out her hatred, Brockton leaves. Laura sinks beside her trunk, now hysterically happy.

Madison returns to tell her that the reporters have said something about her and Brockton, and he must again have her assurance of fidelity. Laura says: "Yes, John, I've been on the level." They are about to go when Brockton comes in casually, as if at home. Madison draws a pistol, but she restrains him.

Laura tells Madison that she was forced by hunger to return to Brockton, despite her steadfast love for Madison. Madison, shamed by his former inability to help, appears willing to forgive her. He orders Brockton out. But Brockton, to prove that he did "the right thing," unctuously tells the whole story of the burned letter. He then leaves. The two are alone.

Brokenly, Laura begs for another chance, but Madison tells her: "You're not immoral, you're just unmoral, and I am afraid there's not a particle of hope for you. In a month you'll recover. With you, it is the easy way, and it always will be." She threatens to shoot herself, but in the face of Madison's taunt that she won't because "it's easier to live," she drops the revolver and he leaves.

Laura sits on the trunk, dazed and weeping. Then she defiantly calls for her maid. "Dress up my body and paint up my face," she cries. "It's all they've left me. They've taken my soul away with them. I'm going to Rector's, and to hell with the rest." A hurdy-gurdy in the street plays a popular café song and Laura, listening, speaks with infinite grief and resignation: "Oh, God—oh, my God!"

The Servant in the House

BY CHARLES RANN KENNEDY

Born February 14, 1871, in Derby, England. He had very little formal education; worked as an office boy and clerk when he was thirteen. At the age of sixteen he began writing—mostly short stories, articles and poems. When he was about twenty-six he became an actor and theatrical business manager, but from 1905 on he devoted himself mostly to dramatic writing. He wrote "The Servant in the House" in 1908. With his wife, Edith Wynne Matthison,

*he was head of the dramatic department at Bennett Junior
College in Millbrook, New York. He died in 1950 at the
age of seventy-nine.*

Manson, a butler, has joined the household of the Reverend
William Smythe, vicar of a forsaken English church. Rogers, a page boy, is awed by the stranger who wears the
costume of his native India. Rogers feels that sometime,
somewhere, he has seen the face of Manson before—a face
of compelling sweetness, dignity and strength. The butler
tells Rogers that he wears his native dress because "people
don't always recognize me in anything else."

The Vicar also feels that he has seen Manson somewhere. He asks the butler's religion, and is told: "My religion is very simple. I love God and all my brothers."
Mary, the Vicar's niece, a wholesome girl in her teens, discloses that today the household is expecting a distinguished
visitor, the Vicar's brother Joshua, whom he had not seen
since a child. Joshua has become the Bishop of Benares, an
almost legendary holy figure with millions of followers.

Left alone with Manson, Mary tells him that she has
never seen her own father, another brother of the Vicar.
She reveals, too, that the coming of the Bishop of Benares
is "rather like a fairy tale." The Vicar's church and study
have been made unpleasant by trouble with the drains, and
the Vicar, unsuccessful in efforts to raise a fund to remedy
it, exclaimed, when reading of the Bishop of Benares:
"Look at the power this chap seems to have at the back of
him! I wish to God I had some of it!" Almost immediately
there came a letter from "your brother Joshua, Bishop of
Benares," saying: "I shall be with you during tomorrow
morning. If anyone will help me, I will restore your
church."

Mary, staring at Manson through the recital, falteringly
asks who he is. He answers only, "I am the servant in this
house," and asks her to "help spin the fairy tale" by wishing
hard for what she wants most. The Vicar's wife interrupts
them, and discloses that another guest of the day will be

her brother James, the Bishop of Lancashire, whom Mary, quoting the Vicar, has described as "a devil," soulless and greedy under the cloak of his office.

The Vicar returns from the odorous church, increasingly miserable. He declares himself a liar in preaching Christianity when he is wronging another brother, the lowly Robert, Mary's father. Robert, unheard of for fifteen years, has asked to visit the vicarage, but because he is only an uneducated "scavenger," has been told that the condition of the drains makes this impossible. The Vicar is incensed when told that the despised James, the Bishop of Lancashire, whom he has never met, is also coming.

The doorbell rings and, assuming that it is her brother James, Mrs. Smythe retires to dress. But the caller is Robert, a crude and belligerent figure in a navvy's costume. Cursing his brother, he declares that drains are his business, and that he has come to see his daughter. Left with Manson, Robert tells him that he and his brother Joshua had sacrificed much to educate William, and were themselves forsaken when he married. The Vicar and his wife took his daughter when her mother died fifteen years ago.

Robert, robed by Manson in the Vicar's cassock while his own coat is being dried from the rain outside, is eating greedily when the Bishop of Lancashire, a pompous churchman, slightly blind and wearing an ear trumpet, is announced. Thinking Robert is William and Manson the Bishop of Benares, he discusses the church as a business property, and asks the secret of the Bishop of Benares' success. Manson's moving description of true faith and sacrifice inspires Robert to tell the Bishop of Lancashire to go to hell, and himself to resolve to do his part for William's church by repairing the drains.

James, still assuming Manson to be his brother-bishop, urges that he lend his fabulous name to the raising of funds for the Society for the Promotion and Preservation of Emoluments for the Higher Clergy, in return for his aid in restoring William's church. The Vicar and his wife enter, the latter expecting to confront Robert and his "evil spirit." Bishop James then learns, to his horror, that Manson is only the butler. The latter informs Mrs. Smythe that he has "cast out" the other "devil," and she, assuming he means Robert, thanks him for having "saved us." Manson answers: "I am trying to, ma'am, but God knows you are making it rather difficult."

Bishop James insists on talking further alone with Manson, and while they are absent, the Vicar reproaches his wife for scheming for his worldly advancement at the cost of his spiritual self. Mrs. Smythe says she is beginning to fear Manson. The butler returns, and when the others leave the room, he burns a five-pound note, given to him by Bishop James. He reflects: "Thou givest thy mouth to evil, and thy tongue frameth deceit. Thou sittest and speakest against thy brother. These things hast thou done, and I kept silence: thou thoughtest that I was altogether such an one as thyself: but I will reprove thee, and set them in order before thine eyes."

Mary is startled by the return of Robert, and rebukes him in the belief that he is a thief. Robert is grief-stricken by her treatment, but keeps the secret of his fatherhood. He is deeply stirred when she tries to comfort him. She confesses that her greatest wish is for the father she has never known. Robert tells her that his own wish is for his daughter, but, in leaving, he identifies himself only as "the bloke wot's a lookin' arter the drains."

The Vicar, angered by Bishop James' offer to help if he wins the patronage of Joshua for the profit-making clergymen's society, declares that he shall break free of his wife's well-meaning influence and his own lies, and restore his self-respect by telling Mary of her father, summoning Robert and denouncing Bishop James. In a painful talk with Mary, however, his wife prevails in keeping the secret concerning the girl's father, and she summons Manson to help get Robert out of the way.

But, dropping his servant's manner, Manson convinces her of the sin and futility of her course, and wins from her and the Vicar the right to be master of the house for one hour "to cleanse it of its abominations." First, he orders Bishop James from the house. James, in a rage, declares:

"If I could have my way with you . . . I would nail you up, sir, for an example!"

Manson answers: "I have encountered similar hostility before, my lord—from gentlemen very like your lordship." As the door slams, the Vicar's wife sinks, weeping, upon a settee, and the Vicar goes to comfort her. Manson lifts his hand in the bishop's sign of blessing. The Vicar and his wife are reconciled in understanding and repentance.

Mary comes in from the garden to reveal her own awakening: she is ready to accept her father, no matter how lowly he may be. As she speaks, Robert, be-mucked from hours in the drains, comes in triumphantly. He declares that, redeemed by Manson's faith and counsel, he has renounced his evil plan to steal "summat" in his visit, and has returned to his own job of "clearing up the muck of the world . . . drains." He has traced a stoppage found in the study, and, braving filth and rats, has found the trouble under the church . . . he could hear the organ playing "The Church's One Foundation."

He is going back into the drain whose dead-end is a noisome burial vault, even if doing so means his death. The Vicar protests, but Robert, proudly proclaiming himself the Drain-Man, asks: "Ain't it worthwhile, to move away that load o' muck . . . if the comrides up above 'av' light an' joy an' a breath of 'olesome air to sing by?" The Vicar cries: "Then, by God and all the powers of grace, you shall not go alone! . . . Off with these lies! . . . This is no priest's work—it calls for a man!" He rolls up his sleeves and prepares to go with his "comrade" brother.

Mary now tells Robert that she knows him to be her father, "because you are my wish come true; because you are brave . . . beautiful . . . good." He embraces her joyously, and the Vicar and his wife take his hands. Manson appears, announcing that the Bishop of Benares "is here." The Vicar asks: "In God's name, who are you?" Manson replies: "In God's name—your brother." He holds out his hand, and the healed Vicar sinks to his knees in tears.

The Witching Hour

*Born in St. Louis, Missouri, January 8, 1857. Before he
entered high school he served as page boy in the Missouri
state capitol and in the House of Representatives in Washington where he acquired an interest in public affairs and
public speaking which lasted all his life. At fourteen he
went back to St. Louis where he worked during the day in
the railroad yards, and studied drawing, acting and playwriting at night. He became a reporter on newspapers in
St. Louis, Kansas City and elsewhere. Went to New York in
1888 where he became business assistant to Julia Marlowe.
The first of his plays to attract attention was "Alabama,"
produced in 1891. After that he wrote and produced many
other plays. "The Witching Hour" was staged in 1907.
Died in Nyack, New York, August 12, 1934.*

Telepathy and mesmerism enter considerably into the conversation of a small dinner party at the luxurious Louisville
home of Jack Brookfield, "square" gambler and politician.
His sister, Alice Campbell, recalls that Brookfield—now a
handsome, middle-aged man—had possessed pronounced
mesmeric powers in his youth, powers apparently shared
by his niece, Viola Campbell.

Telepathy appears evident, too, when young Clay, the
son of Helen Whipple, an old friend, comes to propose
successfully to Viola, and to protest the attention shown
her by another guest, Frank Hardmuth, the county
prosecutor. In talking with Viola of their future, Clay, an
architect, discloses that he has been visualizing with amazing accuracy the jobs he undertakes; he seems always to
glimpse in them the figure of Viola. In designing Brook-

field's library he has even seen the very Corot painting which now hangs there.

Hardmuth tells Brookfield that he, too, has proposed to Viola, but Brookfield replies bluntly that he does not approve of his evasiveness as an official, and terms him "just a little too slick." Brookfield adds: "Frank, some day the truth'll come out as to who murdered the governor-elect of this State. . . . I don't want my niece mixed up in it." Hardmuth is protesting that the killer, Raynor, is already in jail, when Mrs. Whipple interrupts their conversation.

Brookfield suggests to Mrs. Whipple that they renew the romance, broken off in their youth because he refused to give up his gambling. He says he has always felt that she, now a widow, would be coming back to him. Mrs. Whipple recalls that throughout the years she has felt the "nagging" of Brookfield's telepathic power—when he was in college she could not sleep until she had written to him at his psychic bidding. Their conversation is interrupted by the arrival of a Justice Prentice of the Supreme Court who has called to look at the Corot. Thought transference becomes immediately apparent between Brookfield and Prentice, an enthusiast in its study, and he promises Brookfield a book on hypnotism, a power with which he believes the gambler is already unconsciously endowed.

As the Justice leaves, Tom Denning, a drunken guest, rushes in in search of Clay, whom he has been pursuing with a cat's eye stickpin, a stone of which the boy has an inherent fear. Tauntingly, Denning thrusts the pin into Clay's face. As Brookfield enters, Clay, in a frenzy, swings a huge paper cutter in a blind blow that kills his tormentor.

Some months later, in Washington, Justice Prentice and a friend, Justice Henderson, are playing chess and discussing the Whipple case which now has come before the Supreme Court. Clay has been convicted, but the defense has claimed undue influence by the prosecution, and an appeal is pending. As Henderson is leaving, Brookfield is announced; he is accompanied by Viola and Helen Whipple.

Mrs. Whipple reveals that Prentice was a youthful lover

of her mother, and once fought a duel to protect her from a man who was annoying her with a cat's eye jewel. Prentice remembers, and agrees that Clay evidently committed his crime when temporarily insane from the inherited fear. He agrees to favor a new trial. When his visitors have gone, he reflects that the spirit of Helen's mother, dead thirty years, surely has been in the room; a miniature of her dropped from the table just before her daughter arrived.

Several weeks later, another jury is considering Clay's case, and Brookfield, encouraged by his rapidly developing psychic powers, remains at home, concentrating his will upon a friendly juryman. He is disturbed, however, by the appearance of Hardmuth who is furious because Brookfield has told a newspaperman that he, Hardmuth, instigated the assassination of Scoville, the governor-elect. Brookfield refuses to retract his statement, declaring that Raynor, accused of the shooting and now a fugitive in Indiana from Hardmuth's feeble efforts at extradition, had incriminated the prosecutor.

Hardmuth returns to court, and Brookfield confesses to Prentice that he has exposed him now because the prosecutor is about to be nominated for governor and a possible appeal to him for clemency for Clay would be futile. Brookfield and Prentice have been counting, too, on the psychic effect upon the jury of a statewide condemnation of the prosecutor who has so unfairly hounded young Whipple.

Then there is a commotion in the hall and Clay enters— he has been acquitted. As the family, happily filing out with Clay, leave Brookfield and Prentice alone, Hardmuth rushes in and thrusts a derringer against Brookfield's back, just as he is about to press the switch to light a large lamp. Hardmuth shouts a threat to kill Brookfield, but the gambler snaps on the light full in Hardmuth's eyes, and, aided by Prentice's equally potent stare, gazes hypnotically at Hardmuth, saying calmly: "You can't shoot that gun. . . . You can't even hold the gun." Hardmuth drops the weapon; he leaves hurriedly when Brookfield finally permits him to go.

Brookfield now cures Clay of his fear of cat's eyes. Then,

to complete his education in courage and to further a scheme of his own, he sends the youth and Viola to bring back Hardmuth, who is hiding in a Negro cabin. When the fugitive returns, Brookfield reveals that, after all, he is not wholly convinced of Hardmuth's guilt and will help him to safety.

When Hardmuth has gone from the room, Brookfield explains his change of heart to Helen Whipple and Lew Ellinger, a friend with whom he formerly gambled. Brookfield recalls that, a short time before, he had played an experimental game with Ellinger and had unerringly identified the cards, unseen, that were held by his opponent. He had never tried the trick before, consciously, and had been deeply depressed at the thought that he had, even unwittingly, employed a psychic gift to win at gambling. Now he tells his friends: "Suppose, instead of the cards, there's been in your mind a well-developed plan of assassination—the picture of murder. . . ."

Ellinger asks: "Did you drop to him that way?"

Brookfield goes on: "No. Raynor told me all I know of Hardmuth—but here's the very hell of it: long before Scoville was killed I thought he deserved killing and I thought it could be done just—as—it—was—done. . . . I've always had a considerable influence over that poor devil that's running away tonight, and I'm not sure that before the Judge of both of us the guilt isn't mostly mine."

He asks Ellinger and Helen to accompany him as he escorts Hardmuth out of the state, and appeals to Helen to stand by him in his own fight to atone. "You've made your fight, Jack, and you've won," she answers, and gives him her hand.

The City

*Born May 2, 1865, in Elmira, New York, his full name
being William Clyde Fitch. At the age of fourteen he was
sent to a school for boys in Holderness, New Hampshire.
Then he went to Amherst, where he immediately became
associated with the dramatic club and the college paper.
He began writing plays for the dramatic club, as well as
designing costumes and scenery. After graduation he did
some newspaper work in New York, then went abroad
where he traveled and wrote extensively. On his return to
New York after several years, he met Richard Mansfield
who had been looking vainly for someone to write a play
around the character of Beau Brummell. Fitch immediately
set to work on this project, and the result was the first of
his many successes. He afterwards wrote many plays and
achieved great success and popularity. His health began to
fail in 1907 and he died on September 4, 1909. "The City"
opened in New York on December 21, 1909.*

George H. Rand is quite satisfied to be the biggest man in
Middleburg, but George, his ambitious son, and Teresa
and Cicely, his daughters, think life in a small town is
nothing more than dry rot. They beg their father to move
to New York.

Young George is particularly insistent, for his friend
Vorhees, who is progressing rapidly in politics, has an
opening for him. His father protests, however, that he has
been training his son in methods considered honest enough
for Middleburg, where he is solidly established, but that
the line may be drawn differently in the city. Besides, he
adds, city life turns ambition into a greed that is never
satisfied.

As they talk, Hannock, an employee of Rand, appears. The banker tells his son to remain in spite of Hannock's demand for a private interview. Rand then discloses that he has been regularly paying Hannock, a scoundrel and drug addict, to silence his charge that Rand once ruined his, Hannock's, mother. After Hannock, threatening to tell of "shady" deals that he has discovered, leaves with another large bribe, Rand confesses to George that Hannock, though he does not know it, is Rand's own son. He extracts a promise from George that he will give Hannock every brotherly care and consideration, then, exhausted by the scene, he dies of a heart attack.

Several years later, the entire Rand family has been transplanted to New York, but only George appears to have gained by leaving Middleburg. Teresa is planning a divorce from Van Wranken, a wastrel husband, after a marriage in which neither has been faithful. Cicely, unaware of their relationship, is planning to elope with Hannock, whom George has employed as his secretary despite Hannock's continued blackmailing and use of drugs. George, however, has climbed rapidly in politics, and is about to be nominated for governor.

His mentor, Vorhees—whose sister, Eleanor, George is to marry once he is elected governor—comes now to tell him that the party committee is ready to nominate him, and that, if nominated, his election is virtually certain. But Vorhees warns George that the moment he is nominated, his opponents will begin to dig into his past in search of any scandal with which to besmirch him. He asks George if his record is entirely clean. Absolutely, George replies.

Vorhees then tells him, unofficially, that, barring accident, the nomination is assured. George exults: "Oh God, if only I can do it big!" Vorhees reminds him: "You mean do it well," and then discloses that there is one further minor detail: the committee wants George to get rid of Hannock as his secretary because his unsavory reputation is sure to jeopardize the campaign. The shaken George realizes that to dismiss Hannock may mean a scandal, but to retain him means loss of the nomination. His consuming ambition decides, and he agrees to meet the committee's condition.

But now he is confronted by another problem: Van Wranken, the unscrupulous husband of Teresa, threatens a scandal that may very well disrupt George's election campaign. He demands that George influence Teresa to give up Cairns, her lover, and share the children with him. If she will do this, he will agree to a quiet divorce later; if not, he will precipitate a lurid suit. George begs Teresa to agree to her husband's terms until the election is over. "Just think what it means to me!" he pleads. Teresa finally consents, but says: "Go on and rise to be a big man, but somehow, George, today you have become a much smaller man in my eyes. . . ."

George now attempts to solve the problem of Hannock, his last barrier to the governorship. He tells his secretary that he must get another job, but that he will give him a yearly income. Hannock will have none of it, and threatens to tell of a "crooked" deal of George's in which he "gambled" with his partners' money. He then horrifies George with the announcement that he can't be fired—he has just married Cicely. George is at last forced to tell him that Cicely is his blood sister, but Hannock, in a fury, declares that this is only a lie intended to separate him from his bride. At Hannock's declaration that he will never give her up, George calls in Cicely to tell her the truth, but before he can complete his story, the demented Hannock pulls a pistol from his pocket and shoots her dead. Then the telephone brings a message from Vorhees that George has been nominated for governor.

Later that day, Vorhees, at the news of the murder, rushes to George's home to tell him that the governorship is now out of the question. So, too, is his marriage to Eleanor. Vorhees upbraids George for having deceived him as to his reputation and the explosive conditions in his family, declaring that his own pledged reputation is now at stake.

George pleads: "I know it sounds ridiculous, and I don't expect you to understand it, but I've been taken in by myself, too. Intent upon success, I have failed to reckon the cost. I have worked on the assumption—to me it seemed an honest assumption—that the means are justified by the end. I wanted to get to a position where I could do big things and good things." Vorhees relents, reminding George that he is young enough to survive the scandal and disgrace and still succeed. George says he is ready to face it all and make good in an honest way.

The death of Cicely has shocked the Rands into a full realization of their way of life and the consequences of their having left Middleburg. Teresa regrets that the city has taught them to make the worst instead of the best of things, but George contends that it is not the city's fault. He says: "What the city does is to bring out the strongest in us. If at heart we're good, the good in us will win. If the bad is strongest, God help us! Don't blame the city. . . ." Teresa and her husband are reconciled, and George, ready for any punishment, repays his partners for his manipulations with the firm's money.

He goes to say farewell to Eleanor. "You loved me because you thought I was honest," he tells her. "But . . . I'm a trickster, a liar, a thief . . . my only excuse is that I didn't realize what I was doing. I did what others, whom I had been taught to pattern on, did before me . . . what others were doing around me. I accepted cheating for business diplomacy . . . lying as the commercial code . . . stealing as legitimate borrowing. . . . But I should have known better."

He tells her that he is giving everything up, renouncing even her. But Eleanor replies: "The man who has done wrong and can own it up—face life all over again empty-handed, turning his back on everything he has counted on and lived for because he wants to be honest with himself —that, George, is the man I look up to ten times more than the one who is good because he has never been tempted. It is the man who has been tested and failed, and who has come through the failure to make good—that is what makes real character. Today . . . you are a man of that character. Your real self has triumphed. Today you are the man I loved yesterday."

Says George: "Now I know what those people mean who say a man gets all the hell that's coming to him in this world—and all the heaven, too."

Monsieur Beaucaire

BY BOOTH TARKINGTON

Born in Indianapolis, July 29, 1869, his full name being Newton Booth Tarkington. He was educated at Phillips Exeter Academy, Purdue University and Princeton. He received an honorary A.M. from Princeton in 1899, Litt. D. in 1918, Litt. D. from De Pauw University in 1923, and Litt. D. from Columbia University in 1924. He was twice awarded the Pulitzer Prize for literature, and in 1933 received the gold medal of the National Institute of Arts and Sciences. He is probably best known for his Penrod stories which were written between 1914 and 1916, and for "Seventeen," "The Magnificent Ambersons," "Gentle Julia," and "Monsieur Beaucaire" (written in 1900). "The Magnificent Ambersons" was filmed with Orson Welles in the leading role. "Seventeen" and "Monsieur Beaucaire" have been dramatized. Booth Tarkington died in 1946.

At fashionable Bath in England, in the eighteenth century, a group of gentlemen are chatting about two new arrivals —M. Beaucaire, a handsone and consummate gambler about whom little is known beyond the fact that he crossed recently in the same ship with the French Ambassador, and the lovely Lady Mary Carlisle who is quite oblivious to the wooing of several of the titled gallants.

The conversation touches, as well, upon Beau Nash, the arbiter of Bath; the cardroom cheating of the Duke of Winterset, a suitor of Lady Mary who has been virtually beggared by Beaucaire's honest skill with dice and cards;

Captain Badger, Winterset's paid swordsman; and Major Molyneaux, an aide to the English Ambassador at Versailles who has come to court Lucy Rellerton, Lady Mary's companion.

Lucy and other ladies and gentlemen arrive, bringing with them old Mr. Bicksit who has a new bit of scandal from the French court to relate: the French King has secretly clapped into prison Prince Louis Philippe de Valois, Duke of Orléans, for refusing to marry the Princess Henrietta because he does not love her. Molyneaux recalls that the Prince, although he has never seen him, is thirty-three, reputed to be an excellent actor, gambler and swordsman, as well as handsome and gay.

Beaucaire appears, a dashing figure, and is asked to tell what he knows of the Prince. He laughingly declares him his worst enemy and begs leave not to discuss him. Pressed by the ladies to tell something of himself, he mockingly declares that he is the Duke of Orléans. When Molyneaux and Beaucaire are alone, Molyneaux confides that Orléans has escaped to England in the guise of hairdresser to his friend M. de Mirepoix, the French Ambassador, and that he, Molyneaux, has been sent to find and guard him in order to avert any incident that might precipitate a war. He asks Beaucaire's aid in finding Orléans, since he is known to have come on the same boat, and points out that the Prince will not reveal his incognito as he must protect M. de Mirepoix.

Beaucaire refuses to meddle in such weighty matters; but he asks Molyneaux to present him to Lady Mary with whom he has been in love since he returned to her a rose which she had dropped. Molyneaux warns him that she is the haughtiest woman in England, and that her suitors include the Duke of Winterset. Beaucaire withdraws his request, declaring that Winterset himself shall present him.

The men are interrupted by the appearance of Nash, Lady Mary and others who have come to witness a sensational scene: Nash announces that Beaucaire is being publicly expelled as an impostor! Badger, who also was on

the same ship, identifies Beaucaire as a mere barber in
M. de Mirepoix's suite. Beaucaire, restrained by loyalty to
De Mirepoix, as well as by the now enlightened Molyneaux
and his own servant, François, leaves—but with the challenge that any gentleman may find him at his apartment,
ready to play with swords or dice or cards for any stake—
or for only the rose that Lady Mary has given to Winterset.

A month later, Beaucaire's apartment has become the
haunt of the gentlemen, even Nash and Winterset, for
only there can they gamble for huge stakes. Beaucaire, who
continues to win, announces that he is leaving Bath on
the morrow. Molyneaux pleads that he abandon a perilous
plan to meet Lady Mary at last, but Beaucaire declares
that he has never had "jus' one li'l fight," for all his years of
practice in fencing, and persists in his determination to
carry out his plan. Winterset comes to gamble and is
exposed as a cheat. As the price of silence, Beaucaire
compels Winterset to promise to introduce him that
night at the Rellerton ball where he will appear, minus his
mustache and wearing a disguising hairdress, as the Duke
de Chateaurien.

Winterset carries out his bargain, and the unrecognized
De Chateaurien is the lion of the ball. He even captivates
Lady Mary, pleads that she forgive Beaucaire, "who
had written beautiful letters" to France of his love for her,
and asks her to give him a rose. She withholds the token
and leaves, but asks him to take in to supper the ancient
Dowager Countess of Greenbury who is being neglected
by the young cavaliers.

The gentlemen appear. Badger, the best swordsman in
England, goads the Frenchman into a duel. They go into
the garden, with a single witness, and Molyneaux stops the
dance when the witness returns, expecting to hear that
Badger has slain the young Duke. But the witness reports
that De Chateaurien simply toyed with Badger and disabled
him. Then the hero is seen descending the stair with the
aged Countess of Greenbury, as he had promised. Amid
"bravos," Lady Mary gives him a rose from her hair.

Three weeks later, at a party at the home of the rich

AMERICAN PLAYS 69

Squire Bantison, one of Mary's suitors, the guests wager
that De Chateaurien will propose to Mary that night.
Molyneaux warns him that Winterset is bent on revenge,
but the happy Duke explains that François and his servants
are really members of his regiment of guards. François
and Molyneaux are lured away by fraudulent messages
and Winterset arrives with a huge whip, announcing that
De Chateaurien has been exposed as Beaucaire through
recognition of François, and is to be flogged to death by
lackeys.

Beaucaire and Lady Mary, in the garden, are about to
embrace when Winterset and the other gentlemen rush
upon him, crying, "Barber! Kill the barber!" He disables
four of his attackers with his sword, but Winterset grasps
the steel in his gauntlet and Beaucaire is disarmed and
bound. He is about to be whipped when François and his
men, with Molyneaux, return to rescue him. Beaucaire
insists, however, that Winterset be allowed to denounce
him as Beaucaire the barber, and to the shocked Mary he
admits this charge, then collapses from a wound in his
side. He is again told to leave Bath, but declares that in a
week's time he will appear in the Assembly Room.

Here, on the appointed evening, the guests are excited
by the prospect of Beaucaire's return (fourteen bailiffs are
on guard to seize him), as well as by a visit from the
French Ambassador. Lady Mary, from desperate pride, has
been seen often with Winterset, and implies that she is
ready to pay her debt to him in marriage. Molyneaux
appears to tell his beloved, Lucy Rellerton, that he has been
in hiding with Beaucaire for the week while Beaucaire
recovered from his wound. A commotion outside brings
news that the Frenchman has been seen entering the park.
While the hunt is on, Lady Mary enters, and Molyneaux
calls Beaucaire from behind a curtain where he has concealed himself.

Mary reproaches Beaucaire, but he declares that he cannot yet explain. He asks her love for only Beaucaire, the
man. She answers that she cares nothing for names, but
had loved him as an honorable gentleman. Swearing that

he is not a liar, he asks if she will return to France with Beaucaire, a man of honor. She goes to him, crying, "I do not care what you have been! I love you!" A clamor is heard outside and he sends Mary away, bidding Lucy to bring her back in ten minutes.

The gentlemen burst in, but are restrained by Molyneaux, who learns, in vast relief, that the French Ambassador has arrived. Beaucaire orders the dignitary summoned as Lady Mary returns, and exposes the treachery of Winterset. De Mirepoix arrives and identifies Beaucaire as Prince Louis Philippe, now forgiven by his King. The ladies press in to be presented, and the Prince introduces the astonished Mary as his Duchess.

Sherlock Holmes

BY WILLIAM GILLETTE

Born in Hartford, Connecticut, July 24, 1855. Educated in Hartford schools, then at Yale, Harvard and the Massachusetts Fine Arts Institute. Made his first stage appearance in Boston in 1875, and in New York two years later. Appeared many times in London. He wrote numerous plays, collaborated with other dramatists, and adapted stories for the stage. His most notable successes were in "Sherlock Holmes," "The Admirable Crichton," "Secret Service," "Digby's Secretary," and "Dear Brutus." He made a farewell tour of America with "Sherlock Holmes" in 1931–32. Died in 1937.

In a gloomy house in London, the criminals, Jim Larrabee and his wife, Madge, at present using the name Chetwood, are nearing the culmination of a daring blackmail plot. However, to their dismay, they have heard that their intended victims have engaged the services of the celebrated private detective, Sherlock Holmes. Consequently, they are working with feverish speed.

The pair are holding captive pretty Alice Faulkner (on the pretext that she is insane), as well as her aged mother, in an attempt to obtain letters and photographs that will enable them to blackmail a wealthy family of foreign nobility. Alice's sister had died, with her child, after being jilted by the family scion, and his letters would prevent his imminent marriage should the scandal be revealed. The documents are in a desk safe, but Alice has so manipulated the dials that the Larrabees cannot open it. No extreme of torture has induced her to disclose the combination.

Forman, the butler, hints that he knows of the plot, but Madge threatens that she will expose him as a self-confessed forger if he interferes. Forman sends Terese, the maid, who is leaving the household because of the cries of the unfortunate Alice, to Holmes. The Larrabees call in Prince, a safe-cracker, to open the safe; but when he is told that Holmes is involved he hurriedly telegraphs to his chief, Professor Moriarity, king of London criminals, who is waging a deadly feud with the sleuth, and ever seeks opportunity to trap him.

Prince succeeds in opening the safe, but the documents are gone. Alice has taken them. Larrabee is twisting her arm to extort from her their hiding place when the doorbell rings, and the tall, lean figure of Holmes is seen on the threshold. They hurriedly rush Alice upstairs. Prince is assigned to wait outside to attack Holmes should he obtain the papers. The laconic Holmes quickly foils Madge's attempt to masquerade as Alice, identifies Larrabee and Forman as criminals, and compels them to summon the real Alice.

She, bent on protecting her dead sister, is refusing to give up the letters when there is shouting below, smoke pours into the room and Forman reports that the kitchen is ablaze. The Larrabees and Forman rush out, and Holmes, who has seen Alice's eyes dart to a chair upon hearing the alarm, tells her that there is no fire; he has arranged the disturbance in order to learn her hiding place.

He rips open the chair's upholstery and takes the letters, but when she weeps he returns them, saying that she must give them to him willingly. He tells her that she will be safe under his eye hereafter and she leaves the room. Holmes, on his way out, warns the Larrabees that they will be watched. In spite of the warning, they are about to resume the torture of Alice when three mysterious knocks are heard below. Baffled and fearful, they resolve to leave the case to Moriarity.

The next morning, in Moriarity's underground headquarters, the closing net of Holmes is being angrily discussed by the arch-criminal and his lieutenants. Moriarity resolves to decoy the detective's attendants and visit him that night in his Baker Street apartment. Larrabee is brought in. Moriarity, ordering him to get rid of Forman, the butler, as a traitor, and to prepare counterfeit documents, agrees to checkmate Holmes without sharing in the loot.

At Holmes' quarters that night, the detective is amusing himself by his uncanny deductions as to the activities of his friend Dr. Watson who is with him. They are interrupted by the maid, Terese, who reports that Forman (actually one of Holmes' assistants and the mysterious cellar-knocker) has been attacked in the Larrabee home. Holmes is about to go to the rescue when the disheveled Forman comes to report that the Larrabees are counterfeiting the letters. Billy, Holmes' boy servant, brings a letter from Larrabee, inviting Holmes to enter a closed cab at eleven o'clock for a trip to a friend's home where, the letter informs him, he may negotiate for the documents. Holmes sends Terese back with instructions to tell Alice that he is unaware of the counterfeit.

Then, one by one, Watson, Forman and Billy are lured away, and the sinister Moriarity enters, only to be covered by the expectant Holmes' revolver. Billy, his coat torn in wresting loose from his captors, returns and, at Holmes' order, takes a pistol from Moriarity's pocket. The detective's jeering refusal of a truce drives Moriarity to grab furiously for his weapon, but the trigger snaps futilely—Holmes has adroitly removed the cartridges. Billy shows the enraged criminal out.

But, later that night, Moriarity's men are awaiting Holmes in their gas chamber in Stepney where luckless traitors and other victims are put to death. Larrabee also is waiting with the counterfeit letters when Alice, who has followed him, enters. She has come to warn Holmes of the fraud. Learning that his life is in peril, she attempts to buy his safety by revealing that the real letters are behind the shutter of her room; but she is gagged, bound and thrust into a closet when Holmes' arrival is signalled.

The detective, soon aware that he is in a gas chamber by noting the caulking of the room and a lingering odor of gas, knowingly buys the counterfeits for a thousand pounds; he also tempts Larrabee to snatch at added money so that he may charge robbery. He grabs from the closet door a knife hurriedly used to close it, and out pitches Alice. Moriarity's men, in response to Larrabee's whistle, dash in and seize his pistol. Alice declares her readiness to die with him, but Holmes smashes the lamp with a chair, and, decoying his assailants to a window by the glow of his cigar, hustles her safely out the door with him, dropping the bars on his foes.

But Moriarity is not through. His men are seeking Holmes in vain at his Baker Street place—they have even fired the house—and he has sent Prince and Madge to Dr. Watson's office to learn if Holmes is there. Madge is still at Dr. Watson's when there is a commotion outside. Forman, disguised as a cabman, brings in a querulous, supposedly injured old man—Holmes. The latter reveals that the police have trapped all the gang but Moriarity, and, deducing that the arch-criminal is near by in disguise, he permits Madge to signal Moriarity by means of the window shade.

Then little Billy, dressed as a newsboy, arrives to report that Moriarity has emerged from a house across the way and is changing places with a cabman outside, evidently expecting Holmes to enter the cab when he leaves the premises. But the detective, hastily borrowing Watson's heavy Gladstone bag, has the cabman summoned to carry the bag outside. When Moriarity appears, Holmes pretends to help him with the straps to the bag, then snaps handcuffs on his wrists. Moriarity, vowing vengeance, is led out.

But Holmes has one last scene to play. Titled visitors call for the letters, and Alice, summoned earlier, is left in an anteroom where she may overhear the conversation as Holmes, purposely and in presumed good faith, hands over the counterfeit package. Alice, hearing Holmes condemned as a fraud, emerges from the anteroom and presents the real letters (as Holmes had planned) of her own free will.

Left alone with her, he confesses his deceit; but she declares her love for him, and, despite his gloomy view of his own unworthiness, he takes her in his arms.

The Old Homestead

BY DENMAN THOMPSON

Born October 15, 1833, near Girard, Pennsylvania. Moved to Boston in 1850, and drifted to other cities in very minor roles with theatrical troupes. Had some theatrical training with the Royal Lyceum Company in Toronto. In 1875 he wrote a brief sketch of rural Yankee types which he later expanded into a full-length comedy called "Joshua Whitcomb." Later it was developed into a four-act play and called "The Old Homestead." Thompson acted exclusively in it almost to the time of his death on April 14, 1911.

Anxiety gnaws at the heart of Joshua Whitcomb, the master of the Old Homestead at Swanzey, New Hampshire. He is "hard as a hickory nut and spry as a kitten at sixty-four," his farm is flourishing, but he worries constantly. His son Reuben has gone to New York, and the father has had no word from him for several months. When a group of city folks, including Frank Hopkins, son of a former schoolmate of "Uncle" Josh, come up to the farm for a holiday the old man proceeds to unburden himself.

It seems that Reuben had been a cashier in the Cheshire Bank in the near-by town of Keene. One day a party of sharpers from Boston had gone to the bank. While Reuben's attention was diverted, a member of the party "got into the vault and stole a lot of money." Reuben was arrested, "charged with stealin' something," his father says, "that he didn't know no more about than the man in the moon." Though he had later been acquitted and his name cleared, he had felt humiliated and had brooded over the incident. He finally threw up his job, going off to New York. Uncle Josh's nightly slumbers are now disturbed by unhappy dreams, and he tells Frank Hopkins that he intends to go to New York to look for his son.

A mysterious stranger has appeared in the vicinity of the farm. One of the farm-hands mistakes him for a scarecrow, and Rickety Ann, who helps with the housework, fears that he may be "a wild man escaped out of a menagerie." The "wild man" turns out to be a harmless tramp. His name is Happy Jack, and he describes himself as "the champion deadhead of America, the star truck rider of the world." He explains that he rides from one end of the country to the other on the trucks beneath railway cars. He admits that he drinks more than is good for him, and he frankly confesses that he is ashamed to go home because he is a "wreck."

As Uncle Josh elicits the life story of Happy Jack, the farmer is haunted by memories of his wandering son. He urges Jack to stop drinking and return home. "Do you ever think of your mother?" he asks. "How she watched you all through the cares and dangers of childhood. Worked for you! Prayed for you! I tell you, boy, you owe that mother more'n you kin ever repay." He continues, "Will you go home if I give you money enough to pay your fare? And stop drinkin'?" Uncle Josh hands a five-dollar bill to Jack, exhorting him to try and "be something." "You're a young man yet; it ain't too late," he says. Jack replies with determination: "Well, I will! And if I don't win I'll give old John Barleycorn the toughest scuffle he ever had for the underhold."

A little later, Uncle Josh journeys to New York. On the evening of his arrival he is entertained by Henry Hopkins, his former schoolmate who is now a millionaire. Hopkins' wife and daughter are people of fashion; his mansion is gorgeous and resplendent. The city folks are alternately amused and horrified at Josh's indiscretions. He refers to the *portières* as "brush fence" and "whip lashes." He turns upside down in a rocking chair and cries, "Gosh, I thought I sot on a cat," as he jumps up from an upholstered one. When he comes suddenly upon a statue of the Venus de Medici the merriment swells to a roar. "If I'd put that up in my cornfield," Josh says, "I'll bet I'd be arrested before night."

Uncle Josh spends more than a week tramping up and down the New York streets, and he sees more misery and wickedness in that time than he ever thought could exist in a civilized community. In front of Grace Church on Broadway, he talks with his friend Hopkins. When Hopkins leaves, Josh questions a policeman, listens to a Salvation Army band, and meets an apple-woman. He almost gets into a fist fight with a local character who is known as "the Hoboken terror," and he wants to arrest a postman whom he sees taking letters from a mailbox. A policeman comes to the rescue and straightens out matters.

While Josh is around the corner looking for Reub, Happy Jack reappears. He is followed by Reuben. It is evident that Reuben has been drinking, and the policeman threatens to lock him up. But Happy Jack, who has now become a reformed character and who remembers how, only a few weeks before, a farmer up in New Hampshire had helped him in his hour of need, intercedes in behalf of the drunkard, and saves him from the disgrace of imprisonment. He gives Reub a dollar and sends him away to "brace up." Then, with an exclamation of astonishment, he runs into Uncle Josh.

At first Josh fails to recognize Happy Jack, suspecting

him of being a swindler. But when Jack repeats the actual words that he addressed to Josh when they parted, and even returns the five dollars that he had handed to him, Uncle Josh melts into friendliness. Jack asks whether Josh has been successful in his search for his son. The organ is playing in Grace Church. As the two men converse, a commotion is heard. Voices are shouting, "Good night, old fellow," et cetera. Reuben enters, staggering, and Jack comments, "Here comes my dollar investment, and about as drunk as they make them." Josh recognizes his son and, as the latter falls to his knees, bends over him. Inside the church a choir sings "Calvary."

On the following New Year's Eve, a large company of relatives and friends assembles at the Old Homestead in honor of a great event, the impending return of Reuben. A sleighing party has gone over to Keene to meet the prodigal son and escort him home. Hickory logs are crackling. An old clock ticks in a corner. Bunches of corn, strings of dried apples, and slices of pumpkin decorate the walls.

Reuben gets a resounding welcome when he arrives. In his wake comes Happy Jack who is almost as warmly received. "You two boys," says Uncle Josh, "should be friends for life." "It can be done," answers Jack. "How?" asks the astonished farmer. "Mother," responds Jack, "is still a widow." At this there is a general guffaw.

Uncle Josh retires for a talk with his son, and returns in a few minutes with joyous news. He addresses Aunt Matilda: "Til, it's all settled. Reub and me had a good talk. We hev agreed on every p'int. He works the old farm on shares. Takes possession tomorrow, New Year's Day." Reub and Tilda discuss the happy turn of events as Uncle Josh is about to start the night's entertainment. There are two country fiddlers. Before they start to play, Uncle Josh addresses the whole company: "Hold on! I want to say a word to our neighbors afore they go. Now you fathers that hev got wild boys, I want you to be kind o' easy with them. If they are kind o' foolish now and then, forgive them. Like as not it's as much your fault as it is theirs—they might have inherited it, you can't tell. And mothers—well what's the use of sayin' anything to you, bless your smilin' faces. Your hearts are always bilin' over with love and kindness for the wayward child! Now don't let this be your last visit to the Old Homestead. Come up in June when all natur' is at her best—come on, all of ye, and let the scarlet runners chase you back to childhood." As Uncle Josh concludes, the musicians strike a few chords while the guests, amid laughter and jollity, seek partners and positions for the Virginia Reel.

Uncle Tom's Cabin

BY HARRIET BEECHER STOWE

Born in Litchfield, Connecticut, June 14, 1811, daughter of Lyman Beecher, the most distinguished Congregational minister of his time. Received her education at Hartford Female Seminary, then moved to Cincinnati where her father was head of Lane Seminary. There she met and married Professor Calvin Ellis Stowe, one of the instructors. In 1851–52 "Uncle Tom's Cabin" appeared in the anti-slavery paper, National Era. *Published in book form in 1852, it met with immediate success. Later, it was translated into many languages and was dramatized. Mrs. Stowe died July 1, 1896.*

A common tragedy of Negro slavery in the old South is being enacted in the Kentucky cabin of Eliza, servant of Mrs. Shelby, and George, her husband, an intelligent and spirited young slave on the neighboring Harris property. George's master has climaxed a protracted campaign of cruelty and humiliation by ordering him to give up Eliza and marry a girl on his own plantation. George tells Eliza that he can stand the torment no longer; he intends to escape to Canada, hoping to earn enough money there to buy his wife and their little boy, Harry.

But more misery is in store for them. Shelby, a kindly man, facing loss of his plantation through debt, is forced to sell Eliza's boy, Harry, to Haley, a slave trader, together with his most trusted and valuable slave, Uncle Tom, his faithful and devout manager.

Eliza overhears Shelby telling his wife this news, and fights her way through the snow with Harry to the cabin of Uncle Tom and his wife, Aunt Chloe. She tells them that she is determined to try to reach George, who has made his escape and is supposed to be on his way to Canada. Aunt Chloe urges Uncle Tom to try to escape also. Uncle Tom, however, rather than cause his master to lose his plantation and force the sale of all the other slaves, decides to stay, trusting that God will somehow deliver him.

Eliza, with little Harry, walking all day, reaches a tavern by the Ohio River. If the two can manage to cross to Ohio their escape will be virtually sure, but the river is full of huge cakes of floating ice. Phineas Fletcher, a good-hearted countryman who has sold his slaves at the demand of his Quaker sweetheart, and who also is waiting to be ferried across to the other side, provides shelter for Eliza and Harry. Soon they are seen by Haley and his henchmen —Marks, a lawyer, and Tom Loker—who have come in pursuit, and Eliza, with Harry in her arms, leaps upon an ice cake and floats from sight as her enemies rush for a boat.

At this same time, a Mr. St. Clare returns to his home in Kentucky with his little daughter Eva, his cousin, Miss Ophelia, a spinster from Vermont who is to be his house-keeper, and Uncle Tom whom he has bought while on a steamboat journey. Eva's mother is a languid, selfish woman, and Uncle Tom is directed to devote himself entirely to the child. The two become inseparable, Uncle Tom frequently reading to her from the Bible and teaching her hymns. Another addition to the household is Topsy, an impish Negro girl who is assigned to serve Miss Ophelia.

Eva's love goes far to reform Topsy, to whom no one before had ever shown kindliness.

Back at the tavern on the Kentucky side of the Ohio, Phineas Fletcher reveals that Eliza and Harry have safely crossed the river with his help, and now Phineas' sweetheart has sent him back to look for Eliza's husband. George enters the tavern, and, although he is disguised, the shrewd Phineas recognizes him when he greets Wilson, a former master, and exposes a brand mark upon his hand. Phineas hides George in a cellar when Haley, Marks and Loker suddenly appear. He delays them while George escapes to join Eliza.

Haley and his followers are relentless in their pursuit of the slaves; Phineas, adopting Quaker dress to please his sweetheart, sets off with George and Eliza to the north. Marks, Loker and their men overtake them with a warrant for their arrest, and Phineas, Eliza, George and Harry are trapped in a rocky pass. George shouts his defiance as a man now on free soil, but Marks shoots at him and Loker rushes to capture him. George fires at Loker who is then seized and thrown over the rock by the exultant Phineas.

At the St. Clare home, Uncle Tom has won his master away from drink, but he is concerned by little Eva's cough and her growing weakness. Eva asks Tom to sing a hymn picturing angels "robed in spotless white," and tells him that soon she is going to Heaven with "the spirits bright." She tells her father that she has been unhappy because of the miserable life of the slaves, and asks St. Clare to promise to free Uncle Tom "as soon as I am gone." With Uncle Tom kneeling at her bed, the child, smiling feebly, dies with a vision of Heaven before her.

St. Clare later tells Tom that he intends to free him so that he may return to his wife and children. Tom chooses to remain, however, until he sees his master happier in Christian work; his loyalty strongly impresses St. Clare, who is grief-stricken over the loss of Eva. But he comes home, fatally stabbed, and berates himself to Uncle Tom for his failure to free him; now it is too late. St. Clare dies, saying, "Eva, I come!" Uncle Tom is put up at auction with Emmeline, a fifteen-year-old Negro girl, and both are bought by Simon Legree, a particularly vicious and brutal slave-owner.

Meanwhile, Miss Ophelia has adopted Topsy and has taken her back to her Vermont home where an old admirer, Deacon Perry, successfully sues for Miss Ophelia's hand—after some difficult moments when the unmarried lady explains that Topsy is her "daughter." Gumption Cute, a distant relative of Miss Ophelia and an acquaintance of Marks, arrives to share her home, but is quickly ousted by Miss Ophelia and Topsy when he attempts to order the Deacon away.

At Legree's plantation, Uncle Tom's misery is assuaged only by a lock of little Eva's hair and a silver dollar given him by Shelby. Emmeline rebels at Legree's attentions and he orders Uncle Tom to flog her. The old Negro refuses. Legree whips him, demanding, "Ain't you mine, body and soul?" Uncle Tom declares his soul is beyond the tyranny of Legree, and he is ordered flogged "within an inch of his life."

The repentant Shelby, meanwhile, appears in New Orleans, hoping to repurchase Uncle Tom from St. Clare and restore him to his family. By chance, he meets Marks who tells him of St. Clare's death and agrees to guide him, for a fee, to the Legree plantation. Marks later meets Cute, back from Vermont, and their conversation discloses that it was Legree who stabbed St. Clare because he had intervened in a quarrel to protect Cute. The two are the only witnesses to the quarrel and they agree to confront Legree with a warrant for his arrest. If Legree refuses to buy their silence they will arrest him.

At Legree's place, Emmeline and Cassy, another slave girl, have run away. Legree (after a brief period of reformation brought on by the sight of the lock of little Eva's hair—it had reminded him of his mother whom he also had beaten) demands that Uncle Tom tell him where the girls are or be put to death. Tom refuses and Legree strikes him with the butt of his whip. Tom is carried out, forgiving his tormenter, as Shelby, Marks and Cute arrive.

Shelby goes in search of Tom, and Marks confronts Legree with the warrant. Legree strikes at Marks who draws a pistol and fires. Legree cries: "I am hit! The game's up!" He falls dead. He is carried off by two laughing slaves. Shelby reënters, supporting Uncle Tom. Tom recognizes him, and cries: "Mas'r George! Bless de Lord! It's all I wanted. They haven't forgot me! . . . Now I shall die content! . . . Don't call me poor fellow! I have been poor fellow but that's all past and gone now. I'm right in the door, going into glory! Heaven has come!" He dies, and Shelby covers him with his coat, kneeling over him.

Sun-tinted clouds are next seen, with little Eva, robed in white, on the back of a white dove, as if soaring upward. Her hands are extended in benediction over St. Clare and Uncle Tom who are kneeling and gazing up at her.

BRITISH PLAYS

Design for Living

BY NOEL COWARD

NOEL PIERCE COWARD *was born at Teddington, near London, December 16, 1899. When he was a young boy, Coward suddenly went off to a ballet school. He was noticed by Charles Hawtry of the Garrick Theatre, with whom he subsequently acted. He joined the army during the first World War but never reached France. In December 1918, he returned to the London stage as an actor, but it was a few years later, while he was appearing in his own play, "The Vortex," that he was catapulted to fame as the* enfant terrible *of the English stage. Following "The Vortex" came a host of witty, sophisticated plays that captured, for many, the essence of vitality, recklessness, and self-indulgence of the 1920's and 1930's. Among his outstanding successes were "Private Lives," in which he appeared with Gertrude Lawrence, "Hay Fever", "Tonight at Eight-thirty", "Blithe Spirit", and "Cavalcade," a spectacular panoramic drama which embodied both the pathos and the patriotism of the years of the first World War. In addition to his talents as playwright and performer, Noel Coward displayed his flair as a composer in such plays with music as "Bitter Sweet" and "Conversation Piece," and his brilliant lyrics adorn such songs as "Mad Dogs and Englishmen" and "Don't Put Your Daughter on the Stage, Mrs. Worthington." More recently his musical play "Sail Away," which he also directed, has been a Broadway success. In 1933, he enjoyed one of his greatest triumphs, co-starring with Alfred Lunt and Lynn Fontanne in "Design for Living."*

In a shabby Paris studio, Gilda, an attractive woman of about thirty years, is preparing coffee when she hears a knock at her door. She carefully closes the door to the bedroom, then admits Ernest Friedman, a middle-aged art dealer who has come to show a picture to her companion, Otto, an artist.

Gilda tells him that Otto is asleep, after an attack of neuralgia, and explains her own dark mood: "I'm sick of this studio. It's squalid! . . . I wish I were a nice-minded British matron, with a husband, a cook and a baby." Asked what has upset her, she replies: "Glands, I expect! Everything's glandular." When Ernest further inquires why she doesn't marry Otto, she shouts, with a glance at the bedroom door: "I love him! I love him!" More calmly, she continues: "I respect him as a person and as an artist. To be tied legally to him would be repellent to me and to him, too. It's not a dashing Bohemian gesture to Free Love; we just feel like that, both of us."

Gilda starts slightly when Ernest tells her that their dear old friend Leo has returned to Paris with a lot of money from his playwriting, and asks how she and Otto will feel toward him. She denies there will be any jealousy, and adds: "I think you should grasp the situation a little better, having known us all for so long. . . . Leave us to grapple with the consequences, my dear. Look at us clearly as human beings—rather peculiar human beings, I grant you—and don't be prejudiced by our lack of social grace. . . . But I would like you to understand one thing absolutely and completely: I love Otto, whatever happens. I can't explain now, but, darling Ernest, there's a crisis on— a full-blooded, emotional crisis." This rather unsettles Ernest.

Gilda is just describing herself as "a too loving spirit tied down to a predatory feminine carcass," when Otto unexpectedly barges in. He has come from Bordeaux. He notes the restraint of Gilda and Ernest, and the latter explains wryly: "Gilda has neuralgia. It's glandular."

Gilda hurriedly bustles Otto and Ernest out "to meet Leo" at his hotel, and, when they are gone, from the bedroom emerges a distracted Leo to ask what they shall do now. Gilda demands to know who he loves best, herself or Otto, but he answers that this isn't really important. He says to her: "What we did was inevitable. . . . It doesn't matter who loves who the most; you can't line up things like that mathematically. We all love each other a lot, far too much, and we've made a bloody mess of it! That was inevitable, too." Both are taking the blame for the preceding night upon themselves when Otto returns. They confess. Otto, scorning their appeals to be "rational" and to remember that Leo, too, felt "shut out" when he first went off with Gilda, stamps out, condemning them both.

Eighteen months later, Leo and Gilda are living together in London, and Leo suggests that they be married. Gilda isn't interested: it would upset her moral principles and, besides, she thinks Otto would hate it. They agree that they both still love Otto, but were right in what they have done. Leo asks if she thinks that they'll all be together again, and Gilda vehemently says she wouldn't want it so. Then Leo leaves for a week-end party.

While he is away, Otto, back from a successful exhibition of his paintings in New York, walks into their home. After a bit of casual conversation, he and Gilda rush into a tight embrace. They try to unravel the trio's tangled lives, and Otto argues: "According to a certain code, the whole situation's degrading, and always has been. . . . But we're not doing harm to anyone else. We're not peppering the world with illegitimate children. It's no use you trying to decide which you love best, Leo or me, because you don't know! . . . A gay, ironic chance threw the three of us together and tied our lives into a tight knot at the outset. . . . The only thing left is to enjoy it thoroughly. . . . It's my turn again—— That's only fair, isn't it?" Said Gilda: "I

—I suppose so," and Otto vaults over a sofa to take her in his arms.

A surprise caller, next morning, is Ernest who is on his way to permanent residence in New York; he suggests that he needs Gilda as a housekeeper. She explains, a bit excitedly, that Leo is asleep, has been ill, and will be unable to say good-bye to him. She tells Ernest, too, that today she is free and unattached and is going away, possibly to Berlin. She saw the light last night, she says, and the light is "the survival of the fittest." She leaves a note for Leo; then, on second thought, another. She gets a dressing case and leaves with Ernest, slamming the door defiantly.

Otto, in pajamas, later emerges from the bedroom. Soon Leo returns, calling eagerly ahead to Gilda that he has had to come back, he can stand absence no longer. Otto tells him that that is exactly *his* explanation, and confesses that he has passed the night with Gilda, it was "inevitable." Leo snorts that this was unspeakably vile of them both, but asks helplessly what they are to do now. Then they find Gilda's identical letters to them: "Good-bye, my clever little dear! Thank you for the keys of the city!" They drink a great deal of brandy and eventually fall to weeping at the prospect of the lonely years ahead without Gilda; but they find some solace in plans to enjoy their success together.

Two years later, Gilda, now Mrs. Ernest Friedman, a successful decorator, is startled when Otto and Leo, in evening dress and elaborately debonair, walk in. Now beautifully gowned and confident, she presents them to friends, with whom she has been to the opera, and suggests that they come to lunch with her one day and tell her of their adventures. She adds: "You'll have to forgive me if I'm not quite as helpful as I used to be; my critical faculties are not so strong as they once were. I've grown away, you see."

When the friends leave, she insists that Otto and Leo go too, but she slips them a latchkey and whispers that they are to return in ten minutes. When they all have gone, Gilda stands still, staring after them, her eyes filled with tears—then she strides about the room in agitation. Suddenly she snatches up her cloak and bag and runs out.

The next morning, Ernest returns to be greeted by Otto and Leo—in Ernest's pajamas. They tell of their visit, explaining that they went to bed when Gilda failed to appear. Ernest is outraged at their casual announcement that they have come back for his wife, and at Leo's explanation: "We love her more than anyone else in the world and always shall. . . . She is far from contented. We saw her last night and we know." Otto adds: "She could never be contented without us, because she belongs to us just as much as we belong to her."

Then Gilda returns; she had fled to find time to think alone, and has decided: "I'm going away from you, Ernest. Some things are too strong to fight against. . . . I'm mad with joy! I thought they had really forgotten me . . . that my heart would be sick and lonely for them until I died. . . . I took refuge in your gentle, kind friendship, and tried to pretend to myself that it was enough, but it wasn't. . . . I can't possibly live without them, and that's that. We're all of a piece, the three of us. Those early years made us so. From now on we shall have to live and die our own way. No one else's way is any good; we don't fit."

There is no explanation to satisfy Ernest, and there is none that the three feel is necessary; the situation is as they would have it, whatever he may think. Ernest declares he shall never understand "this disgusting three-sided erotic hotch-potch," and marches out of the room, unforgiving. In the hall he stumbles over some canvases, and Gilda, Leo and Otto give way to uproarious laughter.

The Barretts of Wimpole Street

BY RUDOLF BESIER

"The Barretts of Wimpole Street" was read and refused by twenty-seven New York producers before Katharine Cornell accepted the part of Elizabeth Barrett on the urging of her husband, Guthrie McClintock, and opened the play in Cleveland in 1931. Since then, the story of the Wimpole Street family has played to enthusiastic audiences in every important capital of Europe, and has had several successful runs on Broadway. Besier, an English dramatist born in Java in 1878, had previously had the play produced at the Malvern Festival in England. His first play opened in London in 1908, and the next year Mrs. Patrick Campbell starred in his second offering, "Don," a comedy. Besier also collaborated with Hugh Walpole in dramatizations of "Kipps" and "Robin's Father." In addition to independent playwriting, he did translations and adaptations from French dramas until his death in 1942. "The Barretts of Wimpole Street," however, has been his most outstanding achievement.

Dr. Chambers looks at Elizabeth Barrett in concern. "It is this increasingly low vitality of yours that worries me. No life in you—none . . ." he tells her.

"Well, Doctor, if you shut a person up in one room for years . . . you can't . . . expect to find her bursting with life and vigor!" Elizabeth retorts. In delicate health, she has spent most of her life on her sitting-room couch in the Victorian London household dominated by her stern father, Edward Barrett. Her six brothers are mere automatons, the eldest of her sisters is an acquiescent ghost, and Henrietta, the youngest daughter, is forced to see Captain Cook, the young man whom she loves, without her father's knowledge, for Barrett has a fanatical prejudice against marriage for any of his children. Elizabeth has long since given up hope of living a normal life, and has found escape in writing the poems which express her unfulfilled dreams. She has her dog, Flush, and she lives vicariously through her brothers' and sisters' limited experiences.

Dr. Chambers insists that Elizabeth must take more interest in her health. She must obey his instructions. Elizabeth guiltily remembers that there is a tankard of porter, which the doctor has prescribed for her, unfinished on her table. She pleads with him to substitute something else, since she finds this drink utterly repulsive. Chambers laughingly agrees that perhaps hot milk will suffice. Her father visits Elizabeth in great displeasure, however, when he learns that a change has been made. He commands her to drink the porter. Then, because he loves this eldest child of his more than his other children, he changes his tactics. He tells her that she will make him unhappy if he must force her, out of fear, to do what is best for her. She must understand that he is acting in her best interests. Elizabeth docilely obeys her father—then collapses in tears when he leaves her for the night.

Next day, Robert Browning, a high-strung, impulsive young poet who has read and admired Elizabeth Barrett's work, comes to call. Elizabeth usually refuses to see strangers, but she has consented to receive Browning from sheer weariness of repeatedly refusing him. "Do you remember the first letter I wrote you?" Robert asks her. "'I love your books with all my heart—and I love you too.'" Elizabeth assumes that he speaks with the impassioned admiration of one poet for another, but he convinces her that he is actually in love with her. She reminds Robert that she is a dying woman. Robert angrily forbids her to even think such a thought again.

Three months later, Dr. Chambers is amazed at the improvement in Elizabeth's health. He is at a loss to explain her rapid increase in strength. She herself is well aware that Robert's growing affection for her has changed her entire outlook. Robert has given her the will to live. She and the doctor have planned that she spend the next winter in Italy where the climate will help to complete her recovery. Robert also intends to winter abroad. But Edward Barrett bitterly censures Elizabeth for contemplating this journey, even though Dr. Chambers has made it plain that his daughter's health depends upon her going. The father cannot actually forbid her to carry out her plans, since Elizabeth has an income of her own, left to her by her mother, but he plays upon her feelings of love and duty to him.

Robert learns of Barrett's attitude. He insists that Elizabeth marry him immediately and go to Italy with him. Elizabeth is unwilling to burden her lover with an invalid wife. She feels that she would cause the world to condemn him were she to die during the journey. Robert assures Elizabeth that he loves her enough to risk anything that might come. Indeed, he loves her more than her father loves her, for Barrett has proven that he considers his own need of his daughter more important than her recovery.

The Barrett household has now taken on new life. Elizabeth has been able to receive more visitors, take walks and make calls. Belle Hedley, a vivacious cousin, has come to stay with the Barretts until her own approaching marriage. Oddly enough, Barrett does not disapprove of marriage for his attractive niece. He tells Elizabeth he will be relieved when Belle is safely out of the Wimpole Street house with her husband. Meanwhile, Henrietta has continued to see Captain Cook in secret. When Barrett is called away from London on business, both Browning and Cook take advantage of his absence to see the sisters more frequently.

On the day when Barrett is expected to return, Elizabeth receives a letter from him which contains the news that he has taken a house in the suburbs of London, for he fears her "feverishly restless mode of life in London will . . . affect her harmfully, both physically and morally," if continued. Robert calls on Elizabeth just after she has learned of her father's new plans. He immediately decides that they must be married the next Saturday when Belle's father has invited all the family to a picnic. Elizabeth can feign illness and they will be secretly married. Then she can return home for a brief rest before traveling to Italy. But Elizabeth will not agree to this arrangement. She is still obsessed with the idea of duty to Barrett, as well as the injustice of marrying Robert when she feels that she can give him so little. However, she agrees to consider Robert's proposal and to write him her decision before she sleeps that night.

After Browning leaves, Henrietta, who has been entertaining Captain Cook downstairs, insists that he be allowed to visit Elizabeth. The Captain has just been decorated by Queen Victoria. Elizabeth and Henrietta are admiring his full-dress uniform when Barrett returns, unexpectedly early. Cook departs hastily, greatly embarrassed by Barrett's very evident disapproval of the laughing scene which he interrupts. Barrett now accuses Henrietta of deceiving him by carrying on a clandestine and indecent affair under his roof. He is unreasonably enraged and demands that Henrietta swear she will never see Cook again—if she does not, she must leave his house. Poor Henrietta has no choice; young Captain Cook cannot support a wife for many years to come.

Elizabeth tries to intervene, but she only incurs her father's anger without swaying his decision in the least. "I shall not see you again until . . . you have repented of your wickedness," Barrett tells Elizabeth. He goes out. The moment the door closes behind him, Elizabeth summons Wilson, her maid. After receiving Wilson's promise that she will accompany her mistress and Robert to Italy, she sends the girl to Browning with a note, telling him that she accepts his proposal.

After her secret marriage to Browning, Elizabeth returns home. In a week's time, after quietly resting, she feels equal to traveling. She and Wilson are in the midst of packing for the journey when Henrietta brings a letter to Elizabeth. Opening it, Elizabeth discovers that Captain Cook has chosen this method of carrying on a secret correspondence with Henrietta. Elizabeth approves of Henrietta's disregard of her promise to their father and regrets that she can do no more to help the lovers. Barrett enters. He surprises them, for, true to his word, he has not come near Elizabeth for the past ten days. He looks at Henrietta suspiciously. Has she kept her promise? Henrietta coolly lies to him, then leaves for a rendezvous with Cook.

Barrett now tries to justify his attitude to Elizabeth. He confesses that he has been miserable during the time he has not permitted himself to see her. "It's time a little reality were brought into your dreams of life," he tells her, brutally. "Do you suppose I should have guarded my house like a dragon from this so-called love if I hadn't known, from my own life, all it entails of cruelty and loathing and degradation and remorse?" Elizabeth remembers her own mother's untimely death, Barrett's paradoxical attitude toward Belle. She realizes that it is not in Barrett's nature to love or respect a woman. Since he knows no tenderness, he can only feel the baser instincts—and despise these instincts for their power over him. Barrett leaves. Elizabeth calls Wilson, saying to her: "I can't stay here any longer. . . . I've never really known him. He's not like other men. He's dreadfully different——" Then Elizabeth Browning leaves her father's house to join her husband.

An hour or two later, Elizabeth's sisters and brothers are dumbfounded when they discover the notes Elizabeth has left for each of them in her room. She has also left a letter for Barrett. It is unbelievable to them that Elizabeth, of them all, should have dared defy their father. Barrett has heard their excited voices. Now he comes to quiet his unruly children. Henrietta hands him Elizabeth's note. He reads it silently. Walking to the window, he stands looking out into the dark, slowly tearing the letter to shreds. Half to himself, he murmurs: "Yes—I'll have her dog." He turns to one of his sons. "Octavius . . . her dog must be destroyed at once." His children are appalled at this new manifestation of their father's cruelty—the merci-lessness of a man who will destroy anything reminiscent of a person he cannot dominate. Henrietta tries vainly to con-trol the triumph in her voice. She turns to Barrett and says: "In her letter to me, Ba writes she has taken Flush with her."

Journey's End

BY ROBERT CEDRIC SHERRIFF

Born in Kingston-on-Thames, June 6, 1896. Educated at New College, Oxford, he was first employed on the staff of the Sun Insurance office. He began writing plays for an amateur society. The first London performance of "Journey's End" was produced by the Stage Society at the Apollo Theatre, December, 1928. This play was soon translated and performed in every European language, and toured extensively in the United States and the British Empire. Sherriff has also written novels and screen plays.

Before San Quentin on a March evening in 1918, in a gloomy, littered British dugout, Second Lieutenant James Raleigh, a boy of eighteen in a very new uniform, reports for his first active duty.

He confides to middle-aged Lieutenant Osborne that he has schemed to join this unit to be with its Captain, Dennis Stanhope, who, although three years his senior, had been his hero at school. He recalls how Stanhope had disapproved of smoking and drinking and Osborne gently warns him that he must expect a considerable change in the Captain who has been three years in active service. Down the dugout steps comes Stanhope, himself hardly more than a boy, but pallid under his tan and with dark-circled eyes. He is tall and slender, with broad shoulders; his hair is carefully brushed and his stained uniform well cared for. He calls at once for whisky, but stops short when Osborne presents Raleigh. He appears not to see the boy's hand, and, in a low voice, says only: "How did you—get here?" After mess, he casually assigns Raleigh to duty.

Later, as he sits drinking, he shows Osborne a photograph of Raleigh's sister and says: "I don't know why I keep it, really. Yes, she is waiting for me . . . she doesn't know that if I went up those steps into the front line without being doped with whisky I'd go mad with fright." He goes on: "I'll stick it out now. It may not be much longer. . . . But it's rather damnable for that boy—of all the boys in the world—to have to come to me. Raleigh's father knew mine, and I was told to keep an eye on the kid. I met his sister . . . and just prayed to come through the war, and do things, and keep absolutely fit for her. . . . After that awful affair on Vimy Ridge . . . there were only two ways of breaking the strain: one was pretending I was ill—and going home. The other was this." (He holds up his glass.) "I didn't go home on my last leave. I couldn't bear to meet her, in case she realized. I've hoped I'd get fit and then go back to her."

He suspects that Raleigh will write home of his secret, and, as his whisky takes effect, declares he will censor Raleigh's letters—"cross out all he says about me. Then we all go west in the attack and she goes on thinking I'm a fine fellow, forever—and ever." Osborne helps him to bed and tucks the blankets around him.

The next day, Stanhope resumes drinking as soon as he awakens. He tells Raleigh, who has a letter for posting, to leave it unsealed, that he will censor it. Raleigh, who has called him Dennis, embarrassed, starts to return it to his pocket, but Stanhope tears it from his hand and shouts: "Don't 'Dennis' me! Go and inspect your rifles." Raleigh whispers, "Right," and goes quietly up the steps. Stanhope sinks down at the table, his head between his hands, and Osborne reads the letter: ". . . Dennis looks tired, but that's because he works so frightfully hard. . . . A sergeant told me . . . that Dennis is the finest officer in the battalion, and the men simply love him. I'm awfully proud to think he's my friend." Stanhope walks heavily into the dugout's shadows.

That afternoon, the Colonel orders a daylight raid to learn from prisoners of the coming imminent attack; rejecting Stanhope's request to lead the party, he selects Osborne and young Raleigh. Osborne warns the other officers to

keep from the delighted Raleigh the fact that the raid is
"murder." A few minutes before they start, Osborne and
Stanhope say an awkward farewell, and Osborne talks at
random to keep Raleigh's mind from the coming ordeal.
They speak of the English countryside and Raleigh invites
Osborne to visit his home. "I should like to—awfully," Osborne replies. They go up the stairs. Soon violent gun fire
sounds. Gradually the noise dies, and a German prisoner,
who had been carried back by Raleigh, is brought down to
be questioned by the Colonel.

Stanhope comes in. In a dead voice he reports that
Osborne has been killed with six others. Raleigh comes
dazedly down the stairs, his hands bleeding. The Colonel,
promising him a Military Cross, guides him to Osborne's
bed. The Colonel leaves, and Stanhope in the dusk stares
at the letter, ring and watch which Osborne has left to be
sent to his wife. He stands over Raleigh and asks: "Must
you sit on Osborne's bed?" He leaves.

That night, Stanhope, drinking champagne with two
other officers, becomes angry when told that young Raleigh
has declined to join them and has eaten with the men in
the trenches. When Raleigh arrives he shouts and trembles
in his denunciation of the boy. Raleigh blurts: "Oh! Good
God. Don't you understand? How can I sit down and eat
that, when—Osborne's—lying out there——" Stanhope replies
brokenly: "You bloody little swine! You think I don't care!
. . . My best friend—and you think I don't care! You think
there's no limit to what a man can bear?" Raleigh tries to
comfort him, but Stanhope turns upon him: "For God's
sake, get out!"

Toward dawn, a heavy bombardment approaches the
sector and Raleigh comes from his dugout. Stanhope orders
him up to the trench. Raleigh turns shyly, says, "Cheero,
Stanhope." Stanhope answers, "Cheero, Raleigh. I shall be
coming up soon." The firing increases, but as Stanhope
prepares to leave, a soldier comes down the steps bearing
Raleigh, unconscious. He has been hit in the spine. Stanhope orders him laid on Osborne's bed, calls for stretcher
bearers and bathes the boy's face.

Raleigh opens his eyes and Stanhope says, smiling: "Well, Jimmy, you got one quickly." Raleigh apologetically tries to rise, saying: "I—I can't go home just for a knock in the back. I'm certain I'll be better if—if I get up." He again tries to rise, and cries out: "Oh—God! It does hurt. What's —on my legs? Something holding them down——" Stanhope brings him water and sits beside him with a hand on Raleigh's arm. "I say, Dennis," Raleigh says at length, "don't wait if—if you want to be getting on." Stanhope answers gently, "It's quite all right, Jimmy." "Can you stay for a bit? . . . Thanks awfully," Raleigh replies. Then he whispers: "Could we have a light? It's—it's so frightfully dark and cold." A moan is heard from the bed as Stanhope gets a blanket. Stanhope gently lifts Raleigh's hand, then lowers it and takes the candle back to the table. He sits on a bench and stares listlessly at the dead boy.

A soldier scrambles down with an urgent call. Stanhope takes up his helmet, runs his fingers over Raleigh's tousled hair, and goes stiffly up the steps. A shell bursts on the roof and blows out the candle, the door timbers sag, falling sandbags block the passage—leaving only darkness and the faint sound of gun fire.

Rain

BY JOHN B. COLTON AND CLEMENCE RANDOLPH
Based on a story by W. Somerset Maugham

W. SOMERSET MAUGHAM *was born in Paris, January 25, 1874. His father was solicitor to the British Embassy in Paris, and, although Maugham was of pure English descent, he spoke French long before he spoke English. Both his parents died when he was very young, and he was sent to Kent to live with an uncle. Here he lived in a rigid, uncongenial atmosphere; he was shy and his health was* poor at this time. His greatest novel—"Of Human Bondage" —reflects the influence of these years, and is almost entirely autobiographical. When he was thirteen he was sent to King's School in Canterbury, and later to Heidelberg. He was intensely interested in writing, but his uncle insisted that he choose some other profession, so he entered St. Thomas' Hospital, London, to study medicine. He was qualified as a member of the Royal College of Surgeons in 1898. Though he never practised medicine, except in the slums of London during his internship, his training was very valuable when he enlisted with a Red Cross Ambulance Unit in the first World War. He had tried to please his uncle, but he was always obsessed by the desire to write. For ten years after leaving St. Thomas' he wrote, and starved, in Paris. His luck changed in 1907 when he wrote his first successful play, "Lady Frederick." This was followed by a number of successful drawing-room comedies and melodramas, including "Our Betters" and "The Circle," which has been described as "an almost perfect serious comedy." Best known, however, is a play based on Maugham's short story, "Miss Thompson," the dramatization of which was the work of John B. Colton and a collaborator, Clemence Randolph. This play was produced under the title of "Rain." Next to writing, Maugham's ambition has been to travel, and he has gone around the world many times, living in America for long periods. In the second World War he was assigned to work in the British Ministry of Information in Paris, but was overtaken by the Nazis and disappeared for a long while. Subsequently he escaped and returned to England. After the war, Maugham retired from writing, and made his home on the French Riviera until deciding to live in England again.

JOHN B. COLTON was born in England in 1889. His father was a British consul at Yokohama, so Colton spent his early years in Japan. He later came to the United States and became a journalist here, serving on the staff of the Minneapolis Tribune. He went to Hollywood, where for some

*time he wrote scenarios. In 1922, he collaborated with
Clemence Randolph in adapting Somerset Maugham's
story, "Miss Thompson," to the stage. His own best-known
play is "The Shanghai Gesture," written in 1925. In 1932
another of his plays, "Saint Wench," was produced in spite
of much criticism and unfavorable comment.*

The quarantining of a mail boat bound for Apia brings
together an oddly assorted group at the tiny South Seas
port of Pago Pago as the rainy season is starting its nerve-
fraying succession of intermittent drizzles and downpours.

Coming ashore are Dr. McPhail and his wife, a pleasant
middle-aged couple on their way to Apia; the Reverend
Alfred Davidson, missionary, a tall, high-strung man with
penetrating, relentless eyes and a deep voice, dressed in a
loose black alpaca suit, white shirt and stringy bow tie,
and his wife and co-worker, "a religiously withered woman"
of forty, with sharp features and hair tightly drawn into a
knot at the back.

Also aboard, but second class, was Sadie Thompson, a
friendly, "wind-blown creature, the victim of her own good
humor, fond of life and taking its rebuffs smilingly." She is
of medium height and slender, and her face, with traces
of hard beauty, is ablaze with cosmetics. She wears a lace
coat, a dress of a violent salmon color, a wide-brimmed
straw hat topped by a huge purple plume, and white-
topped shoes with tassels dangling from their tops.

The stranded passengers find little at Pago Pago beyond
the general store and hotel run by Joe Horn, a philosophical
trader in his late fifties, and his native wife, Ameena. The
hotel is a frame building of two stories, with an iron roof
and a semi-public living room back of the store. The others
appropriate the upstairs quarters, and a storeroom on the
first floor is cleared for Sadie.

She promptly organizes a little party for the few Marines
stationed here, with the help of a bottle of liquor and a
phonograph she has brought from Honolulu. But Mrs.
Davidson objects to dancing on the Sabbath and Sadie

and the boys withdraw to her room. Davidson declares he
believes Sadie a fugitive from Iweili, the recently raided
red-light district of Honolulu, and strides into her room to
prevent "having this house turned into a brothel." He is
heard shouting "Scarlet woman!" He pushes the phonograph off the table, but is quickly tossed out by a Marine.
He and Sadie exchange furious stares.

Two days later, a conversation between Horn and Mc-
Phail reveals that Davidson is pressing a relentless campaign against Sadie. He has vainly urged Horn to put her
out of the hotel, has asked the island Governor to have her
deported to the States, and has reported O'Hara, the Marine
who ejected him from the party, for drinking. Sadie has
become subdued, fearful; her phonograph, when she is
alone in her room, sounds to McPhail "dismal—like a cry
for help."

But it reminds Davidson of his "duty": he sends for
Sadie and offers her a gift, "the infinite mercy of our Lord."
She must pray for forgiveness, he says, or accept "destruction"; he is not going to permit her to go on to Apia. He
calls her "a harlot out of Iweili," and Sadie cries: "You're a
liar! Who in Christ's name do you think you are? . . .
You lay off me! . . ." Davidson seizes her arm and attempts to make her kneel. "God is waiting," he says. But
Sadie spits in his face. Davidson declares, glaring: "You
are doomed, Sadie Thompson!"

He hurries off, and O'Hara comforts Sadie by telling her
that even if Davidson bars her way to Apia, she can get
back to the States. But Sadie appears terror-stricken at the
thought of either the States or Honolulu. O'Hara urges her
to go to Sydney where he is going in six weeks' time when
he receives his discharge from the Marines. He has good
friends in Sydney—Biff and his wife Maggie, who met in
Iweili; Maggie and Sadie would be great friends. Sadie asks
if they have children and, told that there are two, cries, a
new light in her eyes: "Sure, Handsome, I'll go to Sydney!"

But Davidson has influenced the Governor to deport
Sadie to the States, and her appeals for permission to continue to Sydney are useless. She faces the smugly victorious

Davidson and shouts: "You—you dirty two-faced mutt! I'll bet when you were a kid you caught flies and pulled their wings off—I bet you stuck pins in frogs—just to see 'em wiggle . . . while you read 'em a Sunday school lesson . . . you—you—psalm-singing son-of-a——" O'Hara hustles her away before she can finish.

Later, however, she apologizes to Davidson, and explains that she cannot "go straight" in San Francisco, she has been "framed" there and a penitentiary sentence of three years awaits her. She begs for a chance, and Davidson offers her "the finest chance you have ever had"—to repent. He urges her to go back to serve her sentence "to prove to God you are worthy of His mercy." The tormented Sadie storms at him, calling him a witch burner and torturer. She cries, "Hang me and be damned to you!" and runs to her room.

Four days later, the load of fear, the ceaseless rain, loneliness and doubt have crushed her; she has been praying with Davidson almost steadily and, as Horn says, is "beached and delirious with his psalm stuff." O'Hara, who has been confined, at last comes with his chums to take her to an island where she can catch the Sydney boat. He wants later to marry her. He finds a wan, beaten creature in a frowsy bathrobe who is tremulously grateful to him, but she tells him she cannot go. Davidson has entranced her with a vision of redemption and glory, and now he answers her half-hearted cry for him. She sends O'Hara away, offering to suffer his punishment, too, but Davidson assures her that each must bear his share of the cross.

Davidson goes out triumphantly to walk in the rain, and Mrs. Davidson tells the McPhails that he has been spiritually exhausted from his prayers for Sadie, that he has been having strange dreams that puzzle him, dreams of the mountains of Nebraska. She discloses that their marriage has been "entirely a contract of the spirit." McPhail, comparing memories later with Horn, reflects that the "mountains" of Nebraska are hills "rounded, smooth . . . curiously like a woman's breast."

When the others have retired, Sadie comes shakily from

her room and calls, "Reverend Davidson!" She is troubled again, and wants his assurance and prayer. Coming in from the rain, he finds her huddled in Horn's chair. He tells her ecstatically: "Out there in the rain . . . I looked into the awful groves of Asteroth, where Solomon went to find the secrets of joy and terror. I saw Asteroth herself—I saw Judas. Sadie—you don't have to go back to San Francisco. . . . You are redeemed!"

She asks: "What other sacrifice could I offer—that is all I have got to give? I only hope I will go through with it right." He bends over her and whispers reverently: "From now on you will be strong—beautiful . . . radiant . . . you will be one of the daughters of the King." She smiles wistfully: "Am I? Pray with me, Mr. Davidson—when you pray, everything seems all right." Sadie goes back to her room. He stands irresolutely outside her door for a moment, his head bowed and hands convulsively clasped in struggle, then slowly steps inside, closing the door.

The next morning, the raucous phonograph is heard, and Sadie steps forth again, jauntily but cynically, in her plumage. She tells O'Hara: ". . . You know, I'm radiant—beautiful—— Ha-ha-ha! . . . You men! You're all alike. Pigs—pigs!" She assures O'Hara that she doesn't mean him, that she is ready to go to Sydney if his invitation stands. It does.

Says O'Hara: "Sadie, Davidson has killed himself. They found him on the beach this morning in the water with his throat cut." She answers slowly: "Then I can forgive him. I thought the joke was on me. I see it wasn't . . ."

Outward Bound

BY SUTTON VANE

Born in England in 1888. He was wounded early in the first World War, and was sent home suffering from shell shock. Later, he returned to France to appear in plays behind the lines. The most popular of these was "The Thirteenth Chair." When he wrote "Outward Bound" no producer would accept it, so he financed the first production himself in a small suburban theater near London. The play soon moved to London, and opened in New York in 1924 with Leslie Howard, Alfred Lunt and Margalo Gillmore in the cast. It was revived in 1939, and has been filmed twice.

The few passengers on what appears to be a small ocean liner are casually grouped in the lounge whose bar is presided over by Scrubby, an elderly Englishman in a steward's uniform. They are getting acquainted and otherwise following the usual first-day routine of fellow voyagers.

Tom Prior, a slight and nervous young drunkard, has ordered a drink from the serene and kindly Scrubby. A young couple, Ann and Henry, are apparently under peculiar strain and seem dependent upon each other's nearness. Mrs. Cliveden-Banks, a smartly frocked old harridan, is being happily snobbish, especially to a motherly charwoman, Mrs. Midget. The Reverend William Duke, an earnest young clergyman, and Mr. Lingley, a loud and officious business tycoon of some sixty years, complete the list.

Prior is rapidly becoming disturbed at the trend of the conversations: virtually everyone is as vague about his destination as he himself is. Henry and Ann are groping to remember if they have sinned in some way—they know that something has happened to them and fear the consequences. Henry is worried, too, about Jock, his pet dog, and asks Ann if she thinks there is a heaven for dogs. He recalls something vague about not turning off the gas, but wishes he could remember how they got here—after having wanted to for so long.

Prior has heard part of their talk, and goes to Scrubby to confirm his fears: "We are all dead, aren't we?" Scrubby hesitates, then answers quietly: "Yes, sir, we are all dead. Quite dead. . . . You'll get to know lots of things as the voyage goes on." The terrified Prior asks: "Where . . . where are we sailing for?" "Heaven, sir . . . and Hell, too," Scrubby replies. "It's the same place, you see."

That night in the lounge the lights are on but curtains are drawn over the portholes; the occasionally opened door reveals only utter blackness outside. Mrs. Midget, suffering the brusqueness of Lingley and the clumsy persecutions of Mrs. Cliveden-Banks, has just told how she has sacrificed her life for her son—keeping her identity secret to guard him from the shame of her station in life while financing his college and playboy years—when Prior enters, pale and tense.

He says to them that they are all trapped, but—with the exception of the blustering Lingley and the worried Duke —they are inclined to laugh at him. He then tells them of his talk with the steward and of his later search of the ship. There is "no captain, no crew, no nothing," he says. There is only the steward, who now sits cross-legged, high in the rigging. Only Prior hears a muffled drum. Duke goes out to investigate. He returns to report the liner quite normal, but when the women have left he declares Prior wholly right.

The men discuss what to do. Lingley offers: "To begin with—well, somebody ought to ring a bell." Duke finds the situation "very interesting, from a professional point of view, of course." Lingley recovers his composure enough to demand an explanation from Scrubby, but is told only that he is indeed dead and that "to get out of this" he must await the Examiner. Scrubby says that they have learned earlier than usual because of the "half-ways" aboard, but advises them: "There's nothing to be done. Just go on as if nothing has happened."

Lingley is still angrily unconvinced; Duke is puzzled but calm; Prior has another drink, but his mind is turning to his life as "a fearful rotter"; Henry and Ann huddle together, afraid only that they will be separated; Mrs. Midget is amiably indifferent, and Mrs. Cliveden-Banks is shaken, but confident that a Cliveden-Banks can come to no harm.

Lingley calls a meeting, offering to represent them all before the Examiner. He asks for any helpful information they may wish brought forth, but Mrs. Cliveden-Banks desires only that the Examiner be informed that she is—or was—Mrs. Cliveden-Banks; Prior says he is merely a young drunk; Duke agrees with Prior that Lingley is a pompous old idiot, sharing their blue funk but trying to hoodwink the Examiner. Duke declares himself heartbroken at the idea of "being sacked" from his job.

A siren is heard. The ship has made port. Prior hysterically confesses his fear, asking for prayer. Duke recites a simple prayer of his childhood. The Examiner comes aboard cheerily—he is the late Reverend Frank Thomson, large, elderly and jovial, dressed in white drill and a topee, but wearing a clergyman's collar and black bib. Duke recognizes him as "Grease Spot," an old friend, and Thomson calls for all the news before beginning his official duties.

First he tells Duke that he is to live with him in his "digs near your work, right in the center of the parish," and the tortured Duke at last understands that he is to go on with his beloved "job." Thomson chooses him to be his assistant, and the rest are sent to the deck to await their turns. Henry and Ann, however, are not on the list; they are referred to by Thomson as "half-ways."

Lingley is called first; he is sharply reprimanded for his rascality in business and told, "Come, off you get." Mrs. Cliveden-Banks is next, and is greeted as "only a bad harlot" who must live again with her late husband until she learns to be a good wife. She protests that she could not stand the look in her husband's eyes. Thomson tells Duke that her husband has always known of her cheapness, but never revealed that he knew. He comments: "I hope he beats her—but I know he won't. Anyway, she'll get her punishment . . . the eyes that made her run away." Thomson warns her that now everyone but her husband will know of her sins—he will have forgotten.

Tom Prior asks for utter oblivion, but Thomson tells him that he must go on like the others and, in time, learn to forget his woes. Mrs. Midget interrupts Prior's examination to offer to take care of him, but Thomson tells her that Tom is not yet on her plane—there is a little cottage by the sea waiting for her. If she is bent upon accompanying Tom it will mean that she must live in the slums. Mrs. Midget insists, and at length Tom agrees. Mrs. Midget happily follows him off the ship. "Good-bye, Mrs. Prior," the Examiner calls after her. She has been fearful that Tom will find out that she is, in reality, his mother, but the Examiner has assured her that she may go on serving him in secret. "It's 'Eaven, that's what it is, it's 'Eaven," she exclaims rapturously.

The bewildered and frightened Henry and Ann come forward, but the Examiner says: "Not yet, my children," and goes out. They are left aboard the ship. The eerie drum is heard again. Henry imagines that Jock, his dog, whom he remembers staring in at the window of their flat, has barked, and there has been a tinkling of glass, accompanied by a breath of different air. Scrubby tells them now that they must always be left behind, like himself, because they are "half-ways"—those "who ought to have had more courage to face life." Then they remember that they killed themselves in a hopeless, unmarried love.

Henry is assailed by a longing to return to life long enough to right the wrong he feels he has done to Ann. He goes on deck by himself to think more clearly. "Don't let him go too far, madam," Scrubby warns Ann. "Call him, now." Henry answers her cry, but faintly, and then there is no further reply or sight of him. Useless to search, says Scrubby. "He lives again; the dog . . . perhaps broke through." Ann, in spite of the steward's counsel that it is impossible, exerts her utmost will to follow Henry.

"Henry!" she calls. "Henry! . . . It's Ann, dear. . . . Are you in the flat?" The drum is heard again. "It's speaking, Henry, the little wedding ring, that wasn't a wedding ring at all—put it on my finger again. . . . Don't leave me alone forever. . . ."

The drum stops, and Henry reappears. He says to her: "Quick, dear . . . there's only a second or two . . . I've come to fetch you home, dear! . . . We've such a lot to do . . . and such a little time to do it in. Quick! Quick!" They go out together, hand in hand. The drum resumes softly as Scrubby watches them go.

The Green Goddess

BY WILLIAM ARCHER

WILLIAM ARCHER *had had forty-three years' experience as dramatic critic on London newspapers when he wrote "The Green Goddess," a play which proved to be an important hit on the stages of two continents and a noteworthy contribution to English drama. The immediate success of this, his only play, produced in 1920, made Archer financially independent, and he retired from his journalistic duties which had included positions on* The Tribune, The Nation *and* The Star, *all of London. As an English critic, this Scottish-born writer had been held in high esteem for his judgment and faithfulness to his own idea of what constituted good criticism—"making the best of the actual without losing sight of the ideal." Archer was a freethinker, a spiritualist, an early student of psychoanalysis and the Freudian theory of dreams. In fact, "The Green Goddess" was written from an idea recollected from a dream. Archer was an ardent admirer of Shaw, Granville-Barker and Ibsen, translating many of the latter's plays into*

*English. He was a friend of everyone of importance on the
English stage during his lifetime. George Arliss, who
played the part of the Raja in "The Green Goddess," contributed greatly to the play's spectacular success. The most
important of Archer's published works includes five vol-
umes of dramatic criticism, written from 1884 to 1905
when he was critic on the London* World. *He died in
1924.*

Dr. Basil Traherne, Major Anthony Crespin and Crespin's
wife, Lucilla, struggle out of the wreckage of an airplane
which Basil has been attempting to pilot to Crespin's
Indian post. They emerge into the strange courtyard of a
temple which they discover to be sacred to a huge green
idol. They have landed in a remote region of the Hima-
layas. The Mongolian-featured men who press close about
them do nothing to make the English party feel at ease.
Basil, a distinguished scientist and excellent linguist, learns
from a native who understands Russian that they are in
Rukh. The Raja, who has seen the crash, will presently
come to deal with the survivors. Lucilla recalls that, while
on the plane, she read a newspaper account of three men
from Rukh, soon to be executed for murdering the Political
Officer at Abdulabad. Supposing that the news has not
traveled to this lonely spot as yet, and fearing retribution
from the Raja should the story be known, Basil finds the
paper, tears out the report, then burns it.

Close inspection discloses the fact that the plane is a
total loss. Anthony then berates Basil and Lucilla for having persuaded him to fly from England, but Lucilla reminds
him that he was once delighted at the opportunity.

"I thought we'd get to the kiddies a week earlier," Anthony explains. "They'd be glad to see me. . . . They
don't despise their daddy." The Crespins are on strained
terms, for the Major has spent most of his leisure either
"in his cups" or with other women. "It shan't be my fault,
Anthony, if they ever do," Lucilla answers him, "but you
don't make it easy to keep up appearances." She is dis-

gusted with Anthony's weakness, though she is also determined to make their marriage satisfy convention and safe-
guard their children.

The Crespins' marital problems seem unimportant when
the Raja, a handsome, polished Oriental, arrives to escort
them to his palace. He seems to take perverse pleasure in
torturing his unwilling guests. Discovering the mutilated
newspaper from which Basil has torn the fatal story, he
informs the group that he has already heard that three
of his subjects are to be executed—furthermore, the men are
his half-brothers. The superstitious natives have decided,
he tells them, that the two Englishmen and the lady have
been brought to Rukh by the Green Goddess for sacrifice,
in payment for the lives of her followers. Obviously, the
European-educated Raja does not share this belief, but he
is willing to make use of his people's superstition to satisfy
his desire for revenge. Basil and Anthony stand for everything he hates in the conquering English race; his absolute
power has been diminished through the efforts of such "old
Army" men as Anthony and clever scientists like Basil.

The captives are treated with utmost respect and courtesy in the Raja's palace. They know, nevertheless, that
their host will kill them in two days, for the Raja has
received the news that his brothers are to be executed in
that time. Suddenly, the Raja offers Lucilla the choice between becoming his queen, having her children brought to
her at Rukh—and death. Lucilla declines his offer, feeling
that she can never face her children if she should submit
to the man responsible for the murder of their father and
her friend.

On the day before the scheduled sacrifice, Basil and
Anthony decide that they have but one chance to outwit
the Raja. Should any news of their plight come to the outside world, English justice would move swiftly and mercilessly. The news of the execution to take place in Abdulabad has come through a wireless set, concealed somewhere
in the palace. If it can be located, Anthony, who is familiar
with Morse code, can send a message to the nearest air-
drome. Then they can but hope that it will be possible for

rescue to reach them before it is too late. Secrecy is important, for, should the Raja discover that he has been duped, he will probably kill the three immediately and destroy all evidence of their presence in Rukh.

The Raja, far from being a fool, realizes that such a thought may occur to the Englishmen. He is not convinced by Anthony's pretence of knowing nothing of wireless transmission. As a test, the Raja takes his prisoners to the wireless room. He has his Prime Minister, Watkins, a renegade Englishman, tap out a message: "The lady has come to terms. She will enter his Highness's household." Anthony, understanding that the Raja is trying to trick him into betraying his knowledge, suddenly gains the necessary poise and courage to deceive their jailer by keeping silent. The Raja, satisfied now that none of the party can send a message, concludes that the only course open to them would be an attempt to bribe Watkins to send a call for help. And the Raja trusts Watkins implicitly, for the renegade is wanted for murder by the English police and therefore cannot betray the ruler of the only place in which he can safely hide.

Basil and Anthony do indeed attempt to bribe Watkins. It amuses the Raja to know that his Prime Minister pretends to accept their money, then takes the captives to the wireless room where he taps out a false message. What the Raja does not know is that Anthony, detecting that Watkins has tricked them, throws him out of the window and works the wireless key himself. But the Raja hears the disturbance in the wireless room and rushes in in time to interrupt Anthony with a revolver shot. "How much . . . did you get through?" the ruler asks him. "Curse you— none," Anthony replies, weakly. He dies.

The next day, Basil and Lucilla are led to the temple of the Green Goddess. Anthony's body has been placed at the Goddess's feet. The Raja tells the two that they are to join Anthony—unless, of course, Lucilla wishes to reconsider and to accept his offer of becoming his queen. The victims are left alone, for the Raja hopes Basil will persuade Lucilla to save herself. However, Lucilla refuses to let him die

alone. Basil, moved by her decision, tells her that he has
loved her for years, but has been silent until now out of
respect for her marriage. Lucilla admits that she returns
his love. Basil says, regretfully: "We have sacrificed to an
idol as senseless as this." He points to the figure of the
Green Goddess. Facing imminent death, he and Lucilla
suddenly realize that, just as the natives give the idol
human lives, as the Raja betrays his knowledge and his
people's faith to vengeance, as Anthony gave up decency
and happiness to drunkenness and debauchery, so they
have sacrificed "all the glory and beauty of life" to
convention.

The Raja now returns, to receive Lucilla's second refusal.
He reminds her that he has the power to make her a slave
if she will not be his queen. Basil leaps at the Raja's throat.
The priests, who have followed their leader, seize him, and
the Raja tells Basil he has committed an unpardonable
offense by laying violent hands upon the man most sacred
to the Goddess. Death alone will not atone—the natives
will insist that the culprit be tortured. Lucilla offers to
submit to the Raja if he will save Basil. The Raja agrees to
tell the people that the Goddess has spoken and to ask
that the Englishman merely be imprisoned—on the condition, of course, that she will be his queen and will not
attempt to escape from Rukh.

Suddenly, there is the sound of motors overhead. Looking up, the Raja sees twenty circling airplanes. He realizes
that Anthony had lied to save Basil and Lucilla. Anthony's
message, then, had been received in time. An English
flight lieutenant lands his plane and is escorted to the
temple courtyard. He demands the release of the prisoners,
but the Raja laughingly reminds the lieutenant that the
Rukh soldiers outnumber the pilots of the planes. Every
plane overhead is loaded with bombs, the Englishman
warns the Raja. Unless a signal is immediately given that
the prisoners are safe, Rukh will be blown to bits. The
Raja is defeated. He reflects that his position is indeed
embarrassing, since he must now account for Anthony's

death. He will probably be forced to join other exiled kings.

The Raja looks after Lucilla as she and Basil are escorted to the planes—and safety. Philosophical, unabashed to the end, he murmurs: "Well—she'd probably have been a deuce of a nuisance."

Justice

BY JOHN GALSWORTHY

Born in Surrey, England, in 1867. He was educated at Harrow and at New College, Oxford. His first novel, "Jocelyn," appeared in 1898. Galsworthy is almost equally distinguished as both novelist and playwright. "A Man of Property," published in 1906, initiated the series of novels known as "The Forsyte Saga," dealing with the affairs of a well-to-do English family. Galsworthy devoted the years 1906–18 almost entirely to writing for the stage. His plays, frequently dealing with social problems, include, in addition to "Strife" (1909) and "Justice" (1910), the following: "The Silver Box," "Joy," "The Pigeon," "The Mob," "The Skin Game," "Loyalties," and "Old English." Galsworthy received the Order of Merit in 1929 and the Nobel Prize in 1932. He died in 1933.

A few hours before William Falder, a sensitive young junior law clerk, can carry out his plan to leave the country with Ruth Honeywill, wife of a drunken brute, and her two children, he is trapped by his employers in a small embezzlement.

Cokeson, the chief clerk, and Walter How, junior partner, feel that Falder should not be treated harshly for a first offense in which emotional disturbance evidently weighed heavily; but Walter's father, James How, observes that Falder's guilt might have been blamed on another clerk, and decides: "I don't see how it's possible to spare him. Out of the question to keep him in this office—honesty's the *sine qua non*. . . . Equally out of the question to send him out among people who've no knowledge of his character. One must think of society." Detective-Sergeant Wister takes the young clerk to jail.

Two months later, his trial counsel pleads that Falder, only twenty-three, stole the money in a moment of aberration to help Mrs. Honeywill, who herself could have gotten otherwise only a separation order, with inadequate protection from her bestial husband—her destiny the workhouse or the streets. He establishes the distress of Falder before the theft and calls to the stand Mrs. Honeywill, a pale, quiet woman of twenty-six, unpretentiously dressed.

She testifies that she has not lived with her husband for some four months and, while she and Falder love each other, they have not been intimate. She had fled to Falder on July seventh (the day of the theft), bruised and half-choked by her husband, and Falder had wept because he had no money. On July eighth he had given her "a windfall" to clothe herself and the children for their intended flight to South America. She declares her love for Falder "the only thing in my life now." Falder admits the theft, pleading his grief at the misery of Ruth and his intent to repay the money.

Frome, his lawyer, points to Falder's irresponsibility at the time in defense of the woman he loves, and notes his "not strong" face, suggesting that he be justly acquitted of criminal intent and treated as a person who is ill. He adds: "Is a man to be lost because he is bred and born with a weak character? . . . Justice is a machine that, when some one has given it the starting push, rolls on of itself. Is this young man to be ground to pieces under this machine for an act which at the worst was one of weakness? Imprison him . . . and I affirm to you that he will be lost."

The Crown counsel ridicules the plea of temporary insanity and the "romantic glow" of Ruth's appearance. The judge charges the jury, with particular emphasis upon whether Falder's conduct at the time was such as to warrant a lunatic asylum, and the jury shortly finds him guilty.

Pronouncing sentence, the judge says that the defense of temporary insanity appears to have been only a device to plead for mercy. He adds, of Falder's relations with Mrs. Honeywill: "I am not able to justify to my conscience a plea for mercy which has a basis inimical to immorality. . . . The Law is what it is—a majestic edifice, sheltering all of us . . . you will go to penal servitude for three years."

Falder's head falls on his breast as he is taken away. Ruth leaves, crushed, as the judge, at Frome's request, orders her name stricken from press records of the case.

On Christmas Eve, the prison Governor receives Cokeson who has been visiting Falder. Cokeson tells him that Falder is an orphan; one sister is an invalid, and the husband of another won't permit her to see her brother. He asks if Falder can't be allowed to exercise with the other convicts, but learns that he must be in separate confinement for three months. Cokeson reports that the youth had said: "A day, shut up in your cell thinking and brooding as I do, is longer than a year outside. I can't help it; I try—but I'm not built that way, Mr. Cokeson." Tears had trickled through the fingers Falder clasped over his face.

Cokeson further says that Ruth, who had planned to earn a living for herself and the children while waiting for Falder, has been forced by poverty to go back to her husband, and the agonizing news has reached Falder. He urges that Ruth be allowed to see the prisoner. But the Governor, who has called the chaplain and doctor to testify that Falder is retaining his health and sanity, declares himself unable to grant this permission. Cokeson leaves. Life is to go on for the youth, surrounded by broken criminals to whom a trifling sound in the corridor is a Heaven-sent diversion.

The Governor, in his routine Christmas rounds, urges Falder to "settle down . . . It's no good banging your head against a stone wall." Falder, breathless at the chance to

talk, says that he can sleep very little. He tries to smile: "I
was always nervous . . . I feel I'll never get out." The
Governor urges him to read. He answers: "I don't take the
words in . . . I can't help thinking of what's outside. . . .
In my cell I can't see out at all. It's thick glass, sir."

The doctor says that he can no more recommend Falder
than a dozen others for a change, and the Governor walks
away. Another prisoner bangs madly on his metal door,
and Falder, panting violently, throws himself in despair
against his own door, pounding it with his clenched fists.

Two years later, Ruth again calls to see Cokeson. She
has been forced, after all, to leave her husband. She tells
Cokeson that she ran across Falder yesterday. She says:
"He can't get anything to do. It's dreadful to see him." He
had been provided with a job, but his secret had been
learned by fellow-workers and he had been too sensitive to
stay. Another job had not lasted.

Cokeson suggests that the not unprosperous-appearing
Ruth may help him, but she says: "Not now." She confesses that she could not endure life again with Honeywill,
and that for nine months she had struggled to support her
children at trifling wages as a seamstress, but the load had
been too much; she accepted the attentions of her
employer.

She has really come to beg another chance for Falder in
his old office; Falder is waiting in the street for the decision.
He now comes in—paler, thinner and older, his clothes ill-
fitting. He timidly takes Cokeson's hand as Ruth goes outside to wait. He is "afraid" of strange offices, and has
slept three nights in the park. He says: "Nobody wishes
you harm, but they down you all the same. This feeling—
it's crushing me."

The partners enter, and Falder is sent into an adjoining
office while Cokeson speaks for him. The elder How at
length tells Falder that he may have a job if he gives up
Ruth. Falder insists that she is all he has lived for; only last
night had he been able to find her. All Ruth now lacks is
money to free herself from her husband, he is sure. Walter
How is willing to help her get a divorce, but as Falder

goes to the window, Cokeson whispers to the partners that Ruth has "not been quite what she ought to ha' been . . . she's lost her chance."

James How calls Ruth in, and Falder jubilantly tells her that a divorce is now possible. How stops him sharply with: "I don't think that's practicable, Falder." He tells Ruth that Falder must break with her, significantly adding: "You see what I mean?" She miserably agrees, saying, "I want to do the best for him." At length Falder realizes what she has done.

He covers his face with his hands. James How, relenting, says: "There, there! I'll give you your chance, Falder. Don't let me know what you do with yourselves, that's all." Ruth goes into a side office as someone knocks, and Falder, who has shrunk from her timidly offered hand, now follows and seizes her by the shoulder as the door conceals them both.

The visitor is Detective-Sergeant Wister, seeking Falder for failure to report regularly to the police and for getting a job with a forged reference. The Hows and Cokeson attempt to shield Falder, but Wister sees his cap and opens the other door—to hear Ruth urging: "Oh, do!" and Falder replying: "I can't!"

Wister enters. He comes swiftly out with Falder, who half drags his captor to the stairs. The others hear a thud, and Wister returns with Falder's body. Falder has jumped, breaking his neck.

Ruth recovers from a faint to kneel by Falder's body, crying endearments. As she stares at the body, Cokeson says: "No one'll touch him now. Never again. He's safe with gentle Jesus!"

Strife

BY JOHN GALSWORTHY

For months directors of the Trenartha Tin Plate Works, on
the English-Welsh border, and its employees have been
deadlocked in a bitter strike, neither side willing to consider
concessions to end the conflict, even though the strike is
accompanied by harsh suffering among the workers' families and threatens collapse of the industry.

The directors now have come from London, under the
leadership of the "bitter-ender," John Anthony, to meet
with a committee of the strikers, headed by the equally
stubborn David Roberts, at the home of Francis Underwood, Anthony's son-in-law and manager of the plant. But
there is little prospect of compromise, in spite of the efforts
of Simon Harness, a union official, to bring peace.

Edgar, Anthony's son and a director, protests before the
meeting: "There's great distress among those strikers. . . .
There's no necessity of pushing things so far in the face of
all this suffering—it's cruel. . . . This may mean starvation
to the men's wives and families." But his father gruffly
orders: "No surrender!" He later tells the strikers: "There
can be only one master." Roberts declares that the men
will starve before they give in, and the meeting is ad-
journed until five o'clock that afternoon.

At half-past three, in the kitchen of the Roberts home
where the invalid Mrs. Roberts is propped in a chair before
the fire, are gathered some of the strikers' wives and
daughters to recite their hardships. Someone has given Mrs.
Yeo a sixpence, the first money she has seen in a week.
There has been nothing but bread and tea in Mrs. Bulgin's
home for four days, and she keeps the children in bed—
"They don't get so 'ungry when they're not runnin' about."
Madge Thomas, daughter of a striker, declares the strikers
would go back if it were not for the unbending pride of

Roberts, and his wife says: "You won't beat Roberts!"

There is a knock at the door and Enid, Underwood's wife, comes to reproach Mrs. Roberts, who once was her maid, for returning some jelly she has sent. She declares Roberts' pride responsible, and Mrs. Roberts replies that Enid's father, too, is stubborn. Enid sadly admits this, but appeals to Roberts, who has just come home: "Please . . . try to give way a little—for your wife's sake, for everybody's sake."

Roberts jeers: " 'For my wife's sake, for everybody's sake' —for the sake of Mr. Anthony!" Enid asks why he is so bitter against her father, and he answers that Anthony stands for tyranny. She says: "I suppose you think it brave to go on with the struggle?" He retorts: "Does Mr. Anthony think it brave to fight against women and children?" This talk, too, is fruitless, and Roberts goes off to address a strikers' meeting. Mrs. Roberts calls plaintively: "Don't be too stubborn with 'em, David. Think of the women—and the children." Roberts answers: "No surrender!"

At the meeting, Harness, urging compromise, has won over the men, but Roberts arrives and storms: "So you'll listen to these men from London? You love their feet on your necks, don't you? Well, I don't. I say—fight! . . . Surrendering's the work of cowards and traitors! You know who's your enemy? . . . Capital, a thing that buys the sweat o' men's brows, an' the tortures o' their brains, at its own price. . . . But you've got it on its knees now. When I went this morning to those old men from London, I looked into their very hearts. They were afraid! . . . Hold out just a little longer and give me a free hand. Our fight is won!"

Madge Thomas makes her way to the platform. "Your wife, Mr. Roberts. She's dying!" He goes on automatically: "I tell you, men, the fight is——" then leaps down from the platform and rushes through the crowd. Madge says: "He needn't have hurried. Annie Roberts is dead."

At five o'clock, at the Underwood home, the directors are awaiting a delegation of the strikers. Edgar and Enid, in an adjoining room, are discussing their father with grave concern. Edgar says that since his father will never give in—"It's a sort of religion with him"—the wavering directors will vote him down, compelling him to resign as chairman. Enid protests: "Oh, Ted, you mustn't let them! He's so old; it would kill him!" Edgar answers that they must consider the justice of the issue and the suffering of the workers. Enid reminds him that her father has been warned of a stroke and that Edgar's first duty is to him. He replies: "I wonder——" and goes into the meeting, where there is the sound of hot debate.

Anthony enters, laboriously lowers himself into a chair and gruffly rejects the urging of others to compromise on the best terms possible, both to save the industry and to avert starvation of the men's families. Told by Edgar that Mrs. Roberts is dead, Anthony answers only: "War is war." Nothing will sway him. Reluctantly, the directors vote to compromise. Says Anthony: "Very well, I resign. . . . After fifty years! . . . You have disgraced me, gentlemen. Bring in the men."

The delegation enters, Harness the spokesman in place of Roberts. He is about to offer the strikers terms when Roberts hurries into the room. He first apologizes for his delay, because of "something that—has happened . . ." and then, before Harness can speak, declares: "Go ye back to London, gentlemen. We have nothing for you. By no jot or tittle we abate our demands. . . . Ye may break the body, but ye cannot break the spirit. . . ."

But he learns that he is no longer speaking for the men; they have rejected him, just as the directors have rejected Anthony, and he finds himself alone with his humiliated foe. Says Roberts: "And so they've licked us both, Mr. Anthony." Anthony struggles up from his chair and the two men face each other for a few minutes in mutual defiance and fanatic stubbornness, yet, at the same time, in grudging respect. Then Anthony, aided by Enid and Edgar, walks slowly from the room. Roberts goes.

Says Harness to Anthony's secretary: "A woman dead, and the two best men both broken!" The secretary adds:

"D'you know, sir, these terms are the very same we drew up together, you and I, and put to both sides before the fight began? All this . . . and what for?" Says Harness sardonically: "That's where the fun comes in!"

Disraeli

BY LOUIS NAPOLEON PARKER

*Born in Calvados, France, October 21, 1852. He was edu-
cated at Freiburg and at the Royal Academy of Music in
London. He was the director at Sherborne School, Dorset,
for nineteen years, during which time he composed many
songs, cantatas, etc. He resigned in 1892 to devote himself
to playwriting. His first play, "A Buried Talent" (1890),
introduced Mrs. Patrick Campbell to London. Others of
his well-known works are: "Rosemary" (in which Maude
Adams and John Drew appeared), "Pomander Walk,"
"Joseph and His Brethren," and "Disraeli," written for
George Arliss. He has written over a hundred plays, and
wrote, staged and composed the music for many pageants
in England. Although he had been in America for long
periods, he made his home in England. In 1928 he published his reminiscences in a book called "Several of My
Lives." He died in 1944 at the age of ninety-one.*

The uncannily clever Disraeli, Prime Minister of England,
is a disturbing week-end guest of the Duke and Duchess
of Glastonbury at a house party in the early seventies.
Telegrams, dispatches and letters for him arrive at all
hours, and now he has casually instructed that no less a
personage than Sir Michael Probert, Governor of the Bank
of England, be summoned from his guest chamber for a
private talk with him.

Probert arrives testily, and Disraeli carefully shuts all the doors and windows before disclosing his topic. The time is ripe, Disraeli says, for England to buy the Suez Canal before the watchful Russia can anticipate her and thus snatch at India while the British are alone, with France and Germany crippled by war. Disraeli asks that the Bank of England provide the necessary credit until Parliament meets. Probert scornfully refuses, and Disraeli "goes to Moses" in the person of the Jewish banker, Hugh Meyers.

The Prime Minister, however, still finds time to play Cupid to Lady Clarissa, piquant daughter of his host and hostess, and young Charles, Viscount Deeford. Clarissa has just indignantly rejected a proposal of marriage from the stuffy Charles who has neglected, in his stilted pronouncement, to say that he loves her. Disraeli jolts Charles from his country squire's viewpoint and, to the delight of Clarissa, appoints him as a secretary—"to teach him what it took me many years to learn." The beautiful Mrs. Travers, another guest who, throughout the week-end, has been most interested in all of the Prime Minister's activities and conversations, asks quickly what this may be. "Dear lady," he says, "that a ditch dug in sand gives the best soil for celery."

Back in Downing Street, Disraeli finds Lumley Foljambe, one of his secretaries, more than properly interested in the papers in his private office. Foljambe says he has come to ask that he be allowed to handle more important matters, but Disraeli deftly interrupts him "accidentally" departing with dispatches from Russia.

While, in an inner room, Meyers and Disraeli are agreeing on the financing of the canal purchase, the clumsy caution of Charles convinces Foljambe, despite Disraeli's ruse to divert him, that the monumental deal is on. Clarissa and Mrs. Travers arrive while they are talking, and while Charles and Clarissa are in a balcony garden together, Mrs. Travers signals Foljambe with the tapping of a paper knife on the table. She tells him that Disraeli and Meyers evidently are agreed, and that he should start at once for Cairo, going first by way of Ostend to Trieste for instructions.

Disraeli enters in time to catch the word "Ostend." After the others leave, he is surprised to see Foljambe hurry in while he is idly tapping on the table with the paper knife. He realizes that Mrs. Travers and Foljambe have exchanged vital information, and learns that Charles has unwittingly indicated the import of the conference with Meyers. He calls for Foljambe, but the secretary has gone.

Disraeli then tells Charles that he has known for weeks that Foljambe is a spy and has kept him purposely under his eye, meanwhile duping him with false papers. Now Foljambe is off to warn Russia, and England may be beaten to the purchase of the controlling shares in the canal held by the spendthrift Ismail, Khedive of Egypt. Clarissa and Charles are brokenhearted, but in her disappointment that Charles had not been selected to race to Egypt to undo the harm, Disraeli has an inspiration: he feels that Charles' guileless face will serve better than the wiles of a professional diplomat, and he hustles him off on the trip without delay.

Disraeli invites the lonely Clarissa to his estate while Charles is absent, and is careful to see that his wife invites Mrs. Travers also. Then comes a cable in code from Charles that "the celery is ripe to cut," meaning that the canal has been purchased and the check accepted. All is jubilation at the Disraeli estate.

But disaster threatens with a hurried visit from Meyers, who tells the stunned Disraeli that he is bankrupt; a ship with bullion has been scuttled by conspirators, mysterious rumors have been shrinking his credit since he agreed to finance Disraeli's coup, and his debts have been bought up. Utter disgrace faces Disraeli, but he tells Meyers to keep his bankruptcy a secret as long as possible while he hopes for a miracle.

Mrs. Travers arrives and Disraeli feigns illness. Mrs. Travers asks news of Charles, and Disraeli hands her the cable. He watches her in a mirror while she reads it, slyly picking up the code sheet near by and crushing it in her hand. She makes an excuse to go to the garden, but Disraeli manages to tell Clarissa to give her no chance to

decode the cable. While the two are absent, he instructs
his wife to summon Sir Michael Probert, of whom Mrs.
Travers has accidentally reminded him.

When Mrs. Travers returns, Disraeli playfully takes her
hand and admires her fingers, then extracts the code sheet
from her glove. He tells the now defiant woman that at
last he has recalled meeting her in Geneva, years ago, when
she and her companion, Mr. Lumley, were decoys in Russian pay who tempted refugees back to Siberia and death.
He says that he knows Lumley is now Foljambe and that
their plotting has been futile—the canal has been bought
by England.

Mrs. Travers retorts that Meyers is bankrupt, his check
only waste paper. Disraeli says weakly: "I—I am a child
in your hands." Probert comes and Disraeli explains the
crisis, appealing again that the Bank of England shall
underwrite the credit. Probert refuses anew, but Disraeli,
in a chill warning that England itself may be disgraced,
threatens to smash the bank and ruin its directors. Probert
signs, validating Meyers' check. Disraeli gallantly hands
Mrs. Travers her scarf. She walks slowly to the door, pausing to smile and nod pleasantly in farewell.

The departing Probert mutters: "It is outrageous that a
man like you should have such power!" Clarissa joyously
exclaims: "Oh Mr. Disraeli; thank God you have such
power." Disraeli replies, whimsically: "I haven't, dear
child; but he doesn't know that."

Finally, in the great reception room in Downing Street,
before a brilliant throng, Disraeli is hailed for having made
his Queen the Empress of India. He announces royal
honors for Meyers, Probert and Charles—whom Clarissa
has now accepted.

The Passing of the Third Floor Back

BY JEROME K. JEROME

Born in Walsall, Wales, May 2, 1859. Because of family poverty, he went to work at an early age, first as clerk, then as a reporter on London papers, and later as an obscure actor. His stage knowledge helped him to become dramatic critic on the London Sunday Times, *but his first real success came when he wrote "Idle Thoughts of an Idle Fellow" and "Three Men in a Boat." Then he became editor of* The Idler *and* Today. *His best-known play, "The Passing of the Third Floor Back," in which Forbes-Robertson starred, was first produced in 1907. He died on June 14, 1927.*

A small back room on the third floor of a dreary London boarding house is vacant, and Stasia, the slatternly girl-of-all-work, has put a card in the window, hoping that it will attract, possibly, a nobleman in disguise. Now a stranger comes in search of a lodging, and Stasia announces him to the flinty Mrs. Sharpe, the landlady. The caller has evidently stirred Stasia oddly, for she is smiling dreamily; whether he is "a gentleman," young or old, she hasn't noticed.

Mrs. Sharpe finds him a slightly stooped figure in somewhat shabby clothes, his long coat rather old-fashioned, and his staff quaintly suggestive of the days of pilgrimage. His age is uncertain—his eyes seem to reflect many sorrows, but when he smiles his face is radiant with youth; he seems "important" only in the atmosphere of dignity that he brings, and in a marked simplicity and gentleness. He relieves Stasia of a heavy tray and places a chair for Mrs. Sharpe—strange courtesies in this house. He says that he is a wanderer—"a traveler for pleasure," in Mrs. Sharpe's correcting phrase.

Mrs. Sharpe tells him loftily of the "little circle of persons of more or less distinction" which the house boasts, and offers the room at a pound above her usual price. She angrily finds herself correcting the figure when he pleasantly accepts her terms. He says: "Women are so wilful." He takes her hand and, with a smile, continues, "And you kind women are the worst of all." Mrs. Sharpe, shown unaccustomed kindness and trust, now smiles and gives the harassed Stasia an hour off.

The stranger finds that the "select circle" comprises Major Tompkins, retired, a distinguished-appearing, lazy and penniless fraud; his bickering wife; Vivian, his pretty daughter, weary of poverty and humiliation; Joey Wright, a retired bookmaker of sixty years, reputed wealthy, who is courting Vivian with her father's eager approval; Christopher Penny, a young artist who loves her but whose poverty she cannot endure; Jape Samuels, a shady promoter, and his jackal, Harry Larkcom; Miss Kite, a simpering spinster of forty, struggling to conceal her age with paint and dye, and Mrs. Percival De Hooley, a snob because she is a cousin of a baronet.

Stasia tells Vivian of the new lodger. To Vivian's question, "What's he like?" Stasia replies only: "This ain't all the world, is it? All a-lyin' and a-cheatin' and a-snarlin'—despisin' one another—and ourselves. Ain't there anything else?" Says Vivian: "Yes. There are sweet thoughts, and fine feelings, and self-respect. But such things, Stasia, are only for rich folks."

Mrs. Tompkins doesn't like the newcomer. She muses: "I can't explain it. He makes you feel uncomfortable." Says Mrs. De Hooley: "He reminds me of somebody I've met somewhere . . . long ago." Jape Samuels finds him not his idea of a gentleman. Wright also disapproves—"spoils the party"—and Larkcom thinks: "He's got no conversation—not what I call conversation." Says the Major: "I hate a man with eyes that you can't get away from."

Vivian, who has dressed for a theater with Wright,

stands transfixed when the stranger appears and their eyes
meet. She decides suddenly not to go with Wright, and
hurries to her room. The newcomer chats with Larkcom,
who is playing the piano, and compliments him as a
talented and sincere musician. Larkcom finds himself ceas-
ing his impudence and telling the stranger of his hope to
be an entertainer; he is stirred by the new lodger's earnest
sympathy and encouragement.

Miss Kite calls him gushingly, but under his quiet, grave
eyes she tells her sorrows, too, even confessing that she is
forty. He views it as a "beautiful age," but urges that she
acquire a vanity that will make her proud of her own
undisguised beauty, character and distinction. She cries:
"I hate you, because you have made me see myself as I
am!" She goes to her room.

Joey Wright accuses the stranger of influencing Vivian
not to go out with him. He answers: "May it not have been
merely her Better Self pleading to her?" He tells Wright
that Vivian would be unworthy of him if she married him
only for his money. He smiles and calls Wright "Sir
Joseph," his nickname in the days when he was a generous
and kindly bookmaker, and tells him that he shall free
Vivian to marry the impoverished Christopher, himself
finding happiness in her happiness. . . . "He would be a
great gentleman who could do that." Wright thoughtfully
leaves.

The Major is speaking jeeringly of his wife, and the
stranger says: "I remember her well—as a girl." But he
identifies himself to the Major only as "a friend you have
forgotten." He recalls Mrs. Tompkins as a lovely girl, and
the Major as a gallantly jaunty figure, chivalrous and
tender. The Major, subdued, presents Mrs. Tompkins
who has stormed downstairs to berate her husband. She
thinks she does remember the stranger as one she knew
when she was young, and he congratulates her smilingly
on the happiness of their continued love. The Major asks
his wife to go to the theater with him on the tickets Wright
has given him. He even fetches her cloak and calls her

"dear." She finds herself softly calling him "John." Samuels
drily comments that the age of miracles has begun.

Mrs. De Hooley recalls that she once knew the stranger,
too. She asks him if they met in society, but he tells her
it was "in the days when you were a great lady, before you
came down in the world," forsaking a sister who had
sinned. Mrs. De Hooley weeps in shame, but smilingly goes
to her room when he tells her: "Love goes all the way . . .
it is the Helpless and the Fallen that hold in their hands
the patents of nobility."

The stranger revives Christopher's courage and faith in
his art, and bids him marry Vivian in spite of his poverty.
As Christopher goes to burn some cheap works he has been
selling to Samuels, the promoter attempts to interest the
stranger in some worthless stock. He offers figures, but the
stranger says: "You are—is it not so?—a Jew?" At Samuels'
snarling anger, he continues that if he is a Jew "your word
would be sufficient . . . the word of a Jew. So many of
the noblest men I have known, men I have loved, have
been Jews. It is a great race—a race rich in honorable
names." He accepts Samuels' offer with thanks, but the
promoter withdraws it; if anything went wrong, he explains, he would feel as if he had sold his race for a few
hundred pounds.

Stasia comes in with a pair of earrings, the gift of Larkcom. The stranger tells her that they do not become her,
that they are not pure. He tells Stasia that the father she
has never known was a gallant gentleman, a dear friend.
She asks if she can be his friend, too, and he holds out his
arms. She goes to him, but stops. "I was forgetting: I'm a
bad 'un," she says. He answers: "Did I ask?" He then
kisses her gently and sends her away. She throws the
earrings in the fire.

Vivian comes in, and she and the stranger are alone before the fire. She demands: "Who are you? . . . You look
at me out of crowds. . . . What is it that you want with
me?" He says he has come to plead with her for Christopher, that her Better Self will not let her forsake him.
"You will marry your lover. With him you will walk the

way of sunlight and shadow." Again she demands his name: "I know your voice. I hear it in the wind. . . . Who——" Awe comes into her tone. She stares at him, then cries: "You are——" She is about to kneel. He stretches out his hand and stays her, saying: "—A fellow-lodger. Good night."

Through the stranger's coming, understanding and love transform the house. Mrs. Sharpe recovers her pride; Samuels renounces trickery and bears his head high; the Major is happy at work as a salesman and in the restored love of his wife; Mrs. De Hooley finds contentment in discarding her snobbery and helping her sister to set up as a dressmaker; Wright is happy in helping Christopher, who has regained his own enthusiasm and hope; Larkcom is making progress as a musician; Miss Kite appears without paint and dye, an ordeal happily passed through owing to the kindly tact of all the lodgers; Vivian is to marry Christopher, and Stasia is content in her new-found pride of family.

Now the stranger is leaving. Stasia flings her arms about him, and cries: "Oh, it was such a muddle before you came—life! Everything! I couldn't make head or tail of it. And all the while it is beautiful." She conquers her tears, tries to smile, and puts out her hands to him: "It was so kind of you—to come." The stranger takes her gently in his arms and says: "I came because you wanted me." But now he must go. "I also am a servant. I have my work," he tells her. He takes up his staff and goes out into the fog. A shaft of sunlight steals through the fanlight and bathes Stasia's radiant face.

If I Were King

BY JUSTIN HUNTLY MC CARTHY

Born in 1860, the eldest son of the British historian, novelist, and journalist, Justin McCarthy. The son was educated at University College School and at University College, London, and began to write when he was twenty-one. He became definitely identified with the theater when his famous play, "If I Were King," appeared about 1900. This dramatization of François Villon's story furnished Sothern with one of his best roles, and is further significant because the young and struggling artist, John Barrymore, was commissioned to do a poster for it. In 1920 this play was made into a musical comedy, "The Vagabond King." McCarthy wrote many popular histories in collaboration with his father, and was most successful in the field of the historical novel. He traveled widely in Europe, Egypt, Palestine, and America. He died on March 21, 1936, after a long illness.

With the Burgundian army at the gates of Paris and his abused people near revolt, the weak and superstitious Louis XI of France is moved by a tale of Haroun al Raschid to go in disguise among his subjects to learn the true state of the realm. He is light of heart because last night he dreamed that he, rooting as a swine, found a great pearl in the gutter, but he would have crushed it had not a star fallen from heaven and prevented him from doing so.

Now, with his friend Tristan Hermite, Louis has come at night to the Tavern of the Fir Cone where the Company of the Cockleshells, "the worst rats and cats in all Paris," are roistering. Among them Tristan points out the poet-rogue, François Villon, King of the Cockleshells, "good at pen, point and pitcher"; René de Montigny, Villon's friend, and Huguette du Hamel, called the Abbess "for her nunnery of light-o'-loves."

Villon, handsome and magnetic even in his rags, is telling his cronies of his latest adventure: he sent verses to a lovely lady of the court whom he followed into church, and soon he was lured into a beating for his pains. He continues to call for liquor, for which Louis has been paying, and the disguised King suggests that he may be drinking too much. There is nothing else to do, says Villon, "while a nincompoop sits on the throne."

"No doubt you could do better than the King if you were in his place," Louis sneers. Villon then recites a grandiose poem in which he pictures a realm reglorified "if Villon were the King of France." Tristan whispers: "Shall I hang him tomorrow?" Louis answers vaguely: "We shall see. . . . He has set me thinking of my dream . . . in the streets of Paris I found a pearl—well, well!"

The rabble has rushed out to see a fight, Louis and Tristan are playing cards and Villon nods by the fire when a muffled woman, recognized by the masqueraders as Lady Katherine de Vaucelles, kinswoman of the King, enters and approaches Villon. Tristan leaves, and Louis hides behind a curtain as she awakens the amazed poet. It is his girl of the church! She shows the verse he sent to her. "If I were king . . . to swear allegiance to your eyes and lips and hair"—and asks if these are only idle words. Villon declares: "My words are my life. I love you!"

Katherine answers that then he can serve her well, for her enemy, the man who ordered Villon to be beaten, is coming to the inn in the person of Thibaut d'Aussigny, Grand Constable of France. He means to betray the King to the Duke of Burgundy, and she asks that Villon kill him—for her and for France. Villon escorts her to a gallery from which she can point out the Constable to him and then escape, unseen.

Soon the hulking D'Aussigny arrives, dressed as a common soldier, and plots with De Montigny to enlist ruffians to kidnap the King. As he leaves, Villon, feigning drunkenness, provokes a duel and runs him through. Katherine

tosses the victor a knot of ribbon as the police arrive, but
D'Aussigny is not dead. He identifies himself, and orders
Villon hanged forthwith. Then Louis removes his hood
before the awed crowd, ordering Villon into his own
custody.

The next day, Louis has been assured by his astrologer
that the dream of the pearl may well mean that there is,
in the depths, one who may save the state, and that such
a one would have potent influence for seven days from this
day. Tristan comes to report that D'Aussigny has escaped
to the Burgundian camp and that the "tavern rabble,"
including Villon, is in custody.

Louis tells Tristan, again in the manner of Haroun al
Raschid, that he will appoint Villon, on his awakening from
a drugged sleep, as the Count of Montcorbier and Grand
Constable of France. "His antics may amuse me, his lucky
star may serve me, and his winning tongue may help to
avenge me on the froward maid," remarks the King. So
Villon awakes and fancies himself dreaming, what with his
royal bed, his richly dressed and perfumed body, and his
obsequious attendants—but he carries his grandeur like a
born noble. And he has an uproarious time as judge of the
tavern crew, all of whom fail to recognize in him their
old leader. He mysteriously reminds them of their secret
crimes and sins, but frees them all, giving them gold and
roses, food and drink. To Huguette, who tells him that
Villon has disappeared, he gives his ring.

Then Katherine, bidden by the King to take to the
Grand Constable her plea for Villon, appears, and Villon,
assuring her that he will only banish the rascal, renews
his wooing. He asks what he can do to win her favor, and
she reminds him that, as Grand Constable, he is chief of
the King's army. "For the man who shall trail the banners
of Burgundy in the dust," she says, "I may, perhaps, have
favors."

Villon's elation is short-lived, for Louis tells him, mockingly, that, in punishment for his insolence, he must make
a choice: he may have seven days of this splendor and love,
with his last task the hanging of Master François Villon;

or he may swallow his boasting and be whipped into the
street, again a ragamuffin. Katherine passes, and the King
mutters to himself: "How if my lady virtue who flouted
me could be lured to love this beggar man——" He then
tells Villon that if he shall win Katherine within the week,
he may go free with her. Villon hears Katherine singing
his own song, and instantly chooses his week of glory.

A herald comes from Burgundy to demand surrender,
and Louis ironically calls on his Grand Constable to speak
for him as "if Villon were the King of France." Villon's
answer is flaming defiance, promising blow for blow. Katherine, explaining her cry of gratitude to Louis, says: "It
means, sire, that a man has come to court."

Villon, while preparing his strategy and reuniting the
people by his wise and generous reforms, comes upon
Huguette, disguised, in the garden. She recognizes him at
last, and reveals that D'Aussigny, with De Montigny and
his men, is plotting again to kidnap the King and turn him
over to Burgundy. Villon conquers his temptation to let
the kidnapping dissolve his own peril, and poses as the
King when the kidnappers arrive. Trapped by Villon's men,
D'Aussigny attempts to stab him, but Huguette throws
herself between them and receives the dagger thrust. She
dies bravely, first asking a kiss from her idol, Villon.

Villon, having pardoned and recruited from the kidnap
band many of his old Cockleshells, proves himself to Katherine, by the ribbon she has given him, as her poet of the
tavern. After having earlier promised her heart, she condemns him: "You have stolen my love like a thief; you
have crucified my pride. I hate you!" The sneering Louis
reminds Villon that he must hang tomorrow, but Villon,
now welcoming the gallows because of the loss of Katherine's love, declares that his love has bidden him to save
France, and that tonight he fights for her.

Villon triumphs over the enemy and returns, with Burgundy's banners, to face the gallows. Louis now wishes to
relent, but his counselors have warned that Villon's popularity already is threatening the throne. When the hero's
fate is evident the crowds roar angrily, but none accepts

Louis' challenge that they produce a substitute for Villon.

Then Katherine comes to offer her life in exchange for Villon's, but the King refuses to accept. She asks Villon to kill her and himself with his dagger, and at these belated proofs that at last she loves him, he demands his right to be married before death, that he may die by the sword like a soldier.

But Katherine saves the day; she reveals that with the wedding, the commoner Villon becomes her vassal, and that by law she alone now holds over him the power of life and death. Louis warns her that her marriage also means that she must decline to her husband's beggar's estate, but she finds this "a little price." Villon cries: ". . . A star has fallen to me from heaven . . ." and in the phrase Louis sees the realization of his dream. He proclaims Villon and Katherine free to find their happiness.

The Admirable Crichton

BY JAMES MATTHEW BARRIE

Born in May, 1860, in Scotland, he was educated in the Scottish schools, graduating from the University of Edinburgh in 1882. Early in his life he became interested in writing and journalism, and worked for a while for newspapers and magazines in Edinburgh. His sketches soon won him recognition—especially his writings about Scottish peasant life—and when "The Little Minister" appeared, his success was assured. In 1892 he moved to London and commenced writing plays. Five years later, the stage version of "The Little Minister" appeared. This was followed by "The Admirable Crichton," "What Every Woman Knows," "Peter Pan," "The Twelve Pound Look," and many other well-known plays. Barrie was made a baronet in 1913, receiving the Order of Merit in 1922. He died in London on June 19, 1937.

Crichton, butler to the Earl of Loam, is pained, as usual, as he prepares for his Lordship's monthly gesture—a tea at which his Lordship and his guests mingle with the servants on a basis of "equality." Lord Loam likes to think of himself as a democrat, but Crichton is steeped in class consciousness and the conviction that there can be no true equality either in the fashionable world of society or in the servants' quarters.

Among those at this month's uncomfortable tea party are the widowed Earl's young and beautiful daughters, Lady Catherine, Lady Agatha and the haughty Lady Mary; Lord Brocklehurst, a somewhat inane youngster who is engaged to Lady Mary; Mr. Treherne, a pleasant young clergyman; and Lord Loam's nephew, the Honorable Ernest Woolley, a perpetrator of feeble epigrams. Lord Loam makes his customary observation that class barriers really are artificial, but Crichton deferentially insists that they are the natural outcome of civilized society—that there must always be a master and servants.

Loam, having an important announcement to make, ends the debate. He tells them that he, his daughters, Treherne and Ernest are going on a long yachting trip, and, to prove his contempt for excessive luxury, there will be only one maid to serve the three girls. The daughters are indignant, and when the maids hear of this they all "give notice" immediately. The ladies are left to do with the services of Tweeny, the scullery girl. Loam's valet, denied the company of three maids, also leaves, and Crichton, who has not been wholly cold to Tweeny's love for him, offers to replace him. The party ends, Lady Mary pondering Crichton's contention (despite his happiness as a butler to aristocrats) that, should all return to a primitive setting, Nature would decide who would be master.

Two months later, the yachting party has been shipwrecked on a Pacific island. Everyone but Crichton and Tweeny—who are capable of dressing without help—now goes about barefoot and half-clad. Lord Loam has been lost in the accident. Ernest is engaged in writing an account of the disaster in which he recounts that the crew was

lost and that Lord Loam gave his life to save a servant
who had fallen overboard. Agatha points out that it was
really Crichton who dived in to save Lord Loam, but
Ernest retorts that the report may be printed in the English
papers, and that while Loam was lost in trying to be first
into the lifeboat, after all he *is* an English peer.

Ernest puts the report in a bottle, throws it into the sea,
hoping it will be picked up for eventual publication, and
assumes leadership of the party. He does no work, however, and Crichton begins to realize that English class
distinctions are hardly adequate to the island. He tells
Lady Mary that "no work, no dinner" will undoubtedly
change Ernest's habits. With Tweeny's help he provides a
hut for shelter and cocoanuts for food; he also makes a fire
by using an eyeglass lens.

Suddenly, out of the jungle crawls Lord Loam—he has
somehow managed to save himself. He briskly directs
Crichton to cease idling and be about his work. The butler,
Tweeny and Treherne prepare supper. Loam and Ernest,
meanwhile, cannot agree upon which of them is to be
leader; they call upon Crichton to decide. Crichton first
respectfully proposes that Ernest be ducked in a bucket
for his epigrams. This Crichton does. Loam preens himself for his firmness of spirit, but Lady Mary observes that
it was Crichton who was firm.

Loam, now resentful, attempts to put Crichton in his
butler's place, but, on being reminded that different qualities of leadership are now required, dismisses him from
service with orders to "go." Crichton, still respectful, refuses
so long as Loam needs his help, and Lady Mary says that
if Crichton won't go, they shall leave him. They all troop
off, but as night falls they silently drift back to the fire
and the smell of Crichton's supper. Lady Mary, the last to
come, remains outside the circle, her teeth clenched in
helpless fury.

Two years pass. Crichton's ingenuity, skill and strength
have now made him the accepted master, and the others
are his virtual servants. He has built a comfortable house—
with conveniences—even including electricity; he has ar-

ranged over the island rescue beacons that can be illuminated by a central switch in case a ship is sighted. But
the party cares little about rescue; they are content, especially Crichton and Mary, who are now in love. Crichton,
who now calls Loam "Daddy" instead of "Your Lordship,"
and himself is called "Gov," has come to feel that Tweeny
is certainly an inferior, and he has a touch of condescension
in his attitude toward the deferential Lady Mary.

Crichton decides that he will marry Mary, and, although Tweeny's eyes are tearful, there is general festivity
while the "wedding skirt" is being made. Loam is playing
a concertina and dancing has begun when there is the
sound of a cannon shot. Crichton investigates, returning
to report a ship a mile offshore. Mary pleads that he allow
the ship to leave without signaling her, but Crichton, in
loyalty to his master, pulls the switch of the electric light
system, and soon sailors arrive to take them off the island.
"Come, everybody," says Loam. "Come, Crichton." Says
Crichton: "Yes, my Lord."

Back in England, all resume their former roles quite
naturally. Ernest publishes a book on their adventures—
with most of the glory for himself, an occasional kind word
for Lord Loam and no mention whatever of Crichton. But
Crichton silently forgoes claiming either credit or the love
of Lady Mary, who resumes her engagement with
Brocklehurst.

His mother, Lady Brocklehurst, however, is not quite
sure that Mary has been every bit the young English lady
while on the island, and decides to question the honest
Crichton. She points out to her son in advance that if
Crichton begins any of his answers with "The fact is—" it
will be unfortunate, for this phrase generally denotes a lie.
She first asks a few pointed questions of Ernest and Lady
Mary who tell nothing, but unhappily preface their eva-
sions with "The fact is——"

To Mary's consternation, Lady Brocklehurst summons
Crichton and demands the truth. Crichton promises to give
it to her. Lady Brocklehurst demands to know, first, if
everyone was equal on the island. No, he replies, the social

distinctions were preserved there as in England; the servants' teas of Loam's home were discontinued "at the 'Gov's'
orders." And was there any—shall we say—sentimentalizing
going on among the young people? Crichton answers truth-
fully; yes, there was.

Lady Brocklehurst calls upon Tweeny to tell which gentleman was involved in this "sentimentalizing," but Agatha
comes to the rescue with the reminder that she and Ernest
are engaged to be married, and Lady Brocklehurst, taking
this as a complete explanation, is satisfied.

Brocklehurst brings on a new crisis when he commends
Crichton as an excellent fellow and invites him, if ever he
leaves Lord Loam, to enter the service of himself and Mary
after they are married. Lady Mary drops her guard for an
instant to give an agitated veto—this would be impossible. Lady Brocklehurst, suspicious again, asks why
"impossible"?

But Crichton unhesitatingly sacrifices his contentment to
protect his master's family; he announces to Loam that as
soon as he can be replaced, he is leaving service entirely.
Treherne asks what he intends to do, but Crichton doesn't
know. The family goes in to dinner, Mary lingering to
say farewell to Crichton.

She asks him if he despises her, and the truthful Crichton makes no answer. She declares him the best man
among them all, but he reminds her that England is not
the Pacific island. She says that then there is something
wrong with England, and the admirable Crichton respectfully concludes the leave-taking with the protest that not
even from her, my Lady, can he listen to a word against
England.

Peter Pan

BY JAMES MATTHEW BARRIE

It is six o'clock at the home of the Darling family in a leafy London street, and Nana, the nurse (a large Newfoundland dog, for the Darlings cannot afford a regular nurse), is preparing to put the three Darling children to bed. She turns down the covers, opens the taps for the baths with her nose, and finally brings in Michael, the youngest, on her back.

Mrs. Darling, the loveliest of ladies, comes to say good night to her children, for she and Mr. Darling are going out to dinner. As she enters the nursery, she thinks she sees a strange little face outside the window, but is reassured when she finds Michael, Wendy and John all accounted for.

She tells Mr. Darling that once before a strange little boy had been seen in the house, but that he had escaped out the window when Nana leaped at him. It is her opinion that he has come back to get his shadow which had been snipped off by the window closing, but she cannot explain a tiny ball of light which had darted about the room while the boy was there. But Mr. Darling (in a testy mood because one of his jokes has gone awry) quiets his wife's fears and insists upon chaining Nana downstairs. The parents then leave for their party.

The children fall asleep. Soon a little ball of light appears in the darkened nursery, darting into bureau drawers and wardrobe. Then, through the window flies Peter Pan, dressed mostly in autumn leaves and cobwebs. The light guides him to the drawer where his shadow has been left, and as he is trying to stick it back on again with soap, Wendy awakens. She and Peter talk. She tries to put her arms about him when he tells her that he hasn't any mother, but he warns her that no one must ever touch him.

Wendy sews on Peter's shadow for him and, in lieu of a kiss (he doesn't even know what one is), gives him her thimble; he reciprocates with an acorn button from his clothing. Peter explains that he ran away the day he was born "because I heard Father and Mother talking of what I was to be when I became a man. I want always to be a little boy and have fun." So he ran away and lived with the fairies. Fairies, he tells her, are the laughter of new babies, but one dies every time a child says: "I don't believe in fairies." He explains that the ball of light is Tinker Bell, a fairy who mends the fairy pots and kettles. She and Peter speak the fairy language (like a tinkle of bells), but Peter declares that she is quite "a common girl"; a little jealous of Wendy, she is given to saying "silly ass" and pulling Wendy's hair. Peter tells Wendy that he lives in the Never Land with the Lost Boys—the children who fall out of their prams. He has come to the nursery to hear stories to carry back to tell them. When Wendy boasts that she knows many stories, Peter induces her to come with him to Never Land to be a mother to the boys. He then sprinkles fairy dust on all the Darling children and off they fly—just as the suspicious Nana, who has broken her chain, returns, bringing the Darlings from the party.

In Never Land, which has a forest and a lovely lagoon beyond, the six Lost Boys, all clad in the furs of animals which they think they have shot, are awaiting Peter. They are Nibs, Peter, Curly, the First and Second Twins, and Slightly, who declares his name is Slightly Soiled because that is what his mother had written on his pinafore. They all scurry through holes in hollow trees to their underground home when Captain Jas Hook, a fearsome pirate with an iron hook for a right hand, approaches in a boat with his villainous crew, bawling a grisly chantey of the Spanish Main.

Hook is constantly bent on capturing the boys. He particularly wants Peter, for Peter once worsted him in combat and threw his arm to a crocodile, and now the crocodile is trailing Hook to eat more of him. Fortunately, the creature has also swallowed a clock, and so far the ticking in its stomach has warned the pirate of its approach. Just as the pirates come after the boys, the ticking is heard again and they flee, followed by their enemies, Indian Tiger Lily and countless of her braves of the Piccaninny tribe.

Wendy now approaches, flying among the treetops in her white nightgown. The boys, at Tinker Bell's jealous urging, and thinking her a strange sort of bird, try to shoot her down with a bow and arrow; but the missile strikes Peter's "kiss," the acorn, and Wendy is unhurt. Peter, followed closely by the sleepy Michael and John, who wears a stovepipe hat, arrives. They all quickly build a little house around Wendy, using John's hat for a chimney. Wendy gathers all the boys together to tell them bedtime stories, while Peter stands guard outside against pirates and wolves. The glow of inquisitive fairies dots the darkness.

The Darling children and the Lost Boys now begin a fascinating series of adventures. They try to capture mermaids in the lagoon; they rescue Tiger Lily from Marooners' Rock where the pirates have tied her, and the boys battle and defeat the pirates (the villains had hoped to capture Wendy to be their mother).

But Wendy, somewhat miffed because Peter feels only a filial respect for her, begins to worry about her parents. Peter, sorrowfully remembering his desertion of his own mother and father, agrees that the children should go home. The boys are rebellious—until Wendy has an inspiration and invites them all home with her. Peter refuses to go, but he plans to have the Indians and Tinker Bell guide them home. They have reckoned without Hook, however. The pirates, in a dastardly attack, defeat Tiger Lily's braves and capture the children. Hook leaves poison for Peter, who is asleep. Tinker Bell drinks it to save him, but she is revived in time when Peter calls upon all children who believe in fairies to clap their hands as a sign of faith.

Peter trails the pirates and their captives to the pirate ship where the children are about to be made to walk the plank. By a succession of gallant and wily maneuvers, he frees the boys, and in a hot battle the pirates are defeated. Peter himself engages Hook, baffling him with the brilliance of his swordplay. Hook cries: " 'Tis some fiend fighting me! Pan: who and what art thou?" Peter (at a venture) answers: "I'm youth, I'm joy. I'm a little bird that has broken out of the egg." Hook, defeated, finally resigns himself to the waiting crocodile, and the children, accompanied by Peter, fly off to the Darling home. Here Nana, as usual, though now a little cynically, has laid out their night things. Mr. Darling, in remorse, is living in Nana's kennel.

Peter at first wants Wendy to stay with him always, but, moved by seeing Mrs. Darling's tears ("Come on, Tink; we don't want any silly mothers"), he opens up the window for the children to fly in. The Darlings joyously welcome their offspring and happily adopt all the Lost Boys. Nana assumes the importance of a nurse who will never have another day off. Wendy flies to Peter, who is playing his pipes outside, and asks if he would like to say anything to her parents about a very sweet subject—about her; but Peter only says "No." Mrs. Darling wants to adopt him, too, but as he won't consider school and manhood, it is settled that Wendy may visit him once a year in Never Land to do his spring housecleaning for him.

A year later, in Never Land, Wendy (now a little older and unable to see the ageless Peter quite as clearly) has finished cleaning Peter's house and is going home. She says, pleading that Peter call for her again next year: "If another little girl—if one younger than I am——" She can't go on; she wishes she could hug him, but he draws back. She says resignedly: "Yes, I know," gets astride her broomstick (she no longer flies as easily) and soars homeward.

"In a sort of way he understands what she means by 'Yes, I know,' but in most sorts of ways he doesn't. It has something to do with the riddle of his being. If he could get the hang of the thing his cry might become: 'To live would be an awfully big adventure!' But he can never quite get the hang of it, and so no one is as gay as he. With rapturous face he produces his pipes, and the Never birds

*and the fairies gather closer till the roof of the little
house is so thick with his admirers that some of them fall
down the chimney. He plays on and on till we wake up."*

The Liars

BY HENRY ARTHUR JONES

*Born at Grandborough, Buckinghamshire, September 28,
1851, the son of a farmer. He began to earn his living at
an early age, but, being interested in literature, he spent
his spare time studying. His first play—"Only Round the
Corner"—was produced at the Exeter Theatre, but his real
debut as a dramatist was made in 1882 with his play,
"The Silver King." After the financial success which this
work brought him, he was able to write a play "to please
himself"; this was "Saints and Sinners," and it ran for two
hundred performances. Because of the way it dealt with
middle-class life and religion in a country town, it caused
considerable disturbance, and Jones was finally obliged to
defend his position in an article in the* Nineteenth Century.
*For the next twenty years he wrote a great many plays,
"The Liars" appearing in 1897. He died in 1929.*

A dangerous flirtation between the susceptible Lady Jessica Nepean, young wife of the gruff and thoughtless Gilbert Nepean, and Edward Falkner, whose exploits against African slave-dealers have made him a social lion, is disturbing a regatta house party at the home of spineless Freddie Tatton and his wife, Lady Rosamund, sister of Jessica.

Others at the party, who share in the fear that Jessica will go too far with the honorable and deeply smitten Falkner, are Colonel Sir Christopher Deering, Falkner's

companion in Africa; George Nepean, Gilbert's brother;
Dolly Coke, cousin of the sisters, and her husband, Archibald; Beatrice Ebernoe, whom Falkner rescued in Africa
and the death of whose husband he had avenged, and
Mrs. Crespin, a rather malicious friend.

Jessica and Falkner have gone for a row on the river,
and George has threatened to tell his brother of his suspicions concerning the two. When the couple return, Rosamund and Dolly urge Jessica to discourage Falkner, but she
answers them, and her husband as well, quite airily. She
tells Gilbert, who is going away that night, that Falkner is
only paying her attentions that should be her due. Gilbert
warns her to see Falkner no more, declaring that he will
show no mercy if she goes too far.

But Jessica intimates to Falkner that she will meet him
the next night at a little hotel, the Star and Garter, near
the home of her cousin Barbara, where she is to be a guest.
When she has gone, Sir Christopher appeals to Falkner to
drop the romance, pointing out the scandal that is sure to
follow, and their slim chance for happiness. Falkner persists, however, and turns down an urgent government request that he return to Africa where a new crisis is in
prospect.

The next night, at the Star and Garter, Falkner has
arranged an elaborate dinner in a private dining room.
Jessica arrives, coquettishly dressed. She explains, tongue
in cheek, that she took the wrong path to the station and
came here quite by accident. Falkner, declaring his love
for her, embraces her, but she struggles free, sending him
out of the room on a trumped-up pretext. Going to the
window to recover her composure, she finds herself facing
George, her brother-in-law, who stands on the veranda.

She tells George that she is dining "with a small party,"
but Falkner comes back and there is a long and awkward
pause. George says: "Gilbert must know of this. You understand?"

Lady Rosamund happens by with Freddie, and Jessica
implores her to share in the dinner party in order to fool
George. Lady Rosamund cannot, she and Freddie must

dine with Mrs. Crespin; but with Jessica's pen she writes a
note to George, asking him to call at her home tomorrow
noon for an explanation that will clear Jessica. The sisters
plan to say that they were to have dined at the hotel and
that Falkner had entered accidentally before Rosamund
came.

Jessica's maid now appears with a message that Gilbert is
arriving home in London that night, and Jessica hastens to
get a train. Sir Christopher appears and volunteers to help
Falkner eat the dinner, but the latter takes a London train,
leaving the food to the appreciative Christopher. Christopher finds Jessica's pen.

The next day, at Rosamund's apartment, Jessica learns
from her sister that George will call—but that he plans,
nevertheless, to tell Gilbert of the hotel incident. Just then,
Sir Christopher comes in to return Jessica's pen. She tells
him the whole story, appealing for his advice. He urges her
to tell the truth, but she assures him that her indiscretion
will never be repeated. He eventually agrees to help pacify
Gilbert, as does the docile Freddie.

Confusion enters with Mrs. Crespin, who reveals that she
has just met George, on his way to meet Gilbert at the
station; she has told him that Rosamund and Freddie dined
with her the previous night. Jessica still is determined to lie
rather than tell the truth. She is groping for a story concerning how some other woman dined with her when Cousin
Dolly arrives. Dolly agrees to be the fictitious dinner guest,
but she is puzzled by one point: if Jessica left in dismay
at being confronted by George, did Dolly leave with her
without dinner, or remain to eat the dinner alone?

Agreement on this point is forestalled by the appearance
of the coldly disdainful George. Dolly glibly tells the pre-
arranged tale of being with Jessica. George goes to fetch
Gilbert so that he may draw his own conclusions. Dolly
(by this time hazy even about where the dinner was) recalls that she must take Archibald to the dentist. Archibald enters, and it is necessary to explain to him why
Dolly must stay. Only when Jessica breaks into tears, and
Sir Christopher appeals to his generosity and love of family,

does he agree to help—but only to the extent of keeping silent.

George and Gilbert now enter. Gilbert impatiently demands an explanation and, when Jessica refuses to speak because of his curtness, he turns to Coke. Coke pleads that he doesn't know the particulars, and Gilbert then quizzes Sir Christopher. Sir Christopher advises Gilbert to take Jessica home—and, by kindness, win the truth from her. Gilbert is adamant, and Rosamund bids Dolly tell the story. She gets off to a good start, but Gilbert's adroit questioning soon leaves her and the now flustered Archibald in a muddle over whether or not she ate dinner on her return, what time she got home, and whether or not Archibald was at home when she returned.

Gilbert is indignantly demanding the truth when Falkner arrives, unaware of the revised story. He says blandly that he appeared at the hotel when Jessica was dining with Rosamund; but, when another tangle results, Jessica calmly urges him to tell the whole truth. Falkner does so. He declares that Jessica is guilty only of a passing folly, seeking amusement at his expense. Proclaiming his deep love for her, he leaves with a final: "Now you've got the truth, and be damned to you. . . . Lady Jessica, I am at your service—always!"

Later, at his flat, Sir Christopher, packing to go to Africa, tells Beatrice that he has three tasks: packing, persuading Falkner to return to Africa with him, and inducing her to marry him. She finally consents, and leaves to get ready as Gilbert arrives to obtain evidence for action against his wife. Sir Christopher finally convinces him that Jessica is guiltless—that prosecution would only throw her into Falkner's arms. Gilbert leaves, resolved to accept Sir Christopher's advice—to take his wife to a good dinner and try to regain her love.

Falkner comes to Sir Christopher with a note from Jessica saying that she has at last appreciated his love and will send for him. Soon Jessica and Rosamund come to seek Sir Christopher's counsel. He tells Falkner and Jessica the truth: that their affair can bring only shame and sorrow to them. Jessica sadly agrees. They are interrupted by Gilbert, returning to say that he can't find his wife, and Rosamund also hides behind a curtain where Jessica had gone with Falkner to say farewell.

Sir Christopher, after Gilbert declares his love for Jessica, calls the women and the three leave, Jessica and Falkner exchanging a last furtive glance through a parting in the curtains. Falkner decides to forget his grief in Africa.

The Second Mrs. Tanqueray

BY ARTHUR WING PINERO

Born in London, May 24, 1855, and educated in London. In 1874 he was engaged as an actor at the Theatre Royal in Edinburgh. In 1876 he went to London, where he acted first at the Globe Theatre and later as a member of the Lyceum Company for five years. The first of his plays to attract attention was "The Money Spinner," produced in 1880. His first serious play, "The Squire," was finished the next year and showed more of the qualities of his later work. "Trelawney of the Wells" is the best known of his earlier comedies. "The Second Mrs. Tanqueray" (1893) aroused great discussion when it was first produced, and was soon translated into French, German and Italian. The role of Mrs. Tanqueray has attracted many famous actresses—among them Mrs. Patrick Campbell and Eleonora Duse. Pinero was knighted in 1909. He died in 1934.

Aubrey Tanqueray, a cultured and wealthy widower of forty-two, says farewell to three old friends at a dinner in his apartment, for the next day he is to marry Paula Ray, also known as Mrs. Jarman and Mrs. Dartry, who will not be accepted in his circle.

When the others have gone, he tells one of the trio, Cayley Drummle, who has lingered, that he is fully aware of Paula's past, but is deliberate and even defiant in his intention to marry her, confident that a life of happiness and good repute may be built upon a miserable foundation. Paula has never met a man who has treated her well, he adds, and there is much in her of goodness. He plans to leave at once with her for his country place in Surrey which has been leased for a score of years since his first wife died. He has a daughter, Ellean, who, still under the influence of her chill and religious mother, is prepared to take final vows soon in an Irish convent where she has passed most of her nineteen years. Tanqueray, only last month, visited her in the hope of dissuading her from doing so, but failed.

As Drummle leaves, Paula comes in. She is about twenty-seven, beautiful and innocent-appearing in her superb evening dress. She laughs at Tanqueray's concern over her unconventional call. Presently she hands him a letter which gives in detail a list of her "adventures." She tells Tanqueray to read it, and, after doing so, to call off the wedding if he chooses. Instead, he burns the letter. Paula says that she would have killed herself had he left her; she cannot endure further misery. As she goes for her cloak, Tanqueray idly opens and reads one of his letters which has come by post. It is from Ellean; she believes "her mother in heaven" has counseled her to go to her father. "Dear Father, will you receive me?" she writes. Tanqueray stares at the letter, then abstractedly sees Paula to her carriage.

A few months later, Tanqueray, Ellean, who has relinquished her intention of becoming a nun, and Paula are living at his Surrey home, but the happiness he had hoped for has not been realized. Paula constantly distresses him with her complaints of boredom, as well as by her jealousy of the aloof Ellean about whom Tanqueray's love appears to be centering. She is angry and disappointed, too, because none of Tanqueray's friends have called, particularly

Mrs. Cortelyon, the nearest neighbor, who was a friend of the first Mrs. Tanqueray.

At length Paula demands that Tanqueray influence Ellean to show some affection for her. She says to him: "She is your saint. . . . Do you imagine that makes me less jealous? Aubrey, there are two sorts of affection: the love for a woman you respect, and the love for the woman you love. She gets the first from you. I never can. If Ellean cared for me only a little . . . I shouldn't be jealous then." Paula herself tries to win Ellean over, attempting to kiss her, but Ellean shrinks from her. The scene is interrupted by Drummle, who has ended a stay at the Cortelyon home to become the Tanquerays' house guest.

Drummle tells Tanqueray that Mrs. Cortelyon, now driving up to the house, has relented for her dead friend's sake, and has consented to call. She also wishes to take Ellean on a trip abroad, back to the world Tanqueray has closed to her. Paula treats Mrs. Cortelyon with studied insolence, but Ellean impulsively goes to her and takes her hand. It is arranged that Ellean accompany Mrs. Cortelyon on her trip. When the visitor has gone, Paula upbraids Tanqueray for her "loss" of Ellean. In revenge, she invites to their home as house guests the insipid and drunken Sir George Orreyed and his recent bride, an actress of doll-like beauty, utter stupidity and an infamous past.

A few weeks later, the Orreyeds have arrived and are installed, and Tanqueray and his wife are speaking only in the presence of others. Paula confesses to Drummle that, in her jealousy, she has intercepted letters for her husband from Mrs. Cortelyon and Ellean. She gives them to Tanqueray later, however, but accuses him of sending Ellean away because he doesn't consider his wife a fit companion for the girl. Tanqueray admits the truth of this, but convinces Paula that he has acted for the best. She has just asked another chance to prove her worthiness of Ellean and has left the room, when Mrs. Cortelyon and Ellean return.

Tanqueray lamely explains that their letters were accidentally delayed. When Ellean has gone to her room, Mrs.

Cortelyon tells Tanqueray that in Paris Ellean has met young Hugh Ardale, a heroic soldier invalided home from India, and that the two have fallen in love. Mrs. Cortelyon approves the youth, but she quickly brought Ellean home when her letters to Tanqueray went unanswered. Ardale came with them and is visiting her. She asks Tanqueray to see her home on the chance that he may meet Hugh informally. Her father asks Ellean to be "very gentle" to Paula, and leaves.

Young Ardale slips up to the window to see Ellean, but he retreats into the shadows when Paula is heard entering the room. Ellean goes to Paula and, to her amazement, kisses her, declaring she wants to behave differently toward her; she asks if it is too late. Paula cries, "No, no!" and weeps in happiness. Ellean tells her of her romance, then, at Paula's excited insistence, brings Ardale into the room.

But, on seeing Hugh, after a look of startled recognition, she sends Ellean out of the room. She insists that Ardale, who had once been her own lover, give up the girl. "She kissed me tonight! I'd won her over! I've had such a fight to make her love me and now—just as she's beginning to love me, to bring this on her! . . . I'd made up my mind to turn over a new leaf from tonight . . . tonight!" she tells him. Ardale pleads that he and Paula must keep silent, but she declares it is her duty to tell Tanqueray. Hugh leaves, threatening to kill himself if he loses Ellean.

When Tanqueray returns, Paula tells him that she had listed Ardale in the letter Tanqueray had burned on their wedding eve. She says: "Ardale and I once kept house together. Why don't you strike me? Hit me in the face— I'd rather you did! Hurt me! Hurt me!" A note for Paula from Ardale is brought in, announcing that he is returning at once to Paris, and imploring her: "For God's sake, do what you can for me." Tanqueray decides it is best to let matters stand thus.

Ellean comes in to bid her father good night, and he tells her that she must not see Ardale again. Ellean asks if his reason is because of Hugh's former dissolute life in London. She says that Hugh had confessed his past and

that she had forgiven him everything. Tanqueray refuses
to explain further. He goes to his room in misery, after
Ellean asserts her suspicion that Paula, who said at their
introduction that she had met Ardale in London, has carried gossip to Tanqueray.

Paula, white and drawn, enters from the veranda. As
Ellean accuses her, she replies: "It was my—my duty—to
tell your father what I—what I knew." Ellean retorts:
"What you knew! You can only speak from gossip! . . ."
Then she stops abruptly and backs slowly away from
Paula. She cries, "You—you knew Captain Ardale in London!" She runs to the door, but Paula seizes her by the
wrist, shaking her and demanding an explanation. "You—
you think I'm that sort of creature, do you? . . . You've
always hated me! You shall answer me!" Ellean replies:
"I have always known what you were . . . from the first
moment I saw you!"

Paula forces her to her knees, crying hysterically that
what she says is a lie—that she has always been a good
woman. Tanqueray enters. Ellean says faintly that the
scene has been her fault; she does not wish to see Ardale
again. Tanqueray reflects that there is nothing to do but
return Ellean to the convent; he and Paula will go away
to make a fresh start. He rejects Paula's offer to leave him,
but she insists that they can never forget this night or the
nightmare life that has preceded it, and she forecasts the
day when age will end her attraction for him.

Paula goes to her room as Drummle approaches. The
two men are talking when Ellean appears at the door, crying: "Father! I—I want you! Go to Paula, quickly!" As he
passes her, she seizes his arm: "No, no; don't go!" He
shakes her off and goes.

Ellean tells Drummle: "I—I went to her room—to tell her
I was sorry—it's horrible . . . killed . . . herself. But I know
—I helped to kill her. If I'd only been merciful!"

Trelawney of the Wells

BY ARTHUR WING PINERO

Rose Trelawney, popular ingenue of the "Wells" Theatre
in London, is about to be married to Arthur Gower, grandson of Vice Chancellor Sir William Gower. Her fellow-
players, members of a rather shabby little troupe, are giving her a farewell party in the room of Mr. and Mrs. Telfer,
also of the cast, at Mrs. Mossop's lodging house.

Mrs. Mossop and Ablett, the grocer who is to assist with
the service, are preparing beer and a cold lunch. Mrs.
Mossop tells Ablett that Arthur, an orphan, lives in aristo-
cratic Cavendish Square with his grandfather and a great-
aunt, who have insisted that Rose withdraw quietly from
her stage life and, before their consent to the marriage is
given, live with them "for a short term." They are sending
a carriage for her later in the day.

Tom Wrench, a cheery but awkward actor of thirty
years who always draws the poorer roles, arrives to have
his frayed cuffs trimmed for the occasion. He is followed
shortly by Imogen Parrott, now graduated to the more
lofty Olympic Theatre. Imogen jeers at Tom's hopeless
love for Rose. Tom confesses himself a failure, too, in his
effort to sell the realistic plays which he has written.

Others arrive: Telfer, an elderly actor of sonorous speech
and uncertain aitches; Gadd, a flashily dressed young man;
Colpoys, a low comedian on and off the stage; Mrs. Telfer,
a faded queen of tragedy; Avonia Bunn, an untidy girl
with the airs of a suburban soubrette; Arthur Gower, a
handsome, boyish figure, and Rose, nineteen and beautiful,
but somewhat professionally extravagant and free in gesture and movement.

Rose tells Imogen that she is going to live with the
Gowers "on approval," and the company joins in a lunch

marred only by Colpoys' clowning and Ablett's serving of one of his gloves by error. There are toasts, and Rose, in tears, declares that she will remember them always, even though she "shall have married a swell," and that her happiest years have been those in which she was known as Trelawney of the "Wells." Arrival of the carriage ends the leave-taking; the carriage must be back promptly for the use of Miss Trafalgar Gower, Arthur's great-aunt.

Rose's new life in the stuffy tyranny of the Gower home soon becomes almost unbearable. The elder Gowers nap for an hour after dinner, and during that time there must be utter silence; there are innumerable rules and customs, and even Arthur's visits (he must not live in the house while Rose is there) are rigidly chaperoned. One evening, Rose defiantly plays the piano, protesting against her ceaseless repression. Sir William ominously calls Arthur for a private talk.

Discord and a fierce rain storm end the evening. The others have retired when Rose receives a scribbled note telling her that some of her old friends of the "Wells" are outside and wish to see her. She summons them in out of the rain—Avonia, Gadd, Colpoys and Tom. Gadd is slightly drunk; he and Avonia have just been married because they can live more cheaply together.

The visit of Rose's former pals ends in a noisy row when Gadd slaps Colpoys, provoking a fight. They overturn furniture, accompanied by shrieks from Avonia. Sir William enters with Trafalgar and Arthur. He scores them all as "a set of garish, dissolute gypsies," and orders them out of the house. Rose prepares to go with them, declaring: "Yes, Arthur, if you were a gypsy, as I am, as these friends o' mine are, we might be happy together. But I've seen enough of your life, my dear boy, to know that I'm no wife for you." She declares she will never see him again, and is going back to the "Wells."

In Mrs. Mossop's lodging house, a conversation between Tom and Avonia discloses that Rose's return has hardly been a triumph; she has somehow lost the gusto that once made her popular, has become subdued and ladylike, and her pay has been cut in half. But Tom insists that she is fitted now for real drama, such as the play he has written centering about characters like Rose and Arthur. He confides in Avonia that he has heard from Arthur: Arthur has left home to become an actor in Bristol.

Rose returns with the news that she has been dismissed because she cannot enact the trashy parts of the "Wells" troupe. She regrets now that she did not endure the Gowers. She says, sadly: "There was a chance for me to be womanly and patient, and I proved to them that I was nothing but—an actress. . . . We are only dolls, with heads stuffed with sayings out of rubbishy plays. . . . They were real people—real!"

Imogen comes in with the news that she has induced an uncle to help finance the renting of the Pantheon Theatre for the production of Tom's play. They are excitedly discussing raising the rest of the funds when Sir William calls to see Rose. He demands to know the whereabouts of Arthur. Sir William approvingly notes the change in Rose, and accepts her apologies. Avonia tells him of Rose's ill fortune; he learns, too, that Rose's mother played opposite Edmund Kean, Sir William's youthful idol. His memory fired, he even dons Rose's keepsakes, the property orders and sword that Kean once wore. Tom then enters to talk of his hope of getting his play produced. Sir William, now eager to help Rose and aglow in the trappings of Kean, agrees to provide the necessary money.

A troupe of players is recruited and Tom's play goes into rehearsal. Sir William, hat well pulled down to conceal his face, is a fascinated spectator. He is well aware that one of the parts is based upon the character of Arthur. Gordon, the actor who is to play the part, arrives—Arthur, summoned by Tom who has not revealed the presence of Rose in the cast.

Arthur and Rose are reunited, and Sir William grudgingly intimates his forgiveness when it is pointed out that Arthur may become a splendid gypsy, like Kean. Tom resumes rehearsal, calling: "Mr. Gordon and Miss Rose Trelawney! Miss Trelawney! Trelawney—late of the 'Wells'!"

He grips Arthur's hand and bows his head on Rose's shoulder: "Oh, my dears—let us—get on with the rehearsal."

The Importance of Being Earnest

BY OSCAR WILDE

Born in Dublin, Ireland, October 15, 1856, his full name being Oscar Fingall O'Flahertie Wills Wilde. His father was a famous surgeon and his mother a poet. He was educated at Trinity College, Dublin, and at Oxford where he won distinction as a poet and classicist. He became famous as a wit, poet, novelist, and dramatist, and was for a time the acknowledged leader of the aesthetic movement in London. His reputation collapsed, however, when he was convicted of immoral practices and sentenced to two years' imprisonment. His best-known novel is "The Picture of Dorian Gray," published in 1891. In addition to the play, "Lady Windermere's Fan," he wrote three other full-length comedies: "The Importance of Being Earnest," "A Woman of No Importance," and "An Ideal Husband." His short poetic tragedy, "Salome," was the basis for an opera by Richard Strauss. After his release from prison, where he had written the moving autobiographical sketch "De Profundis," Wilde went to France. He died in Paris on November 30, 1900.

Young Jack Worthing arrives in London from his country place, bent upon proposing marriage to the Honorable Gwendolen Fairfax, lovely cousin of his friend, the waggish Algernon Moncrieff.

Dropping in at Algy's flat, he meets the first obstacle to his intention—his friend confronts him with his lost cigarette case which is inscribed: "From little Cecily, with her fondest love to her dear Uncle Jack." Algy demands an explanation of both the Cecily and the "Uncle Jack," for he has known and introduced Worthing as "Ernest" Worthing.

Jack explains that Cecily, just eighteen and excessively pretty, is his ward, the granddaughter of old Mr. Thomas Cardew who adopted him when he was a baby. As a conscientious guardian, he adds, he has found it helpful to be known in the country as Jack and in town as Ernest, since he can attribute the escapades of Ernest to a fictitious brother. When Gwendolen is won, he plans that Ernest, of whom he has told her nothing, shall conveniently die in Paris.

Their talk is interrupted by the appearance for tea of Gwendolen and her mother, the formidable Lady Bracknell. The latter is lured into the music room by Algy, and Jack at once proposes to Gwendolen. Gwendolen confesses that she has always loved him passionately, principally because it has been her lifetime ambition to love someone by the name of Ernest, "a name that produces vibrations." Worthing suggests that he really doesn't like the name, that he thinks Jack is ever so much nicer, but Gwendolen disagrees. She finds no "vibrations" in the name of Jack.

Jack's suit is further complicated when Lady Bracknell, told of his proposal, sends Gwendolen to her carriage and examines the young man as to his eligibility. Jack is forced to confess that he doesn't know who he is: he was found by Mr. Cardew in a handbag in Victoria Station, and was named Worthing simply because Mr. Cardew had a ticket for Worthing. Lady Bracknell replies that she cannot allow her only daughter to marry into a cloakroom and form an alliance with a parcel.

Lady Bracknell leaves in indignation, but Gwendolen slips back to tell Jack that she still finds his Christian name fascinating; she says she will write to him daily. Algy, intrigued by the description of Cecily, notes on his cuff the address of his friend's country place as Jack confides it to Gwendolen.

Soon after this, Cecily, during Jack's absence from the manor house, is thrilled by the arrival of Algy who has assumed the role of the wicked brother Ernest. Algy is

enchanted by Cecily who confides that she has long been
in love with him in fancy; too, she tells him that it always
has been her hope to be married to someone whose name
is Ernest. She is quite sure, on the other hand, that she
could give only respect and divided attention to anyone
named Algernon, for instance.

Meanwhile, Miss Prism, Cecily's governess, and the Reverend Canon Chasuble who are chatting together in the
garden, are shocked by the appearance of Jack who enters
in deepest mourning, with black hatband and black gloves,
to announce lugubriously the sudden death in Paris of
brother Ernest who suffered a sudden chill. Jack's gloom is
not lightened when the radiant Cecily hurries from the
house to tell him that, on the contrary, Ernest has come
home to atone for his wickedness. Cecily and Chasuble,
with difficulty, induce Jack to shake hands with the beaming Algy. Alone, Jack orders Algy to end his masquerade
and to leave at once, but Algy blandly remains.

Into this confusion comes Gwendolen who is received
by Cecily. Gwendolen is interested to hear the Cecily is
the ward of "Mr. Worthing" and, further, that her hostess
is engaged to marry Mr. Ernest Worthing. Gwendolen indignantly suggests that there must be an error: she says
that she became engaged to Ernest only the previous afternoon.

Further hostilities between the two girls are interrupted
by the appearance of Jack and Algy. At length the men
are forgiven when both explain their dual identities and
add that each has arranged to be re-christened Ernest.
Their joy, however, is short-lived; Lady Bracknell has
traced Gwendolen to the manor house and arrives now in
a state of fury.

Attacking first the case of her nephew Algy, she is somewhat mollified to learn that Cecily is of excellent family,
besides having a plump fortune of her own, soundly invested. She concedes that Cecily, now that she looks at
her, has really solid possibilities.

But as for Jack and Gwendolen, Lady Bracknell is
adamant, even when Jack, as Cecily's guardian, refuses his

consent to the wedding of Cecily and Algy so long as he cannot marry Gwendolen. The issue is deadlocked; Jack is declaring that "a passionate celibacy is all that any of us can look forward to," when Canon Chasuble arrives to announce that all is in readiness for the christenings and that Miss Prism is on her way.

At the mention of this name Lady Bracknell starts in surprise and demands to see her at once. Miss Prism, arriving soon after, pales at sight of Lady Bracknell.

"Prism," demands Lady Bracknell in a severe, judicial voice, "where is that baby? Twenty-eight years ago you left Lord Bracknell's house in charge of a perambulator that contained a baby of the male sex. You never returned."

Miss Prism confesses that she is guilty, but knows only that she left the infant in a handbag in Victoria Station, having confused it in a fit of abstraction with the manuscript of a rather lurid novel she was writing. Jack dashes to his room—to return triumphantly with the very handbag! It is now made plain that he is the son of Lady Bracknell's sister. Consequently, he has in Algernon a scapegrace brother.

And Jack's true name (after his father) is finally established: it is Ernest.

Lady Windermere's Fan

BY OSCAR WILDE

Two tea-time callers considerably upset Lady Windermere as she is happily preparing for her coming-of-age party that evening and admiring an unusual fan, the gift of her husband.

The first caller, the dashing Lord Darlington, intimates, hypothetically, that she should console herself with him because her husband is untrue to her; the second, the gossipy Duchess of Berwick, tells her bluntly that all London knows that Windermere is in the toils of a mysterious and fascinating Mrs. Erlynne.

Lord Darlington she dismisses with the observation that life is a sacrament; its ideal is love and its purification is sacrifice; and, she continues, because a husband is vile, should the wife be vile also? But the charge of the Duchess is supported when Lady Windermere finds, in a secret account book of her husband's, a record of large sums given to Mrs. Erlynne.

Later, Windermere, while not wholly explaining Mrs. Erlynne, tells his wife that he loves only her and their child, but he insists that she invite Mrs. Erlynne to her party. Mrs. Erlynne, he pleads, has atoned for a wrong of twenty years ago and seeks only to restore her place in society by being received by the scrupulously respectable Lady Windermere. Windermere, his appeal refused, himself finally sends the invitation—in spite of his wife's threat to strike Mrs. Erlynne across the face with her fan.

Lady Windermere's courage fails when Mrs. Erlynne, "looking like an edition de luxe of a wicked French novel, meant specially for the English market," arrives and dominates the party. Lady Windermere takes refuge on the terrace with Darlington, who again pleads with her to leave Windermere and come to him. Rejected, he warns her that he is leaving England the following day.

Meanwhile, in the drawing-room, Mrs. Erlynne is informing Windermere that she is prepared to accept, next day, a proposal of marriage from Lord Augustus Lorton, an amiable but wealthy bore, one of the guests at the party. She demands of Windermere a considerable annual settlement as an additional attraction to Lorton. Mrs. Erlynne and Windermere leave for the terrace to discuss the matter further.

Lady Windermere, seeing them go out together, in a jealous rage writes a note to Windermere, then leaves for the apartment of Lord Darlington, resolved to accept his proposal. "It is he who has broken the bond of marriage," she decides. "I only break its bondage."

Mrs. Erlynne, returning alone to take leave of her

hostess, is told by a servant that Lady Windermere has gone, leaving a letter. Mrs. Erlynne reads the letter and sinks into a chair, exclaiming: "Oh, how terrible! The same words that twenty years ago I wrote to her father, and how bitterly I have been punished for it! How can I save my child?"

She tells Windermere that his wife has retired with a headache and wishes him to say farewell to the guests. She induces Lord Augustus to take Windermere, on some pretext, to his club for the night, and then hastens to Darlington's rooms where Lady Windermere, now shaken by indecision, is awaiting him. Lady Windermere finally agrees to return to her husband, after Mrs. Erlynne, without revealing their relationship, pleads with her and promises to disappear from their lives forever.

As the women are about to leave, voices, including that of Lord Windermere, are heard outside. Mrs. Erlynne thrusts Lady Windermere behind a window curtain with the injunction to slip away at the first opportunity; she herself prepares to face the men; but, hearing also the voice of Lord Augustus, she hides in an adjoining room. The men enter. One of them soon notices a fan on the sofa. Windermere, recognizing it as his wife's, is about to search the rooms and is starting toward the stirring curtain when Mrs. Erlynne emerges dramatically. She diverts their attention, and Lady Windermere glides unnoticed from the room.

"I am afraid I took your wife's fan in mistake for my own when I was leaving your house," Mrs. Erlynne tells Windermere. Lord Augustus turns away as the other men smile.

The next morning, with Windermere still unaware of his wife's absence of the night before, Lady Windermere is gratefully pondering the self-sacrifice of Mrs. Erlynne. She is about to tell her husband of the whole incident when they are interrupted by delivery of the fan, accompanied by Mrs. Erlynne's card. Over her husband's protest, Lady Windermere instructs the butler to ask Mrs. Erlynne in.

Their visitor, casually apologizing for taking the fan, says that she is leaving at once for permanent residence abroad. "The English climate doesn't suit me," she tells them. "My . . . heart is affected." She asks for photographs of Lady Windermere and her baby, and her hostess leaves to get them. Alone with Mrs. Erlynne, Windermere scornfully reproaches her, disclosing that she has been blackmailing him to protect his wife from the knowledge that the mother she had been told was dead had actually abandoned her for a lover, and now lives—a notorious divorcée —under the assumed name of Mrs. Erlynne. He taunts her cruelly with the scene of the night before in Darlington's home, and forbids her ever to see her daughter again.

Mrs. Erlynne replies: "Don't imagine I am going to have a pathetic scene with her and tell her who I am. I have no ambition to play the part of a mother, and why should I interfere with her illusions? I find it hard enough to keep my own. I lost one illusion last night. I thought I had no heart, but I find I have, and a heart doesn't suit me. Somehow it doesn't go with modern dress. I am going to pass entirely out of your lives. If you tell her, I shall make my name so infamous that it will mar every moment of her life."

Lady Windermere returns with the photographs and, alone for a moment with Mrs. Erlynne, promises, at the latter's insistence, that she will forever remain silent about her visit to Darlington's apartment. Mrs. Erlynne asks one more favor—the gift of the fan. She is about to go when Lord Augustus enters. In spite of his coldness, Mrs. Erlynne prevails upon him to see her to her cab. She leaves with a final meaningful glance at Lady Windermere.

A few moments later, Lord Augustus returns, bursting with joy. Mrs. Erlynne has "explained everything." The Windermeres are startled, but he tells them that Mrs. Erlynne had visited Darlington's rooms only in search of Lord Augustus in order to accept his proposal—provided he agrees that they shall leave England.

Lord Windermere says: "Well, you are marrying a very clever woman."

And Lady Windermere adds: "Ah, you're marrying a very *good* woman."

Charley's Aunt

BY BRANDON THOMAS

Born in Liverpool, England, December 25, 1856. Was edu-cated to be a civil engineer, but because of his success as an amateur entertainer, he decided to become an actor. He came to America only once, in 1885, in a play called "A Pantomime Rehearsal." Although he was well known in England, and had acted in many plays there before he came to America, he was known here principally as the author of "Charley's Aunt"—an immediately successful play which had run 1,466 consecutive times in England. It has been often revived, and has been translated into every important language since it was first produced. Thomas died June 19, 1914, in London.

Charley Wykeham, an undergraduate of St. Olde's College, Oxford, learns at a fortunate time that he is to have a luncheon visitor—Donna Lucia d'Alvadorez, an English-born aunt who has been supporting him, an orphan, in college. Charley has never seen this aunt, since she had gone to Brazil before his birth and later had married, on his deathbed, a millionaire Brazilian whose secretary she was.

The time is fortunate because Amy Spettigue, the girl Charley loves, is about to leave for Scotland, and the aunt's presence will permit him to invite Amy to his rooms; here he hopes to win her hand in marriage. He has also invited Kitty Verdun, ward of Amy's testy uncle. Kitty is loved by Charley's friend, Jack Chesney. Charley and Jack decide that a good sixth at luncheon would be Lord Fancourt Babberley, called Babbs, a jolly little undergraduate with a penchant for amateur theatricals.

Babbs reveals that he, too, is in love. He has recently made a yachting tour of the Mediterranean, and at Monte Carlo met an English officer, Delahay, who was dying in poverty. Delahay earlier had beggared himself and his young daughter at gambling, and the generous Babbs had financed him, through gambling "losses" to him, until he died. Babbs had been smitten with the daughter, but she was brought to England by a woman traveler, touched by her plight, and Babbs has lost track of her.

The girls arrive, but they leave almost at once when they learn that the aunt, the chaperon, has not yet appeared; they promise to return soon. Charley goes off to meet his aunt. A surprise visitor is Jack's father, Colonel Sir Francis Chesney, a handsome soldier lately returned from India. He tells Jack bad news: debts will keep him and his son in limited funds for several years. Jack thinks it would be a splendid idea if Sir Francis were to marry Charley's rich aunt, and invites his father to return for lunch.

But a crisis occurs: Charley's aunt telegraphs that she will be detained for several days. The girls will shortly be returning—what to do? Babbs drops in, garbed and bewigged for rehearsal in a show where he plays the role of a Victorian old lady in a long black-satin dress. The desperate Jack and Charley draft him, willy-nilly, to impersonate Charley's aunt during the time the girls are there. The girls come back, and Babbs, beginning to enjoy his role, puts his arm about Amy's waist as they chat in feminine fashion.

There is consternation among the group, however, when Amy's uncle, Spettigue, is reported approaching. Babbs, as Charley's aunt, is left alone to get rid of him. He lies cleverly enough to achieve Spettigue's departure, and then Sir Francis comes in, dressed for courting, to present another problem. Sir Francis is hardly attracted by the odd-looking old lady, but he is gallantly doing his best when the suspicious Spettigue returns, demanding that the girls

leave at once. When he is told that the old lady is the
fabulously rich Donna Lucia, he quickly changes his tune
and becomes an ardent and rival suitor.

After lunch there follows a dizzy round of maneuvering:
Sir Francis and Spettigue strive to be alone with Babbs in
order to propose; Babbs deftly escapes to stroll with the
girls in the garden, and Jack and Charley furiously try to
get Babbs to leave the girls to them. At length Sir Francis,
alone with Babbs and fortified by brandy, offers his heart
in a flowery speech. Babbs rejects him, declaring he is a
woman with a history, but he offers to be a "sister" to
him. Sir Francis regrets his rejection for Jack's sake, but
for himself is vastly relieved.

Now the situation becomes really complicated: there
appears the real Donna Lucia, a lovely woman in her early
forties, smartly dressed and with an excellent sense of
humor. She is accompanied by Ela Delahay, Babbs' lost
dream girl, whom she has informally adopted since bringing her from Monte Carlo. She has shrewdly invested the
money Babbs lost to Ela's father, and now Ela is quite
independent, hoping to meet Babbs some day to repay
him.

Arriving at Jack's rooms, they find there only Sir Francis.
Donna Lucia recognizes in him the young lieutenant with
whom she was deeply in love a score of years ago. Sir
Francis, thrilled to find her again, tells them that his son is
helping to entertain Charley's aunt, Donna Lucia. The
mischievous and curious Donna Lucia resolves to masquerade as Mrs. Beverley-Smythe (the name of a friend whose
card she finds in her bag). She wishes to learn more of her
nephew as well as to observe the reaction of Sir Francis in
his ignorance of her identity as the rich Donna Lucia.

Amy and Kitty have consented to be the brides of the
young men, and, with Jack and Charley, appeal to Babbs
to get old Spettigue's consent. Babbs is doing his best when
Donna Lucia appears to meet him. Babbs pleasantly announces himself as "Charley's aunt from Brazil, where the
nuts come from." Donna Lucia has a gay time torturing
him with recollections of the dead husband, Dom Pedro,

whom she claims to remember well. Spettigue then invites
the whole party to his own home. Babbs is refusing when
Ela appears, and he, in an appalled realization of his costume, recognizes her. She thinks she knows his voice, and
is disappointed to find that it emerges only from an old
lady. Babbs faints.

At Spettigue's, Babbs is in further misery as his host
resumes his suit; the thought of Ela discovering his identity
is a constant dread, and Donna Lucia continues her teasing. At length Babbs hints that he may accept Spettigue,
although he declares himself not "an ordinary woman," if
Spettigue will permit the girls to marry the men of their
choice. While Spettigue goes to write a letter of consent,
Babbs encounters further difficulties: Donna Lucia catches
him smoking a cigar, and Ela confides in him her love of
the young man who befriended her father.

Donna Lucia, meanwhile, has tested Sir Francis who
declares himself willing to give up the rich aunt to live
with Mrs. Beverley-Smythe in a cottage. They return from
this private conversation in time to hear Spettigue announce his engagement to Babbs (who has left the room),
and give his permission for the wedding of his niece and
ward. Charley, unwilling to win Amy by fraud, reveals the
masquerade, as Babbs returns in masculine evening dress.

Spettigue, furious, declares that he will contest the written permission given in the letter to the girls, but "Mrs.
Beverley-Smythe," observing that it is addressed to Donna
Lucia, seizes it and discloses her true identity. She promises, through her influence, to compensate Spettigue and
all the lovers are united.

Dr. Jekyll and Mr. Hyde

BY ROBERT LOUIS STEVENSON

ROBERT LOUIS BALFOUR STEVENSON *was born in Edinburgh, Scotland, November 13, 1850. He went to school mainly in Edinburgh, and from the age of six showed a strong disposition to write. From infancy through most of his life he was very frail and was so harassed by serious illness and weakened by its aftereffects that the whole course of his life and education was changed. He studied engineering, changed to the law, and in 1875 was admitted to the bar, but never practiced. His main interest was in literature, and he showed increasing literary skill. His best-known book, "Treasure Island," one of the greatest of all adventure tales, was written in 1883. Two of his most popular works, "Kidnapped" and "Dr. Jekyll and Mr. Hyde," were published in 1886. The latter was dramatized. Stevenson traveled extensively for health and for pleasure. The last four years of his life he spent in Samoa, an island in the South Pacific, where he was known as Tusitala (teller of tales). He died in Samoa in 1894 and is buried there.*

The Reverend Edward Leigh, chatting in the garden of his vicarage with his friend Utterson, a lawyer, is telling of a shocking spectacle he has witnessed while on an early morning call to a parishioner—the sight of a strangely misshapen man trampling down, with fiendish glee, a little girl he encountered in the street.

The Vicar seized the man and, with the child's parents, demanded that he make amends. The man readily agreed to pay a hundred pounds, and led them to a dilapidated house where he wrote a check. The Vicar remained up to go to the bank with the parents to cash it, and he recalls that the name on the check was that of Edward Hyde.

On hearing this name, Utterson, pledging the Vicar to secrecy, discloses that their respected friend, the successful Dr. Henry Jekyll, has made a will naming the mysterious Hyde his sole heir. Lanyon, who, with Jekyll, is an admirer of the Vicar's daughter Alice, arrives, but he can throw little light on the mystery beyond hinting that Jekyll had been dabbling in "unscientific balderdash." Jekyll himself now appears, but, when questioned, says only that Hyde is his private concern and that he can rid himself of his detestable acquaintance whenever he chooses.

Later, after telling Lanyon of her affection for Jekyll, Alice and Dr. Jekyll meet in the garden, and Alice confesses to him her love and her admiration for his noble nature. Jekyll tells her that in every man there are two natures—one of good and one of evil—and "he who has them under such control that the good always balances the bad is indeed blessed." Then, aside, he exclaims: "My God! I feel the change approaching. I must go at once to my cabinet."

He excuses himself "to go to his room," and Alice, turning her back, is leaving the garden when Jekyll, dropping his coat and cane, murmurs, "Too late—too late!" He writhes in agony, and suddenly takes on the twisted, dwarfish form of Hyde, his hair falling over his eyes and his features contorted. Alice, turning and seeing him dimly in the dusk, demands to know who he is. Frightened, she backs away, threatening to call for help.

She calls Jekyll's name, but Hyde snarls: "Don't call him—I hate him—I'll kill him if he comes!" He seizes her, laughing wildly, and the Vicar rushes to her rescue. Hyde fells him with his cane and then, in maniacal glee, chokes him. He runs away as voices are heard. As Alice is telling Utterson and the butler of the attack, Jekyll reappears in his own form. He is shocked and grieved to learn that the Vicar has been murdered.

Inspector Newcomen, called from Scotland Yard, traces Hyde to an old house in Soho, but Hyde's housekeeper, an old hag, can tell him little: she says she has not seen Hyde for two months. Jekyll tells Utterson, with

whom Alice is now living, that he is done forever with
Hyde. He gives Utterson a letter from the killer, lamenting
his unworthiness and boasting of a sure means of escape.
Jekyll says that he himself has had a bitter lesson, and
must go on his own dark way in suffering and terror.
Utterson learns later, to his bewilderment, that the letter
was not delivered by messenger, as Jekyll had said it was,
and that the handwriting of Jekyll and Hyde is similar.

Alice goes to Jekyll to thank him for aiding in the pursuit
of her father's murderer. Jekyll is tortured anew by a
vision of Hyde going to the gallows. He resolves that he
must give Alice up; and, since he fears that he will again,
against his own will, take the form of Hyde, determines to
confess everything to Lanyon so that he will be provided,
in case of need, with the drugs to transform him to Jekyll.

A watch is kept for the return of Hyde in the vicarage
garden which adjoins the home of Dr. Jekyll. And one
night Hyde does appear, chuckling that he is going to
scrawl blasphemies over the pages of Jekyll's books. Accosted by Utterson, he bolts into Jekyll's house. When
Newcomen and the others knock at the door, they are
answered only by a surprised Dr. Jekyll . . . there is no
trace whatever of Hyde, the killer.

But the eerie unmasking of this dual personality comes
later in the professional secrecy of the office of Dr. Lanyon,
who, at Jekyll's bidding, has brought to his own office the
drugs for which Hyde calls. Hyde arrives and, sobbing in
relief, hurriedly mixes a draught—adding a powder he calls
"moral power"—then challenges Lanyon to bid him drink
it there that he may witness an experiment in "transcen-
dental medicine . . . to stagger the unbelief of Satan."
He drinks the potion and, to the amazement of Lanyon,
changes to the figure of Dr. Jekyll. He leaves under the
eyes of the bewildered police. Soon after, Lanyon dies of
shock, leaving a letter that Utterson is to open only "after
the death or disappearance of Dr. Jekyll."

At length, a frightened Poole, Jekyll's servant, comes to
Utterson and Alice to tell them that Jekyll, who has
long been avoiding her, has locked himself in his cabinet

for more than a week. "Whatever is in the cabinet," Poole
says, "walks all day and the better part of the night. It's an
ill conscience that creature has got, for it gets no rest, and it
moans and weeps like a woman, and the voice is changed.
. . . It's my opinion that the master was made away with
eight days ago, when we heard him cry out to God." He
says, further, that the creature inside has been crying for a
particular sort of drug, but none that Poole has obtained
has suited its purpose. Utterson and Alice set off with Poole
to investigate.

In his cabinet, Jekyll is suffering the agony of the
damned; he has found that the drug which has always
restored him contains an accidental impurity that cannot
be replaced, and he fears that after he takes the last of his
remaining supply he will turn into the form of Hyde forever. Alice calls to him from outside the door—and he takes
the last of his potion so that he may appear before her as
himself.

She tells him of her forgiveness for whatever he has done
and of her love, and Jekyll, for the moment, is again happy,
but soon he begs her to leave him. She goes, denying that
this is farewell, and calls to him that she will see him again
tomorrow. Jekyll locks the door. He reflects: "Until tomorrow, on which no sun shall ever rise for me; but now my
soul is clear and I can die in peace." He kneels and prays:
"O God, look into my heart and forgive my sins; You
were right—I was wrong to tempt You! Ah, I must pray—
pray to keep away the demon."

The weird and supernatural change to Hyde is beginning, and he starts to laugh in the harsh, scornful voice of
Hyde. He hears Utterson outside, demanding admittance,
and he leaps on a chair and seizes a bottle of poison. He
cries: "They're going to take me to the gallows—but Hyde
won't die on the gallows—he-he-he-he-ha! I've killed two
people already—here goes for the third—Jekyll—I've always
told you I'd kill him." He drinks the poison and falls in
death as Utterson and Poole break in.

East Lynne

BY MRS. HENRY WOOD

*Born in Worcester, England, January 17, 1814, her maiden
name being Ellen Price. She suffered all her life from a
curvature of the spine, and most of her novels were
written in a wheel chair. For many years, after her marriage
in 1856, she contributed articles to magazines. Her first
novel was "Danesbury House," written in 1860. "East
Lynne" was published in 1861 after several publishers had
rejected it, but it did not become popular until an enthusiastic review appeared in the London* Times *in 1862.
Thereafter, it was translated into most European and
several oriental languages. Before her death on February
10, 1887, she wrote a great many other works, mostly
about the lower middle class in England.*

Archibald Carlyle, a lawyer, marries and brings home to
East Lynne, in England, Lady Isabel, from whose dead
father Carlyle had bought the estate. The match is a shock
to Miss Carlyle, his half-sister, and to Barbara Hare, a
neighbor who had always hoped to be his bride. Isabel
kisses Miss Carlyle on arrival, but is rebuffed by the older
woman who suspects that the new bride will be vain and
extravagant.

Time passes. At the Hare home appears young Richard
Hare who is being sought for the murder of Hallijohn,
brother of a girl he had been courting. Richard, in disguise
as a stableman, tells his sister Barbara that he is innocent,
that a mysterious Mr. Thorn, another friend of Miss Hallijohn, was the killer. He needs money; Barbara asks him to
return secretly the following night when she will arrange to
bring Carlyle to him to advise him.

Isabel overhears the servants gossiping about Barbara's

subsequent call on Carlyle, and she begins to grow jealous of her; too, she is increasingly unhappy under the criticisms of Miss Carlyle for her ignorance of home management. Her guardian and relative, Lord Mount Severn, calls to reproach Carlyle for his hasty marriage, but learns that Lady Mount Severn's cruelty to Isabel hurried Carlyle's intent. Lord Mount Severn privately advises Isabel, when she speaks of "liking" her husband, to see no more of Francis Levison, a scoundrel who has been in love with her.

Barbara, awaiting Carlyle in the conservatory, is tortured to overhear Isabel questioning him about her, Barbara, and to hear him deny to his wife that he had ever loved her. She sees Carlyle kiss Isabel while she sings his favorite song, "You'll Remember Me." Later, Levison, now Carlyle's house guest, speaks again of his love for Isabel, but she sternly rebukes him. She hears more servants' talk of Barbara, however, and hysterically demands that Carlyle not marry her should Isabel die.

Isabel's jealousy is further fed when she sees Carlyle escort Barbara to the gate; he has promised to see her brother that night in the grove. Levison tells Isabel that he has often seen her husband and Barbara strolling together in the moonlight. She is further convinced of her husband's disloyalty when he refuses to tell her why Barbara called. Then, too, he cancels a party planned for that night. Levison has overheard Carlyle and Barbara, and tells Isabel that the two are to meet in the grove; she agrees to accompany him there for proof that Carlyle is unfaithful. If he is, she promises to go away with Levison.

Richard, meeting Barbara and Carlyle in the grove, declares that Thorn quite evidently killed Hallijohn with Richard's gun, and that circumstances have wrongly placed the guilt for the deed. Thorn is reported still in the neighborhood, and the three agree that Richard shall remain, in the hope of identifying him. Lady Isabel sees only her husband and Barbara leaving the grove, and, in a fury of jealousy, she decides to flee with Levison, leaving behind her her two children. She pens a note, bitterly upbraiding Carlyle, and goes to France with Levison.

Shame and more suffering come to her as time passes. Levison increasingly neglects her, and, even in spite of the birth of their child, now refuses, since he has succeeded to a baronetcy, to marry her. He tells her that marrying a divorced woman would offend his family, and jeers: "O sin! You ladies should think of that beforehand." To crown her anguish, he tells her that he believes Carlyle to have been wholly true to her. He justifies his former lies by saying that all stratagems are fair in love and war.

Isabel returns the money he has sent, refuses support for herself or her son, and orders Levison from the apartment, refusing even to shake hands with him as he leaves with an ironic "Da-da-ta-ta." She is moaning that she must bear forever the consequences of her sin when Lord Mount Severn discovers her. Isabel tells him that she will find a means to live by selling her jewels and by teaching, but he insists upon settling a yearly income upon her. He leaves her sobbing bitterly, "Why don't I die!"

In the interim, Carlyle has married Barbara. They have decided that Levison, who has returned to England and is a candidate for Parliament in opposition to Carlyle, is, in reality, the murderer, Thorn. Awaiting Richard to make the identification, Carlyle asks Barbara to sing "You'll Remember Me." As she sings, Isabel, in disguise as Madam Vine, arrives. She has sought a place as governess in the Carlyle household, to be near her children. Barbara, not recognizing her, tells her that the children's mother was killed in a railway accident in France. Isabel is recognized, however, by Joyce, her former maid, but cautions the maid to silence as she embraces her boy, William, who, a frail child, is ill.

William soon becomes weaker, and asks Madam Vine, while Carlyle, also not recognizing Isabel, has gone for Barbara, if he will find his mother in Heaven. Isabel tells him that he will, that God will wipe their tears, and cries: "Oh William! In this last, dying hour, try to think that I am your mother." She throws off her cap and spectacles and embraces him. Murmuring "Mother," the child dies.

Levison is arrested and put on trial for murder. Richard

is cleared, Levison is found guilty and is sentenced to be transported for life.

Isabel is now failing in health. Carlyle asks Joyce about the condition of Madam Vine, and, disregarding the maid's frantic protest, decides to see her himself. While he goes for a doctor, Miss Carlyle goes to her room and immediately recognizes Isabel who is not wearing her disguise. They are reconciled, and Isabel asks to see Carlyle for the last time.

He comes to her. She explains her tragic mistake, asking his forgiveness; for her sake, he declares, he wishes that they could be restored to their former happy home. Isabel murmurs: "Archibald, I am now on the very threshold of the other world; will you not say one word of love to me before I pass it? . . . One word of love—my heart is breaking for it!"

He replies: "May He so deal with you as I fully and freely forgive you. May He bless you and take you to His rest in Heaven!" He takes her head in his arms and she exclaims: "Oh, but it is hard to part so! Farewell, my once dear husband, until—eternity!" He echoes: "Until eternity," and she dies in his arms. He lays her gently down and stands in deep grief.

Caste

BY THOMAS WILLIAM ROBERTSON

Born in England in 1829. He began as an actor, but retired from the stage and became a dramatist. His plays, "Society," "Ours," "Caste," "Play," and "School," introduced a new and more natural type of comedy to the English stage than had been seen during the first half of the century. His earlier drama, "David Garrick," was well received and is still popular today. Marie Wilton (Lady Bancroft) was

*the great exponent of Robertson's best female characters
in his plays. He died in 1871.*

In a tawdry little flat in Stangate, London, the Honorable
George D'Alroy, a young army officer, is waiting with his
friend, Captain Hawtree, for the return of Esther Eccles,
a humbly-born dancer in a ballet chorus, with whom he has
fallen in love. The flat is her home, shared by her pert sister
Polly, also a dancer, and her drunken and garrulous old
father.

George has brought his friend to meet Esther, telling
him that he is determined to marry her. Hawtree scoffs at
the idea of such a marriage, reminding George that his
high-born mother, the twice-married Marquise de St.
Maur, would be horrified, and that the rest of his world
would not forgive the union. He points to "the inexorable
law of caste" and warns that the wedding would bring
utter social and personal damnation. George protests that
" 'True hearts are more than coronets, and simple faith
than Norman blood,' " but Hawtree turns the quotation
upon him after the drunken father contrives a "loan" of a
half-sovereign.

Esther and Polly arrive, and Polly, delighting in hum-
bling the upper-class Hawtree, bears him off to help in
the kitchen. George begs Esther to marry him, and she
consents, although fearful of "the difference of our stations."
Meanwhile, plumber Sam Gerridge, Polly's suitor, calls and
is soundly snubbed by Hawtree who leaves airily, still
believing in "social differences."

Eight months later, George and Esther, happily married,
are living in luxurious lodgings in Mayfair. Esther speaks
of herself as his "poor little humble wife," but George is
proud of her and assures her that she is "every bit the
lady." He is restless, however; he has been ordered to
action in India and is screwing up his courage to tell her
so. Hawtree, in uniform, arrives shortly before Polly, whom
George has summoned to comfort Esther when he breaks
the news to her of his departure.

George's mother, returning unexpectedly from Rome and unaware of her son's marriage, is heard approaching. Esther and Polly, in confusion, hide so that he may tell her about Esther alone. The Marchioness, after delivering a loud lecture on the blue blood of the D'Alroys and on George's duty to marry a lady, discloses the secret of his order to India. Thereupon, in comes Polly, supporting Esther. George has just introduced Esther as his wife when old Eccles arrives with Sam, and, offering his dirty hand to the Marchioness, observes: "We old folks ought to make friends."

When Eccles and Sam are presented, she snorts: "Eccles! There never was an Eccles . . . the name breaks one's teeth." Then, boasting of the honor of the D'Alroys, she demonstrates the family courage by offering to fasten George's sword to speed him off to war. George urges Esther to arm him, in order to show her own courage, but she faints instead.

A year later, George has been reported captured and killed in India. Esther and her baby are back in the little flat in Stangate, living with Polly and old Eccles, who has gambled away all of the money left by George. Polly brings in a dress for the absent Esther, who is trying to get work again as a dancer. Sam comes in, jubilantly, to announce that he has bought the plumbing business of old Binks, and he and Polly happily plan their future. She tells Sam that Hawtree, now a major, is back from India, and that he has advised Esther to ask her mother-in-law for aid.

Old Eccles comes home, and Sam and Polly bribe him to mind Esther's baby while they go out to shop. While audibly bemoaning his thirst, the unequal division of property and his own lot, Eccles discloses that he has written to the Marchioness concerning the plight of Esther and her baby. Esther arrives to find a letter from Hawtree, enclosing money and asking if he may call to deliver some papers of George's.

Polly and Sam have just returned to the flat when the Marchioness arrives, sniffs about her and demands that her grandchild be turned over to her. Esther refuses and scorns

her proffered money, declaring she is returning to the
ballet to support her child. The Marchioness leaves with
this farewell: "If anything could have increased my sorrow
for the wretched marriage my poor son was decoyed into,
it would be your conduct this day to his mother." Angry
and sad, Esther retires to her bedroom to rest, taking with
her the baby, in the fear that the old woman will steal it
away.

Sam now formally asks Eccles for the hand of Polly,
and, to Sam's horror, the old reprobate wipes his eyes with
a dirty handkerchief and says: "I'll come and see you often
—very often—every day, and crack a fatherly bottle and
shed a friendly tear." Major Hawtree comes in, and, on being invited to a highly informal tea, concludes to himself:
"'Pon my word these are very good sort of people. I'd
no idea——" There is a knock at the door, and in comes
George, bronzed and healthy. Explanations bring a joyous reunion; George has escaped his captors and has just
reached England from India.

They fear to break the news of his return too suddenly
to Esther, and while discussing the best plan of procedure,
Polly brings out the baby to George who, until now, has
not known he is a father. He asks why Esther has returned
to the flat, and is told that it was necessary to sell her
furniture. Polly tells him that Hawtree had sent money to
help and that Esther herself has been courageous and independent. George exclaims: "There's a woman! Caste's all
humbug."

He recognizes his sword, a map of India and the piano
he had bought Esther, and Polly tells him that Sam bought
them back for Esther, after they were sold, with the money
he had saved for his wedding. Sam and Hawtree, realizing
each other's worth, shake hands. The latter goes to fetch the
Marchioness.

Polly now has an inspiration: she suggests that they
break the news to Esther by re-enacting a ballet, "The
Return of the Soldier"; and, with George waiting in the
hall, she uses the story and a number of excited hints to
prepare Esther. Husband and wife are reunited, when the

Marchioness arrives. Her tears convince Sam that, after all, there may be some good in her. She and Esther are reconciled. But now Hawtree enters in agitation: he has been jilted by the daughter of a countess, who is to marry a marquis.

Says George: "Well, perhaps it's for the best. Caste, you know . . . a marquis is a bigger swell than a major." Hawtree plaintively agrees: "Yes, best to marry in your own rank of life." George replies: "Yes, if you can find *the* girl. But if you ever find *the* girl, marry her. As to her station —— 'True hearts are more than coronets . . .'"

The still stubborn Hawtree protests: "Ya-as. But a gentleman should hardly ally himself with a nobody." George answers: "Nobody's nobody! Everybody's somebody. . . . Caste's a good thing if it's not carried too far. It shuts the door on the pretentious and the vulgar, but . . . let brains break through its barriers, and what brains can break through love may leap over."

Eccles, at Hawtree's suggestion, agrees that for two pounds a week he can go to Jersey and drink himself to death in approximately a year. The Marchioness bends over the cradle, murmuring happily: "My grandson!"

Richelieu

BY EDWARD BULWER-LYTTON

Born in London, May 25, 1803. He was a delicate and neurotic child and, because of his precocious talent, he was difficult and discontented in the various schools to which he was sent. Eventually he reached Cambridge, and, in 1825, won the Chancellor's medal for English verse. He wrote continuously for many years—novels, articles, fantasies—became active in politics and was sent to Parliament for nine years. In 1858 he was secretary of state for the colonies. Despite his political activities, he was an indefatigable writer. He reached the height of his popularity when he published "The Last Days of Pompeii" in 1834, and "Rienzi" in 1835. From these successes he went on to journalism and playwriting, and produced "Richelieu" in 1839. He was created a baronet in 1838. He died at Torquay, January 18, 1873.

At the home of Marion de Lorme, mistress of the Duke of Orléans, and also a spy in the pay of Cardinal Richelieu, Prime Minister to the weakling Louis XIII of France, a plot is being completed for the dethronement of Louis, the elevation of Orléans and the murder of Richelieu who, by means of guile, bribes and the headsman, has been the real ruler of France.

Chief among the plotters are Orléans; Baradas, the King's First Gentleman of the Chamber; and De Beringhen, First Valet of the Chamber. Also in the plot is the Chevalier de Mauprat, "wildest gallant and bravest knight in France," who hates the Cardinal. Because Mauprat has joined in an earlier revolt, Richelieu has unfairly ordered him to die in battle, but, despite reckless valor, he has returned from combat with the sentence of death still pending.

At the meeting, Baradas displays the documents of a plot that would admit the Spanish army to aid in the overthrow of Louis, and he assures Orléans that he will find a desperate man to take the life of Richelieu. Baradas, since childhood jealous of Mauprat and now doubly envious because the Chevalier loves and is loved by Julie de Mortemar, the Cardinal's lovely ward, hopes to imperil Mauprat by assigning him to the task. As he tells him of the murder plan, Huguet, chief of the Cardinal's guard, arrests the Chevalier to take him before the Cardinal. Baradas welcomes the seizure of his rival, and reflects that he himself will yet be Julie's husband—and, perhaps, King.

In Richelieu's chamber, the Cardinal is coolly discussing the plot with his confidant, the Capuchin Joseph, who brings him new details. Joseph also reveals that Louis, to veil his passion for Julie, is planning to marry her to Bara-

das; but Julie arrives and they learn that her heart has been
won by Mauprat. Richelieu bids her wait in another room
while he receives Mauprat, now brought in by Huguet.

Mauprat's fearlessness and candor win Richelieu's admiration, and the Cardinal offers him fame and fortune if
he will marry another instead of Julie. When Mauprat
chooses death instead, the Cardinal sends him to the room
where Julie waits to meet his "executioner." Richelieu then
tells Joseph that they will be married tomorrow, and that
he now counts Mauprat as a strong ally against the plotters.

But the next day, at the Cardinal's Luxembourg house
which has been given to the bride and bridegroom, Mauprat receives a letter from the King, nullifying the marriage
just performed, and ordering that Mauprat shall await the
King's penalty, meantime keeping the royal injunction secret from Julie. The King has sent De Beringhen to watch
the lovers constantly, and Julie is bewildered and humiliated by Mauprat's aloofness. Baradas now convinces Mauprat that Richelieu has planned all this in order to revenge
himself upon Mauprat and increase his favor with the King
by providing a cuckold for Julie. Mauprat, enraged, agrees
to lead a band that will kill Richelieu, and Baradas arranges
to post him outside the plotters' meeting that night at
Marion's so that he shall know nothing of the treason bound
up with his revenge. Julie, told that Mauprat has left
for the day, is summoned to court.

Meanwhile, at the Cardinal's palace, Richelieu hears
more of the plot through Joseph and Huguet, and Marion
comes to tell him that she has induced the traitors to accept
her "brother" to carry the incriminating message to other
conspirators. Richelieu chooses his page, François, to play
the part of the brother and bring the packet to him instead.
But Huguet overhears him planning to merely reward him
with the promise of a colonel's rank, and vows revenge.
Richelieu tells Huguet to enlist twenty faithful guards and
follow him to his Ruelle castle, and he bids Joseph (dangling the hope of a bishop's robes before him) to watch at
court.

At Ruelle, François brings the news that an armored

man, accosting him outside Marion's dwelling, has taken
the packet from him, and Richelieu sends François back to
trace and recover it. Julie then arrives, miserable: she has
rebuffed Louis' advances, but Baradas has told her that
Mauprat has approved the suit. She has escaped through
the Queen's aid. Richelieu assures her that she has wronged
Mauprat, and he has just escorted her to another room
when the Chevalier, with visor down, comes to kill him.
Huguet, in his anger, has formed the Cardinal's "guard"
of plotters.

Mauprat angrily reproaches the Cardinal, lifting his visor
to reveal himself before striking. The Cardinal quickly
dissuades him from the act by revealing Baradas' infamy
and calling Julie to prove his account. The lovers are
reconciled, but now the impatient traitors are heard approaching to make sure of Richelieu's death. The Cardinal
throws himself upon a bed in an adjoining chamber, and
Mauprat tells them: "Richelieu is dead!" He explains that
he has strangled him to create the impression of a natural
death. Satisfied, the plotters ride off to their rewards, Mauprat remaining "to crush eager suspicion."

Huguet comes to Orléans to tell him that Richelieu is
dead, but the false Duke promptly has him clapped into a
cell to die, thus clearing himself of a part in the supposed
murder. François enters to tell of the loss of the incriminating packet, and Orléans and Baradas, realizing that it must
be in Mauprat's possession, send François to regain it
from him. Mauprat appears next day at the palace of the
King and attacks Baradas, but he is restrained when Louis
appears.

A sensation is created when Richelieu walks in, tells
Louis that he must pardon Mauprat, and attempts to reveal
the treasonable plot. But the gullible King, influenced by
the plotters in Richelieu's absence, orders Mauprat to be
imprisoned in the Bastille. Before he is led away, Mauprat
tells François that he has given the packet to Huguet.
Richelieu's talk of treason is smothered by Baradas, who
points to the imprisonment of Huguet as proof that the

traitors have been caught, and Louis refuses to believe that his courtiers can be disloyal.

Now Richelieu is in disfavor with the King who has been ever resentful of his statecraft and power. Louis sends his courtiers and Baradas to the Cardinal's home to fetch Julie to him, but Richelieu draws the "awful circle of our solemn church" about her and openly defies the King. Then, before Baradas, his speech becomes increasingly incoherent, and he falls, in a state of apparent collapse, into Joseph's arms.

François, pretending to be Huguet's son, plays upon the pity of his jailers, and reaches his cell while Baradas is vainly trying to wrest the secret of the whereabouts of the packet from Mauprat. In vain, Julie appeals to the King for Mauprat, but he offers his release only on condition that Julie yield. Baradas, bearing the writ for Mauprat's death, offers her only shame, and she decides to die with her husband.

Then Richelieu, pale and feeble, accompanied by secretaries and state papers, arrives to say that he is resigning his office, but that he first wishes his successors to be informed of the problems of state. The secretaries set forth the grave questions threatening France and Louis, and the King asks Baradas, his new minister, for counsel. Baradas' feeble answers, parried by Richelieu's quick solutions, have begun to sway Louis to an appreciation of the Cardinal's indispensability when François at last arrives with the evidence of the plotters' guilt. Richelieu's triumph is complete.

Granted sole authority by Louis, Richelieu, now rejuvenated, sends Baradas to his doom, reunites Julie and the freed Mauprat, exiles Orléans and De Beringhen, and rewards François and Joseph.

The School for Scandal

BY RICHARD BRINSLEY SHERIDAN

Born in Dublin, Ireland, October 30, 1751, his full name being Richard Brinsley Butler Sheridan. He went to Harrow, then continued his studies under a tutor and at Middle Temple. In 1772 he eloped with beautiful Elizabeth Linley, a singer, immortalized by the painter Gainsborough, and fought a duel with one of her suitors. In 1776 he became part-owner and director of the Drury Lane Theatre in London. Four years later, he entered Parliament and achieved fame as an orator. Sheridan wrote a comic opera, "The Duenna," and two of the most successful comedies in the English language, "The Rivals" (1775) and "The School for Scandal" (1777). He died in 1816 and was buried, with great ceremony, in Westminster Abbey.

At Lady Sneerwell's house, fashionable London's current villainies are being discussed and new ones hatched at a meeting of the School for Scandal, a coterie of ladies and gentlemen who delight in gossip and character assassination. Their present topic largely concerns the affairs of the brothers, Charles and Joseph Surface, and Sir Peter and Lady Teazle.

The conversation of the group discloses that both brothers are seeking the hand of Maria, ward of the elderly Sir Peter. Charles Surface, a pleasure-loving but admirable young man, is honestly in love with her, but brother Joseph, a scoundrel who, so far, has succeeded in concealing his knavery, is smitten only by her money. Sir Peter, also a sort of informal guardian of the brothers, has been hoodwinked by Joseph, and is trying to obstruct the suit of

Charles whom he suspects of advances to his wife, Lady Teazle.

In spite of his scorn of the gossips, Sir Peter is brought to this session of the School for Scandal by the young and vivacious Lady Teazle, an enthusiastic attendant; but he soon departs on business, "leaving his character behind him." The other guests retire to play cards, and Joseph, left alone with Lady Teazle, makes advances to her. She doesn't mind flirtation, but, being jealous of his suit for Maria, rebuffs him. Joseph reflects: "A curious dilemma! I wanted, at first, only to ingratiate myself with Lady Teazle that she might not be my enemy with Maria; and I have, I don't know how, become her serious lover!"

Into this situation, after a long stay in India, comes Sir Oliver Surface, wealthy uncle of the young men. He is told by his agent, Rowley, of Sir Peter's suspicion of Charles, generated by the scandalmongers, and Rowley ventures the opinion that if either is guilty of making advances to Lady Teazle, it is Joseph. When Sir Oliver visits his old friend, Sir Peter Teazle, the latter is outspoken in his denunciation of Charles. Thereupon, Sir Oliver determines to learn which of his nephews is worthy to inherit his estate.

Since neither Charles nor Joseph has seen his uncle in fifteen years, Sir Oliver decides to conceal his identity and to visit each under an assumed name. He goes first to the house of Charles where he is introduced as Mr. Premium, a banker who is willing to make a loan. Charles confesses that he is an extravagant young fellow without any resources as security beyond a roomful of family portraits which he will sell at a bargain. Sir Oliver, deeply pained at his nephew's apparent callousness toward family treasures, is ready to buy them, and Charles offers the lot for three hundred pounds. He refuses, however, to part with a portrait of Sir Oliver, even at a bid of eight hundred pounds. "No, hang it!" he says stoutly, "I'll not part with poor Noll. The old fellow has been very good to me and, egad, I'll keep his picture as long as I can find a place for it." The mollified Sir Oliver leaves, now convinced that Charles is "a dear, extravagant rogue."

Sir Oliver goes now to the home of Joseph, disguised as an impoverished relative of Joseph's mother, and is greeted by this nephew with sanctimonious expressions of sympathy—but no aid, Joseph protesting that he himself has no money. His visitor says that he understands that Joseph's uncle, Sir Oliver, has sent him large sums from India, but Joseph answers: "You are strangely misinformed. Sir Oliver is a worthy man but he is old; and avarice is a vice of old age." Sir Oliver reflects: "Here's gratitude for twelve thousand pounds!" Joseph dismisses him with "my most generous good wishes for your health and spirits," and Sir Oliver decides: "Charles, you are my heir!"

Meanwhile, Sir Peter accuses Lady Teazle of misconduct with Charles. She angrily retorts: "Take care, Sir Peter! . . . I'll not be suspected without cause, I promise you!" And in her pique she visits the rooms of Joseph. As she and Joseph are talking, Sir Peter, who has decided to obtain Joseph's counsel on his troubles, is announced, and his wife hurriedly hides behind a screen.

Sir Peter tells Joseph of his suspicions of Charles, and Joseph glibly condemns his brother, disclaiming relationship if Charles should be guilty. Sir Peter exclaims: "What a difference there is between you! What noble sentiments!" Then he vows his continued affection for his wife: "I love her in spite of everything . . . so much so, indeed, that I have just made two settlements on her . . . eight hundred a year independent while I live, and . . . the bulk of my fortune at my death."

Joseph, reflecting that this declaration will spike his romance with Lady Teazle, is desperately trying to find an excuse to get rid of Sir Peter when his brother is announced. Sir Peter, directing Joseph to question Charles about Lady Teazle while he himself hides in order to listen and determine the truth, hurries behind the screen which conceals Lady Teazle. He retreats quickly, exclaiming, "Hey! . . . There seems to be one listener here already! I'll swear I saw a petticoat!"

Joseph declares that the person he is hiding is a French milliner, and Sir Peter, assured by him that "the milliner" will repeat nothing of the scandal she has overheard, hides in a closet as Charles enters. Joseph, seeing a chance to ruin his brother's character in the hearing of Sir Peter, tells him that Sir Peter has accused him of attempting to win Lady Teazle. Charles blurts: "Who, I? O Lud, not I, upon my word! Why, it's you, Joseph. Don't you remember one day, when I called here, and found you together . . . and another time, when your servant told me——"

Joseph implores: "Hush, Sir Peter . . . is in that closet!" The angry Charles then cries: "Oho! . . . Come forth, Sir Peter!" He hauls him from the closet. Charles and Sir Peter are comparing notes when Joseph is told that Lady Sneerwell, who is also one of his conquests, is downstairs. He goes quickly to see her. Left together, Charles is denouncing his brother, who "pretends to be such a saint," when Sir Peter, agreeing, recalls that Joseph "has a little French milliner hidden there right now."

Charles cries: "Let's unveil her!" and upsets the screen just as Joseph returns. Joseph tries to explain that Lady Teazle came to talk with him about Maria, but she declares: "Don't listen to the hypocrite. I came here, seduced by his insidious arguments, at least to listen to his pretended passion, if not to sacrifice your honor. . . . But I have recovered my senses. . . . Sir Peter, the tenderness you expressed for me, when you did not know I was listening, has penetrated to my heart . . . let my future life bespeak my gratitude." Sir Peter tells her: "You have my fullest confidence, Lady Teazle." To Joseph's weak: "Sir Peter, Heaven knows——" Sir Peter rejoins: "That you are a villain!"

The members of the School for Scandal arrive to extend mock sympathy to Lady Teazle and Sir Peter, but he orders them out with the general observation that they are "fiends, vipers and furies," and an added personal flaying for each as they scuttle away. Then he, Lady Teazle and Sir Oliver bestow their blessings upon Charles and Maria, with the final words:

"And so they're freed from their pernicious friends,
As this our tale in merry laughter ends.
For laughter is the weapon of the wise;
When malice meets with mirth, then scandal dies."

The Rivals

BY RICHARD BRINSLEY SHERIDAN

Young Captain Absolute, son and heir of Sir Anthony
Absolute, arrives in Bath to pay court to the rich and
lovely Lydia Languish. His suit is singularly complicated
because he has made himself known to her as the penniless
Ensign Beverley, the better to intrigue her romantic nature.
Lydia, seventeen, favors the excitement of an elopement,
but Captain Absolute is aware that she will lose two-thirds
of her fortune if she weds without the consent of her aunt,
Mrs. Malaprop. He hopes that Lydia will accept him in
his true name after she has come to love him as Ensign
Beverley.

Lydia also has problems: her aunt has intercepted a
note from Beverley and has confined Lydia to her home;
now she has no opportunity to patch up a petty quarrel
with her lover, and fears that she has lost him. Her friend
Julia tries to console her by saying that, after all, Beverley
is penniless, but Lydia declares herself determined to
marry, before she becomes of age, a man who will care
nothing for her fortune.

She tells Julia that Mrs. Malaprop has not scrupled to
carry on a small romance of her own: she is corresponding,
under the name of Delia, with a fire-eating Irish baronet,
Sir Lucius O'Trigger, who is unaware of her true identity.
Mrs. Malaprop's shrewd maid, Lucy, who acts as messenger between them, is fattening her purse by telling the
impoverished O'Trigger that "Delia" is the beautiful Lydia.

A new complication now arises: Sir Anthony makes a

surprise visit to Bath. He arrives with Mrs. Malaprop at her home to propose a match between his son, the Captain, and Lydia. Mrs. Malaprop, who has an amazing propensity for garbling the English language, orders Lydia to "illiterate" Beverley from her thoughts. But Lydia, unaware of his true identity, refuses to marry Captain Absolute. In spite of her refusal, her aunt accepts his father's proposal, and prepares to dismiss another of Lydia's suitors, Bob Acres, a young man who is somewhat of a bumpkin.

Captain Absolute has learned of the arrival of his father and Julia, who is Sir Anthony's ward, and he summons his friend Faulkland to give him the news about them. Faulkland and Julia are betrothed, but the former is in a perpetual stew of doubts, fears, hopes and wishes, all revolving around his beloved. For amusement, the Captain calls in Bob Acres to report on Julia's health (he is a country neighbor of the Absolutes), and to hear Acres berate his rival, Beverley, not knowing that the latter is, in reality, his friend Absolute. Faulkland, who has been worrying for fear Julia might be ill, hears that she is quite merry in spite of his absence, and is thrown into a new fever of unhappiness.

The testy Sir Anthony calls in order to command his son to marry Lydia, but the Captain refuses—his father neglects to tell her name—and Sir Anthony stamps out, threatening to disinherit him. Fag, the Captain's servant, learns from Lucy that Sir Anthony's choice is Lydia, and this he tells young Absolute. The enlightened Captain hastens to his father to say that he has repented and is willing to court Lydia. Father and son set off to pay their addresses to Mrs. Malaprop.

This lady, after approving the Captain as "the very pineapple of politeness," tells them that she has intercepted another note from Beverley to Lydia—in which, unfortunately, he refers to Mrs. Malaprop as "a weather-beaten she-dragon." The letter also reveals that Beverley has a scheme to see Lydia—with "the old harridan" as an unwitting go-between.

Young Absolute suggests that Mrs. Malaprop punish the

conceited puppy, Beverley, by letting him reach the point
of elopement; then he, Absolute, will himself carry off
Lydia. She agrees, and Lydia is summoned. "Beverley"
whispers to her that he has disguised himself as Absolute,
and the delighted Lydia tells her aunt again that she will
wed only Beverley. Mrs. Malaprop declares Lydia to be
as headstrong as "an allegory on the banks of the Nile."

Meanwhile, Acres, rebuffed by Lydia and blaming the
mysterious Beverley for her coldness, is urged by O'Trigger
to challenge his rival to a duel. A note is written to Beverley, naming that very evening for the duel in King's Mead-
Fields. O'Trigger himself sets out in search of Captain
Absolute (whom he believes to be his rival for "Delia")
with the idea in mind of challenging Absolute to a duel.
Acres, in preparation for his tilt with Beverley, asks young
Absolute to be his second. The waggish Captain declares
that he thinks this hardly proper, but he agrees to deliver
Acres' note to Beverley.

Sir Anthony Absolute now insists on taking his son to
Lydia's home. Here he acknowledges him in her presence,
and Lydia at once realizes that there has been a hoax—
Beverley, of course, is really the Captain. Mrs. Malaprop
agrees to forgive all, and says: "We will not anticipate
the past, our retrospection will now be all to the future";
but Lydia, angry at being duped, declares that indeed she
renounces "Beverley" forever, and flounces from the room.

The Captain, infuriated by Lydia's behavior, leaves at
once. He meets O'Trigger who is seeking to challenge him,
they quarrel and agree to cross swords that evening in the
King's Mead-Fields—where Acres is scheduled to meet
Beverley. Absolute informs his friend Faulkland of the
coming event, giving the latter a new idea for testing Julia's
love for him: he tells her that he has involved himself in a
quarrel and must run away immediately. Julia is ready to
accompany him, but, learning that the story is another one
of Faulkland's concoctions, declares that now she will
never marry him.

Lydia, Julia and Mrs. Malaprop hear from the servants
a confused story of the impending duel—a duel in which

Absolute, Faulkland and O'Trigger are named as the principals—and they hasten to the field to prevent what Mrs.
Malaprop fears is to be "fine suicide, paracide, salavation
and an antistrophe." Sir Anthony, who has met his son on
his way to keep his engagement but who has been deceived
as to the purpose of young Absolute's sword, now learns of
the impending duel, and sets out for the King's Mead-
Fields.

Here, the bloodthirsty O'Trigger is giving Acres some
preliminary instructions in duelling, but so graphically does
he illustrate the lesson that Acres has quite lost his appetite
for combat. Young Absolute and Faulkland arrive. O'Trigger, learning that Faulkland is not Beverley (he has
assumed from the beginning that he was), proposes that
Faulkland fight Acres anyway, just to make a foursome.
Acres hurriedly vetoes this suggestion. Absolute then identifies himself as Beverley. Acres, much to O'Trigger's disgust,
now insists that he cannot possibly fight his friend Absolute.
Absolute and O'Trigger are drawing their swords when Sir
Anthony and the women appear.

O'Trigger greets Lydia as his "Delia," and is unpleasantly
surprised to learn that his correspondent has been, in
reality, the simpering Mrs. Malaprop. He promptly relin-
quishes "Delia" to Absolute. Lydia forgives the Captain,
and he and O'Trigger are quickly reconciled. Faulkland
and Julia also grant forgiveness to each other, and plan to
be married at once. Bob Acres, vastly relieved, renounces
all claims to any wife for whom he must fight, and invites
the company to a party.

She Stoops to Conquer

BY OLIVER GOLDSMITH

Born in Ireland, November 10, 1728. He was educated at Trinity College, Dublin, later studied medicine, but did not practice. He traveled on the continent, and made a meager living by writing and teaching—until he met Samuel Johnson in 1761. Johnson encouraged him, with the result that he settled down to serious writing. Goldsmith is credited with having written the best novel ("The Vicar of Wakefield"), the best poem ("The Deserted Village"), and the best play ("She Stoops to Conquer") of his time. "She Stoops to Conquer" and another comedy, "The Good-Natured Man," were highly successful. They earned him a large income before his death on April 4, 1774.

An exciting and romantic night is anticipated at the English country home of Kate Hardcastle. Kate is to be visited by her father's choice of a husband for her—young Marlow, the son of Charles Marlow, Mr. Hardcastle's old friend. Kate has not yet seen her intended. With him is to come young Mr. Hastings to call on his sweetheart, Constance Neville, Mrs. Hardcastle's niece and Kate's dearest friend. Mrs. Hardcastle hopes for a match between her son, Tony Lumpkin, Kate's half-brother, and Constance, though both Constance and Tony detest each other.

Marlow and Hastings, having lost their way during the post-chaise trip from the city, stop for directions at the Three Pigeons Tavern—where Tony, as usual, is whiling away the evening with drink, flirtations and practical jokes. On hearing the travelers' destination, Tony gets the inspiration for what he conceives to be a great prank: he tells Marlow and Hastings that they can never reach the Hardcastle home at night over the dangerous path that

lies before them, and that, since the Three Pigeons is
crowded, they had best go a mile farther to the Buck's
Head, easily identified by a pair of horns on the door. He
advises them to drive into the yard "and call stoutly about
you." The young men thank him and leave, unaware that
Tony has, in reality, sent them to the Hardcastles' home.

Upon arrival, Marlow and Hastings believe Mr. Hardcastle to be the innkeeper, and they order him brusquely
about, demanding supper and ignoring his attempts at a
host's affability. Marlow insists upon going upstairs to
inspect his bed personally, and while he is absent, Constance walks into the room. When Hastings asks what she
is doing at the "inn," she exposes the hoax. Hastings warns
Constance that the sensitive Marlow must not be allowed
to learn the truth, for he might leave at once, humiliated
because of his rude conduct, and so spoil their own plans.

These plans provide for the elopement of Hastings and
Constance—just as soon as she can get possession of her
fortune in jewels which Mrs. Hardcastle has carefully
locked up. Until she does so, they decide to continue to
carry out Tony's fraud, Hastings telling Marlow that, by
chance, Constance and Kate also are guests at the inn. But
the meeting of Marlow and Kate is hardly auspicious, for
the bashful Marlow blushes and stammers stupid compliments. Kate later tells her father that she will have none of
him: "His awkward address, his bashful manner, his hesitating timidity, struck me at first sight."

Her father is amazed at her words. Says he: "Then your
first sight deceived you, child, for I think him one of the
most brazen sights that ever astonished my senses. He met
me with a loud voice, a lordly air, and a familiarity that
made my blood freeze." He and Kate agree to await
further developments before pronouncing judgment on
Marlow's true nature, and Kate disguises herself as a maid.
Marlow, looking at her closely for the first time, assumes
her to be "a female of the other class" with which he has
never been ill at ease, and he becomes the assured gallant.
He tries to kiss her.

Kate protests: "Pray, Sir, keep your distance . . . I'm

sure you did not treat Miss Hardcastle that was here a
while ago in this obstropalous manner." Marlow replies
airily: "Who cares for Miss Hardcastle? A mere awkward,
squinting thing! . . . But you——" He tries again to embrace her. Kate escapes, but not before the irate Mr. Hardcastle has arrived to see the scuffle. He demands that Marlow leave his house at once. Marlow tells him to bring his
bill and make no more words about it.

Mr. Hardcastle replies: "Young man, from your father's
letter to me, I was taught to expect a well-bred, modest
man, but now I find you no better than a coxcomb and
a bully! But Sir Charles will be down here presently and
you shall hear more of it!" In bewilderment, Marlow calls
to the "barmaid," Kate, to clear up the muddle. She tells
him that he is, indeed, in the Hardcastle home, and that
she lives there as "a poor relation." Marlow, covered with
mortification, is prepared to leave at once, but begins to
realize his love for the maid, and Kate begins to suspect
that he is, after all, quite bearable.

In the meantime, the romance of Hastings and Constance
is not doing well. To clear the path for their elopement,
the helpful Tony, who wants Constance out of the way
because she is a threat to his liberty, has stolen her jewels
from Mrs. Hardcastle and has given them to Hastings. For
safekeeping, Hastings has passed them along to Marlow.
Marlow, who has thought Mrs. Hardcastle only the landlady of the inn, has turned them over to her to take care of.
She thus learns of Constance's intended elopement.

To put an end to this plan and forward her hope that
Tony shall be Constance's husband, Mrs. Hardcastle orders
Constance off to her Aunt Pedigree's, summoning Tony
to drive Constance and herself there at once. Tony agrees,
and the three start off into the night.

Then Sir Charles arrives. He joins with Mr. Hardcastle
in a hearty laugh over his son's bewilderment, though they
assume that the youth, by now, is wholly aware of the
truth. But young Marlow still thinks the maid and Kate
are different persons, and when twitted by Mr. Hardcastle
over his ardent behavior toward his daughter, replies: "By

all that's just and true, sir, I never gave Miss Hardcastle
the slightest mark of my attachment." He leaves the room,
and now the fathers are completely bewildered. They ask
Kate if Marlow has made love to her. "I must say he has,"
she declares. The fathers decide to watch when the young
folk meet again, and they hear Marlow, still believing Kate
to be the poor relation, declare his love for her and offer
marriage.

The two men come forward to reproach him for his
hypocrisy, and Hardcastle says: "What do you have to say
for yourself now, young man? . . . You can address a lady
in private and deny it in public; you have one story for us
and another for my daughter."

Marlow then learns that the maid, in reality, is Kate. He
can say only: "Oh, the devil!" The tangle now unraveled,
the young people are happily betrothed.

Good fortune also comes to Hastings and Constance.
The irrepressible Tony, instead of taking the party to Aunt
Pedigree's, has driven them for hours around the Hardcastle grounds, jouncing through every mud-hole to make
the trip more miserable, before finally bringing the carriage
to a halt at the end of the Hardcastle garden. The exhausted Mrs. Hardcastle is now in no mood to reproach
Tony or even to oppose the match between Hastings and
Constance, although she does insist upon retaining Constance's jewels.

A condition of the custody of Constance's fortune, however, is that the jewels shall be released to her if Tony,
upon coming of age, refuses to marry her. Mr. Hardcastle
then tells Tony: "While I thought concealing your age was
likely to conduce to your improvement, I concurred with
your mother's desire to keep it secret. But since I find that
she turns it to a wrong use, I must now declare you have
been of age these three months."

"Then," says Tony, "you'll see the first use I'll make of
my liberty." He formally renounces Constance, removing
the last barrier to the double match.

The Beggar's Opera

BY JOHN GAY

Born in 1685 at Barnstaple, England. He was educated at the grammar school in the town, and was later apprenticed to a silk merchant. His first known work was a publication called "Wing" which appeared in 1708. His later work, "Rural Sports," which he dedicated to Alexander Pope, marked the beginning of a lifelong friendship between the two men. Through the influence of Jonathan Swift, Gay was appointed secretary to the Ambassador to the Court of Hanover for a short while, and from then on he seems to have had numerous patrons with considerable influence at court. On January 29, 1728, his "Beggar's Opera" was produced, and was such a success with the people that he wrote a sequel, the first musical comedy in English, "Polly." These comedies were an innovation of their time. They satirized the corruptions of the governing class. "Polly" was forbidden at court because it caricatured Sir Robert Walpole; and the Duchess of Queensberry, who was Gay's patroness at the time, was dismissed from the court. However, the Duke of Queensberry gave Gay a home from then until his death in December, 1732. He is buried in Westminster Abbey. "The Threepenny Opera," a successful modernization by Bertolt Brecht and Kurt Weill of "The Beggar's Opera," has demonstrated the enduring popularity of much of Gay's satire.

A lion of the eighteenth-century British underworld is the young highwayman, Macheath, handsome, romantic, courageous and witty. He boasts that he has enough virtues to be classed with the most respectable of criminals, and vices enough to rank him with the most lofty of noblemen. Besides, he tells his thieving friends: "I am not a mere court-friend, who promises everything and will do nothing. We, gentlemen, have still honor enough to break through the corruptions of the world."

Thus confident of his equality with the gentlemen of his time, this rogue does not hesitate to woo Polly Peachum, daughter of a politician who is successfully serving both police and outlaw. Peachum does a bustling business in aiding thieves for a fee and in betraying them for a reward. "A lawyer," Peachum reasons, "is an honest employment; so is mine. Like me, too, he acts in a double capacity, both against rogues and for 'em."

Macheath is a good client of Peachum, and he and his wife have no objection to a romance between Polly and the highwayman—but they are outraged when they learn that she has married him.

Peachum protests: "What! Married! . . . Do you think your mother and I should have lived comfortably so long together if ever we had been married? Baggage!" Mrs. Peachum seconds him: "Can you support the expense of a husband, hussy, in gaming and drinking?" And, when Polly declares that she loves him, adds: "Love him! Worse and worse! I thought the girl had been better bred!"

But Peachum observes that, "in spite of all that may be said against marriage, it has one great advantage": a wife can always become a widow. "The comfortable estate of widowhood," he points out, "is the only hope that keeps up a wife's spirits." He suggests to the horrified Polly that she get possession of all of Macheath's money, accuse him in court, and become a rich widow. He argues that the highwayman is sure to be captured sooner or later, and no doubt would be pleased to have the Peachums, rather than strangers, get the reward.

Mrs. Peachum further argues: "Your duty to your parents, hussy, obliges you to hang him. What would many a wife give for such an opportunity!" Polly scornfully rejects the plan, and the parents, "knowing their duty," decide to betray Macheath themselves. Polly overhears them discussing the idea, and warns Macheath. The highwayman declares: "You might sooner tear a pension out of the hands of a courtier, a fee from a lawyer, a pretty woman from a looking-glass . . . but to tear me from thee is impossible." However, he finally decides to flee, leaving for other haunts and philanderings.

He soon appears at a cutthroats' tavern, near Newgate, as leader of a robber band. He is surrounded by a bevy of trollops, and it is his fickleness which proves his undoing. The jealous girls betray him to Peachum, whom he has deceived into thinking that he has renounced crime, and he is taken to Newgate Prison. Here he is visited by a former acquaintance, Lucy Lockit, daughter of the warden, who reproaches him for deserting her and marrying Polly.

The crafty Macheath, seeing a possible means of escape, promptly denies that Polly is his wife, and suggests that Lucy's vexation may be of "ill consequence to a woman of your condition." He offers to marry her, and asks if she thinks that twenty guineas might move her father to let him escape. Lucy forgives him, promising that she will do everything possible to get him out of jail. She tells him, however, that she would rather see him hanged than in the arms of another woman. Macheath gallantly swears that he would rather be in her arms than hanged, and Lucy, getting the keys to his cell from her sleeping father, quickly frees him. Lucy asks that Macheath take her with him, but the highwayman points out that two cannot hide as well as one, and promises that he will send for her when the hunt for him dies down.

When Warden Lockit, who shares Peachum's trade in both felons' fees and police rewards, finds out what has happened, he tells Lucy that she is a fool, both for failing to make Macheath pay well for his freedom and for believing his avowal of love for her. Lucy now agrees that she has been hoaxed, and envisions a dread future in which Polly will get Macheath's money and Peachum will hang him, completely cheating her out of any compensation.

Now, both Lockit and his daughter, as well as Peachum, scheme to get Macheath back in a cell once more, and the jealous Lucy plans to do away with Polly by poison. She offers a "cordial" of ratbane to Polly as a peace offering, with the reflection that now she shall "get even with the hypocritical strumpet." Polly, suspecting that Lucy is trying to learn her secrets by plying her with drink, begs to be excused. But Lucy is so insistent that Polly is about to drink the poison when she sees Macheath in the clutches of Lockit and Peachum. Cries Polly: "What! My husband again betrayed! Now every glimmering of happiness is lost!"

The two girls forget their rivalry now that the highwayman once more is in danger of the hangman. They fall upon their knees, imploring their fathers to save him. But Lockit says: "Macheath's time has come, Lucy. So let's have no more whimpering or whining." And Peachum is equally determined to share in the reward for Macheath's capture. "Set your heart at rest, Polly. Your husband is to die today," he tells her.

Macheath is sentenced to death, and Polly and Lucy go to see him for the last time. The debonair robber gives them his counsel: "My dear Lucy—my dear Polly—whatsoever hath passed between us is now at an end. If you are fond of marrying again, the best advice I can give you is to ship yourselves off for the West Indies, where you'll have a chance of getting a husband apiece: or, by good luck, two or three, as you like best."

The sorrowful girls are trying to comfort him with the possibility that there may yet be hope for him when a jailor announces to Macheath: "Four women more, Captain, with a child apiece! See, here they come."

Laments Macheath: "What? Four wives more! This is too much. Here, tell the sheriff's officers I am ready."

(In an epilogue, the actors protest this unhappy ending of the play and, as an alternative finale, the author sets Macheath free. "For you must allow that in this kind of drama anything can happen, no matter how absurd. . . . So, you rabble there, run and cry a reprieve for the prisoner." Macheath then falls into the hands of his wives. "So think of this maxim, and put off your sorrow: the wretch of today may be happy tomorrow.")

The Way of the World

BY WILLIAM CONGREVE

*Born in Bardsey, near Leeds, England, February 10,
1670. He went to school in Ireland where his father, a
soldier, had been sent. Later, in London, he studied law
at Middle Temple. His first comedy, "The Old Bachelor,"
met with such instant success, when produced in 1693,
that his career can be said to have started with that brilliant piece. He became manager of the newly established
Lincoln's Inn Theatre, and was under contract to write a
play a year for it. Among the plays which he wrote at
this time were, "Love for Love" and "The Mourning Bride."
These were Restoration comedies, reflecting the moral
laxity of the time. When Congreve's next play, "The Way
of the World," appeared it was greeted in terms of superlative praise, but did not evoke the spontaneous enthusiasm
which "The Old Bachelor" had aroused. Congreve was
later associated with Vanbrugh in the management of the
Queen's Theatre, but because of failing health, he was
obliged to retire. As the result of injuries received in an
accident, he died on January 19, 1729.*

A ribald tangle of deceit among upper-class English
households is revealed as Mirabell, a philanderer, cynically comforts Mrs. Fainall, his mistress. Mrs. Fainall is
complaining that she completely detests her husband, and
asks why Mirabell compelled her to marry him.

Observing that it is well to "have just so much disgust
for your husband as may be sufficient to relish your lover,"
Mirabell reminds her: "If the familiarities of our loves
had proved that consequence of which you were appre-
hensive, where could you have fixed a father's name with
credit but on a husband?" As for his choice of Fainall, he

says: "A better person ought not to have been sacrificed
to the occasion; a worse had not answered the purpose."

Mrs. Fainall's passion for Mirabell, nevertheless, leads
her to help him in his next scheme, even though it involves
her own mother, Lady Wishfort, also infatuated with Mirabell. Mirabell wants to marry the beautiful and wealthy
Mrs. Millamant, niece of Lady Wishfort, but her aunt—
who is also her guardian—is jealously withholding her consent. With Mrs. Fainall's connivance, Mirabell arranges
to have his servant, Waitwell, in the guise of an uncle
called Sir Rowland, pay court to Lady Wishfort. Then,
since he already has accomplished a secret marriage between Waitwell and Lady Wishfort's maid, Foible, he
proposes to expose the scandal. His price for silence is to
be Mrs. Millamant and her fortune.

The scheme perfected, Foible tells Lady Wishfort that
Sir Rowland has seen her picture and is infatuated by her
loveliness. A meeting is arranged, but the plot is overheard
by Mrs. Marwood, another of Mirabell's conquests and herself no mean schemer. Desiring Mirabell for herself, she
promptly influences Lady Wishfort to agree that Mrs.
Millamant shall be married to Sir Wilfull, a rich and
amiable dunce. Then Mrs. Marwood, to make sure of
success, enlists the help of Fainall who is infatuated with
her and jealous of Mirabell. Fainall is a willing tool, complaining: "My wife is an arrant wife, and I am a cuckold.
. . . 'Sdeath! To be out-witted, out-jilted, out-matrimo-
ney'd! . . . 'Tis scurvy wedlock!"

Deceived by her caresses and angered by her reminder
that Mirabell, his foe, may otherwise get Mrs. Millamant's
fortune, Fainall agrees to Mrs. Marwood's plan: she will
write a letter to be delivered to Lady Wishfort when Waitwell, as Sir Rowland, is with her. The letter will expose the
fraud and Mirabell, she says, will be ruined. Mrs. Marwood neglects to tell Fainall of her scheme to save Mirabell for herself.

Lady Wishfort is a-twitter as she awaits the bogus Sir
Rowland. She is informed by Foible that candles are ready,
that the footmen are lined up in the hall in their best

liveries, and that the coachman and postillion, well perfumed, are on hand for a good showing.

Assured by Foible that she looks "most killing well," Lady Wishfort ponders: "Well, and how shall I receive him? . . . Shall I sit? No, I won't sit—I'll walk—ay, I'll walk from the door upon his entrance, and then turn full upon him— No, that will be too sudden. I'll lie—ay, I'll lie down—I'll receive him in my little dressing room—yes, yes, I'll give him the first impression on a couch. I won't lie neither, but loll and lean upon one elbow, with one foot a little dangling off, jogging in a thoughtful way—yes—and then as soon as he appears, start, ay, start and be surprised, and rise to meet him in a pretty disorder."

Sir Rowland arrives. He and Lady Wishfort get along famously at once, and Sir Rowland begs for an early marriage, declaring that his nephew, Mirabell, will poison him for his money if he learns of the romance. The jealous Lady Wishfort promptly agrees, suggesting that Sir Rowland starve Mirabell "gradually, inch by inch." Then Mrs. Marwood's letter, denouncing Sir Rowland as Waitwell, arrives, but Sir Rowland deftly declares the letter to be the work of his nephew, and he hies himself off "to fight him a duel."

Lady Wishfort learns of the deception that is being practised, and turns on Foible: "Out of my house! To marry me to a servingman! To make me the laughing-stock of the whole town! I'll have you locked up in Bridewell Jail, that's what I'll do!"

The frightened Foible confesses that it is Mirabell who has conceived the whole plot, and Lady Wishfort is planning a dire revenge when more trouble comes: Fainall, her son-in-law, demands that his wife turn over her whole fortune to him, else he and Mrs. Marwood will reveal to the world that Mrs. Fainall was Mirabell's mistress before her marriage and that she still is. Lady Wishfort is dazedly reflecting upon this new humiliation when Mirabell comes to her with another plan.

"If," he says, "a deep sense of the many injuries I have offered to so good a lady, with a sincere remorse and a hearty contrition, can but obtain the least glance of compassion, I am too happy. . . . Consider, madam, in reality it was an innocent device, though I confess it had a face of guiltiness. It was at most an artifice which love contrived —and errors which love produces have ever been accounted pardonable."

The susceptible Lady Wishfort offers to forgive Mirabell if he will renounce his idea of marrying Mrs. Millamant. Mirabell offers a compromise: if she will permit her niece to marry him, he will contrive to save Mrs. Fainall's reputation and fortune. If he can do this, Lady Wishfort agrees, she will forgive anything and consent to anything. Mirabell then tells her: "Well, then, as regards your daughter's reputation, she has nothing to fear from Fainall. For his own reputation is at stake. He and Mrs. Marwood —we have proof of it—have been and still are lovers. . . . And as regards your daughter's fortune, she need have no fear on that score, either: acting upon my advice, and relying upon my honesty, she has made me the trustee of her entire estate."

Cries Fainall: " 'Tis outrageous!"

Says Mirabell: " 'Tis the way of the world."

In a closing observation to the audience, he adds:

"From hence let those be warned, who mean to wed,
Lest mutual falsehood stain the bridal bed;
For each deceiver to his cost may find,
That marriage frauds too oft are paid in kind."

The Beaux' Stratagem

BY GEORGE FARQUHAR

Born in 1677, in Londonderry, Ireland; educated at Trinity College, Dublin. He became an actor in Dublin, but, in a fencing scene, he forgot to exchange his sword for a foil and nearly killed a fellow actor. After this incident, he never acted again. He started writing plays, and his first,

"Love and a Bottle," was performed at the Drury Lane Theatre in London in 1698. He married in 1703, but the fortune which he expected to acquire by this marriage did not materialize, and his life was a constant struggle against poverty. The best of his plays, "The Beaux' Stratagem," was finished toward the end of a fatal illness. It was produced three nights before his death on April 29, 1707.

In London in the early eighteenth century, two rollicking young gentlemen, Aimwell and Archer, their money spent and their only alternatives being to marry money or to sell their swords for the wars, conceal their poverty from their gay London friends, and ride into the country to let fate decide their course for them. They are still in possession of their last two hundred pounds, and they have conceived a shrewd plan: by turns one is to play the fine lord, the other his servant, the better to impress the country folk.

They arrive at Litchfield Inn, and Aimwell, taking the first turn at playing the lord, drinks with the garrulous Will Boniface, the landlord, in order to learn of the prospects in the vicinity. The countryside's most notable household, he finds, is that of Lady Bountiful, a wealthy widow whose philanthropy and skill as a healer have made her an idolized figure. She has a young, wealthy and lovely daughter called Dorinda, and a sluggard son, Squire Sullen, who has recently married a comely London lady. Also at the inn are some captive French officers, among them Count Bellair and Foigard, their priest.

Aimwell, to strengthen the impression of his high estate, puts his money in the landlord's strongbox, bidding Boniface to keep it in readiness as he may stay at the inn only a half hour. Boniface, himself in league with the highwaymen, Gibbet, Hounslow and Bagshot, suspects that Aimwell and Archer are thieves, and, to betray them and get their money, he tells his pretty daughter, Cherry, to tease what information she can from Archer while he plies Aimwell with drink and subtle questioning. But Boniface

is outwitted by Aimwell who reveals nothing, and Cherry
only succeeds in falling in love with Archer.

Dorinda and her sister-in-law, Mrs. Sullen, are also curious about the travelers, for Aimwell has gone to church
to meet the rich Dorinda. Dorinda immediately becomes
deeply interested in the handsome stranger. She and Mrs.
Sullen induce Scrub, servant to the Sullens, to invite
Archer (still playing Aimwell's servant) to their home for
questioning. They too are checkmated in their attempt to
get information, but the discontented Mrs. Sullen observes
that Archer is not without charm.

When Archer has gone, Mrs. Sullen and Dorinda carry
out a ruse to awaken Sullen, who has been derelict in this
respect, to his duties as a loving husband. Dorinda has
concealed Sullen in a closet in order that he may hear
Count Bellair woo his wife and she ridicule her husband.
Sullen reacts by rushing out with drawn sword, but is
restrained from attacking Bellair by a pistol leveled at
him by his wife. He scores a point, however, when he observes that he does not care if his wife bestows her favors
elsewhere if she does so secretly and not to a Frenchman—
he detests all Frenchmen. Bellair, whom Mrs. Sullen now
informs, with some exaggeration, that her passion has been
only feigned, notes that her virtue may be very great but
her honesty very little, and invites her to send for him
whenever she needs a fool. All in all, the stratagem has
not done well, but Mrs. Sullen is still in a reckless mood.

A diversion is created when Archer appears, simulating
great concern, to report that his master is outside, suffering
from a fit, and he implores the good offices of Lady Bountiful. Aimwell, feigning coma, is borne in, but quickly regains
consciousness after violently squeezing the comforting
hand of the beautiful Dorinda. When Archer suggests that
Aimwell should not yet venture into the open air, Dorinda
and her sister-in-law escort the men on a tour of the house.
Aimwell and Dorinda stray off by themselves, and only a
determined effort of conscience saves Mrs. Sullen from a
lapse from virtue when the industrious Archer entices
her into her own bedchamber.

As Archer leaves, Scrub tells him that he has overheard
Foigard, the priest, bribing Gipsy, the Sullens' maid, to
conceal Bellair in Mrs. Sullen's chamber that night. Mrs.
Sullen now wonders if, without supernatural gifts, she can
do more than simply avoid the temptation of Archer, and
Dorinda dreams of marrying "Lord" Aimwell and living a
gay life in London. Archer and Aimwell, meanwhile, confront Foigard with a trumped-up charge of treason, and,
in exchange for their silence, win the priest's promise
that he will conduct Archer, instead of the Count, to Mrs.
Sullen's bedroom.

Other developments are in the making for the household
that same night. Boniface has arranged that Gibbet, Hounslow and Bagshot, armed to the teeth, shall rob Lady
Bountiful. Gibbet has already gotten Sullen well besotted
with drink by way of preparation. Sir Charles Freeman,
brother of Mrs. Sullen, whom she has summoned to help
her get free of her obnoxious husband, now arrives at the
inn. Freeman and Sullen, the latter unaware that he is talking with his brother-in-law, fall into conversation. Sullen
becomes indignant when Freeman suggests that he should
not go home to his wife in his drunken condition. "What!"
he exclaims, "not lie with my wife! Sir, do you take me for
an atheist or a rake? I'm a justice of the peace, and must do
nothing against the law." Since Freeman takes her part, he
makes a drunken promise that Freeman shall have his wife
in the morning, with a venison pasty to boot.

At two o'clock the next morning, Cherry, unable to find
Archer, who by this time is concealed in Mrs. Sullen's
closet, runs to Aimwell with the news that the robbers are
leaving for Lady Bountiful's home. Mrs. Sullen, sigh-
ing languorously, is entertaining disturbing thoughts of
Archer: ". . . Suppose him here, dressed like a youthful,
gay and burning bridegroom, with tongue enchanting, eyes
bewitching, knees imploring . . ." She shrieks as she sees
Archer, who steals forth from his closet hiding place and
faithfully acts out her thought. Again, Mrs. Sullen's conscience comes reluctantly to her rescue, and she is sum-

moning resolution enough to scream when Scrub rushes in with word that robbers are in the house.

Archer, drawing his sword, hides as Gibbet enters to plunder, then springs upon the bandit and subdues him, summoning Foigard, who is hiding in Gipsy's chamber, to bind the fellow. Meanwhile, Aimwell has arrived and has engaged in combat Hounslow and Bagshot, who are robbing Lady Bountiful and Dorinda. Archer and Mrs. Sullen appear, and soon the bandits are disarmed. Archer, slightly wounded, contrives that Mrs. Sullen show him to a bedchamber, but this time she is saved by a servant announcing the arrival of Freeman, her brother. It so happens that Freeman is an acquaintance of both Archer and Aimwell. Archer fears that the masquerade will now be spoiled just at the very moment of its almost sure success, for Aimwell is about to propose to Dorinda while she, grateful for her rescue, is sure to be in a softened mood. Aimwell proposes, but under the compunction of his sincere love for Dorinda, confesses that he is a fraud, wearing his brother's title.

Dorinda accepts Aimwell for himself, then hears some good news. As she and Aimwell are about to be married, she tells him that his brother is dead and that he has succeeded to his title and estate. Freeman verifies this report and all are happy, Aimwell with his bride and Archer with Dorinda's ample fortune which Aimwell gives to him.

Bellair arrives to tell them that the inn has also been robbed and Cherry sends to Archer a note disclosing that her father, fearing betrayal by the bandits, has fled. She sends the strongbox, as well as her love, to Archer. The company agrees to seek a pardon for Boniface and to accept Cherry in the service of the Aimwells.

There remains only one problem—the freeing of Mrs. Sullen and her fortune from her husband. This is contrived by Archer, who has recovered from Gibbet all the papers of her estate and, with the consent of Sullen, whose headache from the night before has left him wanting "only

a dram," Archer and Mrs. Sullen lead a final dance, joined
by everybody but Sullen.

The Shoemaker's Holiday

BY THOMAS DEKKER

*Born in London, about 1570. Little is known of his early
life and education. He wrote dozens of plays, some in
collaboration with Drayton, Wilson, Chettle and other
writers of his time—but more particularly with Ben Jonson.
However, he was more famous for the disputes he had with
Ben Jonson than for any of his own writings. He has been
called "the Dickens of the Elizabethan period" because of
the similarity between himself and Dickens in their writings
about life in London, their humorous kindliness and senti-
ment, and their interest in picking odd characters. The only
dramatist who portrayed as vividly the life and manners
of London in that era was Thomas Middleton. "The Shoemaker's Holiday" (the original title of which was "The
Shoomakers Holiday or The Gentle Craft. With the humorous life of Simon Eyre, shoomaker, and Lord Maior of
London") was written in 1600. Dekker died about 1641.*

In the fifteenth century, in London, Rowland Lacy, spendthrift nephew of the Earl of Lincoln, and Rose, daughter
of Sir Roger Oteley, Lord Mayor of London, fall in love,
but obstacles to their wedding seem insurmountable, a fact
which causes them much unhappiness and distress. Neither
of their elders favors the match. Sir Roger has sent Rose
into the country, to Old Ford, and Lincoln has contrived
to have Rowland appointed to head an army leaving soon
to fight in France.

Rowland, however, tells his cousin, Askew, that he must
attend to serious business for three days, bids him com-

mand his troops until he arrives either in Dover or in
France, and shares with Askew the considerable purse
which Lincoln and Oteley have given him. As they talk,
Simon Eyre, who declares himself the shoemaker of Tower
Street, comes with his men, Hodge and Firk, to ask the
release from service of Ralph, another workman who has
been drafted. His release is denied, and Ralph leaves Jane,
his pretty wife, little comforted by an initialed pair of shoes
which he has made for her as a parting gift.

At Old Ford, in the meantime, Rose is informed by Sybil,
her maid, that Lacy has led his troops off to war, and Rose
sends Sybil back to learn if he truly has gone to France.
In reality, Lacy has been reduced to learning the shoemaker's trade in Germany after squandering his travel
fund. He returns to London, and, disguised as a Dutch
cobbler, finds work at the shop of Simon Eyre where he
hopes to hear news of Rose.

Soon Lacy, who calls himself Hans and speaks in broken
English, meets a sea captain whose cargo must be sold at
a rare bargain. Lacy lends his war purse to Simon to buy
the cargo, and Simon, disguised as a rich merchant, makes
so shrewd a deal that he becomes wealthy overnight—with
considerable assistance from Lacy, who has plied the sea
captain with drink.

The Earl of Lincoln has received shameful tidings of his
nephew from Dodger, his spy: a battle has been fought
in France, but Lacy was not there. The Earl sends Dodger
to watch for the truant at Rose's home. Here, Rose out-
rages her father by refusing to marry Hammon, a wealthy
young Londoner who made her acquaintance while hunting at Old Ford. Hammon himself, made somewhat dubi-
ous by Rose's conduct, reflects: "There is a wench keeps
shop in the Old Change, to her will I . . . and will prefer
her love before the world."

Ralph, lamed in the war, comes back to Eyre's shop
seeking Jane; but she, because of a quarrel with Simon's
wife, has gone—where, no one knows. Firk comes with the
news that Simon has been elected Sheriff of London. The
new dignitary invites all his men to make holiday, and to

meet him for a celebration at the Lord Mayor's house at Old Ford where he has been bidden to dinner.

At the home of the Lord Mayor, the shoemakers are merrily dancing when Rose spies Hans. She immediately thinks: "How like my Lacy looks yond' shoemaker." She brings him wine, and although he speaks his thanks in his broken tongue, she is convinced that he really is Lacy. Rose tells Sybil of her suspicion. The maid wagers that when they return to London, Lacy will find a way to meet and wed her. They return to town, and Sybil furthers her wager by going to Eyre's shop to bid Hans come to fit Rose's new shoes.

Shoes are also the means of providing help in Ralph's search for his wife. Jane, working in a London shop, is the girl with whom young Hammon is in love. She has told Hammon that her husband is fighting in France, but he has recalled a letter which says Ralph is among the dead, and Jane is now ready to marry him. She insists that the shoes Ralph made for her as a last gift be duplicated for her wedding. When one is brought to Eyre's shop for a pattern for the new pair, Ralph recognizes it, and learns that Jane is to be married next morning at St. Faith's church.

Lacy, as Hans, goes to Rose's home, deceives her father with his disguise, and finds opportunity to tell Rose to steal to the home of Simon, who is now the new Mayor of London. There they will be secretly married. Rose does as he directs. Sybil then hastens to tell Oteley and Lincoln that she has fled with the shoemaker. The angry Oteley answers: "A shoemaker! . . . I'll not fly after her. Let her starve, if she will: she's none of mine." Firk, to confuse them further, tells Oteley and Lincoln that Hans and Rose are to be married in the morning at St. Faith's. Lincoln now suspects that Hans is Lacy, and he and Oteley prepare to trap the couple at the church. Firk mischievously reflects that they will, in reality, only disrupt Jane's wedding while Hans and Rose are being wedded at the Savoy.

At Simon's house, the new Mayor agrees to help in the wedding of Hans and Rose; he sends his wife to attend at

the ceremony. He promises that he will intercede for Lacy
with the King, who is to be his dinner guest. He also ful-
fills his pledge that, if made Lord Mayor, he will feast all
the shoemakers of the city and set Shrove Tuesday, this
day, as a holiday.

At St. Faith's, Ralph and his shoemaker friends are waiting, armed with cudgels, to take Jane away from Hammon
and restore her to him. He has fitted her shoes that morning, but she has not recognized him as her husband because of his lameness and his war-weathered face. But she
has wept at the resemblance and Ralph feels that she still
loves him. When Jane, Hammon, and his party appear,
they are confronted by Ralph—and Jane flies happily to
Ralph's arms. Unable to tempt Ralph with gold to free her,
Hammon gives the couple twenty pounds to right the
wrong he has done them, and sadly leaves. Emerging from
a three-hour vigil, Lincoln and Oteley also learn, to their
disgust, that the wedding couple is not Hans and Rose.

Dodger, Lincoln's spy, now brings word that Hans and
Rose are already married at the Savoy, and Lincoln and
Oteley hasten away to influence the King to annul the
marriage. The shoemakers hurry to the great new hall
which Simon has built for the holiday feast. Firk leads
the march to the feast, crying: . . . "O my brethren!
There's cheer for the heavens: venison pasties walk up and
down piping hot, like sergeants; beef and brewies come
marching in dry-fats; fritters and pancakes come trowling
in in wheelbarrows; hens and oranges hopping in porters'
baskets, collops and eggs in scuttles, and tarts and cus-
tards come quavering in in malt-shovels!"

Amused by the antics of Simon and the merry feasting
of the shoemakers, the King grants a full pardon to Lacy,
urging Lincoln and Oteley to forgive the lovers. They insist that the marriage be voided, and so the jolly monarch
duly divorces them—only to marry them anew. When Lincoln protests that Rose's blood is too lowly for Lacy, the
King promptly knights Rowland, thus giving Rose a title.

The King grants yet another favor: he names Simon's
new hall the Leadenhall, and grants to the shoemakers the

right to hold two market days there weekly. He joins in the banquet, "and will say, I have not met more pleasure on a day."

Volpone

BY BEN JONSON

Born in Westminster, London, probably in 1573. According to one account, he went from the Westminster schools to Cambridge. Other accounts state that he went to a trade school. He did some acting in his youth, probably with a strolling company, and wrote a few plays. In 1598 he produced one of the most famous of English comedies, "Every Man in His Humor," in which William Shakespeare took part. His career was interrupted for a while because he was imprisoned at this time for killing an actor in a duel. In 1599, however, he was back at work, quarreling with such well-known contemporaries as Dekker, Marston and others. He enjoyed royal patronage which permitted him to travel in France. For the court he wrote numerous dramas of the type known as masques. In addition to these, his writings included tragedies and comedies. Among the latter, "Volpone" (produced about 1605) is preëminent. Under James I, Jonson was poet laureate. He died on August 6, 1637.

Volpone, an elderly Venetian miser, and his servant, Mosca, are operating a droll fraud with huge success. Volpone pretends that he is dying, and he and Mosca convince his greedy friends, in turn, that each of them is to be Volpone's sole heir. To insure Volpone's supposed preference, the friends shower him with rich gifts, each in the expectation that he will soon get them back and inherit the old man's fortune as well.

Their method of operation is well illustrated in the treatment of their first caller of the day, the advocate, Voltore. At his knock Volpone has hurriedly donned his nightcap, jumped into bed and begun to groan piteously. Voltore gives him a costly gold plate and a pious expression of sympathy. Volpone accepts the present with proper thanks, then promptly falls to coughing violently. Mosca whispers to Voltore:

> "He's going fast. And you, sir, are his heir . . .
> Without a partner, sir, confirmed this morning.
> 'Twas I induced him; pray remember this."

There is another knock, and no sooner has Voltore hurried out than in hurries Corbaccio, himself an old man, but also confident that he will inherit Volpone's treasure. Mosca tells him that his master is "very bad," to which Corbaccio replies: "That's good. And has he made his will?" Mosca says the will has not yet been made, and Corbaccio presents a little bag of gold for Volpone. Mosca induces the visitor to make a will leaving his own estate to Volpone, assuring Corbaccio that this gesture cannot fail to bring a reciprocal will from his master. Of course, he adds, Volpone will die first.

Next comes Corvino, the merchant, with a pearl and a diamond for Volpone. He, too, is assured that he is the sole heir of the rapidly failing Volpone. When he goes, Volpone leaves his bed and the two knaves count the day's booty. Volpone, deciding that this is better even than robbing churches, now wants to celebrate their gains with music and dancing, and asks Mosca to find him a beautiful woman.

Mosca recalls that Corvino's wife has an enticing face—skin whiter than snow and lips tempting to "eternity of kissing." Volpone is vastly interested, but Mosca says the wife is "kept as warily as your gold, never comes abroad, never takes air but at a window." Volpone insists that he must see her, however, and agrees to Mosca's suggestion that he disguise himself in order to do so.

So, in the guise of Scoto, a peddler of fake medicines,

Volpone takes up a post outside Corvino's house, with
Mosca in the role of his assistant. He mounts a bench,
bawls that he has a precious ointment that will cure every
ill, and that he will give a vial of this, together with another gift of surpassing value, to the first person who tosses
him a handkerchief. Celia, Corvino's wife, is tempted, and
tosses down her handkerchief. Volpone is offering his mysterious gift—a powder guaranteed to provide perpetual
youth—and beginning an insinuating speech on Celia's loveliness when Corvino appears. Corvino, not recognizing
Volpone, drives him away.

Volpone now is truly smitten with Celia, and demands
that Mosca, even at the cost of all his beloved gold and
jewels, bring Celia to him. Mosca tells Corvino that, unhappily, Volpone is recovering from his ailments; that a
scheming physician, who also has hopes of being Volpone's
heir, has prescribed a fair woman as a bed companion to
strengthen him; and, lastly, that the physician has offered
his own daughter to clinch his hold upon Volpone's affection. Says Mosca to Corvino:

"Signior, prevent him if you can, I pray you,
 Or else you lose your sure inheritance.
 Have you some wench that you can recommend?
 Some kinswoman? Think, think, think, think, think, think,
   sir."

Corvino, declaring that "no man shall cheat me of my
heritage," generously bids Mosca tell Volpone that he will
bring him his wife—but he adds, aside, "and may her kisses
help to end his life." Mosca comforts him by a promise
that, at Volpone's next relapse, they will "just pull the
pillow from under his head, and he'll die for want of air."

But when Corvino brings the reluctant Celia, they arrive too early for the scheming Mosca who has other business afoot. He has told Corbaccio's son, Bonario, that his
father is disinheriting him in favor of Volpone; he has concealed Bonario to witness proof of the fact when his father
calls. Mosca is unable to effect this minor plot, for he has

to withdraw with Corvino in order to leave Celia alone
with Volpone. She is viewing the "invalid" Volpone with
acute distaste when suddenly he springs toward her with
youthful enthusiasm. She screams, bringing Bonario from
his hiding place to her rescue. Bonario, after scratching
Volpone with his sword in the ensuing scuffle, has just
taken Celia away when old Corbaccio appears with the
faithless Mosca. Mosca tells him:

> "Your son, Signior,
>   Acquainted with the purpose of your will
>   (Informed by whom I know not), came to spy
>   Upon you, and he vowed that he would kill you."

Corbaccio says this act, indeed, forces him to disinherit
his son in favor of Volpone. He leaves. Mosca and Volpone
now realize that their tricks are becoming too complex even
for them, and the latter says he already feels "the dampness
of a prison cell." It is Bonario and Celia, however, who go
to prison, accused by Corvino to conceal his own machinations. Voltore, the prosecutor, also to serve his own ends,
convinces the magistrates that the young people are adul-
terers. Not only do Corvino and Corbaccio lie against them,
but Volpone is brought into court on his bed to show that
he couldn't be guilty.

Volpone, chuckling over his hoodwinking of the judges
—a trick which pleases him more "than if I had enjoyed the
wench"—gleefully concocts more sport: he makes a temporary will naming Mosca his heir, then sends out a report
of his own death. Corbaccio, Voltore and Corvino hie
themselves to Volpone's house to count their inheritance,
but they find only a contemptuous Mosca. He orders them
out on pain of exposing them in their villainy.

Voltore is now too angry for caution; he again goes before the magistrates and confesses the whole plot—thereby,
incidentally, exonerating Celia and Bonario. But Volpone
is not yet at the end of his rope. As Voltore tells his story,
he appears, this time disguised as a policeman, and whispers to Voltore that Volpone is still alive and that Voltore

is his heir. The frantic Voltore, on the disguised Volpone's advice, feigns a fit, and when he recovers, professes that his confession was merely delirium. Volpone really is not dead, he says, and the good Mosca certainly is guilty of nothing. Volpone turns to his servant:

> "Methought that all was lost, yet all is well.
> Come, Mosca, tell them that I'm yet alive."

But the greedy Mosca, now the acknowledged heir, tells the magistrates that he has just returned from Volpone's funeral; his master is thoroughly dead. Volpone at last is trapped. He strips off his disguise, tells the whole story and "craves a lenient penalty." But the magistrates are not to be placated: they free Celia and Bonario, send Mosca to the galleys for life, disbar Voltore, condemn Corbaccio to a monastery, and order Corvino rowed around Venice with asses' ears on his head. They send Volpone to prison; his property to be confiscated by the state. Says the chief magistrate:

> "Let all who see these vices thus rewarded
> Take heart and learn the lesson. Mischiefs feed
> Like beasts, till they be fat, and then they bleed."

Macbeth

BY WILLIAM SHAKESPEARE

The exact date of Shakespeare's birth is not known. He was baptized on April 25, 1564, the son of a moderately prosperous citizen of Stratford. He received a sound education in the grammar school, but because of his father's financial losses he did not go on to a higher school. He was probably apprenticed to some local trade. He was married to Anne Hathaway when he was eighteen, but was forced to leave Stratford soon after because of trouble with the authorities—probably because he had been caught poaching on the estates of a wealthy landowner. His activities between 1584 and 1592 are obscure. In 1592 he emerged as a playwright and an actor with "the King's men," a company of players under the patronage of James I. He was the mainstay of this company for fifteen years, writing about two plays a year. Scholars accept thirty-eight plays as the work of Shakespeare, and rank him as the greatest dramatist who ever lived. His comedies include: "A Midsummer Night's Dream," "Much Ado About Nothing," "The Merry Wives of Windsor," "Twelfth Night," and "As You Like It." His best-known tragedies are: "Hamlet," "Macbeth," "Othello," "Romeo and Juliet," and "King Lear." Among the historical plays which he wrote are: "Julius Caesar," "Antony and Cleopatra," "Richard III," and "Henry IV." Performances of Shakespeare's plays in the Globe Theatre, London, of which he was part-owner, filled the house to overflowing. He became prosperous and was able to return to Stratford in 1596, where he lived the life of a retired gentleman, interested in local politics and his farm and garden. He died in April, 1616.

Macbeth and Banquo, Scottish captains journeying homeward after defeating the Norse invaders in battle, are accosted on the heath by three witches. The hags hail Macbeth, first by his present title, thane of Glamis, then as thane of Cawdor, a higher rank, and lastly as one "that shalt be king hereafter." Banquo they greet as "lesser than Macbeth, and greater; not so happy, yet much happier; thou shall get kings, though thou be none." The witches vanish when Macbeth calls upon them to prophesy further.

Ross and Angus, of the court of Duncan, King of Scotland, arrive to welcome the returning warriors. They reveal the truth of the witches' first prediction: the King has elevated Macbeth, for his valor in battle, to be thane of Cawdor. Lust for power now swells in Macbeth, and he reflects:

"Two truths are told
As happy prologues to the swelling act
Of the imperial theme . . .
Why do I yield to that suggestion
Whose horrid image doth unfix my hair
And make my seated heart knock at my ribs? . . .
My thought, whose murder yet is but fantastical,
Shakes so my single state of man that function
Is smother'd in surmise, and nothing is
But what is not."

His envious ambition is further heightened when the
King's eldest son, Malcolm, as Prince of Cumberland, is
named heir to the crown. Macbeth, marking Malcolm as
an obstacle in his path to the throne of Scotland, hastens
to his castle at Inverness where his wife, already informed
by letter of the witches' prophecy and Macbeth's new
honor, is scheming to goad Macbeth to quick action toward becoming King.

Duncan, with his sons, Malcolm and Donaldbain, and a
train of courtiers, arrive at Inverness to spend the night.
Lady Macbeth, realizing their immediate opportunity,
taunts her husband, now wavering in his intention to do
away with the King, into agreeing to murder Duncan that
very night as he lies asleep in the castle. Lady Macbeth
carefully plans their course of action: she stupefies Duncan's guards with drugged wine, laying their daggers ready
for Macbeth to stab the King. She herself refrains from
committing the deed only because Duncan reminds her of
her own father.

Macbeth, in terrible fear and apprehension, slays the
sleeping Duncan, and returns to his wife in a state of horror
and foreboding. Lady Macbeth completes his grisly task
by placing blood-stained daggers near the guards and
smearing their faces with blood. In the morning, the murder is discovered by Macduff, a member of Duncan's
court. The Macbeths join loudly in the lamentations for
the dead King. Macbeth righteously announces that he has
killed the guards whose guilt seems evident. The King's

sons, fearing further violence, decide to flee, Malcolm to England and Donaldbain to Ireland. Suspicion of the murder now falls upon them, and Macbeth succeeds Duncan to the throne of Scotland.

Macbeth's purpose has now been accomplished, but he lives in fear of Banquo who appears to have a suspicion of the truth. Also, he resents the witches' prophecy that Banquo, not he, is to beget a line of kings. Macbeth, tortured almost nightly by "terrible dreams" and fears of exposure, hires murderers to do away with Banquo and his son, Fleance. They succeed in killing Banquo, but Fleance escapes. Now, even with the death of Banquo, there is no peace for Macbeth. At a court dinner, Banquo's ghost appears to him, "shakes his gory locks" and glares at him with blank eyes. Lady Macbeth tries to explain away her husband's evident terror and his strange behavior as an old and recurrent ailment, but the feast is spoiled and she dismisses their guests.

Meanwhile, Macduff has fled to the royal court in England where Malcolm is a fugitive, to implore help in overthrowing Macbeth whose tyrannies by now are oppressing all Scotland.

Macbeth's fears drive him to return to the heath to again consult the witches. They warn him to beware of Macduff, but assure him that "none of woman born shall harm Macbeth," and that he "shall never be vanquished until great Birnam wood to high Dunsinane Hill shall come against him." Macbeth asks if Banquo's issue shall ever reign upon the Scottish throne. In answer, the witches conjure forth a ghastly procession of kings who all look alike, followed by the ghost of Banquo. Macbeth is transfixed in terror as he realizes the meaning of the prophecy. Macbeth immediately sends murderers to Fife, the home of Macduff, and Macduff's wife, children and all of his line are brutally murdered.

In England, Malcolm tests the loyalty of Macduff and, finding him true, tells him that he has obtained an army to return to Scotland to overthrow Macbeth. A Scottish nobleman now comes with the tidings of the murders at

Fife, and the bereaved Macduff vows to kill Macbeth with his own hands.

Now, at last, Lady Macbeth has fallen prey to her own conscience. She has taken to walking in her sleep. An alarmed lady-in-waiting summons a doctor to watch her. Lady Macbeth enters, bearing a lighted candle, her eyes closed. She sets the taper down, begins to rub her hands, as though washing them, and speaks:

"Yet here's a spot. Out, damned spot! out, I say!—One: two, why then 'tis time to do't.—Hell is murky!—Fie, my lord, fie! a soldier and afeared? What need we fear who knows it, when none can call our power to account?—Yet who would have thought the old man had so much blood in him? The thane of Fife had a wife: where is she now?— what, will these hands ne'er be clean?"

Lady Macbeth dies soon after, reportedly a suicide. Macbeth, taking heart from the witches' assurance that he is invulnerable, prepares to fight the approaching army of Malcolm.

But Malcolm has directed his men to bear before them branches from the trees in Birnam wood, in order to conceal their numbers, as they march upon Dunsinane Hill to besiege Macbeth. Macbeth, in overwhelming fear, recalls the witches' words: "Macbeth shall never be vanquished until great Birnam wood to high Dunsinane Hill shall come against him," but he goes out to battle, reassured by the witches' last pledge that "none of woman born" can harm him.

In the struggle, he finds himself face to face with Macduff. As they cross swords, Macbeth boasts of his invulnerability, but Macduff tells him: ". . . let the angel whom thou still has served tell thee Macduff was from his mother's womb untimely ripp'ed."

Macbeth, realizing all is lost, his offer to surrender scorned, cries:

"Yet I will try the last. Before my body
I throw my warlike shield. Lay on, Macduff,
And damn'd be he that first cries 'Hold, enough!'"

Macduff kills Macbeth, and brings to Malcolm and his
leaders the head of the cruel tyrant.

Hamlet

BY WILLIAM SHAKESPEARE

Hamlet, young prince of Denmark, is still shaken by the
recent death of his idolized father and by the marriage,
scarcely a month later, of his widowed mother, Queen
Gertrude, to his uncle, the present King Claudius, whom
he despises. He tells of his despair in soliloquy:

> "O that this too, too solid flesh would melt,
> Thaw and resolve itself into a dew!
> Or that the Everlasting had not fix'd
> His canon 'gainst self-slaughter! O God! God! . . .
> But break, my heart, for I must hold my tongue!"

Horror and anger are added to his grief when the ghost
of his father comes to tell Hamlet that he was not slain by
a serpent as had been announced, but by the poison of
Claudius. He pleads that his death be avenged. The ghost
cautions Hamlet to spare his mother, saying: "Leave her
to heaven, and to those thorns that in her bosom lodge."
Hamlet vows to exact retribution, swearing his companions,
his friend Horatio and a soldier who are with him, to secrecy as to the appearance of the ghost. He refuses, however, "in wild and whirling words," to tell them the nature
of his father's revelation.

Later, in the home of Polonius, the Lord Chamberlain,
his daughter Ophelia, with whom Hamlet has been in love,
tells her father how Hamlet has just visited her, unkempt
and with "a look so piteous in purport as if he had been
loosed out of hell." The girl, who had once returned Hamlet's love but had dismissed him at her father's order, reports that the Prince, "after such perusal of my face as he

would draw it," had sighed brokenly and left her without
a word. Polonius then tells the King and Queen that Hamlet is mad and, to prove it, arranges that he and the King
shall listen, in hiding, at a meeting of Hamlet and Ophelia.
Hamlet, coming to this tryst, reflects:

"To be, or not to be; that is the question:
Whether 'tis nobler in the mind to suffer
The slings and arrows of outrageous fortune,
Or to take arms against a sea of troubles,
And by opposing end them. To die: to sleep;
No more; and by a sleep to say we end
The heart-ache, and the thousand natural shocks
That flesh is heir to, 'tis a consummation
Devoutly to be wished. To die, to sleep;
To sleep: perchance to dream: ay, there's the rub;
For in that sleep of death what dreams may come,
When we have shuffled off this mortal coil,
Must give us pause. . . ."

Before Ophelia, Hamlet forces himself to deny ever having given her the remembrance tokens she tries to return
to him, saying: "You should not have believed me; for virtue cannot so inoculate our old stock but we shall relish
of it: I loved you not. . . . Get thee to a nunnery; why
wouldst thou be a breeder of sinners?" He mocks her,
too, with: "God hath given you one face and you make
yourselves another: you jig, you amble, and you lisp, and
nickname God's creatures, and make your wantonness your
ignorance. Go to, I'll no more on't; it hath made me mad."
The King, listening to this, resolves to send Hamlet to
England after, as Polonius suggests, the Queen shall attempt to placate him.

Meanwhile, Hamlet has arranged with a troupe of players, brought to court by the King and Queen to try to divert Hamlet's mind from his broodings, that they shall enact a scene similar to the murder of his father as recounted
to him by the ghost. He plans to watch the King for evi-
dences of guilt during the performance so that he may determine whether or not he has imagined the ghost. The

King hastily commands the play to end, and Hamlet is convinced of his uncle's perfidy.

The Prince is then summoned to his mother, and Polonius hides behind a tapestry in her chamber so that he may hear what Hamlet has to say. Hamlet, on his way to the interview, sees King Claudius kneeling in prayer. He wishes to kill him then, but forgoes the deed in order that Claudius may not have the advantage over his father of having died confessed. He continues to his mother's rooms, reflecting: "O heart, lose not thy nature; let not ever the soul of Nero enter this firm bosom: let me be cruel, not unnatural: I will speak daggers to her, but use none."

Hamlet's reproaches so alarm the Queen that she calls for help. Polonius, behind the tapestry, echoes her cry, and Hamlet thrusts his rapier through the arras, killing the old man. He then continues his indictment until his mother confesses her shame. The ghost comes to intercede for her and to spur Hamlet to his final purpose. The Queen, to whom the ghost does not appear, now believes her son to be quite mad, and tells the King of this tragic episode. The King plots to have Hamlet killed on his way to England where he has decided to send him.

Ophelia now visits the Queen. The shock of her father's death and Hamlet's behavior have driven her out of her mind, and she babbles childish and lewd songs in a manner pitiful to witness. Laertes, her brother, has hastened home to avenge his father's murder, and his rage is added to by Ophelia's tragic recitation of Polonius' burial. The King tells Laertes that the absent Hamlet is the murderer of Polonius. Word is received that Hamlet, supposedly on his way to England, has outwitted his escorts and is returning home. Laertes and the King then plan to dispose of Hamlet in a fencing match with Laertes—where the latter's foil shall be buttonless and poisoned.

The mad Ophelia, weaving garlands of flowers beside a brook, falls into the stream and, still chanting of love and death, is drowned. At her burial, Laertes throws himself into her open grave to take one last farewell of his sister. Hamlet, who has now returned, follows him, crying: "I

loved Ophelia; forty thousand brothers could not, with
all their quality of love, make up my sum." He challenges
Laertes: "Dost thou come here to whine? To outface me
with leaping in her grave? Be buried quick with her, and
so will I." Bystanders separate the youths.

The fencing match has been arranged. Before it begins,
Hamlet confesses his wrong to Laertes, begging his pardon. The King offers a poisoned cup of wine to Hamlet,
but he refuses it. The Queen unwittingly drinks from the
cup and dies. In the confusion of the scene, the foils are
exchanged and both Laertes and Hamlet are wounded by
the poisoned blade, Laertes dying at once. Hamlet stabs
the King, also forcing him to drink the rest of the poisoned
wine. Claudius then dies. Hamlet, too, soon expires, and
Horatio, his friend, mourns: "Now cracks a noble heart.
Good night, sweet prince, and flights of angels sing thee to
thy rest!"

Julius Caesar

BY WILLIAM SHAKESPEARE

All Rome is in holiday dress for the Feast of Lupercal. Excitement is heightened by the imminent prospect that the
triumvir, Julius Caesar, is to be named king. But from the
crowd a soothsayer calls: "Caesar, beware the ides of
March." The ruler sees another evil portent as Cassius, a
jealous noble, joins in sober conversation with the revered
Marcus Brutus, Caesar's friend. To his loyal companion,
Mark Antony, Caesar says: "Yon Cassius has a lean and
hungry look . . . such men as he be never at heart's ease
while they behold a greater than themselves."

The meeting of the nobles is indeed a dark omen. The
thoughtful Brutus, ever mindful of "the general good and
the name of honor," and fearful that Caesar may prove a
tyrant, is skillfully played upon by Cassius. Cassius says

to him: "Brutus, and Caesar: what should be in that 'Caesar'? Why should that name be sounded more than yours? . . . Brutus will start a spirit as soon as Caesar."

Brutus reluctantly tells Cassius: "What you would work me to, I have some aim." The crafty Cassius goes to prepare, in several different handwritings, petitions praising Brutus and disparaging Caesar, to be left in Brutus' home. He is quick, too, to enlist other nobles in the plot, including his friend Casca, who says of Brutus: "Oh, he sits high in all the people's hearts: and that which would appear offence in us his countenance . . . will change to virtue and worthiness."

Just before dawn, the sleepless Brutus decides that, for the public welfare, Caesar must die. His resolve is buttressed both by reflection that it is now the fateful ides of March, and by reading the false petitions that Cassius has written. In a fearful storm, which seems to bring even further portents of death, Cassius and his conspirators come to Brutus' home. It is there decided that Caesar must be slain that very day at the Capitol where the Senators are expected to name him king. Cassius proposes that Antony, too, be killed, but this Brutus vetoes because "Antony can do more harm than Caesar's arm when Caesar's head's cut off," and because he fears "our course will seem too bloody" to the populace.

Forebodings are felt by Portia, the wife of Brutus, and by Calpurnia, wife of Caesar. Portia senses some desperate plan afoot, and finally Brutus tells her of it. Caesar has heard Calpurnia cry out thrice in her sleep: "Help, ho! they murder Caesar!" Filled with apprehension, she forbids Caesar to leave his home that day. His priests, too, advise him that their portents are dark; but the conspirator, Decius Brutus, flatters him into going forth to the Capitol.

Here the plotters cluster about Caesar, on the pretext of offering a petition which he refuses. They then stab him. At the thrust of his friend Brutus, Caesar cries: "Et tu, Brute? Then fall, Caesar!" He dies.

Brutus directs the conspirators to bathe their hands and swords in Caesar's blood, and to walk among the populace

proclaiming peace, freedom and liberty. Just then Antony's
servant enters to offer his master's hand to Brutus. Brutus
summons Antony, promising an explanation once the populace, now in a state of panic, is quieted. Antony feigns acceptance of this, asking only that he be allowed to conduct Caesar's funeral in the market place. Brutus agrees,
despite warnings from Cassius, but stipulates that Antony
shall not blame the slayers; he shall only, with the pro-
claimed permission of the conspirators, speak well of
Caesar. Alone with Caesar's body, Antony pledges revenge. He awaits the mood of the populace before summoning the young Octavius Caesar, nephew of Julius.

At the market place, Brutus first wins the half-hostile
crowd by an impassioned declaration that while he loved
Caesar, he loved Rome more, and that the elevation of the
ambitious ruler would have meant only slavery for its citizens. He offers to kill himself if his countrymen condemn
him, and there are cries of "Live, Brutus!" "Let him be
Caesar!" Brutus asks the crowd to listen to the eulogy of
Caesar by Mark Antony who enters with Caesar's body.
Brutus leaves, and Antony speaks:

"Friends, Romans, countrymen, lend me your ears.
I come to bury Caesar, not to praise him. . . .
He was my friend, faithful and just to me;
But Brutus says he was ambitious;
And Brutus is an honorable man.
He hath brought many captives home to Rome,
Whose ransoms did the general coffers fill;
Did this in Caesar seem ambitious?
When that the poor have cried, Caesar hath wept;
Ambition should be made of sterner stuff;
Yet Brutus says he was ambitious;
And Brutus is an honorable man.
You all did see that on the Lupercal
I thrice presented him a kingly crown
Which he did thrice refuse. Was this ambition? . . .
I speak not to disprove what Brutus spoke,
But here I am to speak what I do know.

You all did love him once, not without cause;
What cause withholds you then to mourn for him?
O judgment! thou art fleet to brutish beasts,
And men have lost their reason. Bear with me;
My heart is in the coffin there with Caesar,
And I must pause till it comes back to me."

Doubt, as well as awakened sympathy for Caesar and the shaken Antony, now stir the crowd. Antony's victory is complete when he recites the pity of the dead Caesar, with "none so poor to do him reverence." He summons the throng about the corpse, pointing out the rents left in the dead ruler's war mantle by the daggers of Cassius, "the envious Casca" and "the well-beloved Brutus," this last "the most unkindest cut of all." He reveals that Caesar's will has left his estates to the populace. He so inflames the people that they form a riotous mob bent only upon destruction of the conspirators. Brutus and Cassius, fore-warned, flee from the city.

Antony then meets with the perfumed dandy, Octavius, and with Lepidus, of the dead Caesar's court, who are now to be triumvirs to rule Rome. They list the rebels who must die, Antony agreeing to include his own sister's son. Antony then schemes with the easily led Octavius to "divide the three-fold world" among themselves, to prune the amounts paid out in Caesar's legacies, and to discard Lepidus when he shall have served his purpose in taking the blame for their actions. Then he warns Octavius that Brutus and Cassius have raised an army near Sardis, and that they must be defeated at once.

In the conspirators' camp, Brutus has learned that the grieving Portia has committed suicide. He is at bitter odds with Cassius who has been niggardly and suspicious in supplying funds for their troops. The two men are reconciled, but they disagree fatally over tactics for the coming battle at Philippi. The night before the battle the ghost of Caesar appears to Brutus, saying only: "Thou shalt see me at Philippi." Indeed, the battle brings death by suicide to Brutus and to Cassius when their army is defeated. Says Antony of Brutus:

"This was the noblest Roman of them all.
All the conspirators, save only he,
Did that they did in envy of the great Caesar. . . .
His life was gentle, and the elements
So mix'd in him that Nature might stand up
And say to all the world 'This was a man!' "

As You Like It

BY WILLIAM SHAKESPEARE

A chance meeting at the French court of the usurper, Duke Frederick, occurs to brighten the unhappy lives of his pretty niece, Rosalind, daughter of the banished Duke Senior, and the gallant Orlando, youngest son of the recently deceased Sir Rowland de Boys, friend of Duke Senior.

Rosalind has been allowed to remain at the court through the intercession of her inseparable friend, Frederick's daughter, Celia, but she has sorely missed her kindly father, now an exile in the Forest of Arden with a few of his loyal lords. Orlando is made miserable by his elder brother, Oliver, who has denied him his inheritance and forces him to live the life of a peasant on his estate.

Rosalind and Orlando meet when Duke Frederick suggests that Celia and Rosalind attempt to dissuade the slender Orlando from trying his skill with the Duke's wrestler, Charles, an enormous fellow, who, in a general challenge match, has just crippled three brawny youths. Rosalind and Celia plead in vain, for Orlando almost hopes that he may be killed in the bout—as, indeed, the jealous Oliver has plotted with Charles that he should be. However, the wrestler's taunts anger him and he quickly defeats Charles.

Frederick rebuffs the youth when he learns that he is the son of an enemy, and the girls, as the Duke leaves, speak to Orlando in order to make amends for the Duke's discourtesy. Rosalind gives him a chain from around her neck, hinting at her love for him. Orlando is speechless in his new happiness. The day, however, quickly brings trouble for them both.

Orlando is warned to flee—first by a courtier who tells him that Frederick resents the defeat of his wrestler, and again by his father's old servant, Adam, who brings him word that Oliver, his jealousy further heightened by Orlando's victory, is plotting to burn his brother's lodge while he is asleep inside. Adam gives Orlando his small life's-savings, and together they set out to find a new home.

Frederick, who has become angry at Rosalind's popularity and her influence over his daughter, orders her, on pain of death, to leave his dominions at once. Celia decides to share Rosalind's fate, and the girls, accompanied by the court jester, Touchstone, set out to find Rosalind's father. Rosalind dresses herself in the garb of a young man.

At length they come to the Forest of Arden. Here they purchase a cottage, a pasture and a flock of sheep, retaining the shepherd to care for the place. Orlando and Adam, too, arrive at Arden Forest. Orlando, seeking food for his fainting servant, comes upon the greenwood gathering of Duke Senior and his followers who "live like the old Robin Hood of England . . . and fleet the time carelessly, as they did in the golden world." Duke Senior warmly welcomes the son of his old friend, and Orlando and Adam join his band.

Here in Arden, with the sorrows of the court left behind, there begins for the fugitives a merry confusion of identity and courtship. Rosalind, still posing as a young man and calling herself Ganymede, finds upon a tree a mournful verse of love dedicated to Rosalind. Celia, who is known as Ganymede's sister, Aliena, tells Rosalind that she has just come upon the writer of the verse—Orlando. As the girls talk, Orlando appears and the disguised Rosalind teases him about his woodland messages. She professes to know a cure for such lovesickness: she directs Orlando to come daily to her cottage where, pretending that Ganymede is Rosalind, he shall woo him until Ganymede's simulation of the fickle whimsies of girls frees him of his infatuation. Orlando agrees to try the plan.

Love soon becomes contagious. Touchstone courts Audrey, a herder of goats; Silvius, a neighboring shepherd, woos Phebe, a shepherdess, but this match is complicated when Phebe becomes enamored of the masquerading Rosalind. Orlando learns of the whimsies of love from the teasing Ganymede.

Then Oliver, Orlando's evil brother, whom Frederick has stripped of his wealth until he shall deliver the fugitive Orlando, appears in the forest in search of the young exile. Falling into a sleep of exhaustion, he is threatened by a snake and a lioness. Orlando, happening to pass by, recognizes him and, in spite of the way Oliver has treated him, routs the snake and slays the lioness. Oliver repents of his former wickedness and brotherly love is restored. Orlando take Oliver to join Duke Senior's men. Oliver promptly falls in love with Celia, and Orlando arranges for their wedding the following day.

Ganymede tells Orlando, still pining for Rosalind, that by magic she can conjure Rosalind to the forest, and promises that they shall be wed also. Phebe, still in love with Ganymede, and her disconsolate suitor appear. Ganymede tells Phebe: "I will marry you, if ever I marry woman, and I'll be married tomorrow." To Orlando she says: "I'll satisfy you, if ever I satisfied man, and you shall be married tomorrow." To Silvius she promises: "I will content you, if what pleases you contents you, and you shall be married tomorrow."

The next day, Duke Senior and his band are gathered for the festivities. Ganymede extracts from the Duke the promise that, should he bring his daughter, he will give her to Orlando, and from Orlando gains the pledge that he will marry Rosalind. Phebe vows that if she herself refuses to marry Ganymede she will accept Silvius. Ganymede leaves. The Duke remarks that in him he notes "some lively touches of my daughter's favor," but Orlando assures him that this cannot be.

Then Rosalind, in woman's clothes, appears with Celia and there is joyous confusion. All the promises are honored, Phebe saying tartly: "If sight and shape be true, why, then, my love adieu!" The four couples are married. Then to the feast comes Jacques de Boys, another brother of Orlando, with this news:

"Let me have audience for a word or two:
I am the second son of old Sir Rowland,
That bring these tidings to this fair assembly.
Duke Frederick, hearing how that every day
Men of great worth resorted to this forest,
Addressed a mighty power; which were on foot,
In his own conduct, purposely to take
His brother here and put him to the sword:
And to the skirts of this wild wood he came:
Where, meeting with an old religious man,
After some question with him, was converted
Both from his enterprise and from the world,
His crown bequeathing to his banished brother,
And all their lands restored to them again
That were with him exiled . . ."

Duke Senior promises to share the returned fortunes among all, and exclaims:

"Play, music! and you, brides and bridegrooms all,
With measure heaped in joy, to the measures fall."

The Merchant of Venice

BY WILLIAM SHAKESPEARE

Antonio, a merchant of Venice, is asked by Bassanio, his
friend, for a loan so that he may pay fitting court to the
rich and beautiful Portia of Belmont, who prefers him
above her other princely suitors. Though Antonio would
gladly make the loan, his fortune is tied up at sea in his
trading vessels, and the money is sought from Shylock, a
moneylender.

At their meeting, Shylock reflects, of Antonio:

> "I hate him for he is a Christian;
> But more for that in low simplicity
> He lends out money gratis and brings down
> The rate of usage here with us in Venice.
> If I can catch him once upon the hip
> I will feed the ancient grudge I bear him.
> He hates our sacred nation; and he rails,
> Even where merchants most do congregate,
> On me, my bargains, and my well-won thrift,
> Which he calls interest. Curst be my tribe,
> If I forgive him!"

Shylock slyly simulates friendship and offers the money,
on condition that Antonio be willing to sign a bond ("in
merry sport") to forfeit a pound of his flesh. Antonio
agrees to what is apparently a jest, and Bassanio prepares
to journey to Belmont. Shylock's hatred for Antonio is
heightened when, apparently with Antonio's aid, his friend
Lorenzo elopes with Shylock's daughter Jessica, who takes
with her both money and jewels.

At Belmont, Bassanio has won Portia's hand by solving
the riddle of her father's will which provides that she
shall marry the suitor who correctly chooses among three

caskets—one of gold, one of silver, and one of lead. Portia gives him a ring, but warns that, should he part with it, it shall mean the end of their love. Bassanio assures Portia that he will wear the ring until his death.

The lovers' joy is suddenly blighted by the news that Antonio's ships have been lost and that his bond is now forfeit. Portia bids Bassanio pay Shylock treble the required sum, if need be, from her fortune, and he leaves for Venice. In haste, Portia sends a messenger to Bellario, a learned doctor of the law at Padua.

Meanwhile, Shylock, questioned as to what he proposes to do with Antonio's flesh, replies:

"To bait fish withal: if it will feed nothing else, it will feed my revenge. He hath disgraced me, and hindered me half a million; laughed at my losses, mocked at my gains, scorned my nation, thwarted my bargains, cooled my friends, heated mine enemies; and what's his reason? I am a Jew. Hath not a Jew eyes? hath not a Jew hands, organs, dimensions, senses, affections, passions? fed with the same food, hurt with the same weapons, subject to the same diseases, healed by the same means, warmed and cooled by the same winter and summer, as the Christian is? If you prick us, do we not bleed? if you tickle us, do we not laugh? if you poison us, do we not die? and if you wrong us, shall we not revenge? If we are like you in the rest, we will resemble you in that. If Jew wrong a Christian, what is his humility? Revenge. If Christian wrong a Jew, what should his sufferance be by Christian example? Why, revenge. The villainy you teach me I will execute; and it shall go hard but I will better the instruction."

Shylock has Antonio haled into court where the presiding Duke of Venice vainly appeals to the Jew to forgo his cruel forfeit, and Bassanio as vainly offers in payment ten times the loan, on forfeit of his life. But Shylock is unyielding and Antonio is prepared for the ordeal.

Then Portia, disguised in the robes of a doctor of laws, appears to plead mercy for Antonio. Asked by Shylock why he should be merciful, she replies:

"The quality of mercy is not strain'd,
It droppeth as the gentle rain from heaven
Upon the place beneath; it is twice blest:
It blesseth him that gives and him that takes;
'Tis mightiest in the mightiest; it becomes
The throned monarch better than his crown;
His scepter shows the force of temporal power,
The attribute to awe and majesty,
Wherein doth sit the dread and fear of kings;
But mercy is above this sceptered sway;
It is enthroned in the hearts of kings,
It is an attribute to God himself;
The earthly power doth then show likest God's
When mercy seasons justice. Therefore, Jew,
Though justice be thy plea, consider this,
That, in the course of justice, none of us
Should see salvation: we do pray for mercy;
And that same prayer doth teach us all to render
The deeds of mercy . . ."

But Shylock applauds Portia as "a Daniel come to judgment" when she declares that Antonio must yield his pound
of flesh. To her plea that he provide a surgeon to stop
Antonio's wounds, he answers only: "Is it so nominated in
the bond? I cannot find it; 'tis not in the bond." Antonio
says farewell to Bassanio, who vows that he would sacrifice
even his life and his wife if he could spare his friend. Portia
remarks: "Your wife would give you little thanks for that,
if she were by to hear you make the offer."

Shylock is about to take his forfeit when Portia warns
him that the bond permits a pound of flesh but no blood,
and that, should he shed one drop, his lands and goods
are confiscate under the law. Shylock then calls for payment in money instead; but Portia insists he must take the
flesh, and warns him further that it must be neither more
nor less than a pound or his own life and goods are forfeit
by law. Now denied even his principal, Shylock prepares
to go, but Portia points out that an alien who has plotted
against the life of a Venetian must give half his goods to

his intended victim, half to the state. Antonio shows mercy in providing that Shylock's fortune shall be shared with Jessica and that she shall be his heiress.

Antonio and Bassanio are profuse in their thanks to Portia, but she will accept in payment only Antonio's gloves and the ring Bassanio has sworn never to lose. Her waiting-maid, Nerissa, who has served in the guise of Portia's clerk, also demands a ring from her lover, Gratiano, another friend of Antonio and Bassanio. Back in Belmont, Portia and Nerissa, after teasing Bassanio and Gratiano by insisting that they have given their rings to other women, finally disclose the masquerade, and all ends happily.

Romeo and Juliet

BY WILLIAM SHAKESPEARE

In fourteenth-century Verona, in Italy, young Romeo, of the noble house of Montague, and Benvolio, his friend, conceive a daring plan to attend a ball which is being given that night by the Capulets, a rival family which has carried on so bitter and bloody a feud with the Montagues that the Prince of Verona has decreed that further fighting between members of the two houses will bring a sentence of death to the warring parties.

As the ball is to be a masquerade, the youths decide that there is little risk of recognition, and they set forth with their kinsman, Mercutio, and others. They are mingling, undetected, with the other guests when Romeo's eyes fall upon Juliet, not yet fourteen, daughter of Capulet. He vows that he "ne'er saw true beauty till this night." He speaks to her, and soon they know that they are in love. Before the party ends and Romeo's friends induce him to leave, they each learn that the other is a member of the rival house.

Later that night, Romeo comes to worship outside Ju-

liet's window in the Capulet garden. Juliet appears on her
balcony, and Romeo to himself exclaims:

"But, soft! what light through yonder window breaks?
It is the east, and Juliet is the sun! . . .
See, how she leans her cheek upon her hand;
O, that I were a glove upon that hand
That I might touch that cheek!"

Juliet, unaware of his nearness, speaks:

"O Romeo, Romeo, wherefore art thou Romeo?
Deny thy father and refuse thy name;
Or, if thou wilt not, be but sworn my love,
And I'll no longer be a Capulet."

Romeo makes his presence known, saying to Juliet, "I
take thee at thy word." In ecstatic happiness the lovers
pledge their love. Juliet promises to send her nurse to him
in the morning so that she may bring her word of what
plans Romeo has been able to make for their wedding.
Romeo hastens at once to the cell of Friar Laurence, his
confessor, and it is arranged that he and Juliet be married
that very afternoon. Romeo gives this message to the nurse,
also entrusting her with a rope ladder by which he may
secretly reach Juliet's chamber that night. Presently Juliet
comes; they are married, and she slips home again quietly.

A short time later, Romeo joins Benvolio, Mercutio and
others in the street. Tybalt, a Capulet who recognized
Romeo at the party but who had been restrained from
attacking him by old Capulet, appears, ready for a fight.
Romeo, now desiring nothing but peace, refuses to fight
him, and Mercutio takes up Tybalt's challenge. Tybalt
thrusts at Mercutio, fatally wounding him. Romeo, losing
his head, kills Tybalt, and the Prince of Verona, who
quickly hears of this, orders him to exile at once.

But Romeo flees to Friar Laurence's cell, where Juliet's
nurse brings him an appeal from Juliet that he visit her
before his departure. Romeo threatens to kill himself, but
the Friar counsels him to say farewell to his bride and to
escape to Mantua, leaving the Friar to contrive some way

to win the Prince's pardon. Romeo obeys. After a night
with Juliet in her chamber, he leaves Verona, hoping, of
course, for a quick reunion.

Juliet's parents, who have no intimation of her marriage
to Romeo, insist that, in two days' time, she wed young
Paris, a kinsman of the Prince. Juliet, in despair, goes for
advice to Friar Laurence. After some thought, the Friar
decides that she shall take a potion which will be harmless,
but which will make her appear as one dead. In the
meantime, he will see that Romeo is informed of the
stratagem. He will also arrange that Romeo be in the tomb
of the Capulets when Juliet awakens so that he can take
her away with him immediately. That night at her home
Juliet drinks the potion the Friar has prepared. Plans for
her wedding are sadly exchanged for plans for her funeral.

But, through an accident, Friar Laurence's message explaining the plot fails to reach Romeo in Mantua. The
young husband is stricken with grief when he hears from
his servant that Juliet is dead. He obtains poison from an
apothecary and leaves for Verona, determined to die with
Juliet in her tomb. He reaches Verona and, as he and his
servant attempt to pry open the vault where Juliet lies, he
is challenged by Paris who has come to lay flowers before
her tomb. Paris scorns Romeo's appeal to be left to his
grief, and attacks him. Romeo kills Paris, but before Paris
dies he begs to be buried with Juliet. This Romeo promises,
and he drags the body into the vault. Then, gazing on the
flower-shrouded Juliet, he cries:

> "O my love! my wife!
> Death, that hath suck'd the honey of thy breath,
> Hath had no power yet upon thy beauty:
> Thou art not conquered; beauty's ensign yet
> Is crimson in thy lips and in thy cheeks,
> And Death's pale flag is not advanced there.
> . . . I will stay with thee,
> And never from this palace of dim night
> Depart again . . . Eyes, look your last!

Arms, take your last embrace! and lips, O you
The doors of death, seal with a righteous kiss
A dateless bargain to engrossing death!
. . . Thus with a kiss I die!"

As Juliet stirs in awakening, Friar Laurence, having
learned of the failure of his message, arrives at the tomb
to find Romeo and Paris dead. He tells Juliet of the tragedy
and urges her to a nunnery, but the anguished girl refuses.
She says to him: "Go, get thee hence, I will not away."
Friar Laurence leaves, and she cries:

"What's here? a cup, closed in my true love's hand?
Poison, I see, hath been his timeless end:
O churl! drunk all, and left no friendly drop
To help me after? I will kiss thy lips;
Haply some poison yet doth hang on them,
To make me die with a restorative."

She kisses Romeo, and, as voices of the watch are
heard outside, says: "Yea, noise? then I'll be brief. O happy
dagger!" She snatches Romeo's dagger and, stabbing her
breast, cries: "This is thy sheath; there rust, and let me
die!" She falls dead upon the body of Romeo.

Tamburlaine the Great

BY CHRISTOPHER MARLOWE

*Born in Canterbury, England, February 6, 1564. He was
educated at King's School in Canterbury, and from there
went to Corpus Christi College, Cambridge, where he won
his Master of Arts degree three or four years after he had
graduated as a Bachelor of Arts. In 1587 he joined the
Lord Admiral's Company of players in London, and spent
much of his time with such men as Edward Allyn, the
actor, Robert Hughes, the mathematician, Thomas Har-*

*riott, the astronomer, and Sir Walter Raleigh. When his
epic drama, "Tamburlaine the Great," was staged in 1587,
his substitution of blank verse for rhymed couplets led
Ben Jonson to refer to "Marlowe's mighty line." He wrote
three other tragedies which challenge comparison with the
plays of Shakespeare, and are among the greatest in the
history of English drama. They are, "Doctor Faustus,"
"The Jew of Malta," and "Edward II." Because of his
associations, his opinions and his writings, he was considered immoral by some of his contemporaries. The Privy
Council was about to investigate a serious charge against
him when his life was abruptly ended. He was only twenty-
nine years old when he died. It is probable that he was
killed in a tavern brawl in May, 1593.*

Tamburlaine, a lowly Scythian shepherd turned outlaw,
dreams of conquering the whole world. And, indeed, his
progress from leader of a few marauders to master of a
considerable army has amply fed his hopes. His five hundred footmen threatened by a thousand horsemen sent by
the Persian King to crush him, by flattery Tamburlaine has
induced their commander, Theridamas, to join him. Now,
through constant raiding and recruiting, they feel themselves strong enough to defy even the King.

The most precious booty of these raids is the beautiful
Zenocrate, daughter of the sultan of Egypt and betrothed
to the Arabian King. An added spur to Tamburlaine's ambition is his hope of making her empress of the world. At
first contemptuous of this bandit, Zenocrate has at last
been won as his bride by threats, promises and flattery,
but chiefly by the romance of his boundless adventurings.

So Tamburlaine sweeps on to more and more bloody
conquests, his rapacity and cruelty rising ever higher with
each triumph. He defeats and slays the King of Persia;
subdues the armies of Algiers, Morocco and Fez, then
overcomes even Bajazeth, ruler of Turkey. His vanity
further swollen by these great victories, Tamburlaine has
Bajazeth hauled around in a cage, flings him to the ground

to serve as a footstool, and compels the Turkish Queen to labor as a menial. At last Bajazeth, mocked by the guests at one of Tamburlaine's feasts and left unguarded for the moment, kills himself by beating his head against the bars. His Queen follows him in death. Zenocrate is horrified, and reproaches her husband:

> "Ah, Tamburlaine my love, my Tamburlaine,
> Are these the fruits of thy great victories?"

Still there are no bounds to his hunger for domination. He attacks Damascus, which has been reinforced by troops of Zenocrate's father and her former suitor. The Governor sends four virgins to Tamburlaine to ask his mercy, and he replies to their appeal:

> "Virgins, in vain your labor to prevent
> That which mine honor swears shall be performed.
> Behold my sword; what see you at the point?"

One of the virgins answers that they see "nothing but fear and fatal steel, my lord," and Tamburlaine retorts:

> "Your fearful minds are thick and misty, then,
> For there sits death; there sits imperious Death."

And to an attendant he orders:

> "Away with them, and show them Death."

The girls are put to death, and even Zenocrate cannot sway Tamburlaine from his assault upon Damascus. He says to her:

> "I mean to rise upon the topmost peaks
> And be renowned as never emperor was . . .
> And wouldst thou have me buy thy father's love
> At such a loss of my ambition?"

Capturing Damascus, he spares Zenocrate's father but kills her former lover before her eyes. His obsession is now complete, and he boasts:

> "Emperors and Kings lie breathless at my feet;
> The very god of war resigns his place,
> Meaning to make me ruler of the world!"

Through the years he drives himself into more and greater conquests, even though now he and Zenocrate have three grown sons. Of these, Celebinus and Amyrus delight him as promising also to be "a scourge and terror to the world," but the gentle Calyphas he disowns.

Soon, however, Tamburlaine first meets his master, Death, who, despite Tamburlaine's protests, takes Zenocrate. To display his grief he sets fire to a whole city to illuminate her funeral. But his sorrow fails to halt his mad career of slaughter. To teach courage to his sons, he cuts off his own arm unflinchingly. The warrior-sons hold out their arms as token of their bravery, but Calyphas shrinks away, and in a later battle refuses even to fight. The enraged Tamburlaine seeks him out after the fighting, crying to him:

> "Coward, stand up, and I will teach you arms,
> And what the jealousy of wars must do."

His other sons plead with Tamburlaine, but he seizes Calyphas and stabs him to death, shouting:

> "O Jove, receive his fainting soul again
> Whose body is the flesh of Tamburlaine!"

Tamburlaine and Theridamas now storm the fortress of Balsera. Its captain appears on the walls with Olympia, his wife, and their young son. Theridamas appeals to him to surrender, but the captain, knowing the cruelty of Tamburlaine, refuses. The fortress falls and the captain, wounded, urges his wife and boy to flee through a secret passage. They choose to remain, and the son implores his mother to kill him to cheat Tamburlaine. She stabs him and is about to slay herself when Theridamas takes her captive.

Theridamas falls in love with her and, when she scorns him, threatens to take her forcibly. Olympia begs him to leave her honor unsullied, and, in return, offers him a salve that, she says, will make his skin proof against daggers. Theridamas asks why she did not give it to her husband, but she protests there was no time in which to do so. She offers to prove its worth upon herself. She anoints her throat, then goads Theridamas into trying the steel of his weapon against it. He stabs her and she dies. Theridamas mourns only a little, as becomes a follower of Tamburlaine, and returns to war after ordering a proper funeral for Olympia.

This next adventure, however, is to be the last for the insatiable Tamburlaine. King Callapine, son of the humiliated Bajazeth, has vowed to avenge his father. The opposing armies are about to clash when a fever, not a sword, fells Tamburlaine. He rages at his helpless physicians and orders them to bring even God from heaven to rid him of the malady, but "the scourge of heaven must die like any other earthly thing."

At last Tamburlaine decides to die like a god. He struggles from his couch and reels out to meet his end in battle.

Everyman

ANONYMOUS

The author of the English morality play, "Everyman," is unknown. "Everyman" is characterized by Ernest Rhys, editor of the famous Everyman's Library, as "the noblest interlude of death the religious imagination of the middle ages has given to the stage." It is assigned to the reign of Edward IV (1461–83), and is regarded by some authorities as a translation of a Dutch play, "Elckerlijk." Morality plays were performed in England without scenery, often as pageants in the open air. The word "pageant" (from pagina, or plank) was used for the stage, or wheeled car of two stories, before it was used for the show set forth upon it. The actors costumed themselves in the lower room, playing in the upper room which was open at the top so

*that they could be seen and heard by the audience. During
recent years, the Elizabethan Stage Society, under the
direction of Ben Greet, successfully revived "Everyman"
in England and the United States.*

God, reflecting in Heaven upon the failings of Everyman,
concludes that all men are drowned in sin and flout His
commandments; that, in spite of His sacrifice upon the
cross, all have forsaken Him. It is the day upon which
Everyman is to die, and God summons Death to go to
Everyman "and show him in my name a pilgrimage he
. . . must take, which in no wise he may escape."
    Death sets out with a promise:

"Lord, I will in the world go run over all,
    And cruelly out-search both great and small . . .
    He that loveth riches, I will strike with my dart
    His sight to blind and fro Heaven to depart."

Soon he sees Everyman walking on his way. "Full little
he thinketh on my coming," reflects the grim messenger,
as he hails him: "Everyman, stand still; whither art thou
going thus gaily? Hast thou thy Maker forgot?"
    Everyman asks what it is that God desires of him, and
Death replies:

"On thee thou must take a long journey.
    Before God thou must answer and show
    Thy many bad deeds, and good but a few."

Everyman protests:

"Full unready I am such reckoning to give . . .
    O Death, thou comest when I had thee least in mind . . .
    A thousand pounds shalt thou have
    An thou defer this matter till another day."

Death cannot be bribed, but he concedes to Everyman
the comfort of taking with him on his journey a few of his
friends, and Everyman, after reflecting on his companions
so that he may select the most congenial ones, confidently
starts on his quest. He appeals first to Fellowship, with

the reminder that ever before he has found him true.
Fellowship, unaware of the favor to be asked, glibly
replies:

> "And so you shall forevermore.
> Therefore show me the grief of your mind,
> As to your friend most loving and kind."

Then Everyman implores his company on the deathly
journey, and Fellowship promptly cancels his shallow
pledge. In dicing and drinking—indeed in almost everything
—he will gaily go with Everyman, but he concludes:

> "If you will murder, or any man kill,
> In that I will help you with a right good will.
> But if you ask me to help when you die,
> Let another man do it—no, not I."

Everyman turns next to Kindness, but Kindness says:

> "No, by Our Lady, I have the cramp in my toe.
> God speed you now in your way to Hell;
> And so, my cousin, a fond farewell."

Next, he goes to Riches who answers:

> "My job, good friend, is in life to deceive,
> And not in death to comfort and relieve."

At last Everyman has tried all his companions except his
Good Deeds. She is too feeble to help, although she wishes
to stand by him. She explains: "Thy sins have me so sore
bound that I cannot stir." She sends him to Knowledge,
who takes him to Confession, who, in turn, presents him
with a necessary but painful garment, the scourge of
Penance, to help him find the oil of Forgiveness.

Now, garbed in his garment of Penance and anointed
with the oil of Forgiveness, Everyman goes back to Good
Deeds. He finds her restored in health, ready to serve him.
Heartened by her loyalty, Everyman exclaims: "For every
sweetness of love I rejoice." He finds that the presence of
Good Deeds has brought to his side several other friends
—Strength, Discretion, Beauty and Five Wits.

But after Everyman has gone to the priest to receive the Sacrament, and all have journeyed to the edge of the grave, the friends desert him one by one. First to do so is Beauty, with this excuse:

> "What, into this grave? I fear
> That I would smother here."

Next, Strength says, despite Everyman's appeal to "tarry, I pray you, for a little space":

> "Nay, sir, by the rood of grace,
> I will hie me from thee fast,
> Tho thou weep till thy heart brast."

Everyman comments sadly:

> "He that trusteth in his Strength
> Deserves to be deceived at length."

Next, Discretion deserts him, saying:

> "My friend, when Strength is gone before,
> I follow after evermore."

Finally Five Wits goes. Everyman reproaches him, saying: "I thought you were my closest friend." Five Wits answers: "But now our friendship is at an end." Only Good Deeds is left now to follow him into the grave. Everyman reflects:

> "Thou helpest me when all are gone,
> Though I loved thee least of any one."

She answers:

> "When all thy friends and comrades flee,
> Good Deeds alone will speak for thee."

So Everyman, with his sole loyal friend, surrenders himself to Death. The grave closes over them. An angel sings him to sleep, and his purified soul is welcomed to Heaven.

IRISH PLAYS

Juno and the Paycock

BY SEAN O'CASEY

*Born in Ireland, about 1881. He received very little formal
education, not only because his family was very poor, but
also because of a serious eye disease. He went to school for
only three years, then taught himself from dictionaries and
from the textbooks his brothers had used before him. He
first worked as an ironmonger, then as a laborer for several
years, although he was not very strong and was a semi-
invalid during much of his life. While still a young man
he became interested in the Irish National Movement. He
joined the National Club, organizing a dramatic class and
writing plays for it. He submitted several plays to the
Abbey Theatre, but at first they were rejected. Later, however, many of them were accepted and became very successful. He took part in the Sinn Fein movement, and was
an organizer of the Irish Citizen Army. He went to England
in 1926 where, for the most part, he has lived ever since.
Some of his plays are, "Shadow of a Gunman," "The
Plough and the Stars," and "The Star Turns Red." "Juno
and the Paycock," received the Hawthornden Prize in
1926.*

Poverty is pinching ever harder in the two-room home of
the Boyle family in Dublin, with misfortune piling upon
misfortune. Mary, the pretty daughter, twenty-two, is on
strike with her union, and Johnny, the son, has lost an
arm and suffered a crippled hip in the civil warfare. Little

over twenty, he has been left the prey of a constant, tremulous fear.

Alone at work is Mrs. Boyle (whom her husband brightly calls Juno because in June she was born, met her husband, was married and had her son), and her life has crushed, at forty-five, what had once been a woman of good looks and cleverness. Not the least of her burdens is "Captain" Boyle, "struttin' about the town like a paycock," cadging beer money from his wife, adroitly dodging work and bawling ballads with his crony, old Joxer, another loafer. Although he talks knowingly of the high seas, his "Captain" is a filched title born of a single voyage to Liverpool on an ancient collier.

Jerry Devine, a young labor leader, calls to bring word of a digging job that the priest has found for the Captain. He reproaches Mary for having neglected him for a new sweetheart. He urges marriage, but she, telling him that their affair is over, leaves to meet her new friends. The Captain, after shrewd maneuvering to breakfast leisurely, discusses the stars and the moon with the admiring Joxer, complains of his suddenly aching legs (they ache when work is mentioned), and finally is resigned to report for the job when Juno returns with great news: Mary is coming with her sweetheart, Charlie Bentham, a young lawyer, who has tidings "that'll give you the chance of your life."

And, indeed, the smug Bentham has news: a relative has died and left to Boyle and another cousin a fortune that will bring the Captain some two thousand pounds. In his vision of a new and glorious life of wealth, he promises Juno that he is through with such as Joxer: "I'm a new man from this out," he says, jocularly. He clasps his wife's hand and sings emotionally: "Oh, me darlin' Juno, I will be thrue to thee; me own, me darlin' Juno, you're all the world to me."

But two days later, in the flat now refurnished with garish chairs, pictures and huge vases of artificial flowers, the Captain and Joxer are pals again, and Boyle is telling him of the cares of great estates. He has borrowed handsomely against the forthcoming fortune, and Mrs. Madigan, a neighbor, has pawned her blankets and table to provide more ready money. Juno and Mary bear in a gramophone, also bought on the installment plan.

The Captain, as a man of property, sagely tells Bentham how the "whole country's in a state of chassis." Bentham, a Theosophist, is explaining his opinion of ghosts, when Johnny screams in terror; he thinks he has seen the bullet-riddled body of the recently slain Robbie Tancred, a neighbor, kneeling before the Virgin's statue in his room, ghastly in the votive light before it. The Boyles hesitate to investigate, but Bentham does so and reports nothing amiss. The incident is passed over with the arrival of Mrs. Madigan and Joxer. Whisky is served and songs are sung, but a neighbor halts the hilarity for the passing of the Tancred funeral.

Two months later, Mary is dully telling her mother that she has not heard from Bentham for a month—he has gone to England without leaving an address. Mary still loves him, and hesitatingly tells her mother: "I imagine . . . he thought . . . we weren't . . . good enough for him." Juno insists upon Mary going to the doctor, and, as they leave, she demands that the Captain go again to the lawyer to see if the promised fortune has arrived. Boyle, luxuriously reclining, testily declares that he can't haunt the lawyer's office day and night, and calls for another bottle of stout and his leg liniment.

The women gone, Joxer comes in with Nugent, the tailor. Nugent has himself gone to the lawyer for money owed on the Captain's new suit: he has learned that the will was defectively drawn and that the Boyles are not to get a cent—nor are the neighbors from whom they had been lavishly borrowing. He demands the money for his suit, but Boyle jauntily asks the bill, then orders "a good heavy top-coat—Irish frieze if you have it," reckoning that he will then owe Nugent thirteen pounds. Nugent seizes the suit from a chair and leaves with it, ignoring the Captain's distressed cry: "Here, what am I going to dhress meself in when I'm goin' out?" Then Mrs. Madigan appears. "Puttin' aside all formularities," she demands her loan. The

Captain offers a receipt in full, but no cash. Mrs. Madigan, shaking him roundly, bears off the gramophone. Joxer, too, deserts him, jeeringly, as Johnny and Juno return.

Juno arrives with the news that Mary is going to have a baby by Bentham. The Captain first blusters of going to England to bring Bentham back, then mourns: "Oh, isn't this a nice thing to come on top o' me, an' the state I'm in! A pretty show I'll be to Joxer an' to that oul' wan, Madigan!" He demands to see Mary, but Juno says she has left the girl at her sister's, and pleads that she deserves mercy for having helped the family for so long. Boyle, echoed by Johnny, declares that Mary must leave home in disgrace. Juno then threatens to accompany her. They can both go, Boyle declares, in a burst of self-pity.

Juno suggests that they can go quietly away, with no one the wiser, when they get the fortune. Then the Captain tells his stunned wife and son that he has long known that there is no fortune: Bentham had failed in the will to specify names, and now a horde of cousins has appeared, claiming equal rights. Johnny turns upon his father, declaring him worse than Mary for his deceit and continued borrowing. But the Captain, calling Joxer, goes out to drink up the last of his coins, warning that he must not find Mary when he returns, or "I'll lay me han's on her."

Men come to reclaim the furniture, and, just as Mary enters, Juno hurries out to fetch the Captain to stop them. Jerry arrives to tell Mary that Juno has told him "everything," and that he still loves her; but when he learns that she is to have a child, he leaves. The men are carrying out the furniture (Mary, unable to witness the humiliation, has gone) when Johnny screams from his room: the votive light has gone out, and he feels the pain of a bullet in his breast. As he speaks, two Irregulars with revolvers enter softly and drag him off—screaming prayers for mercy—for execution as the betrayer of his friend Tancred.

Later, with most of the furniture gone, Juno and Mary have left with the police to identify the body of Johnny. Juno has decided: "Come, Mary, an' we'll never come back here again. Let your father furrage for himself now: I've done all I could an' it was all no use—he'll be hopeless till the end of his days. I've got a little room in me sisther's where we'll stop till your trouble is over, an' then we'll work together for the sake of the baby."

The Captain and Joxer return to the empty flat, maudlin drunk. Joxer falls on the bed and the Captain subsides on the floor in a sitting posture. He lets fall a single coin and says: "Wan single, solitary tanner left out of all I borreyed. . . . The blinds is down. . . . I'm tellin' you, Joxer, th' whole worl's . . . in a terr . . . ible state o' chassis!"

The Playboy of the Western World

BY JOHN MILLINGTON SYNGE

Born near Dublin in 1871, he went to the local schools and then received his degree from Trinity College, Dublin. Later, he went to Germany to study music, then to Paris where he spent several years writing literary criticism. There he met William Butler Yeats who persuaded him to return to Ireland and continue his writing. He is best known for his plays based, for the most part, on Irish peasant life. Most of these were written during the last six years of his life. "Riders to the Sea" was produced in 1904 by the Irish National Theatre Society, which group later became the Abbey Theatre, under the directorship of Yeats, Synge and Lady Gregory. Among his other plays are, "The Shadow of the Glen" and—perhaps best known—"The Playboy of the Western World" which, when first presented by the Abbey Players in 1907, aroused bitter resentment, as certain of the characters were felt not to be representative of Irish life. He died in 1909.

To an untidy little country saloon on a wild coast of Mayo, in Ireland, there comes a shy, frightened youth, Christy

Mayo, with a tale of having killed his cruel father, with a single blow of a spade, a week ago on a distant farm. He is fleeing the police, and is accepted by Michael James, the publican, and his pretty but tart-tongued daughter, Pegeen, as a hero whom it would be well to hire as pot-boy.

So Christy stays on, and Michael James and his cronies leave for a wake. Pegeen scornfully dismisses Shawn Keogh, her betrothed, a young farmer who fears to stay alone with her until dispensation for their wedding is granted, and Christy tells her—the first woman to allow him a confidential talk—that he has been a cloddish young farmer, shy and unheeded by the girls. But now his ego is inflated at her attention and at the realization that he is, indeed, a sinister figure.

Their chat is interrupted by the Widow Quin, a forthright woman of thirty, who has come, at Shawn's urging, to take Christy to her house to lodge. She tells Christy that he and she will be great company, and he asks if she, too, killed her father. Pegeen scornfully declares that it was a sneaky kind of murder—she hit him with a rusty pick and he died of blood poisoning. The women debate sharply for possession of the thrilling stranger, but Christy elects to stay where he is. He goes to sleep wondering, in his new-found importance, why he didn't kill his father long ago.

Next morning, while Pegeen is out, the Widow Quin is prompt to return, announcing that she has entered him to compete in the sports of that afternoon. Shawn, Pegeen's betrothed, is a visitor also; he offers Christy the half of a ticket to the Western States, his new hat, his breeches with the double seat and his new coat if Christy will leave Pegeen to him. While Christy is trying on the fine clothes, the Widow Quin makes a deal of her own to help Shawn, promising to wed Christy herself in return for a red cow and other tribute.

But Christy, swaggering in Shawn's finery, sees no reason why so rich a field should be abandoned by "a gallant orphan cleft his father with one blow to the breeches belt." He opens the door to seek Pegeen, but staggers back and cries that the ghost of his father is approaching. He hides behind a door. In comes Old Mahon, a squatter with bandaged head, seeking his son. The Widow, enjoying her role, quizzes him, and is promptly told that Christy is a lazy lout, "making mugs at his own self in a bit of glass," a weakling who can neither drink nor smoke and is terrified by girls.

The Widow sends Old Mahon off on a false clue, then jeers at the crestfallen Christy: "Well, you're the walking Playboy of the Western World, and that's the poor man you had divided to his breeches belt!" She assures him that Pegeen will knock his head and drive him off as a liar, and suggests that he would do well to marry her. But Christy determines that he will win Pegeen, promising the Widow a share when he is master of the saloon if she will aid him. She agrees, and Christy runs out to take part in the sports and make a name for himself.

While he is gone, however, Old Mahon returns to the saloon to boast of his cracked head, and the Widow is hard put, despite canny lies, to make him appear a madman and not Christy's father. She can see from the window that Christy is performing heroic feats in the races and games, and she finally induces Old Mahon to believe that he is "a sniggering maniac" and had better escape—that his shy son could not possibly be this champion Playboy of the Western World. Old Mahon slips out. One farmer is suspicious and follows to talk further to him.

Christy, escorted by a cheering throng, returns triumphantly to the house with his prizes. He now calls for the greatest prize of all, Pegeen's promise to marry him. Pegeen fears that he will return to some girl in his own town, but the now eloquent Christy protests: "I will not, then, and when the air is warming in four months, or five, it's then yourself and me should be pacing Neifin in the dews of night, the times sweet smells do be rising, and you'd see a shiny new moon, maybe, sinking on the hills." He goes on to picture the delights of a poacher's life, but cools when Pegeen agrees; he concedes that, after all, her own snug home would be best.

Michael James returns from the wake, drunk, to interrupt with the announcement that dispensations have come for the wedding of Pegeen and Shawn. The latter has accompanied him with the news. Pegeen declares that it is Christy she will wed, and Michael James eggs the young farmer to fight. Shawn flies out the door when Christy picks up a significant spade.

Michael James has overcome his drunkenness enough to give Christy and Pegeen his blessing when there is a shout, and Old Mahon rushes in, followed by the Widow Quin and a curious crowd. Old Mahon knocks Christy down and begins to beat him. Pegeen rushes to her lover's rescue, but learns that the attacker is his father who, indeed, has not risen from the dead. "Do you think I look so easy quenched with the tap of a loy?" he bellows. She turns on Christy: "And it's lies you told, letting on you had him slitted, and you nothing at all! . . . And to think of the coaxing glory we have given him and he after doing nothing but hitting a soft blow and chasing northward in a sweat of fear!"

Christy can find no comfort in the lies of the now exhausted Widow Quin, or in the jeering crowd, and he again is pale with terror as Old Mahon heaps humiliation upon him. A girl in the crowd suggests maliciously that he ask Pegeen to help him, but he says: "I will not, then, for there's torment in the splendor of her like, and she a girl any moon of midnight would take pride to meet. . . . But what did I want crawling forward to scorch my understanding at her flaming brow?" The weeping Pegeen tells Mahon to take him off or she will have him beaten.

Her scorn revives Christy, the champion. As Old Mahon bullies him to come, he seizes a spade and pursues his father into the yard—from whence there comes a yell, then silence. Christy returns, half dazed, and the Widow Quin begs him to run or he will be hanged. But he will not go. He says: "What good'd be my lifetime, if I left Pegeen? . . . Leave me go . . . when I'm thinking of my luck today, for she will wed me surely, and I a proven hero in the end of all."

The men report Old Mahon doubly dead, and Pegeen herself slips a noose over the dazed Christy's arms. He asks what she has now to say to him, but Pegeen replies: "A strange man is a marvel, with his mighty talk; but what's a squabble in your back-yard, and the blow of a loy, have taught me that there's a great gap between a gallous story and a dirty deed." He begs her to free him, to return no more, but Pegeen is merciless; she says that she and her neighbors might hang for his deed.

Christy, having managed to bite Shawn in the leg, is forecasting his dramatic execution before weeping fine ladies when Old Mahon crawls in. He loosens Christy and respectfully bids him to come on and leave the fools of Mayo. And Christy, the proved "master of all fights from now on," grandly orders the old man to lead. "The thousand blessings upon all that's here," he says, "for you've turned me a likely gaffer in the end of all, the way I'll go romancing through a romping lifetime. . . ."

As he leaves, Shawn suggests that their wedding can now go on, but Pegeen cuffs his ear and sends him off. She covers her head with her shawl and loudly laments: "Oh, my grief, I've lost him surely! I've lost the only Playboy of the Western World!"

Riders to the Sea

BY JOHN MILLINGTON SYNGE

A melancholy conspiracy is being enacted in a cottage kitchen on the Irish west coast by Cathleen, a girl of perhaps twenty years, and Nora, her younger sister, who has just entered noiselessly, revealing under her shawl a small bundle.

The bundle contains the shirt and a stocking taken from a drowned man at Donegal, and the sisters, who have been searching for a clue to the fate of their missing

brother, Michael, are fearfully examining them when they
hear their mother moving on her bed in the adjoining
room. Cathleen whispers: "Maybe she'd wake up on us
and come in before we'd done. It's a long time we'll be
looking them over, and the two of us crying."

So Nora suggests that they put them in the loft where
the turf for the fire is stored. Cathleen is hiding them when
Maurya, their aged mother, enters. Cathleen tells her that
she is getting more turf to bake bread for Bartley, another
brother, who is planning a trip to Connemara. Maurya is
fearful, with the wind rising, and hopes that the priest will
dissuade him, but Bartley, entering to get a piece of rope, is
determined to make the dangerous journey.

"We'll be wanting this rope, Bartley, if Michael is
washed up," Maurya protests, "for it's a deep grave we'll
make him by the grace of God. . . . It's a hard thing
they'll be saying if Michael's body is washed up and there's
no man to make the coffin, and I after giving a big price
for the finest white boards you'll find in Connemara.
. . . Isn't it a hard and cruel man won't hear a word from
an old woman, and she holding him from the sea?"

But Bartley, saying he will be gone from two to four
days, takes the rope for a halter; he will ride the red mare,
and the gray pony will run behind on the trip to the boat.
Maurya laments: "He's gone now, God spare us, and I'll
have no son left me in the world." Cathleen remembers that
she has forgotten the bread, and at her urging, Maurya
goes to the spring to give it, with her blessing, to Bartley as
he passes. She takes a stick Michael once brought from
Connemara, and sets out, murmuring that in this place it
is the young who leave their possessions to the old.

The sisters hurriedly examine the shirt and stocking, and
learn that they were Michael's. Mourns Cathleen: "Ah,
Nora, isn't it a bitter thing to think of him floating that
way to the far north, and no one to keen for him but the
black hags that do be flying on the sea?" They hurriedly
hide the relics as Maurya returns, still bearing the bread,
and crying: "I seen the fearfulest thing!"

Cathleen hurriedly looks out in time to see Bartley riding

the mare away, with the gray pony behind him, but old Maurya says tremulously that she had seen Michael, "and he riding and galloping right behind Bartley on the gray pony—with fine clothes on him and new shoes on his feet." Cathleen tells her: "It isn't Michael, for his body is after being found in the far north, and he's got a clean burial by the grace of God." But the girl begins to weep: "It's destroyed we are from this day."

Maurya says dully: "Bartley will be lost now, and I won't live after them. I've had a husband, and a husband's father, and six sons in this house—six fine men—and there were some of them found and some of them not found. There was Stephen and Shawn were lost in the great wind . . ."

Nora and Cathleen hear a crying by the seashore, but Maurya goes on: "There was Shaemus and his father, and his own father again, were lost in a dark night. . . . There was Patch after was drowned. . . . I was sitting here with Bartley, and he a baby in my arms, and I saw women . . . coming in, and they crossed themselves, and not saying a word . . . And there were men coming after them, and they holding a thing in the half of a red sail and water dripping out of it and leaving a track to the door. . . ."

As she pauses, with her hand pointing to the door in illustration of her mournful recital, it opens slowly and old women file in. They cross themselves and kneel. Says Maurya: "They're carrying a thing among them and there's water dripping out of it and leaving a track by the big stones. . . ." Men bear in the body of Bartley on a plank, with a scrap of sail over it; they lay it on the table. One of the women reports: "The gray pony knocked him over into the sea, and he was washed out where there is a great surf on the white rocks."

Maurya kneels at Bartley's head: "They're all gone now, and there isn't anything more the sea can do to me. . . . It's a great rest I'll be having now, and great sleeping in the long nights, if it's only a bit of wet flour we do have to eat. . . ."

Cathleen asks the men to make a coffin out of the

boards Maurya has bought, but there are no nails. One man comments: "It's a great wonder she wouldn't think of the nails, and all the coffins she's seen made already." Cathleen says: "It's getting old she is, and broken."

Maurya sprinkles the body with holy water, places the empty cup bottom upward on the table, lays her wrinkled hands on Bartley's feet. She says: "They're all together this time, and the end is come. May the Almighty God have mercy on Bartley's soul, and on Michael's soul, and on the souls of Sheamus, and Patch, and Stephen, and Shawn, and may He have mercy on my soul, Nora, and on the soul of everyone left living in the world. . . . Michael has a clean burial in the far north . . . Bartley will have a fine coffin out of the white boards . . . What more can we want than that? No man at all can be living forever, and we must be satisfied. . . ."

The Shaughraun

BY DION BOUCICAULT

Born in Dublin, December 26, 1822, son of a French refugee and an Irish mother. Before he was twenty he had won success in his play, "London Assurance," and this was rapidly followed by others. He toured America from 1853 to 1869, and was very popular—the best of his plays at this time being "Colleen Bawn" which made him a fortune. "The Octoroon" was almost as popular when it was first presented in 1861. "The Shaughraun," first produced in London in 1875, won him the reputation of being the best Irish actor of his time. He returned to New York many times, and finally made his home there. He died September 18, 1890.

Captain Molineux, a young English officer commanding a detachment at Ballyraggett, Ireland, finds Claire Ffolliott, a Sligo lady, working at a churn outside her cabin home. He at first takes her for a dairymaid, and flirts with her. Then Arte O'Neale appears, and he learns that Claire and Arte are gentlewomen who have been reduced to poverty by the machinations of their enemies. He wants permission to shoot and fish on the estate, but Claire says to Arte: "Shall I spare you the humiliation of confessing that you are not mistress in your own house, much less lady of the manor?" She turns to Molineux. "Do you see that ruin yonder? Oh, 'tis the admiration of the traveller, and the study of painters, who come from far and near to copy it. It was the home of my forefathers when they kept open house for the friend—the poor—or the stranger. The mortgagee has put up a gate now, so visitors pay sixpence a head to admire the place, and their guide points across to the cabin where the remains of the old family, two lonely girls, live—God knows how. You ask leave to kill game on Suil-a-more and Keim-an-eigh." She crosses to the dairy window. "Do you see that salmon? It was snared last night in the pool . . . by Conn, the Shaughraun. He killed those grouse at daylight on the side of Maurnturk. That's our daily food, and we owe it to a poacher."

The period is that in which the revolutionary movement known as Fenianism is in full blast. Claire's brother, Robert, as Molineux learns, has been transported to Australia because of his active opposition to British rule. It is because Robert's estate has been practically confiscated during his absence that his sister and her cousin are in their present plight. The situation becomes clear when Corry Kinchela, a scampish squireen, appears on the scene and actually gloats over their plight. "I'm just back from Dublin," he says, "and thought I'd stop on my road to tell you the court has decreed the sale of this estate, under foreclosure, and in two months you'll have to turn out."

Molineux has been ordered by his Government to look out for a "schooner carrying a distinguished Fenian hero" which is said to be "hovering about the coast," intending to land her passengers in the neighborhood. This hero turns out to be none other than Robert Ffolliott who,

thanks to the efforts of Conn, the Shaughraun, has succeeded in escaping from Australia by way of America.

In the home of Father Dolan, a local priest, Robert appears in company with his sister, Claire, and his betrothed,
Arte. The priest's niece, Moya, is present. Conn is there,
too; he conveys by means of his speech, his actions and
his demeanor something of the meaning of the word
"Shaughraun." (The Shaughraun is the Soul of every Fair,
the Life of every Funeral, the First Fiddle at all weddings
and patterns.)

Father Dolan disapproves of the drinking habits and ir-
regular life of Conn, but admires his loyalty and his good
heart. For Robert Ffolliott he feels the love that a father
might feel for his son—and, indeed, the elder Ffolliott when
he died had laid a special charge on Dolan to care for his
infant son. But even while the priest is rejoicing over
the safe return of Robert to Ireland, a sinister figure who
had been largely responsible for Robert's arrest and trans-
portation, lurks in the shadows behind the house. It is
Harvey Duff, the rascally accomplice of Corry Kinchela.

Never has a man found a truer friend than Robert finds
in Conn; and never did a man need a friend more than
Robert needs Conn. For Robert is now being stalked as a
felon escaping from justice, and Molineux, in performance
of his duty, is compelled to arrest him again and take him
to prison.

At this juncture, Kinchela receives word that the English Government has granted an amnesty to Fenian prisoners. The news spoils all his plans, for he has hoped to
get possession of the Ffolliott estate and to marry Arte
O'Neale.

Kinchela and Harvey Duff now conspire to betray Robert by offering him the means of escape from his cell—they
plan to shoot him as he makes the attempt. Kinchela visits
Robert in his prison, winning his confidence. He asks: "Is
that ship that landed you within reach?" Robert replies:
"Every night at eight o'clock she runs in shore and lies
to off the coast; a bonfire lighted on Rathgarron Head is to
be the signal for her to send off her skiff under the ruins

of St. Bridget's Abbey to take me on board." Kinchela responds: "That signal will be fired tonight, and you shall be there to meet the boat." He hands a pistol to Robert.

When Robert secretly emerges from his cell a few hours later, Kinchela and four constables are waiting behind a wall nearby. Harvey Duff carries a carbine. But just as Duff is getting ready to fire, Conn drops from a wall on Duff's shoulders and throws him to the ground. Conn creates the impression that it is Robert who has fallen, and in the ensuing confusion Conn and Robert make their escape.

On Rathgarron Head that night Conn plays another trick. The bonfire is lighted; Robert swims out to safety. Conn leads the constables on a false trail and receives in his own body the shots intended for his friend. He falls, apparently lifeless, and is carried on a shutter to the cabin of his mother. Over his (supposed) corpse is held a wake which, when Conn comes to his senses, affords him great amusement.

The next step of the vicious Kinchela and Duff is to organize a band of ruffians, and to kidnap Arte O'Neale and her friend Moya, Conn's sweetheart. The two women are held in a shed overlooking a rocky cave on the seacoast. The topmasts of a ship can be seen beyond the edge of a precipice. Kinchela and Duff are planning to take the women to sea.

In the nick of time a mob, headed by Conn, comes to the rescue. Retribution is effected by violently melodramatic means. Harvey Duff leaps to his death over a cliff. Kinchela is hurt but not killed, and is led off to be dealt with by a legal tribunal. Conn receives the permission of Father Dolan to marry Moya, and promises to mend his ways.

Since Robert, the revolutionary, is now released, under the amnesty, and has nothing to fear from either the English soldiery or the Irish constabulary, his troubles for the time being are over. With Conn his friend, Claire his sister, and Arte his betrothed, he is able to enjoy without anxiety the sunlight of freedom.

FRENCH PLAYS

Cyrano de Bergerac

BY EDMOND ROSTAND

*Born in Marseilles, France, April 1, 1869, the son of a
prominent journalist and economist. He had written several successful plays before his "Cyrano de Bergerac" was
first shown on December 28, 1897, but that play was the
most immediately successful. It was quickly translated into
English, German, Russian, and other European languages.
His "L'Aiglon" was produced in 1900 by Sarah Bernhardt
at her own theater; the title role in this play was one of
the most famous in her repertoire. In 1902 Rostand was
elected to the French Academy. During the first World
War, he wrote mostly patriotic verse. He died in Paris,
December 2, 1918.*

Cyrano de Bergerac, "the best friend and the bravest soul
alive," is a Gascon guardsman, superlative swordsman,
musician, poet and philosopher:

"He might have been a model for Callot—
  One of those wild swashbucklers in a masque—
  Hat with three plumes, and doublet with three points—
  His cloak behind him over his long sword
  Cocked, like the tail of strutting Chanticleer—
  Prouder than all the swaggering Tamburlaines
  Hatched out of Gascony. And to complete
  This Punchinello figure—such a nose!
  My lords, there is no such nose as that nose—
  You cannot look upon it without crying: 'Oh, no,

Impossible! Exaggerated!' Then
You smile, and say: 'Of course,
I might have known;
Presently he will take it off.' "

Cyrano's impudent belligerency is demonstrated to Paris
when he halts a performance at the Hotel de Bourgogne
because a fat actor, Montfleury, has ignored his command
to leave the stage. To compensate the players, he flings
his purse upon the stage, and so for his own dinner he is
reduced to a single macaroon, a glass of water and a grape.

He admits to Le Bret, his friend, that he has punished
Montfleury because the actor dared to smile on his lovely
cousin, Roxane, and confides further that he himself is
hopelessly in love with her—hopelessly because of "this
nose of mine that marches on before me by a quarter of
an hour." He tells of his bitter days, "knowing myself so
ugly, so alone," when he cannot even weep because "that
would be too grotesque—tears trickling all the long way
along this nose of mine."

He is transported with joy when Le Bret tells him that
Roxane had paled at seeing him in a minor duel after
the play, and is made even happier when Roxane's duenna
comes to ask if Cyrano will meet her mistress on the morrow. He arranges a meeting for the morning at Ragueneau's
pastry shop, then goes blithely out on another of his adventures—to rout a hundred ruffians lying in wait for his
poet friend, Ligniere, who has offended their employer, De
Guiche, a powerful nobleman. He kills seven or eight of
the band, then goes to the pastry shop to compose a poem
while he waits for Roxane.

But when she comes his dream crumbles. Roxane tells
him that she loves Christian, a young nobleman who has
just joined Cyrano's company of guardsmen. She asks that
Cyrano protect him. Cyrano, who has not dared to tell her
of his own love, gives his promise. Now a crowd has come
to hail the hero of the street battle. Among the crowd is
De Guiche who offers Cyrano honors and patronage if he
will join him. Cyrano promptly insults him, and De Guiche

warns him not to tilt with windmills, that their long arms
may throw him into the mire. "Or up," Cyrano answers,
"among the stars."

Cyrano, pressed to tell his cadets of the fight, begins his
story. Young Christian, to prove his courage under the
taunts of the Gascons, repeatedly interrupts with jibes at
Cyrano's nose. But the poet only orders the others from the
room, embraces Christian and tells him of Roxane's love.
Christian is overjoyed, but protests that his suit is hopeless
since, when he is with women, he is speechless. Cyrano
promises to help him by lending his wit to Christian's
wooing.

So Cyrano expresses his own hopeless love for Roxane
through the name and person of Christian. He writes her
lyric letters, and one night even lends his eloquent voice.
He and Christian stand in the darkness below Roxane's
balcony while he pours out his heart to her. She, believing
the voice to be that of Christian, pledges her own love.
Cyrano, at Christian's urging, asks for a kiss, and the youth
is climbing upon the balcony to receive it when a monk,
bearing a lantern, appears.

Cyrano, revealed by the rays of the lantern, explains
that he just happened to be passing, and learns that the
monk bears a message from De Guiche who also is in love
with Roxane. The wily Cyrano tells the unlettered monk
that the note contains De Guiche's instructions that he shall
at once marry Christian and Roxane, and the monk enters
the house to perform the ceremony. But De Guiche suddenly appears. Cyrano, to gain time for the wedding, falls
at the nobleman's feet and insists that he is a man from the
moon. In the darkness, and with an assumed voice, he
fools De Guiche with a fantastic story until the lovers
are safely married.

But the angry De Guiche is not yet defeated; in the current war with Spain he has been appointed to command
the regiment that includes the Gascony cadets, and he
orders that Cyrano and Christian march with him at once
to besiege Arras. The drums are heard and Christian is
forced to leave. Roxane pleads with Cyrano to guard him

well and to see that he writes often to her. From the field of battle Cyrano not only writes daily letters, signed with Christian's name, but hazards his life to get them through the lines.

Soon there is word that the enemy is to attack, and Christian says that he wishes he could write a beautiful letter of farewell to Roxane. Cyrano tells him that it is already done and shows the letter to him. Christian notes that a tear has fallen on the paper. In spite of Cyrano's denial, he begins to suspect his friend's tragic devotion. Just before the final battle, Roxane gets through the Spanish lines with a carriage full of food; she insists upon remaining with her husband.

But Christian, realizing at last that he has won Roxane through the masquerade of Cyrano's love, exposes himself on the ramparts and is killed. Roxane reads the letter found on his body and exclaims to Cyrano: "Wasn't he an exquisite being? . . . A profound soul? . . . See, there are tears on his letter! His tears!" Says Cyrano: "Yes, Roxane." She throws herself upon Christian's body as the cadets charge into defeat.

Fifteen years later, Roxane is in a convent, still devoted to the memory of Christian. She is visited each Saturday by Cyrano, now reduced to utter poverty because of his arrogant independence of the nobles. But his enemies want a greater revenge, and one Saturday a block of wood, thrown from above, fractures his skull. But, his cane tapping as usual and the bandage round his head concealed under his white-plumed hat, he manages to reach the convent. Roxane speaks again of Christian's last letter, and Cyrano asks if he may read it aloud to her.

He begins: "Roxane, farewell, I am going to die!" Then suddenly the truth dawns upon Roxane. She cries: "It was you! Those tears are yours!" He stoutly denies his love, but at last replies, "But the blood was his." Then he tells her of his injury: "My battlefield a gutter—my noble foe a lackey, with a log of wood! It seems too logical: I have missed everything, even my death!"

Roxane sobs her love for him, and he asks "a double

meaning to your widow's weeds, and the tears you let fall
for him may be for a little—my tears." At last he struggles
to his feet and draws his sword against death. Cries he:
"I can see him there—he grins—he is looking at my nose."
He lunges, too, at his ancient enemies—falsehood, compromise, cowardice. Exhausted, he drops his sword and
falls, his last boast that he takes with him one thing without stain—his white plume.

Camille

BY ALEXANDRE DUMAS, FILS

*Born in Paris, July 27, 1824. He had a carefree childhood,
early developing the extravagant tendencies which his father, the famous author of "The Count of Monte Cristo,"
had always shown. When his debts approximated $10,000,
he took to literature in order to earn a living. In 1848 he
wrote "La Dame aux Camelias"; a year later he dramatized
it. The play was at first condemned by the censor, and
suffered many vicissitudes before an important minister
of Napoleon intervened in its favor. It was then accepted
by the public, attracting large audiences, and the role of
the frail, tragic heroine was played by many great actresses; among the most famous early interpreters were
Sarah Bernhardt and Eleonora Duse. From the time of the
play's success, Dumas lived the life of a brilliant and
prosperous dramatist. He was elected to the French Academy in 1874. He died November 27, 1895.*

Camille Gauthier, a frail and beautiful Parisienne of many
loves, is awaited in her luxurious apartment by the Count
De Varville, a persistent but so far unsuccessful admirer.
As he chats with her maid, Nanine, the strange story of
Camille's career is unfolded:

Camille had been an embroideress until her loveliness freed her from the workshop (Nanine says: "There are many evil things said of Madam, and with truth"). Two years ago, becoming ill, she had gone to the springs at Bagneres where she had met Mademoiselle de Meuriac, daughter of the Duke. The girls, who appeared to be twins in their close resemblance, became inseparable until Mademoiselle de Meuriac, who suffered the same illness, died.

The aged Duke then took Camille under his protection, treating her as another daughter; he introduced her into society and, as De Varville says: ". . . tonight she is at the opera, the Queen of the Camellias, fifty thousand francs in debt." But earlier, in the Duke's absence, her story had become known, and the sneers of the society which the Duke had ruled had driven her back to her own old gay circle in Paris.

Camille arrives with her friends, Olympe and Gaston, who are sweethearts. For supper Camille summons from across the way her friend and milliner, Madame Prudence. Prudence tells Camille that she has a guest, and is bidden to bring him, too; he is Armand Duval, son of the Receiver-General at Tours, a young man who has shyly loved Camille for two years but has feared to seek an introduction. Camille is interested in him, and seats Armand beside her.

Gaston plays a polka on the piano and the company dances; but Camille, coughing, is compelled to excuse herself to rest. Armand follows her to her room and pleads: "Ah, Camille, let me be your nurse—your doctor. I will guard you like a brother—shield you from this feverish excitement, which is bringing you to your grave—surround you with a thousand little cares that will make you in love with life—then when you are strong and well and can enjoy it, I will be as your guiding star and lead your thoughts to find content in a home more worthy of you."

But Camille, although moved by Armand's sincere love for her, declares that she is only "a woman of the world—friendless, fearless—loved by those whose vanity she gratified—despised by those who ought to pity her." She protests that she is also fretful and expensive—a union between them would never do. She urges Armand to marry a girl of his own merit, and to forget her. But he declares he will have no other, that he will love her for eternity. Finally, in ecstasy, she declares: "Alas, my life may be happy yet—it cannot be long. . . . When this little flower is faded, bring it back to me again."

A few days later, Camille, aglow with her first true love, rents a little house in the country and asks Armand to live there with her for the summer. He, however, withholds assent, suspecting that the money for the house may come from a rival. He sees De Varville, whom Camille has summoned to pay her debts with her own funds, enter the apartment. In a fit of jealousy, he writes that he is quitting Paris. But he returns to beg forgiveness, and Camille tells him of her hope of recovery of both health and spirit— that she may be worthy of a home with him—and they are reconciled.

They go to the country for three months, and there find utter happiness together. Although Camille still feels herself unworthy to be Armand's wife, she tells Nichette and Gustave, her friends who are to be married: "I have so much happiness, why ask for more? To be near the man I love—to hear his voice—to know his truth! Oh, my dream of life has grown so blissful, peaceful, calm, I would not dare to wake it by wearying heaven with a wish beyond the present." She is secretly planning to sell her Paris house, pay her debts, and live simply with Armand in a little apartment, forsaking altogether her old life of luxury.

But the past that she thinks she is successfully erasing rises to turn her dream to dreary tragedy. In Armand's absence, his father appears at their retreat to confront her with the news that Armand is trying to sell a property left by his mother; M. Duval accuses her of ruining his son. She convinces him, however, that she has known nothing of the transaction. She herself is taking nothing from Armand, having received money from the sale of all the trappings of her old life.

M. Duval tells her that the scandal of her life with

Armand is threatening the happiness of Armand's sister whose fiancé will withdraw if the affair is not ended. Camille offers to leave Armand until after his sister's wedding, but M. Duval demands that the parting be final; he convinces the stricken girl that there can be no happiness for them, that she cannot marry Armand and thus make him "the idle jest and scorn of every honorable man."

Camille sadly agrees, but decides that her only course to free Armand is to make him despise and hate her, and she swears that he shall never know why she has ended their idyl. Armand returns. Leaving him to greet his father, she begs him that, should they ever be parted, he will recall her love and never curse her. When Armand comes back she is gone, leaving behind this note: "An hour after you have received this letter, Armand, I shall be with the Count De Varville."

A month later, Camille has resumed her feverish life in Paris. The desperate Armand has followed her, and goes at once to a dance at the home of Olympe where Camille and De Varville are expected. Camille attempts to leave when she learns of Armand's presence, but the Count refuses. She overhears Armand declare that he will gamble with the Count and, with the gold he wins, buy her return to the country with him—that she left him only because he was poor.

Armand does gamble with the Count; he wins. Camille, fearing a duel, confronts Armand and begs him to leave Paris. He taunts and insults her, then breaks down and begs her to go away with him. She is loyal to her promise to his father, however, and, to disillusion him once and for all, declares that she loves De Varville. Armand, in a fury, throws a shower of gold and bills upon her before the guests, and De Varville challenges him to a duel.

Months later, Camille, gravely ill and impoverished, and living in a shabby room, is reading a letter from M. Duval: Armand has fled Paris after wounding De Varville, but the latter has told Armand's father of her loyalty. He, relenting, has written to inform Armand, bidding him return to her. She is now awaiting her lover. For a time she dreams that she may recover to find happiness again with him, but when he appears, remorseful and begging her to live for him, she declares it is too late.

Weakly, she tells Armand that death is welcome—the memory of her guilt would forever haunt them. She gives him her picture and some faded flowers—the flowers he had picked for her the morning of their parting in their country home. She asks him to plant others like them on her grave, murmuring: "Oh, how strange! All the pain is gone! Is this life? Now everything appears to change. Oh, how beautiful! Do not wake me—I am so sleepy." As Armand frantically cries her name, she dies.

Hernani

BY VICTOR HUGO

Born at Besançon, France, February 26, 1802, his full name being Victor Marie Hugo. He was the son of a general who fought under Napoleon. He was taken by his father to Italy and Spain, and, at an early age, cherished the ambition to be a poet. While best known as the author of the humanitarian novel, "Les Misérables," which was published when he was sixty years old, Hugo was the author of a long series of plays. "Hernani" was produced in Paris in 1830, and marked the climax of a struggle between the classicists and the romanticists in French literature. Three years before, Hugo's preface to his drama, "Cromwell," had made him a leader among the romanticists. Other of Victor Hugo's plays are: "The King Amuses Himself" (the basis of Verdi's opera "Rigoletto"), "Lucrezia Borgia," "Ruy Blas," and "Mary Tudor." He was elected a member of the French Academy in 1841. For nearly twenty years Hugo was an exile from France because of his political views and activities. During part of this period, he lived on the island of Guernsey in the

*English Channel. He returned to France in 1870, and was
elected a member of the National Assembly. He died on
May 22, 1885. On the day of his funeral, more than a
million people lined the streets of Paris.*

The castle of Don Ruy Gomez de Silva is the setting of a
tragic romance: although betrothed to Don Ruy, her uncle,
young Doña Sol loves the outlaw, Hernani, and they meet
secretly each night. This night, however, as her attendant
is awaiting Hernani, there enters a third figure, a mysterious young man who says he is Don Carlos. He forces the
servants to hide him in a closet before Doña Sol and the
outlaw appear.

Unaware of his presence, Hernani asks her to choose
between him and her uncle. He reminds her that he is a
hunted man, although of noble blood: his father, in a
feud with the royal family, has been hanged, and Hernani
has sworn to avenge him. Doña Sol declares her love for
him despite his perils. They are planning to elope the following night when Don Carlos emerges from his closet and
identifies himself only as "a man who, like yourself, is in
love with Doña Sol."

The two men have drawn swords when Don Ruy enters
and demands their names. Says Hernani: "I am a man
in search of the King," and Don Carlos for the first time
fully shows his face—he is the King of Spain. He explains
that his grandfather, the Emperor, has just died, and he
has come to ask the aid of Don Ruy in his ambition to
succeed him. The Duke turns then to Hernani, but in a
generous impulse the King declares him one of his followers. Hernani reflects: "I am one of your followers, O
King! I'll follow your footsteps until I avenge my father's
death!"

But, by the next midnight, Don Carlos has regretted his
generosity and has ordered Hernani's arrest; for now he
also loves Doña Sol and has come to frustrate the elopement and to take the girl. He gives the signal Hernani had
arranged, and Doña Sol comes from the castle. The King

seizes her. As she calls for her lover, Hernani and his followers, far outnumbering the King's men, rush in and the
outlaw exultantly gives Don Carlos a chance for his life in
a duel.

But the King will not fight, and Hernani, repaying his
enemy's earlier chivalry, snaps his own sword upon the
pavement, allowing the King and his men to leave. His
gallantry, however, has made the elopement impossible:
the roads will be guarded; even now the alarm bells for
his capture are heard. He flees again into hiding and Doña
Sol returns sadly to the castle.

Now Doña Sol's uncle, old Don Ruy, fearful that he will
lose her and "insanely jealous, yet ashamed of my jealousy," has ordered that she marry him this very night. He
is awaiting her when a pilgrim is ushered in. Doña Sol
appears in her wedding dress, and the pilgrim tears off his
robe, revealing himself as Hernani. He cries: "I, too, am
to be wedded tonight. . . . My bride—how ardently I
long for her!—is Death." He urges Don Ruy to have him
arrested, but the nobleman refuses to harm a guest and
goes to have the castle guarded against his capture.

On his return, he finds Doña Sol in Hernani's arms. He
reproaches him, and is concealing him in a secret wall
chamber when bugles announce the arrival of the King.
Don Carlos demands the surrender of Hernani, but Don
Ruy refuses, choosing even to die with the outlaw before
betraying a guest. Don Carlos orders the Duke's arrest,
and Doña Sol scornfully declares he lacks a Spaniard's
heart. He tells her:

"It is you that have caused the wrath that is in my heart.
In your presence a man becomes an angel or a monster.
Had you willed it so, you could have made me great and
noble—the lion of Castile. But your disdain has transformed
me into a tiger." To Don Ruy he says: "Very well, be
faithful to your guest, and faithless to your King. I pardon
you, but I take your niece, Doña Sol, as a hostage."

He leaves with his men and the girl, and Don Ruy re-
leases Hernani from his hiding place to tell him what has
happened. The outlaw discloses to Don Ruy that Don

Carlos has only coveted Doña Sol, and begs that he be allowed to join in pursuit of the party. He offers his life in gratitude, and, as a token, removes his horn from his girdle and gives it to Don Ruy, saying: "Whenever you decree that my time has come, blow on this horn, and I will be ready to go to my death." He gives his hand in the pledge.

But Don Carlos is not captured. Don Ruy and Hernani now plot with others for his overthrow. They meet at night in the vaults of Charlemagne's tomb and draw lots to determine who shall kill the King. Hernani is chosen, to his great joy. Don Ruy begs the honor, offering in return to restore the outlaw's horn and release him from his oath—even to yield Doña Sol to him, but Hernani chooses revenge.

Then the booming of a cannon, signaling the election of Don Carlos as Emperor of Europe, is heard. Soldiers rush into the vaults—the King had been warned of the plot. The conspirators are quickly disarmed; Don Carlos orders that only the nobles shall be held. Hernani steps forward with a claim to be included among them. "I am," he declares, "the Duke of Segorbe and Cardona, Count of Albaterra, and Lord of more domains than I can name. I was born in exile when my father was slain by order of the King."

Don Carlos, magnanimous now as the Emperor, says: "So you are the son of sires with whom my sires dealt unjustly. . . ." He not only pardons Hernani but bestows upon him Doña Sol for his bride. He also forgives the other plotters, and calls upon the brooding Don Ruy to forgive Hernani as well. But the nobleman declares: "I will never forgive nor forget!" Later, among the merrymakers at the wedding of Doña Sol and Hernani, is seen a sinister figure with eyes burning behind his black mask.

At last the guests are gone and the lovers are alone. Doña Sol, at the balustrade, cries happily: "The torches are out. The music is done. Night is alone with us. No cloud in the sky. All things are at peace. Peace . . . calmness . . . joy." Hernani adds: "Joy, joy forever. Our sorrows are at an end." Then there comes the blast of a horn from the darkness. It is Don Ruy, the man in the black mask, come to demand the pledged life of Hernani. He hands a cup of poison to Hernani, who pleads: "For pity's sake, wait until tomorrow. Give us at least this one night of love!"

Don Ruy answers inexorably: "For you tomorrow will never come. You die tonight."

Doña Sol begs for "an hour for my love—just one short hour!" But her uncle answers: "The grave is open, and I cannot wait."

The bride snatches the cup and drinks half of the poison; Hernani drinks the rest. As they meet in a last embrace, Don Ruy's jealous spirit pursues them into death. He stabs himself and falls dead at their feet.

The Barber of Seville

BY BEAUMARCHAIS

Born in Paris in 1732, his full name being Pierre Augustin Caron de Beaumarchais. Son of a watchmaker, he learned his father's trade and was appointed watchmaker to King Louis XV when he was twenty-two. He married the widow of a court official, and took the name of "Beaumarchais." He wrote a sentimental drama, "Eugénie," in 1767. This was followed by his "Memoirs" which were very widely read. During the next few years he was in the King's service, at one time inducing the French government (secretly) to give money and ammunition to the American colonists in their war against Britain, and carrying on, privately, an enormous traffic in arms to America. During this period, he also produced the two comedies for which he is most famous—"The Barber of Seville" and "The Marriage of Figaro." They are both best known today through their adaptation for opera by Rossini and Mozart, respectively. In 1792, following the outbreak of the French

*Revolution, he was accused of treason to the republic
and was imprisoned. He was later released, and sought
refuge in Holland and England. He returned to Paris in
1796, and died there May 18, 1799.*

Happy-go-lucky Figaro, roving barber of Seville, is strolling
the streets with his guitar when he chances upon a former
employer, the young Count Almaviva, and consequently
a problem in romance well suited to his roguish wit. The
Count has seen and fallen in love with Rosine, a beautiful
young lady who is the ward and unwilling fiancée of Dr.
Bartholo, an old tyrant who generally keeps her well concealed behind locked doors.

Disguised as a poor student, the Count comes each
morning to glimpse Rosine when she can elude Bartholo
and appear at her window. It is here beneath her window
that he has met Figaro. Rosine has just managed to drop
a note written on the score of a song, "The Useless Precaution." It reads: "I don't know who you are, but your
devotion excites my curiosity. . . . Sing a few words to
the tune of the song on this sheet. Disclose your name,
your rank and your intentions to the unfortunate Rosine."
He takes Figaro's guitar and sings: "My name is Lindor,
sweet, and I adore thee!" She replies: "Thy love and adora-
tion I return. . . ."

The elated Count declares he must save her from Dr.
Bartholo, and Figaro, warning that Bartholo plans to wed
Rosine the next day, offers a plan: Figaro is the Doctor's
apothecary as well as his barber, and he will drug the
servants; then the Count can enter the house in the guise
of an army officer who must have lodging but is apparently
too drunk to wish for flirtation. This is agreed upon after
Figaro, holding out his hand, observes: "It is gold that
greases the wheels of love."

Next, Figaro is waiting in Rosine's room while she writes
a note to the presumed poor student, Lindor. He hides
in a closet when Bartholo appears to voice suspicion that
the barber has drugged the servants. The Doctor says he

is going to lock her window blind now, and she flounces from the room as Don Bazile, her music teacher, comes to warn Bartholo that Count Almaviva is walking the streets in disguise, evidently seeking Rosine. He advises Bartholo to slander Lindor and agrees to arrange the wedding, but he hints that "gold makes the strongest link in the matrimonial chain."

Figaro slips out to urge the Count to hasten, and Almaviva soon appears at Bartholo's house in the role of a drunken trooper. He whispers to Rosine that he is Lindor and hands her a letter; but, after outraging Bartholo with his jeers, he is ordered out of the house. Bartholo demands the letter, but Rosine deftly exchanges it for a harmless note from her cousin. Bartholo then leaves. Rosine reads Almaviva's note and exclaims: "Ah, it's too late! He asked me to start a quarrel with my guardian, so he could carry me off in the scuffle. . . . Now he is gone and I'm to be wedded to my evil fate. . . . What shall I do?"

But the Count tries again, in a new disguise. He tells Bartholo that Bazile is ill and that he, his pupil, has come to help prepare for the marriage. Bartholo urges that he allay any suspicions Rosine may have by saying he has come to give her a music lesson. The Count happily agrees, but the jealous Doctor seats himself before them. He nods sleepily, however, and the Count again identifies himself to Rosine as Lindor. Their kisses awaken Bartholo, and Figaro comes to the rescue.

He suggests that Bartholo go with him to be shaved, but the Doctor orders that he be shaved where he is, and gives Figaro his keys to fetch the utensils. Behind his back, Figaro winks and holds aloft the key to the window blind. Then, by making a clatter in Bartholo's room, he lures the Doctor out to investigate. The Count hurriedly whispers: "Good old Figaro! . . . You are going to escape tonight, through your window. He will unlock your blind with that key which he showed us."

Bartholo and Figaro have returned, the barber again making meaningful gestures with the key, when another crisis confronts the conspirators: Bazile enters. Bartholo tells him that "his pupil" has reported him ill, and Bazile exclaims: "This young man?" He is further confused when Bartholo, at the Count's whispered warning that "Rosine mustn't suspect anything, you know," enjoins Bazile in another aside: "Don't say that he is not your pupil. Rosine must be kept in the dark."

When Rosine adds to his confusion with another whisper: "The less you say, the better," Don Bazile whispers to Figaro: "What the devil is the meaning of all this? Everybody seems to have a secret." The Count breaks the chain of whispers by handing Bazile a purse and telling him: "Go to bed. You're sick." This cue is joyously received by all the plotters who chorus that Bazile indeed looks sick and should go to bed. Bazile agrees that, come to think of it, he does feel rather funny. He leaves abruptly.

Figaro begins to shave Bartholo, standing between him and the lovers, but the wary Doctor spies them as they are about to embrace and shouts an accusation. Rosine leaves angrily, and Figaro says: "I don't blame her. A young woman and an old man! Why, sir, you're mad!" He goes out. The Count declares: "I quite agree with Figaro; old man, you're mad." He, too, departs. Now Bartholo, distrusting his own eyes, wonders if he really did see them embrace. Suspecting, too, that he may be going mad, he calls for Bazile.

It is nearly midnight, and he orders Bazile to bring the notary to marry him and Rosine before morning. Bazile tells him that the notary can't come before four o'clock as he has to marry Figaro's niece. Bartholo's suspicions are now confirmed, since he knows Figaro has no niece. To spoil the plot, he tells Rosine that Lindor is untrue to her and is making sport of her love by giving her letters to Count Almaviva. Rosine believes him, and in her humiliation confesses that she and Lindor were to escape that night through the window, but that she will marry her guardian instead. Bartholo gleefully goes off to bring the police to trap Lindor.

While he is absent, the Count and Figaro enter through the window, and the reproachful Rosine is startled to learn that her lover is not the poor student Lindor but the noble, Count Almaviva. Don Bazile returns with the notary, and the Count instructs the official to marry him and Rosine. The protesting Bazile, handed the Count's purse, says: "I'm always convinced by a heavy argument."

The ceremony is no sooner over when Bartholo bustles in with the police. He cries: "What's this? You have stolen my bride?" The Count replies: "Yes, and you have stolen her property." Bartholo calls him an "impertinent young student," and Figaro warns: "Be careful, you are speaking to his Excellency, the Lord Count Almaviva." Bartholo quickly protests that he is the Count's humble servant and Almaviva shows mercy: he could have Bartholo arrested for misuse of his ward's money, he declares, but will let him keep the fortune if he will withdraw his claim upon Rosine.

Don Bazile: *Friend Bartholo, always listen to a weighty argument.*

Bartholo: *But to think that I have been outwitted in spite of all my precautions!*

Figaro: *All your foolishness, you mean. An old man's defense against the wiles of young love may well be called "The Useless Precaution."*

The Misanthrope

BY MOLIÈRE

Born in Paris, January, 1622, his real name being Jean Baptiste Poquelin. He had a good education at the college at Clermont, and ample opportunity to develop an interest in the stage, as many of the friends of his family were actors. On leaving Clermont he was sent to the law school at Orléans, but left the latter to join a traveling troupe of players. It was at this time that he assumed the stage name of Molière. The troupe was at first unsuccessful, but later

performed before King Louis XIV and obtained royal pa-
tronage. The star of the troupe was Armande Béjart, whom
Molière married and for whom he wrote many of his
plays. In rapid succession a series of masterly dramatic
comedies was produced. In addition to "Tartuffe" and
"The Misanthrope," the following are among the best
known of his plays: "Les Précieuses Ridicules," "A Physi-
cian in Spite of Himself," "The Miser," and "Le Bourgeois
Gentilhomme." "Tartuffe" portrays a religious hypocrite,
and the play was bitterly attacked; for years Molière was
not permitted to give it publicly because of the strong
animosities it aroused. About a week after the first showing
of "The Imaginary Invalid," in February, 1673, Molière re-
turned from the theater suffering from cold and inflamma-
tion, and suddenly died. A great crowd attended his
funeral, but the Archbishop of Paris forbade the clergy to
perform a religious ceremony.

Alceste, a gentleman of Paris, announces to his friend
Philinte, during a conversation at the home of Célimène,
that he is outraged by the insincerity of society—he would
have no word spoken that is not from the heart. Philinte
protests that custom demands pretense—in many cases
plain speaking would become ridiculous. But Alceste declares himself so grieved by the flattery, selfishness and
deceit about him that he intends to break with all mankind,
and to voice nothing but the truth thenceforth.

He is particularly bitter because of a lawsuit against a
despised citizen who continues to be received everywhere
with smiles, and declares that in court he will depend only
upon reason, his just right, and equity. If he loses, he will
be convinced of the wickedness and perversity of all men.

Philinte asks if his war against the human race is to
extend to Célimène, the lady he loves. He wonders why
Alceste is cold to Eliante, her sincere cousin, and the
prude, Arsinoë, yet suffers the malicious wit of Célimène.
Alceste replies that her charms conquer his scruples, but he

expects that his love will purify her heart of the vices of the times.

They are interrupted by Oronte, also a suitor of Célimène, who asks Alceste to criticize some of his verses. Philinte is conventionally approving, but Alceste bluntly tells Oronte he had better put the sonnet in his closet and seek someone else to flatter him. Philinte forestalls blows, but at their parting Alceste slips in his intention sufficiently to say: "I, sir, am your most humble servant."

Célimène arrives, and Alceste reproaches her for fickleness, but she soothes him with the pledge that it is he alone whom she loves. However, she also receives Acaste and Clitandre, additional admirers who arrive with Eliante, and Alceste informs her that he will not leave until she makes her choice.

During the conversation, Célimène acidly criticizes everyone mentioned, and Alceste rebukes the gentlemen for encouraging her slander by flattery. He declares he will not leave until they leave, and they decide to stay as long as he does. The deadlock is broken when a guard arrives to summon Alceste before the Marshals of France who wish to avert a duel between him and Oronte. When he has gone, Acaste and Clitandre make a compact that the first to have a proof of Célimène's love shall leave the field free to the other.

Now the prudish Arsinoë, whom Célimène views as simply envious, arrives to give her some advice "as a matter of duty"; she says that people are talking about Célimène's conduct—"not that I believe that decency is in any way outraged." Célimène retorts that Arsinoë's prudery and too fervent zeal also are a topic, and that Arsinoë (so others say) would do well to concern herself less about the actions of others and take more pains with her own. The conversation warms to the point where Arsinoë intimates that Célimène's admirers are drawn not entirely by her virtue, when Alceste returns. For the moment—left alone with Alceste—Arsinoë warns him that Célimène is untrue to him, and induces him to accompany her to her home where she claims proof of it.

Philinte, meanwhile, returns to Célimène's house to tell
Eliante that Alceste has maintained his stubbornness before
the Marshals, and only with difficulty has been induced to
modify his criticism of Oronte's sonnet and be reconciled.
Eliante declares herself willing to love Alceste should he
fail with Célimène, and Philinte asks that he, too, be considered should Alceste and Célimène wed.

At this point Alceste storms back. "It is all over with
me. . . . My love . . . Célimène deceives me and is faithless . . . I have in my pocket a letter in her own handwriting . . . intended for Oronte," he declares. He appeals
to Eliante to accept him in revenge, but she is skeptical
of the constancy of his anger. Célimène is shown the letter;
she first intimates that it was not written to Oronte but to
a woman; then, angered by his chiding, she tells him that
it was sent to his rival, and that Alceste would please
her by leaving. Alceste, however, declares he must submit
to his love for her.

He is summoned home by an urgent message, and now a
new blow falls on him: his faith in justice is shattered at the
loss of his lawsuit, and the victor and Oronte are ascribing
to him authorship of a scandalous book; he is in danger of
arrest. He hurries back to Célimène's home to test her
love—and finds Oronte there. Both men demand that she
choose between them, but she insists that gentler intima-
tions suffice.

Arsinoë, Eliante, Philinte, Acaste, and Clitandre now
join them, the latter two to confront Célimène with her
compared letters to them. The missives ridicule Acaste and
Clitandre as well as Alceste and Oronte. Clitandre declares
he will expose her faithless heart everywhere; Acaste deems
her beneath his anger, and in indignation Oronte leaves
Célimène to Alceste. Arsinoë deplores the treatment of
Alceste, but he tartly tells her he will manage his affairs,
and in any event will not turn to her.

Célimène admits her wrong, but declares she is only
concerned that Alceste is injured—the others she despises.
He tells her that he is willing to forget her crime if she will
accompany him into solitude; that "after the scandal which

every noble heart must abhor, it may still be possible for me to love you." She will accept marriage, but not the wilderness, and Alceste declares that since she is not disposed thus "to find all in all in me," he now loathes her.

He tells Eliante that he feels unworthy of her with only the remainder of a heart, and she and Philinte decide that they will marry.

Alceste wishes them happiness, adding: "Deceived on all sides, overwhelmed with injustice, I will fly from an abyss where vice is triumphant, and seek out some small secluded nook on earth, where one may enjoy the freedom of being an honest man."

Tartuffe

BY MOLIÈRE

The household of Orgon is in a ferment because he has installed as a privileged guest the sanctimonious and always hungry Tartuffe. Orgon refuses to believe ill of his idol, and tells his brother-in-law, Cléante: "If you only knew him, dear brother! He is a man who—well—he is a man! His converse has weaned me from all earthly love—and I could see my brother, children, wife, and mother all die before my eyes and never shed a tear. . . . The very first time I saw him, at church, I felt the presence of a godly man. He was kneeling—on both knees—and praying so fervently that he drew the eyes of the entire congregation. When I left the church, he ran before me to offer me the holy water at the door. . . . And when I gave him money, he distributed part of it to the poor. . . .

"I asked him to come to my house—it was an inspiration from Heaven—and from that day on, everything has been well with us. . . . He even watches ever the virtue of my wife; he seems to be six times as jealous of her as I am. . . . You have no idea how scrupulously pious he is: why, the other day I heard him censure himself for having killed a flea!"

Cléante calls Orgon mad, and Orgon retorts that Cléante is an atheist. The brother-in-law declares he is only distinguishing between true piety and hypocrisy, that Tartuffe has "set up a trading booth on the road to Heaven" and is selling counterfeit prayers for real gold. Orgon frigidly bids him good day.

Dorine, the maid, when Orgon returns from a business trip and asks how the household—especially Tartuffe—has fared, also fails with her irony to move her master. To Orgon's persistent inquiries about Tartuffe, she tells him that his wife, Elmire, has been ill with a fever and has been bled, but the fat Tartuffe has been stuffing himself with meat and wine without pause. Orgon is concerned only for the "poor man."

Orgon's admiration for the oily intruder has extended even to offering his daughter Mariane as his bride. She is in love with the young Valère, but Orgon tells her he dislikes Valère because he doesn't go to church regularly and that she must marry Tartuffe. Valère, hearing of the decision, comes in a rage to reproach Mariane who has lacked the courage to defy her father. Valère threatens to abandon her, and the resentful Mariane tells him to go— and good riddance. But Dorine, the maid, brings them together to end their quarrel.

Another who is anxious to oust Tartuffe is Damis, the son of Orgon by a former marriage, who hides in a closet to watch Tartuffe. He sees Elmire meet with Tartuffe to protest his mating with Mariane. Tartuffe tells her that he is overjoyed to find himself alone with her, and toys with her knee (merely admiring her gown), and with the lace yoke of her dress (investigating its exquisite workmanship). Then he denies that he plans to marry Mariane—his heart is elsewhere. In Heaven, no doubt, Elmire replies, and Tartuffe passionately declares his love for the mother. Elmire threatens to tell her husband of his conduct, winning from Tartuffe the promise that he will forward the marriage of Mariane and Valère.

Damis tells Orgon what he has seen and heard, but Orgon will believe no evil of Tartuffe and, cursing Damis, sends him away. He declares Tartuffe now his son and heir, and Tartuffe piously says: "Heaven's will be done in everything. . . ." Cléante later appeals to Tartuffe to undo this wrong, but the latter asserts that it would be against the interest of Heaven for him to intercede for Damis; that he is the humble instrument of the Lord, called upon to save Orgon's estate from ignoble hands.

Elmire is no more successful in her effort to turn Orgon against the parasite, but she does prevail upon him to hide under a table to witness the conduct of Tartuffe, who comes eagerly at her summons.

Elmire: *I've been thinking about those passionate words of yours.*

Tartuffe: *Ah, madam, are you ready to listen to them now?*

Elmire: *Perhaps.*

Tartuffe: *The thought of your love, madam, is the one beatitude of my heart. How happy my heart would be if you could grant me a positive proof of your love!*

Elmire: *But how can I grant what you request without offending Heaven?*

Tartuffe: *Never fear about that. I know the ways of Heaven. If our love remains secret, Heaven itself will shut its eyes. A secret sin is accounted no sin at all.*

Elmire: *But what about my husband?*

Tartuffe: *He's a man we can both lead by the nose. . . .*

He is about to embrace Elmire when Orgon emerges, refuses to listen further to Tartuffe's hypocrisy, and orders him from the house. Now Tartuffe drops his pious mask and declares that it is Orgon, not himself, who shall leave the house. He stalks arrogantly from the room, and the dumfounded Orgon recalls that indeed it is Tartuffe's house: in his rage at Damis, Orgon at once deeded it to Tartuffe. Further, he finds that the rascal has made off with a box which he had entrusted to him—a box containing incriminating documents left for safekeeping with Orgon by an exiled friend, a revolutionist. Thus Tartuffe has the means also to denounce Orgon as a traitor.

Tartuffe mercilessly employs his every treacherous power to ruin the man who befriended him; he not only sends a bailiff to eject Orgon and his family, but hurries straight to the King with his story that Orgon has befriended an enemy of the Crown. Valère runs in to warn Orgon to flee, but Tartuffe and a King's officer are close behind him. Orgon denounces Tartuffe, who replies only: "I forgive your insults. Heaven has taught me to be patient in all things." To the officer, he adds: "Pray, sir, do your duty."

But the officer turns upon the amazed Tartuffe and announces that he, not Orgon, is going to prison. To Orgon the officer explains: "You, sir, may dismiss all your fears. The King has sharp and discerning eyes . . . he has seen through this scoundrel's hypocrisy. . . . In accusing you, Tartuffe has incriminated himself." He says further that the King has granted to Orgon a full pardon for aiding his exiled friend and, besides, has restored his property.

The happy Orgon accepts Valère as his son-in-law, hoping that the wretch Tartuffe may "reform his ways, and learn that base deception never pays."

Phèdre

BY JEAN RACINE

Born at La Ferté-Milon, France, in December, 1639. He was a diligent and apt student at both the Collège de Beauvais (a grammar school) and Port Royal. In Paris he associated with Boileau, La Fontaine, and Molière. Through some odes and sonnets written to Louis XIV, he attracted the attention and interest of the King, and received certain "gratifications" for several years. Now began a series of dramatic representations that established Racine's reputation as the greatest modern tragedian in the

*classical tradition. The series opened with "Andromache"
(1667), and ended with "Phèdre" which started a bitter
competition with disastrous effects on Racine's genius. This
competition resulted from the rivalry of a second theatrical
company which, with ample financial resources, produced
another version of "Phèdre" and, for the time being,
eclipsed Racine's play. He was so disturbed by the difficulties of his situation, after thirteen years of unbroken success, that he stopped writing. Soon after this he married,
and his life became domestic rather than dramatic. During
the next twenty years he wrote only two plays. He died
April 12, 1699.*

A morbid love triangle involving King Theseus of Athens,
his wife, Phaedra (which in French is Phèdre), and his son
by a former marriage, Hippolytus, is revealed by the Queen
to her nurse while the family is staying at Troezen, in the
Peloponnesus, during Theseus' absence at war. Phaedra
has not eaten or slept for three days, and tells the nurse,
Oenone, that she wants only to die.

"And you want to betray your child?" Oenone protests.
"The day that robs him of his mother will see him en-
slaved to Hippolytus. For if you die, Hippolytus usurps the
throne; but if you live, the throne belongs to your son."
Phaedra reveals that she can no longer endure her shame,
that it is for Hippolytus that she dies.

"Hippolytus? Your husband's son? And your own son's
rival for the throne? Aye, shame to you indeed!" the nurse
exclaims. Phaedra answers: "I hate my life, Oenone, and I
hold my love in horror. In death I wish to purify my
heart. I must bury this guilty passion in the grave. . . ."

But here enters Panope, a waiting-woman, with news
that Theseus has been reported dead, and Oenone promptly
points out to Phaedra that now she must live to protect the
interests of both her young son and Hippolytus from another heir, Arica, an Athenian woman of royal blood now
living in Troezen as an exile. The nurse suggests that Hippolytus remain as King of Troezen and that Phaedra's son

assume the throne at Athens. Phaedra reluctantly agrees.

Hippolytus, unaware of the Queen's passion for him, has long loved Arica but has kept silent because of a blood feud between their families. Now, with Theseus dead, he goes to tell her of his love and to propose that he shall rule in Troezen, Phaedra's son in Crete, and that Arica shall take her rightful place on the throne of Athens. He has just confessed his love to the receptive Arica when Phaedra enters and is left alone with him.

The Queen appeals to Hippolytus to help protect her son's succession. Hippolytus attempts to comfort her with the possibility that Theseus may still be alive, but Phaedra exclaims: "The King is dead . . . and yet he lives . . . he lives and breathes in you, Hippolytus. . . . I seem to speak to him when I say 'I love you!'"

Hippolytus is aghast, and reminds her that Theseus is his father and her husband, but Phaedra goes on: "I have not forgotten. I love you and I feel guilty of my love. You cannot hate me half as much as I hate myself. I did not come to make this vile confession; I came to plead for my son . . . but my heart is too full of love for you. Come, take your revenge, punish my hateful passion, rid the world of an offensive monster! Here is my heart. Pierce it with your sword!"

Hippolytus stands dazed. The Queen, declaring that she will stab herself, seizes his sword and runs from the room. As she leaves, Theramenes, tutor to Hippolytus, hastens in to tell that Phaedra's son has been elected King of Athens, and that King Theseus now is reported still alive. Hippolytus goes to search for Theseus, to "give the scepter back to worthy hands."

Theseus does return and Phaedra is in terror, fearing either that Hippolytus, whom she now hates for scorning her love, will expose her to the King, or that she will betray herself even should he keep silent. She hopes again for death, but Oenone urges a plot whereby Hippolytus shall die instead: the Queen shall accuse him first, offering his sword as evidence that he has come to her. Phaedra recoils at the thought of herself slandering an innocent man, but allows Oenone to accuse him.

Theseus summons Hippolytus and condemns him: "Traitor, how dare you show yourself to me after you have tried to defile my bed with your adulterous lust! . . . Never set your foot again upon this soil! . . . And to thee, O Neptune, Lord of the Sea, I utter this solemn prayer: avenge a father's wrong, and overwhelm with thy waves this son who no longer is a son of mine!"

The dumfounded Hippolytus protests that he is guiltless; but, to spare his father, he refrains from telling of the Queen's infidelity. He replies only: "I might be pardoned if I told the truth but it concerns your honor to conceal it. . . . Know this, my father, I am innocent . . . I love not Phaedra, but Arica." Theseus will not believe him, nor will he relent later when the conscience-stricken Phaedra pleads for him. But when the King mentions that Hippolytus, in his denial, has revealed his love for Arica, the jealous Queen makes no further effort to save the exiled youth.

Hippolytus goes to Arica who implores him to tell the truth to his father. He answers: "To do this would but bring disgrace upon my father's name. . . . The gods are just . . . sooner or later, Phaedra will be punished. . . ." Hippolytus and Arica plan to flee from Troezen, and he goes to prepare for the journey.

Theseus goes to warn Arica against Hippolytus, who declares: "My love can see his true nobility. . . . I could tell you a tale . . . but your son has forbidden me to speak." The King begins to suspect that there may be more of the story than he has heard from Oenone and the Queen, and sends for the former to question her again. But Oenone, to atone for her crime, has plunged to her death in the sea, and Phaedra, too, has attempted suicide. This convinces Theseus, and he sends for Hippolytus to ask his forgiveness. But Theramenes, the tutor, brings these tidings:

"Your son is no more. . . . He was driving his chariot on the seashore when Neptune sent a towering billow upon the land, with a sea-monster reaching out of the foam. Hippolytus stopped the chariot and gave battle to the monster." The horses, he continues, galloped away in fright, the chariot collapsed, Hippolytus was entangled in the reins and dragged to the shore. Before dying, he told Theramenes: "The gods have robbed me of an innocent life. Tell my father to treat Arica tenderly."

Phaedra enters and Theseus tells her: "Madam, you have triumphed. . . . My son is killed. . . . Accept your victim. . . . You have had your wish. . . ."

Phaedra answers: "I will have my wish now. Your son is guiltless, and I, the guilty one, will soon be dead. A subtle poison runs through my veins. . . . Already as through a thickening mist I see the husband to whom my presence is an abomination. My eyes are closing upon the light that they defiled." She dies. Theseus says:

"Would that her memory would die with her forever! . . . The gods deprive, and the gods restore. They have taken away my son, and they have given me a daughter. Arica shall be my child. . . ."

The Cid

BY PIERRE CORNEILLE

Born in Rouen, June 6, 1606, he was educated by the Jesuits of Rouen. At the age of eighteen he was appointed an advocate, and later an "advocate to the admiralty." His first play, "Mélite," was produced in 1629 and was extremely popular. In 1634 he met Cardinal Richelieu and, for several years, was employed, with four other writers, in putting Richelieu's ideas into dramatic form. He incurred Richelieu's displeasure, however, and his great jealousy at the time of the presentation, in 1636, of "The Cid," based on the life of the eleventh-century Spanish soldier and national hero. "The Cid" was Corneille's masterpiece and

*marks the beginning of modern French drama. It was fol-
lowed by other tragedies—"Horace," "Cinna," and "Poly-
eucte"—and by a comedy, "The Liar." The breach between
Corneille and Richelieu was healed, and the latter allowed
Corneille five hundred crowns a year. There followed years
of prolific writing—comedies, tragedies, verse—but, from
1674 until his death on September 30, 1684, Corneille produced little more than an occasional poem.*

Rodrigue, a young cavalier, is loved by Urraque, Princess
of Spanish Castile; but, as she cannot be the bride of a
commoner, she consents, in "a mingled sense of joy and
pain," to Rodrigue's betrothal to Chimène, daughter of
Count Gomez.

Rodrigue's romance, however, soon meets with tragedy.
Diegue, his father, is tutor to the King's son, a position
coveted by Count Gomez. The jealous Count strikes
Diegue, and the latter challenges him to a duel. Gomez
scornfully refuses: "You are too old to fight a powerful
swordsman like me. . . . I draw my weapon only against
a worthy opponent."

The humiliated Diegue begs Rodrigue to avenge him,
and the son faces the cruel problem of whether to fight his
beloved's father or leave undefended the honor of his own.
He reflects: "Whatever course I follow, misfortune follows
me." But honor triumphs over love and he kills Gomez in
a duel. He thus earns not only the hatred of Chimène but
the anger of the King, for the Count was a valuable soldier.

Chimène, alive with the desire to avenge her own father,
condemns her lover before the King, demanding justice.
Diegue defends his son and offers himself for punishment
instead. The King defers his decision to await the opinion
of his councilors. Rodrigue, mourning that "sharper than
death to me is the knowledge of her hatred," goes to
Chimène to offer his life as a sacrifice to her father's memory. Chimène agrees that he should die in atonement. She
tells him: "My strength must equal yours. Like you, I

must prove my courage for my father's sake. If I let you live, you must hate me for my cowardice. By your death alone can I prove myself worthy of your love."

Rodrigue replies: "It is sweet death that comes through your dear hand," and she finds that she cannot strike him. She bids him: "Go hide yourself from the King . . . leave me to my shame . . . your life is dearer to me than my honor."

But instead of hiding, Rodrigue replaces the dead Count Gomez as leader of the Spanish army and defeats the Moorish invaders. Summoned to court, he explains to the King that he had not dared to ask the monarch's consent to join in the battle, and had wished only to die in his service rather than in prison while his comrades were fighting. The King promptly dubs him the Cid, the Hero of Castile, and grants him full pardon for the killing of Gomez.

Chimène, again steeling herself against her love, protests the pardon. When the King rejects her plea that Rodrigue pay with his life, she calls for a cavalier to avenge her honor, his reward for Rodrigue's head to be herself as a bride. The King objects to so risking the life of the valuable Cid, but Rodrigue's father seconds Chimène's appeal, saying that it is only right that his son should pay his debt upon the field of honor. Sancho, a young gallant, challenges Rodrigue to win Chimène, and the Cid goes to bid her farewell.

He tells her that he is going to his death, and has come to salute her. "Why must you die?" she asks. Rodrigue replies: "To satisfy your hatred with my life. . . . Your champion shall find me an easy adversary. . . . I shall offer no defense, for I shall feel that it is your hand that is wielding Sancho's sword."

Chimène protests: "That would be the act of a coward! . . . You would allow the conqueror of my father to be conquered by this unskilled stripling?" Rodrigue insists that he has lost her love to save his honor, and now shall lose his life to regain her love.

"Live, Rodrigue," Chimène decides, "and deliver me from Sancho's arms. Go, fight him, help me to fulfill my duty to my father, but plan a sure defense. . . . And when you come back, if your heart still beats for your poor Chimène, why then—who knows? Forgive my blushing confession, and go."

The elated Rodrigue goes forth with the cry: "Come on, Castile, Navarre, Morocco, the flower of Spain! My single sword I'll match against your combined power! I'll have my honor and my love again. I'll fight the world and win —for my Chimène."

Chimène awaits in torment the outcome of the duel, reflecting that if Rodrigue wins, she will marry the slayer of her father; if Sancho wins, her bridegroom will be the slayer of her lover—the victory of either will bring her a husband "steeped in blood that I adore." Then Sancho enters and offers her his sword. She cries: "What! dripping with my lover's blood? How dare you show yourself to me!" He implores her to hear his report, but she will not listen to his "boastful tale of murder." The King enters with Diegue, and she finally confesses her love for Rodrigue, lamenting that he is now dead at her command.

"Now that she is no longer ashamed of her love, speak to her, sire," old Diegue urges, and the King tells Chimène that Rodrigue still lives. Sancho, now given opportunity to speak, says that Rodrigue, after disarming him, mercifully returned his sword and bade him place it as a trophy at Chimène's feet. The King assures her that she has vindicated her honor and now may accept Rodrigue's love.

Rodrigue enters, accompanied by the forlorn Princess Urraque. She is still in love with him and can properly marry him since he has become a noble, but for love of Chimène she forgoes her own happiness and brings Rodrigue and Chimène together. Chimène smilingly murmurs: "I accept my verdict. It is a royal command, and I obey."

The King directs, however, that the marriage wait a year, "for time cures all and conquers all"; Chimène will dry her tears for her father's death and Rodrigue will expel the Moors. The King urges him to "let the name of Cid become a terror to the foe, and the love of Chimène an

290FRENCH PLAYS

inspiration to your friends." Rodrigue obeys, and says: "I
thank your majesty for your kindly words, and I will do
my best to be worthy of them. My arm is iron and my
heart is flame to wed my love and win a glorious name."

BELGIAN PLAYS

Pelléas and Mélisande

BY MAURICE MAETERLINCK

Born at Ghent, Belgium, August 29, 1862, of Flemish extraction. He was educated at the College Sainte-Barbe, then at the University of Ghent where he was enrolled as a barrister. His literary career began in 1889 when he published a volume of verse, "Serres Chaudes," and a play, "La Princesse Maleine." He remained virtually unknown, however, until an article about him was published in the Paris Figaro; in it he was referred to as "a Belgian Shakespeare," and, because of the enthusiasm of the author of the article, Octave Mirbeau, and the excellence of the passages he quoted, Maeterlinck became famous overnight. "The Blue Bird" was produced with great success in America, and may fittingly be called a children's classic. "Pelléas and Mélisande," written in 1892, was set to music by Debussy and is one of the great modern operas. Other of Maeterlinck's plays are, "Monna Vanna" and "Sister Beatrice." In 1940 he came to live in the United States. He died in 1949.

At an imagined castle in an imagined land, maidservants are washing the steps, gate and threshold of the castle, but a porter mocks them: "Scrub on. Pour on water . . . pour on all the water of the Flood! You will never be able to wash this castle clean. . . ."

At the edge of a spring in a twilight forest, Mélisande, a lovely young girl, is discovered by Golaud, the grandson of King Arkel. She cries that she will throw herself in the water if he touches her. Golaud reassures her, and asks if anyone has hurt her. Yes, she says, everyone. Where has she come from? She answers, "I have come from far away . . . I am lost." He bids her to come with him, but where he does not know. "I, too, am lost," he tells her.

Golaud takes her to his grandfather's dreary castle where people walk with heavy hearts. Here, old King Arkel says, its people see "only the reverse of their destinies—we never get what we long for most. . . . And yet, whatever happens may be right in the end. . . ." Golaud learns nothing more about Mélisande, but he marries her. With them live Yniold, Golaud's son by a first wife, and his brother, Pelléas, the younger grandson of King Arkel.

Pelléas at length realizes that he is coming to love Mélisande. He attempts to leave the castle, but his father is ill and bids him remain. Struggling with his problem, he walks on the seashore and meets Mélisande. He tells her that he is going away. Her sorrow at this news is revealing, but their innocent relationship continues; they meet again at an abandoned spring called "Blind Man's Well" because it is reputed to have restored sight.

Mélisande, at the spring's edge, plays with her wedding ring and it falls into the water. "I threw it too high, toward the sun," she explains to Pelléas; but later, she is afraid to tell Golaud the truth. "I dropped it at the seashore," she says, "but I know where it is." Golaud bids her find it, suggesting, when she pleads fear of going alone, that she ask Pelléas to accompany her.

She answers: "Pelléas? . . . With Pelléas? . . . Oh, I am so unhappy . . . so unhappy! . . ."

Pelléas again attempts to leave the castle, but is dissuaded. He comes upon Mélisande at a tower window, combing her long hair and singing:

> "My hair falls foaming
> Down from the tower;
> It waits for thy coming
> This long, long hour.
> This long, long hour . . ."

Pelléas calls to her: "I have never seen so many stars.
. . . Bend forward, Mélisande, that I may look at your un-
bound hair. . . . Lean out and let me touch your hand,
Mélisande. . . . I leave tomorrow." She answers: "If you
go, I will not give you my hand. . . . Will you stay?"
Pelléas says that he will stay awhile. As Mélisande leans
out to touch his hand her hair falls over him.

"All your locks, Mélisande, all your locks have fallen
about me," he murmurs. "I hold them in my arms . . . I
bathe my face within them . . . They are sweet, sweet as
if they fell from Heaven. . . . You are my prisoner tonight,
Mélisande—all night, all night. . . ." Golaud comes upon
them, watches them for a moment, and sadly speaks: "You
are children . . . Do not play in the darkness . . . What
strange children!"

Later, Golaud sits with Yniold under Mélisande's window and asks the child if "little mother" is often with Uncle
Pelléas. The boy answers: "Yes, yes . . . Always, when
you are not there. . . . They weep . . . They seem to be
afraid. . . . Kiss? Oh, yes . . . once . . . When it rained."
Golaud lifts the child to see above the sill, and the boy
reports Pelléas and Mélisande within: "They just stand and
stare . . . They never close their eyes . . . Take me down,
little father. . . . I am terribly afraid. . . ."

One day, Golaud flies into an unexplained rage; he seizes
Mélisande by her hair, forcing her to the ground. She declares this the end of his love, and, at a fountain in the
forest, keeps a rendezvous with Pelléas who is leaving at
last. Now they openly confess their love, lingering until
they hear the palace gates closing. Happy that they cannot
go back, they embrace—then see Golaud approaching.
They pray that he will kill them both. They kiss each other.
Pelléas cries: "The stars are descending!" Mélisande is crying out, "On me, too!" when Golaud's sword pierces his
brother. Mélisande flees, her husband in pursuit.

The servants, talking of the tragedy, report that both
Golaud and Mélisande have been found outstretched before the castle gate, Golaud wounded by his own sword
and Mélisande dying, though hardly scratched. Says one:

"Ah me, and she was delivered of her babe only three days ago." Pelléas, another declares, was found at the bottom of Blind Man's Well.

The physician finds that Mélisande's wound could not have killed a bird, yet she is "dying without a reason . . . just as she was born without a purpose." Golaud laments: "I have killed her without a cause! . . . They had kissed like little children . . . merely kissed. . . . They were brother and sister. . . . And I, in spite of myself, I killed them!"

Mélisande awakens. At Golaud's plea for forgiveness, she asks what it is that she is to forgive. He replies: "I have wrought you so much evil, Mélisande. . . . I see it all so clearly now—when it is too late. . . . Tell the truth to a dying man, Mélisande. . . . Did you love him—with a forbidden love? . . . Were you . . . were you guilty?"

She answers: "No . . . we were not guilty. . . . The truth. . . . The sun is down . . . I am so afraid of the great cold. . . ." Her baby is brought to her, but she can only look sorrowfully upon it and mourn: "She is so little . . . and she is weeping. . . . I pity her. . . ." She closes her eyes. Golaud begs her to listen, pleading: "It was not my fault! . . . It was a power beyond me!"

But old Arkel silences him: "Hush! . . . She must not be disturbed. . . . The human soul likes to depart in silence . . . alone."

ITALIAN PLAYS

Six Characters in Search of an Author

BY LUIGI PIRANDELLO

Born in Sicily in 1867, he was educated in Rome and at the University of Bonn, and was professor of Italian literature at the Normal College for Women in Rome from 1897 to 1921. He first wrote short stories and novels. His first play to receive recognition was "Six Characters in Search of an Author." It was produced in Rome in 1921 and quickly won international fame. After that, many of his works which had been written earlier became widely read. His outstanding literary qualities were his wit and intellectuality, and his plays and novels are usually based on philosophical problems. Other of his well-known plays are: "Henry IV," "Each in His Own Way," and "As You Desire Me." The last named was made into a motion picture starring Greta Garbo. He won the Nobel Prize for literature in 1934. He died two years later.

A theatrical company is rehearsing a comedy when six strange Characters intrude, seeking to have their dramatic story completed. They are a Father, Mother, Stepdaughter, Son, Boy and Girl. The Father explains that the author who created them has dropped them right in the middle of the tale.

The Mother, he says, is his wife, but she is in black because she is a widow—the widow of her lover. The Son is her only legitimate child; the Stepdaughter, the Boy and the Girl are children of the lover, now dead. The

Mother has come back to her husband with her illegitimate brood, but the Son protests that "the whole thing is so vile!" The Stepdaughter interjects: "Especially that incident in Madame Pace's house of ill fame," where, apparently, the Father had unknowingly consorted with her. The theater manager quickly calls for a clearing up of the tangle.

The Father starts at the beginning: A clerk at his office fell in love with his wife, and she with him, so he discharged the clerk and turned out his wife. They went to another town, and there had three children. With the lover's death, they returned and nearly starved because the Mother shrank from asking help of her husband.

The Stepdaughter and Mother found work at Madame Pace's establishment, where the Mother was a milliner and the Stepdaughter one of the pretty girls whom Madame Pace supplied to rich gentlemen. The Father met her there and, he says, the Mother interrupted them "in the nick of time." But the girl contradicts this maliciously: "Almost in time!" The Father then took them all to his home.

The Stepdaughter interrupts: "Not a home, but a mere lodging. This Son of his regarded us as intruders who had come to disturb the kingdom of his legitimacy. It was his unbearable behavior that made me so defiant—that transformed me from his father's guest into his father's mistress." The Father concurs in blaming the Son, declaring that his sneers are bringing tragedy for the Boy and Girl.

The manager agrees that here they have the material for an excellent drama, but he has never been an author and can't help them. The Father offers a solution: the Characters will play their parts and the actors then can re-enact the scenes, with the manager recording the lines and action as the Characters proceed.

But the Characters, when the professional actors attempt to mimic them, find that they are unreal. The Stepdaughter protests: "You don't begin to understand us. For example, when I met this man (pointing to her father) at Madame Pace's establishment, I told him I was wearing black in mourning for my father. And what do you think he answered? 'Let's put an end to this mourning; let me help you take off this little dress.'"

The manager protests that such a scene would create a riot, that a professional artist cannot afford to tell the truth, and that a dramatist cannot tell everything about his characters; he must be selective. The Stepdaughter declares: ". . . Kill our parts, if you wish. But you can't kill us, our passion, our bitterness, our shame, our remorse, our disgust. Go on with your artificial scenes . . . make a mere pretense of it all when I embrace this man, closing my eyes and letting my head sink on his breast—like this— when suddenly my mother comes in and cries out——"

The Mother rushes between the Stepdaughter and Father, crying: "My daughter! . . . Let her go, you brute! . . . Don't you know she is my daughter?" The manager agrees that this is a perfect ending for a first act.

At length the Characters are ready to play the last act. The setting is the garden of the Father's house, a house into which the Mother and her three children have moved despite the Son's indignant protest. The manager orders the last act, adding: "Let's see how cleverly we can turn an illusion into a reality." But the Father corrects him, contending that they are turning a reality into an illusion.

It is the Characters who are real, he asserts, and the manager, the authors and the actors are merely fantastic and unreal; living characters die, but characters in drama are immortal. The manager protests that he has never heard of a fictitious character who steps out of his part and makes up speeches never intended by his author, but the Father stoutly insists that every experienced author knows that he is wholly at the mercy of his characters and must follow wherever they lead him.

The six Characters attempt to carry out their story to a logical conclusion. The Father and Mother strive to make the best of a bad situation, and to establish some semblance of harmony in this strange family, but evidently it cannot be: the Stepdaughter cannot adjust herself, and the Son relentlessly persecutes her and the Boy and Girl in his self-righteous scorn. At length the Boy, with growing realization of the sorry pattern of his home, makes a tragic resolution.

The Stepdaughter interjects: "Let the Son tell about it . . . he was to blame for it all. . . ." The Son first refuses: "Let me alone! I don't want to tell! The original author didn't want to tell, either. That's why he refused to put us on the stage." The Father compels him, however, with the reminder that he is "too real to quit," and the Son goes on: "I was walking in the garden . . . I came near the fountain . . . the Child, there in the water . . . I was about to jump in to the rescue when I saw the Boy standing there and staring . . . at his drowned little sister. . . . And then——"

He is interrupted by a shot from stage trees where the Boy has hidden himself. The manager rushes to the spot: "Is he wounded?" One of the actors replies: "He's dead!" Another actor adds: "But the whole thing isn't real! It's only make-believe!" Says the manager: "Reality? I've never seen anything like it. . . . To hell with it all! I've lost a whole day on account of these crazy people—a whole day!"

The Mistress of the Inn

BY CARLO GOLDONI

Born in Venice, Italy, February 25, 1707. The young Goldoni ran away from home with a Venetian company of players. He began to study law in Venice, and continued his studies in the Papal College at the University of Pavia, from which he was expelled for writing an abusive satire. His first play, "Amalasunta," was a tragedy, but he later turned to writing comedy, and is now recognized as the real founder of modern Italian comedy. Molière was his example. Goldoni was a prolific writer, and, in addition to "The Mistress of the Inn," he wrote "The Coffee House,"

*"The Good-Humored Ladies," "The Beneficent Bear," and
many other plays. In his old age in Paris Goldoni, caught
by the French Revolution, was reduced to extreme misery.
He died in 1793.*

Mirandolina, mistress since her father's death of his prosperous inn in Florence, is remarkable for her lively charm
and her deft juggling of innumerable admirers. But now
all her wit is challenged by the courting of three men,
as well as by the equally interesting indifference of another.

Offering the boasted "protection" of a lordly title is the
Marquis di Forlipopoli who remains at the inn solely because of his admiration for its mistress. But the offer of the
title is counterbalanced by a poverty and a stinginess incon-
gruous in so snobbish a figure whose most frequent phrase
is: "I am who I am and must be shown respect."

Wealth is offered by the Count Albafiorita, also attracted
to the inn solely by Mirandolina, upon whom he continually
showers costly presents. He loses no opportunity to call attention to his riches and generosity, and to taunt the Marquis upon his thin purse; but he confesses that so far his
suit has been without success.

Also in the lists is Fabricus, serving man at the inn,
whom Mirandolina's father had suggested as her prospective husband. Fabricus is blandly maintaining his role of a
waiter, however, through all of Mirandolina's guileful maneuvering, but he himself never knows whether she favors
him or not. The Marquis and the Count are quite aware
of his position, and they somewhat favor so respectable
and convenient a match for their admired one.

The indifferent guest is the Cavalier di Ripafratta who,
jeering at the Marquis and the Count for their worship of
Mirandolina, declares: "As far as I am concerned there
isn't any danger that I'll get into any dispute with anyone
about women. I have never loved them, I have never had
any use for them, and I have always thought that woman
is an unbearable infirmity for men. . . . I have been in this

hotel three days and I don't see anything especially remarkable about her."

As the three guests chat, Mirandolina appears. The Marquis attempts to lure her to his room, but she demurely informs him that the waiter is available. Equally demurely,
she refuses diamond earrings offered by the Count, but
finally accepts them "so as not to displease" him. The Cavalier bluntly criticizes the linen provided, and Mirandolina, reflecting that she has never seen such a savage man,
decides to order him from the inn.

Later, however, she reflects: ". . . That Cavalier . . .
why does he treat me so brusquely? He's the first guest
. . . who hasn't been delighted to be in my society. . . .
To despise me so is something that makes me angry. He
a woman hater? . . . Poor fool! Probably he hasn't found
the one who knows how to handle him. . . . I'm going to
enter the lists with him. Those who run after me soon bore
me . . . My whole delight is in seeing myself served, de-
sired and adored . . . I treat everyone well, but I'll never
fall in love with anyone. I like to make fun of these exaggerated ardent lovers, and I want to use all my skill to
conquer, strike down and shake to their depths these cruel
and hard hearts which are the enemies of us who are the
best thing that beautiful Mother Nature has produced."

So she tells Fabricus that she will deliver the linen, and
soothes his jealousy with another intimation that she cares
nothing for her guests—Fabricus is to be the favored one.
She straightway visits the Cavalier (who has just lost his
morning chocolate and a loan to the penniless Marquis),
and presents linen so fine that he must admit that she is at
least an obliging woman. He is pleased as well by her
frankness when she tells him that she listens to the Count
and Marquis only to better her inn's business.

A few minutes of Mirandolina's shrewd flattery and the
Cavalier is impelled to agree that she is most pleasing, but
he is sure that he could never sacrifice his freedom for her.
He invites her to return, however, and Mirandolina decides,
while accepting more gifts from the Count and Marquis so

as not to displease them, that she would rather humble the Cavalier than have the finest of jewels.

For the Cavalier's dinner she sends a delightful and special meal, but he observes that he is leaving tomorrow. "Let her do her worst for today, but she will discover I'm not so weak," he reflects. Mirandolina appears with a ragout made by her own hands, and he soon finds himself—at her hint that she is strangely attracted to him—asking her to share his wine and his meal. They are interrupted by the Marquis—but not until the Cavalier is perilously near his doom. He decides that his safety demands that he flee the inn at once.

He attempts to evade her, but she personally brings him his bill—oddly small. She is weeping. The Cavalier is about to leave in confusion when she employs her chief weapon, a faint. He returns with water, murmuring in surrender: "Courage, courage. I am here, dear. I'll never leave you now." The Count and Marquis arrive to taunt him, and in a rage he throws down the water jug and leaves. Mirandolina recovers and reflects: "My task is done. . . . All I have to do is to complete my victory, to make my triumph public to the discomfiture of presumptuous men and to the honor of my sex."

The Cavalier cannot go. "Dragged by the devil," he finds Mirandolina, after sending to her a gold flask which she returns, much to the pleasure of Fabricus. She has justified her flirtation with the thought that she only wants the Cavalier "to confess the power of women without being able to say that they are self-seeking and venial." She torments him by throwing his gift in a basket, being overly kind to Fabricus in his presence, jeering at his past contempt for women, and, finally, by leaving him. When he has gone, she sends a servant for the flask, but the Marquis has salvaged it already.

The humiliated Count and Marquis, realizing that they have been duped, decide to leave. Now, Mirandolina, alarmed by the Cavalier's fury, thinks that she had better marry Fabricus. She says, reflectively: "After all, with such a marriage I could hope to protect my honor without det-

riment to my freedom." The Cavalier, whom she had
promised to visit in his room at his demand for an explanation, returns, threatening to break down the door. He is
restrained from doing so by the arrival of the Count and the
Marquis. The Count provokes him, and the Cavalier demands the Marquis' sword to fight, but he finds only half
a weapon in the scabbard. Furious, he is about to attack,
even with this poor makeshift, when Mirandolina and
Fabricus appear.

Mirandolina stops the fight, telling the Count and Marquis: "The Cavalier in love with me? He denies it, and
denying it in my presence he mortifies, humiliates me, and
makes me recognize his strength and my weakness. . . .
A man who cannot bear the sight of women . . . I cannot
hope to make him love me. . . . I tried to make the Cavalier fall in love with me, but all to no purpose. Isn't it true,
sir! I have done my best, but I have accomplished
nothing."

She declares that the Cavalier will prove that he is still
heart-whole by approving her marriage to Fabricus. The
Cavalier leaves, after stormily declaring: "Yes, curse you,
marry whom you will. . . . I curse your flattery, your
tears . . . you have made me see what baleful power your
sex has over us, and you have taught me to my cost that
it isn't enough to despise it—we men must flee from it."

Mirandolina announces that, from now on, Fabricus is
to be her only concern. She asks the Count and Marquis
to go elsewhere, reminding them: "May you profit by what
you have seen . . . and whenever you may find yourselves
hesitating as to whether you ought to yield or give in, may
you think of the tricks you have learned, and remember the
Mistress of the Inn."

SPANISH PLAYS

The Bonds of Interest

BY JACINTO BENAVENTE

*Born in Madrid, Spain, August 12, 1866, his full name
being Jacinto Benavente y Martinez. He studied law at the
University of Madrid, but failed to complete the course.
For a time he traveled with a circus, then joined a com-
pany of actors. His first play, "Thy Brother's House," was
a comedy which appeared in 1894. In addition to "The
Bonds of Interest" (1907), he is the author of "Saturday
Night," "The Evil Doers of Good," "The Prince Who
Learned Everything out of Books," and "The Passion
Flower." The plays of Benavente superseded those of José
Echegaray, and, as editor of the* Vida Literaria, *Benavente
gathered about him famous writers, and gave form and
substance to a new cultural movement. He traveled
through the United States and Spanish America, directing
the production of his plays. In 1922 he was awarded the
Nobel Prize for literature. He died in 1954.*

In the early seventeenth century, Leander and Crispin, two
"freeborn subjects of the Kingdom of Roguery," arrive at
an inn. They are equipped with only Crispin's shrewd wit,
Leander's imposing appearance, and some fine clothes as
their hope of fortune, for they are penniless fugitives from
justice. Crispin is confident that effrontery and their talents
will prevail, however, and directs that Leander pose as a
distinguished personage (saying as little as possible) while
he plays the part of his servant and builds about his companion an aura of wealth and greatness.

Crispin's plan works flawlessly at the start: his arrogant demands for the best for his master (who presumably is on a secret mission of state) provide sumptuous lodging and credit—provisions extended as well, at his order, to two other penniless adventurers, a soldier called the Captain and a poet, Harlequin. Crispin demands cash credit for them, also, and wins from them the allegiance of arms and poesy for his project.

"In the same boat" of poverty and pretense is the faded beauty, Doña Sirena. At her imposing home, her adopted niece, Columbine, tells her that the tailor has refused further credit, and the musicians and servants, unpaid, refuse to appear for an elaborate party she has planned for that night. The party is a most important one to Doña Sirena: she hopes to make a match for Silvia, daughter of the rich merchant Polichinelle, and to fatten her own purse, for she has contracted with several nobles to win Silvia for them—one is sure to be the lucky husband. Her only other hope of recouping her fortunes is Columbine, but the latter is in love with the penniless Harlequin.

But Crispin, learning from Harlequin of Doña Sirena's plight, appears with flattery and a profitable proposal: his distinguished master will provide everything—servants, musicians, soldiers and fireworks, plus a hundred thousand crowns for Doña Sirena—if she will invite him and arrange his wedding to Silvia, the heiress. Leander appears with the retinue he has promised, and is so fulsomely praised as a nobleman of exceeding estate by Crispin, Harlequin and the Captain, that Doña Sirena capitulates.

She arranges the first dance for Leander and Silvia, and Crispin hastens to bolster the campaign by a talk with Polichinelle in which he reminds the merchant of his days in the prisoners' galleys—days shared by Crispin—and of the mysterious fate of his first wife in Bologna, his first master in Naples and a usurious Jew in Venice. Offered money for his silence, the crafty Crispin suggests that, instead, the merchant quickly separate Silvia and his "hated" master Leander—because Leander, too, is an insinuating scoundrel and will surely bewitch her.

Crispin plots that parental objection shall only increase Silvia's infatuation for Leander; indeed, this is the case when old Polichinelle rudely dismisses him. Leander is made sad, however, for he has come to love Silvia in a hopeless fashion. But she again seeks him out and they embrace in the garden. Here Crispin accomplishes another coup: he has engaged some ruffians to feign an attack upon Leander, promptly placing the blame upon Polichinelle. Then he stirs Harlequin to write verses that will inflame the citizens against the merchant.

Columbine comes with the news that Silvia has fled to the home of Doña Sirena; she will not return to her father's house except as the bride of Leander. The success of Crispin's plot is now threatened by the conscience of Leander, who declares his love will not permit him to deceive her. Crispin points out that the situation has become desperate, with the dupes beginning to demand something more than talk to repay their outlay: Signor Pantaloon, who has been moved by the innkeeper's credit to finance their house; Doña Sirena and a horde of tradesmen are beginning to clamor. But he vows that he and Leander will be saved. Says he: "It will be enough to accept what others offer. We have intertwined ourselves with the interests of many, and the bonds of interest will prove our salvation."

Doña Sirena now appears with Silvia, proposing an immediate marriage to hasten her fee. She also tells them that Polichinelle has betrayed them to the law; a writ has arrived from Bologna, and a lawyer who had been prosecuting them at the time when they decided to flee has arrived. Silvia enters, and, disregarding Crispin's entreaties, Leander confesses his deception. His confession only strengthens Silvia's infatuation. She hides in a rear room as Polichinelle, officers and tradesmen, clamoring for their money, burst in.

Crispin soon impresses them all with the fact that if the match of Leander and Silvia is prevented, their money will be lost. He declares that Polichinelle cannot oppose the union because Silvia already has run off with Leander, a

rapscallion, and Polichinelle certainly will not want to pub-
licize the fact. The others greedily see Crispin's logic, but
Polichinelle believes him to be lying; Crispin promptly
suggests an "inventory." He throws back a curtain to reveal Silvia and Leander, Doña Sirena and Columbine.

All now agree (Polichinelle unwillingly) that love must
prevail, and that scandal must be avoided. Leander refuses to accept Silvia's fortune to pay his debts, and
Crispin prevails upon the others, while promising that they
shall have their money, to cancel his debts as a formal gesture to permit him to wed. Polichinelle imposes only one
condition: that Crispin must leave Leander's service.
Despite the latter's grief, Crispin announces that he is going
to leave it anyhow.

He assures Leander that his sorrow will not last long,
and adds: "I can be of no further use to you. With me, you
will be able to lay aside your lion's skin and your old man's
wisdom. What did I tell you, sir? Between them all, we
were sure to be saved. And believe me now, when you are
getting on in the world, the ties of love are nothing to the
bonds of interest."

Leander protests: "You are wrong. For without the love
of Silvia I should never have been saved."

Crispin retorts: "And is love a slight interest? I have
always given due credit to the ideal and I count upon it
always. With this the farce ends."

Silvia answers, to the audience: "You have seen in it
how these puppets have been moved by plain and obvious
strings, like men and women in the farces of our lives—
strings which were their interests, their passions and all the
illusions and petty miseries of their states. . . . But into the
hearts of all there descends sometimes from Heaven . . .
the invisible thread of love, which makes these men and
women . . . almost divine . . . and whispers to us still that
this farce is not all a farce, that there is something noble,
something divine in our lives which is true and which is
eternal, and which shall not close when the farce of life
shall close."

Life Is a Dream

BY CALDERÓN

Born in Madrid, January 17, 1600, Calderón, whose full name was Pedro Calderón de la Barca, was educated at the Jesuit college in Madrid and later studied law at Salamanca. He served as a soldier between 1625 and 1635, and during this period was writing plays. In 1635 Philip IV called him to Madrid as a court dramatist, and a year later knighted him. In 1651 Calderón became a priest. Some of his best work consists of autos sacramentales—*allegorical pieces of a religious character. Other of his plays are* comedias de capa y espada—*plays in which the characters wear cloaks and swords. Of his plays, 118 dramas and over 70 autos are extant. Four of the best known are: "Life Is a Dream," "The Fairy Lady," "The Mock Astrologer," and "The Wonder-Working Magician." Calderón died in 1681.*

Victim of his father's belief in mystic omens, the young Polish Prince, Sigismund, has been held a prisoner, ignorant since infancy of his identity, in a lonely dungeon in the mountains. His sole companion is his tutor, the nobleman, Clotaldo. It had once been foretold that Sigismund would be the death of his mother, a cruel monarch whose rule would partition Poland, and the conqueror of his father; indeed, the Queen had died in childbirth, lending credence to the prophecy.

To the dungeon come two wayfarers—Rosaura, a Russian lady disguised as a man, and Clarin, her servant. Rosaura has come to Poland to revenge herself upon her betrayer, Astolfo, Duke of Muscovy, and bears a sword given to her by her unmarried mother, Violante. The sword had been Rosaura's father's; her mother, without naming him, has bidden her display it among the Polish nobles—in the hope that her father will see it and perhaps aid her.

Rosaura and Clarin see Sigismund, chained and clad in the skins of beasts, in his dungeon. He cries out his sorrow and rage at his fate to them, but Clotaldo and the guards appear and close his door. Clotaldo, threatening death to the trespassers for visiting the forbidden tower, demands their arms. Rosaura yields the sword and Clotaldo learns its story. He recognizes Rosaura as his "son," although he does not tell her that he does so. He decides to confide in Basilius, the King, and to ask mercy for her.

At the court, Astolfo is wooing the Infanta Estrella. He is the nephew of Basilius, she the King's niece. On this day, the King has said he will decide who is to have the throne when he, aged and tired, abdicates. Astolfo proposes that he and Estrella marry and share the rule. Estrella, however, doubts his love, since he wears the portrait of another girl on his breast.

Basilius reveals to the couple and the court the story of his son Sigismund, and his resolve to test the prophecy: Sigismund, drugged, is to be brought to the palace and awakened as King Sigismund; if he rules with wisdom and kindliness, he shall remain, but if he is indeed cruel and violent, he will be returned to his dungeon, told that his kingship was only a dream. Basilius has pardoned Rosaura and Clarin, and Rosaura has resumed her woman's garb. Posing as Clotaldo's niece, she has become an attendant of Estrella.

Presently Sigismund, lost in amazement, is ushered to the throne in regal dress. He believes himself to be dreaming, but reflects: "Why perplex myself and brood? Better taste the present good, come what will some other day." Clotaldo appears, and Sigismund promptly orders him executed because he has been his jailer. He insults Astolfo, voices a passion for Estrella and, reproached by a servant, throws him out the window to his death. He sees and dimly remembers Rosaura's face, orders the courtiers away, and is about to assault her when Clotaldo intervenes. Sigismund is on the point of stabbing his tutor when Astolfo enters

and draws his sword to save him. Basilius arrives in time
to prevent bloodshed, but tells Sigismund that he will
awake to find the day only a dream.

Astolfo, meanwhile, continues to woo the still skeptical
Estrella, and, in order to convince her, goes to get the
portrait to surrender to her. Estrella asks Rosaura to receive
it from him for her, and Astolfo, returning, recognizes
Rosaura as the woman in Russia whom he had once loved.
She demands the portrait, snatching it from him as Estrella
appears. She then tells the Infanta that it is her own
portrait that she has just dropped; Astolfo had picked it
up. She declares that Astolfo intends to surrender hers and
keep his own love's picture from Estrella. Rosaura's revenge
succeeds, for Estrella, vainly demanding the token from
Astolfo, leaves him in scorn.

Back again in his dungeon, Sigismund awakens and tells
Clotaldo of his "dream." He resolves that "to live is but
to dream; man dreams what he is, and wakes only when
upon him breaks death's mysterious morning beam." He
says that he will now restrain his rage and ambition.
Drums and trumpets are heard, and soldiers come to set
him free; they wish to be ruled by their natural Prince, not
the foreigner, Astolfo.

But Sigismund, disillusioned, refuses to return. "Dis-
abused, I now know well, life is but a dream—a vision,"
he tells them. He finally decides, however, to dream again;
to dismiss Astolfo and test the prophecy that he will
trample upon his father; he is determined this time "to do
what's right, since we even in dreams should do what's
fitting." As his first step of reformation, he permits Clotaldo
to rejoin Basilius.

Rosaura, again in man's dress, joins the forces of Sigismund, still determined to kill Astolfo. Sigismund restrains
the temptation to ravish her, reflecting: "Let us seek then
the eternal, the true fame that ne'er reposeth, where the
bliss is not a dream, nor the crown a fleeting glory." He
goes to battle the forces of Basilius and Astolfo. He is
triumphant, capturing Basilius. The old King bows his
neck, but Sigismund raises him and prostrates himself in

token of his new self. He points out the fallacy of portents and declares: "He who would be victor o'er his fortune must succeed by wise prudence and self-strictness."

He directs that Astolfo shall, in justice, give his hand to Rosaura. Astolfo protests that he cannot marry a nameless woman, but Clotaldo reveals that he is her father. For Estrella, Sigismund proclaims: "I propose from mine own hand as a husband one to give her." He takes her hand. Of Clotaldo he says: "I can give him but these open arms wherein he will find what e'er he wishes." But when the soldier who first freed him asks reward, he sentences him to his old dungeon: "For the traitor is not needed once the treason is committed." He concludes:

> "Why this wonder, these surprises,
> If my teacher was a dream,
> And amid my new aspirings
> I am fearful I may wake,
> And once more a prisoner find me
> In my cell? But should I not,
> Even to dream is sufficient;
> For I have thus come to know
> That at last all human blisses
> Pass and vanish as a dream,
> And the time that may be given me
> I henceforth would turn to gain;
> Asking for our faults forgiveness,
> Since to generous, noble hearts
> It is natural to forgive them."

GERMAN AND AUSTRIAN PLAYS

Grand Hotel

BY VICKI BAUM

Born January 24, 1888, in Vienna, Austria, her real name being Hedwig Lert. She went to Germany when she was twenty-one, played in an orchestra for three years, and taught music. In 1916 she married the conductor, Richard Lert. Purely by accident, a friend saw some stories on her desk which she had written for her own amusement, and was so interested in them that he took them to a publisher who accepted them immediately. After the publication of her two first books, she gave up writing, devoting herself to the care of her two small children. It was six years before she resumed any literary work. She was persuaded, against her judgment, to dramatize her novel, "Grand Hotel," and it was immediately successful. She was invited to come to New York for the opening in 1931. She planned to stay two weeks—and has been here ever since. She has written almost entirely for the movies since 1932. A recent novel of hers is "Hotel Berlin '43."

Within thirty-six hours in the routine of Berlin's sumptuous and glittering Grand Hotel, the lives of a colorful group of strangers intermingle and come to dramatic climaxes of death, triumph, heartbreak and ruin.

Among the guests at the hotel are Grusinskaia, a celebrated Russian dancer in her late thirties, still beautiful but fading in popularity with her public; Baron von Gaigern, young and engaging, but a gambler and a thief; Preysing, a coarse, middle-aged industrialist who is facing the collapse of his business; Kringlein, a bookkeeper in Preysing's plant in Fredersdorf, who, incurably ill, is pitifully trying to get a taste of the luxurious life in his few remaining days; and Flaemmchen, a young stenographer, too pretty for an office. Lesser figures, with their own joys and tragedies, move through the turbulent current of life at the Grand Hotel; adding color and contrast to the ever-changing scene, which is old, yet ever new.

Gaigern, although fascinated by Grusinskaia, is awaiting a chance to steal her famous pearls. He has vainly tried to exchange accommodations with Witte, the dancer's conductor, whose room adjoins hers. However, Witte, moved by poor Kringlein's appeal to the desk clerk for a room as good as Preysing's—("I want to live well, just as Mr. Preysing does. I am sick. I am tired," he tells the clerk)—gives up his room to the bookkeeper. Gaigern immediately strikes up an acquaintance with him.

Grusinskaia and her retinue enter the lobby on their way to a performance of the dancer at the theater. Grusinskaia, informed by telegram that her Budapest engagement has been cancelled because of lack of interest, superstitiously blames her pearls for her misfortune, and has them sent back to her room. Gaigern overhears her instructions. For purposes of his own, he plans a "big night" of pleasure for Kringlein and Flaemmchen with whom he has been flirting. But Flaemmchen has already been engaged by Preysing to type a paper for him—a document needed in a vital business merger he is seeking. Gaigern accompanies Kringlein to the latter's room, offering to make the bookkeeper a "man of fashion." As the first step in this direction, he sends him off to the barber shop. As soon as he is gone, Gaigern tries a skeleton key in the lock of Grusinskaia's door.

He enters her room, finds the pearls, and is about to slip them into his pocket when the entrance of a chambermaid forces him to hide behind a costume case. Next, Grusinskaia's maid comes in, seeking her mistress. Then Witte and Grusinskaia's manager arrive. It seems that when the dancer appeared at the theater there was no applause—

only hissing from the audience. Grusinskaia disappeared during the intermission. She now comes in, and finally induces everyone to leave her. She weeps in self-pity before her mirror. Suddenly she attempts a few dance steps, but collapses, crying: "Never! You cannot dance again. . . . Finished——"

Then, in the mirror, she sees Gaigern emerge from behind the costume case. She recognizes him at once as a constant and not unwelcome spectator at the theater. Gaigern tells her that he is hiding in her room because he loves her. "Poor Grusinskaia," he says to her. "Were the people bad to you? Are you afraid? Do you cry because I love you?" She sobs: "I was so alone, always alone—nobody—and suddenly you were there and said that word. No, I am not afraid. . . . You love me. . . ." She tells him then of all her lonely years, and when he pleads that he must stay and help her to forget them, she whispers, "Just for a minute," but falls into his arms.

The following morning, Gaigern confesses to her that, even though he really has loved her, her pearls have been his objective. He tells her that he has been forced to steal the pearls because of his urgent need for money. He asks her if she understands. She cries that she does, and hugs him to her. Called for a rehearsal, she finds herself once more inspired to dance. She insists that Gaigern shall come with her when she leaves the next day on tour. She will give him money. Gaigern promises to be on the train tomorrow, but he will not take her money; he has a whole day in which to get some.

In the meantime, Preysing has lied in order to put over a deal which will save his business. Now, almost hysterical with relief and victory, he feels that he must celebrate—must do things he has never done before. He thinks of Flaemmchen, and goes to find her dancing with Gaigern. Gaigern induces her to give Kringlein, dressed in his new clothes, the great thrill of his first dance. "For the first time in my life," exclaims the bookkeeper, "I am happy!"

The dance over, he takes Flaemmchen to Preysing who has brusquely attempted to interrupt the dance by calling for Flaemmchen's services. Preysing, sneeringly remarking that Kringlein may well be an embezzler to be able to afford the Grand Hotel, discharges him from his employment when Kringlein resents his order to go. He angrily shakes the bookkeeper and flings him against the bar. Kringlein cries: ". . . You can't fire me. You can't do anything to me any more. I am ill—I am going to die very soon. By the time you fire me I'll be dead already!" Sobbing, he runs from the room.

But in his own room, dressing in his faultless new clothes, Kringlein recovers his composure and consents to go to a gambling room with Gaigern, to whom he has lent money. They gamble and Gaigern loses everything, but the excited Kringlein wins a huge amount and calls for champagne for everyone. He then collapses. While a doctor is treating him, Gaigern steals his bulging wallet. But when he sees Kringlein's terror at the loss of his means of a few more days of happiness, he relents and returns it to him.

While this is happening, Preysing has induced Flaemmchen to accompany him to a conference in England and to precede the trip by spending a night with him. His room adjoins Flaemmchen's; he goes into hers and clumsily makes advances to her. As they talk, Grusinskaia returns from the theater and enters her room near by. Her last performance has been a great triumph—she has danced "as if she had found wings or a great love." She talks now of Gaigern, and of their meeting tomorrow on the train. But Gaigern, threatened by thieves from whom he has been borrowing, is at that moment letting himself into Preysing's room (Number 170), by a picklock, desperate for the money he needs.

Preysing hears him, returns to his room to discover Gaigern, and finds that his wallet is missing. Gaigern gives it back to him, but Preysing insists that he will send him to jail. He reaches for the telephone. Gaigern threatens him with a revolver, but Preysing hurls a lamp at him. There is a struggle, a shot—and Gaigern lies on the floor, dead. Preysing is trying to quiet the hysterical Flaemmchen when Kringlein appears. He helps Flaemmchen to recover her clothes, then calls the police.

Preysing appeals to Kringlein to report that Flaemmchen was with him throughout the night. He offers Kringlein money to avert the scandal that will ruin him when the police come. Kringlein bends over Gaigern. He says: "He looks content; it cannot be so hard," and leaves Preysing to face the police and disaster. He sets out for Paris with Flaemmchen, who is to have his winnings "when it's all over."

Grusinskaia has been calling Gaigern's room—there has been no answer. Witte and her manager have finally persuaded her to wait for him no longer. They tell her that the train is leaving at once for Prague, and Witte assures her that Gaigern will be on it. She cries: "Witte, stay here . . . bring him with you . . . come on the next train. Tell him that he must travel with us. Must! Must!" She is hurried away, and a few moments later Witte, unable to find the Baron, follows them.

As he goes, a man comes to the desk downstairs to ask for a room. He is assigned to Number 170, a large room with bath.

Anatol

BY ARTHUR SCHNITZLER

SCHNITZLER *was born to Viennese Jewish parents in 1862. He first became interested in the theater through knowing many celebrated stars of the day who came to his father, a famous throat specialist, for treatment. Though Schnitzler studied medicine and was finally admitted to the medical faculty of the University of Vienna, he found time from his studies to form the Young Vienna Group, a literary and artistic movement which had a profound influence upon Austrian literature and drama. By the time "Anatol," the first of Schnitzler's plays, and "Liebelei," the play which established his reputation in 1893, had been produced, Schnitzler had given up medicine completely to devote his entire time to writing. All of Schnitzler's early dramas are concerned with some version of the man-versus-woman theme which figures in "Anatol," and are imbued with his philosophy that, while mankind as a whole justifies no faith in its future greatness, the immediate happiness of the individual is of utmost importance. His later plays and his short novels, especially those written just prior to his death in 1931, reflect his growing skepticism, his hatred of injustice and a morbid fear of old age and death.*

Anatol, a handsome Viennese romanticist, has been searching for someone to fulfill his ideal of romantic love. Max, his more realistic friend, visiting him in his apartments, finds Anatol torturing himself by thoughts of Cora, a pretty little seamstress whom he loves insanely. How can he know she is faithful? "Oh, it will drive me mad! If I should implore her . . . all is forgiven in advance . . . but only tell me the truth . . . she would lie to me as before," he tells Max. Max suggests that Anatol hypnotize Cora; then she will certainly speak the truth.

When Cora happens to come in, she agrees to the idea, although she does not know its purpose. Once under the hypnotic spell, Anatol, who has asked Cora several unimportant questions, finds he cannot bring himself to inquire whether she has been faithful. While tormenting himself with doubt, he lacks the necessary courage to demand the truth. Instead, he invents excuses: in her hypnotic state Cora might think that she had been untrue in loving another before meeting Anatol, even in looking with slight interest upon another man. Max tells Anatol he is avoiding the issue, that Cora will very well understand the meaning of his question.

Anatol asks Max to leave the room for a moment. He will question Cora alone; Max must not know if his love has betrayed him. Alone with Cora, Anatol still lacks the

courage to interrogate her. He awakens her. Max, returning to the room, is quite aware that Anatol has not
broached the all-important subject. He realizes that Anatol
would rather keep his illusions, beset as they are with
doubt, than to know reality. Anatol comforts himself with
the thought that even if he does not know Cora to be
faithful, she has told him she loves him, even while hypno-
tized. Max, looking at the lovers, reflects: "Women can
lie even when in hypnosis—but they're happy—that's one
important thing."

But Anatol is not satisfied with Cora for long. On Christmas Eve he is shopping for a present for another girl when
he meets Gabrielle, securely and quite dully married, who
offers to help him select his gift. She must know the sort
of woman who is to receive it if she is to make an appropriate selection, she tells him. Anatol describes to her
the young, affectionate creature who has made him her
whole life—for the present. (Anatol always adds "for the
present" to any avowals he may make or receive.) He
dwells on the pleasure he knows with this new love . . .
says that he finds her always waiting for him . . . glad
when he comes to her. Gabrielle, moved by his story, buys
some flowers for the girl. "Tell her," she commands him,
"'these flowers, my sweet little girl, were sent to you by a
woman who, perhaps—might know how to love as well as
you—but hasn't the courage.'"

Anatol is not capable of maintaining a whole-hearted,
simple devotion to one woman, and he decides to leave
Vienna—to begin a new life, free and alone. The night
before he goes away, he brings a package to Max for safekeeping. He tells him that the package contains envelopes
filled with mementos of his former loves—those loves who,
were he to call them all to him now, would come, "one
from a simple tenement home, another from her husband's
gorgeous drawing room," several from stage dressing
rooms, "one from the grave . . . one from here—another
from there . . ." He fingers the souvenirs—a curl, a wisp of
veil, a verse. "Maiden with the well-pricked fingers . . ."
Anatol reads from an envelope. "That was Cora, wasn't

it?" Max guesses. "What's become of her?" "I met her just recently—as the wife of a cabinet-maker," Anatol replies. Max picks up another envelope and reads the inscription aloud: " 'Episode.' But there's nothing in this—just a little dust." "Dust?" Anatol answers. "That was a flower once." A flower—it had been worn by Bianca, a circus acrobat. Anatol knew her for only two hours, yet he tells Max that he gave her something to remember always.

Max surprises Anatol when he remarks that he knows Bianca, too—in fact, she is coming to call this very evening. When Bianca arrives and greets Max, she turns to Anatol and cannot remember him at all. His dream of her undying memory is spoiled, for their brief affair had been only an "episode" to her as well as to him.

Anatol's search for true love leads him from Vienna, and, eventually, to the arms of Emile, a woman who confesses to him that she has sold her love, or thrown it away, countless times. Anatol loves her, nevertheless, and is resolved to make her his wife. Then comes a day when she surprises him in the act of ransacking her desk. He has found two jewels hidden there—he had thought she had thrown away every keepsake of her past when she came to love him. There is a ruby—and she explains that it fell from a locket she had worn the first day she fell in love. She immediately promises to throw it away, although surely he cannot be jealous of the first man she knew, a man who means nothing to her now, except for the remembered sweetness of her first woman's emotion. The other gem, a rare black diamond, clearly has no sentimental connotations. "Why did you keep this one?" Anatol asks. "Why —it's worth a quarter of a million!" Emile answers. Disgusted at this reaction which he deems worthy only of a harlot, Anatol throws the costly bauble into the fire, then leaves Emile. She instantly forgets him in an effort to rescue the valuable gem from the flames.

So Anatol continues to drift from one woman to another. Back in Vienna, he becomes involved with Annie, a ballet dancer. They both agree that, should the time come when they no longer love each other, they will part honestly before either is unfaithful. Anatol does meet "someone else," and is untrue to Annie. By appointment, one evening, he meets Max in a restaurant. He is expecting Annie, he tells Max, and has screwed up his courage to tell her that their affair is over. Anticipating tears and recriminations on her part, he wants Max to be present in order to relieve the strain. However, when Annie arrives, she turns the tables on Anatol by telling him that she has fallen in love with a fellow dancer. Anatol, his vanity wounded, taunts her with the truth. He has been untrue to her for a long time, he says. Annie confesses that she has deceived him also, but adds that she would never have been so inconsiderate as to tell him this unless he had shown the same lack of respect for her pride.

A woman named Elsa is Anatol's next love. She is married to an uninteresting, but prosperous, business man. Anatol tries to persuade her that theirs is the "great romance" and that they must go away from Vienna in order to be together always, instead of limiting their love to a few stolen hours. Elsa refuses. Anatol suddenly realizes that Elsa has been his only because she is restless and craves excitement. He forces himself to think of her as "just one more!"

Anatol at last decides to marry a suitable "nonentity." Max, coming to pay him a visit on the morning of his wedding day, discovers that, after his wedding-eve party, Anatol had visited a carnival, determined to have one last fling before losing his freedom. At the carnival he met Ilone, a former love, and she has come home with him. Max is now thoroughly disgusted by this last outrage of Anatol's. Things grow complicated when Ilone, unaware that Anatol is to be married that afternoon, insists that she and Anatol spend the day alone together. When Anatol explains this will be impossible because of his scheduled wedding, she makes a scene, swearing to stop the ceremony. Anatol and Max finally quiet her, and Anatol goes off to meet his bride.

Ilone is planning to prevent the nuptials in some way when Max reminds her, "He can come back to you—it will be the other who is forsaken." Ilone now realizes that this will be her revenge. She consents to let Max take her home. "And now bid farewell to these rooms," he tells her. "Not farewell—I shall come back," she replies. Indeed she will—and countless others like her—for Anatol has so dissipated his emotions that he himself does not have the quality of faithfulness he has so long sought in others.

The Weavers

BY GERHARDT HAUPTMANN

Born in Obersalzbrunn, Silesia, Germany, November 15, 1862. He went to school in Breslau until his father failed in business. Then he was sent to stay with an uncle, and was strongly influenced by the musical and artistic atmosphere of the home. He showed a talent for sculpture, and for two years attended classes at the Royal College of Art in Breslau. Later, he studied at the University of Jena. After leaving the university, he went to Italy. His first important dramatic work was called "The Weavers," a play exposing the plight of Silesian wage earners. His plays, "The Festival of Peace" and "Lonely Lives," were radical social documents. From his early mood of social protest he passed to the idealistic and mystical attitude which inspired "Hannele," "Florian Geyer," and "The Sunken Bell." In his late years, he was showered with honors—degrees from Columbia, Oxford, Leipzig, Prague, the Nobel Prize in 1912, and almost every honor and medal the German government could offer—and a Hauptmann cult sprang up. He was compared to Goethe, and was followed by disciples who took down his most casual remarks to pass on to posterity. He was the only world-famous German author of his day who remained in Germany during the second World War. He died in 1946.

Into Dreissiger's textile plant in Peterswaldau, Silesia, in the eighteen forties, there files a line of men, women and children, half-starved, emaciated and humble with the humility of beggars. They are weavers, delivering their webs for a payment measured by the greed and flinty heart of Dreissiger and his equally arrogant and cheating staff.

One by one they bring their webs to be tested and weighed—the men flat-chested, sallow and stooped; the women pale and anxious. One weaver's wife, in tears, appeals for a few pennies in advance; her husband is sick, her children are without bread and their credit has been exhausted. But there is no sympathy for her, nor for any of the equally downtrodden weavers, at Dreissiger's.

Old Father Baumert has come, clutching the body of his pet dog. There is no food in his house and little meat on the starved dog, but it is something and he has had the animal killed. "I didn't have the heart to kill him myself," he says. Only the young weaver Becker speaks out, and he is summarily discharged. As he gets his money, a sickly boy faints from hunger. Dreissiger prescribes water for him.

At Father Baumert's dilapidated house are his wife, their crippled son, August, and two young daughters, busy at the winding wheels, as Father Baumert returns home with the dog for a rare feast—they have had no meat in two years. He brings with him young Moritz Jaeger, a former weaver just discharged from the army, who has saved the incredible fortune of thirty shillings, and has as well a bottle of brandy and a silver watch.

Father Baumert, who could hardly wait for the dog to be roasted, eagerly eats a morsel, but has to leave the room. He cries: "It's no good! I'm too far gone! Now that I've at last got hold of somethin' with a taste in it, my stomach won't keep it."

But, warmed by the brandy and talk of their miserable plight, Father Baumert urges Jaeger to champion the weavers. The young man tells him that he and Becker have just given Dreissiger "a piece of our mind." They sang for him a song, "Bloody Justice, or Dreissiger's Song," voicing the misery of the weavers and the threat of justice to come. Baumert and Ansorge, another weaver, are stirred to fury and agree that Dreissiger's tyranny must end.

Other weavers are discussing their sad situation at a tavern when there passes the funeral of a comrade. The sight fans their resentment. "A lucky thing for him. . . . He's been goin' around like a livin' ghost for years. . . . An' what a corpse! It didn't weigh ninety pounds!" they say. Jaeger, Baumert and other workmen enter, and the weavers' rage is stirred anew when Becker leads them in singing the new song. Even Wittig, the blacksmith, joins in the demonstration.

A policeman orders them to be silent, but Wittig jeers at him. He tells the workers: "The only way to get anything is to fight!" Becker agrees and, roaring the song, the men surge into the street. Only old Baumert says reluctantly: "If we could only manage the thing peacefully!" Jaeger is arrested and brought before the police superintendent at Dreissiger's home where the official had been summoned. He is ordered to stop the weavers' rioting by the most drastic means.

Jaeger, made confident by the shouts of his friends outside, jeers at Dreissiger, the police official and his pastor, the hypocritical Kittelhaus, but is bound and hustled out to be taken to jail. Dreissiger and Kittelhaus, deploring the "humanitarians" who have aroused the weavers, prepare to play cards, but the crowd has freed Jaeger and storms the house. Kittelhaus is mauled by the crowd, but the frightened Dreissiger manages to escape with his family from the town.

The weavers pour into the house, smashing everything below stairs, flooding into the luxurious drawing room with cries of "Where's the cruel brute? . . . If we can eat grass, he may eat sawdust. . . . We'll hang him whenever we catch him! . . . We'll take him by the legs and fling him out at the window, onto the stones! . . . If we can't lay hands on that brute Dreissiger himself we'll at any rate make a poor man of him!" They tear and batter the home to wreckage. Becker rallies them now to march on to Bielau, where the steam power looms are.

At a miserable weavers' hut in Bielau are old Hilse, his blind wife, his son, Gottlieb, and the latter's wife, Luise. Old Hilse, a palsied ex-soldier who lost an arm in battle, has just led the morning prayer and the weaving has begun when a rag dealer brings news of the revolt at Peterswaldau and the march on Bielau. Gottlieb leaves to return to the police one of Dreissiger's spoons that his daughter, aged seven, had picked up, and returns excitedly to report that the weavers, armed with poles and axes, have arrived. Father Baumert has urged him to join them, but he has run home.

Old Hilse cries indignantly: "An' that man calls himself your godfather an' he bids you take part in such works of wickedness? Have nothing to do with them, Gottlieb. They've let themselves be tempted by Satan, an' it's his works they're doin'!" Gottlieb would join them, but he obeys his father in the face of the scorn of Luise, who reminds old Hilse: "You an' your piety an' religion—did they serve to keep the life in my poor children? In rags an' dirt they lay, all the four—it didn't as much as keep them dry. . . . It was cryin' more than breathin' with me from the time each poor little thing came into the world till death took pity on it."

Now the weavers, flushed with brandy and victory—for a leader of the manufacturers has capitulated—rush into the house in an endeavor to recruit more rebels, but old Hilse clings to his faith in justice in the hereafter and to his mute acceptance of the weaver's life. Soldiers are heard approaching to put down the rebellion. Luise, shouting scornfully in answer to an inquiry as to her husband's stand: "I've got no husband," leads the rush to face the muskets.

Outside, a volley of gunfire is heard, and several of the weavers are seen to fall. One is brought in, with a bullet in his ear, and Gottlieb dashes out to the side of Luise, who is "jumpin' in front of the bayonets as if she was dancin' to music." Old Hilse takes his place at his weaving.

He says: "My heavenly father has placed me here. . . .
Here we'll sit an' do our bounden duty." There is another
volley, and old Hilse, mortally wounded by a bullet
through the window, falls over his loom.

His granddaughter enters to tell them that the weavers
have routed the soldiers and are storming on with their
conquest of the factories. She sees the slumped body of
Hilse and calls to him in fright. He is silent. Blind Mother
Hilse cries in alarm: "Come now, Father, can't you say
somethin'? You're frightenin' me."

Faust

BY JOHANN WOLFGANG VON GOETHE

*Born in 1749 in Frankfurt on the Main, in Germany, the
son of wealthy parents. He studied law and medicine at
Leipzig and Strasbourg, and published his first book in his
early twenties. Poet, dramatist, novelist, philosopher and
student of science, he had tremendous influence on German
letters and thought. From 1775 Goethe lived in Weimar
where, as principal minister of state to the Duke Charles
Augustus of Saxe-Weimar, he built the state theater into
the greatest in Europe. It was in this theater that his own
dramatic works first appeared—"Goetz von Berlichingen,"
"Faust," "Iphigenia in Tauris," "Tasso," "Clavigo," "Stella,"
"Count Egmont," etc. "Faust" is Goethe's greatest dramatic
poem and also his greatest work. Its theme was used by
Gounod in his famous opera. The first part of "Faust"
was completed in Goethe's youth. He was working on the
second part throughout his life. He died in 1832.*

Mephistopheles has debated with God the worth of a creation that only destroys the men it rears, and he has denied
as well the essential goodness of man. God has singled out

the saintly old scholar, Faust, to prove that there is at least one good man on earth. But the Devil has declared Faust like the rest: "Give him to me but for a little while and I will damn his soul eternally." God has accepted the wager, contending: "While man's desires and aspirations stir, he cannot choose but err; yet in his erring journey through the night, instinctively he travels toward the light."

The Devil, descending to earth to tempt the aged scholar, finds him utterly disappointed by his life: "Has all my learning taught me only this—that men, self-tortured, everywhere must bleed? That, seeking life, they blindly rush to death?" Mephistopheles offers him a new life, with restored youth and himself as his slave, if Faust will be his slave in the next world. Faust, planning now to live from pleasure to pleasure, agrees to become the Devil's slave when he has reached the apex of bliss, and the bargain is sealed in a drop of blood.

Mephistopheles then transforms Faust into a handsome young man. The two set forth to join merrymakers at Auerbach's Tavern where the Devil draws drink from a wooden table and turns it into fire. A Witches' Kitchen is their next stop, and here the Devil gives Faust the draught that imbues him with sensual love. Then, in the street outside, he sees Margaret, a fresh and lovely young girl, and offers his escort, but she rebuffs him. He tells the Devil of his passion for her, and, disregarding Mephistopheles' sardonic observation that Margaret has just returned from confession, demands that he hold her in his arms that night or he will break his pledge.

The Devil contrives a meeting of Faust and Margaret (who, in the German original, is known as Gretchen) in a neighbor's garden, and the girl is enchanted by the charm and intelligence of her visitor. She prays that he will come again. Faust indeed appears again, but this time to urge that she admit him to her room while her mother sleeps. To overcome Margaret's fears of discovery, he gives her a sleeping potion for her mother, and the lovers have their meeting. But it ends in tragedy: the potion kills the mother, and Margaret is to have a child.

Margaret's brother, Valentine, just home from service
with the army, hears of her disgrace and seeks out Faust
to avenge her. They fight; Faust stabs the youth who dies
with a curse upon his sister. Faust now seeks supernatural
pleasures, and at the Witches' Sabbath joins the evil spirits
in their weird play. But he cannot free his mind of the
tragic Margaret and orders the Devil to take him to her.

However, he finds that it is too late; Margaret has been
imprisoned, accused of the murder of her baby, and she
rejects Faust's offer of rescue. Preferring to face her punishment with the help of God, she dies. So ends Faust's
adventure in sensuality—without finding the supreme moment of bliss that would warrant his surrender to Mephistopheles. He is eager now "to bare his breast to every
pang, to know all human joy and sorrow," and to share
with his fellow men "the shipwreck of mankind." (Part
One ends with Faust's glorification of Margaret as the
symbol of eternal womanhood.)

In Part Two, the frustrated Mephistopheles tempts him
with pleasures of another sort, and takes him "out of the
little world into the great world." He presents him at the
court of the German Emperor, where his talents quickly
earn for him the Emperor's gratitude and the honors of a
councilor. But these rewards, too, are empty to Faust. He
recalls the thrills of his romantic life, and conjures from
the ages the spirit of Helen, to which he supplies lifeblood.
He attempts to woo her, but Helen, symbol of the beauties
of antiquity, eludes him, leaving nothing in his unhappy
hands but her cloak.

So, "with his very walk a series of falls," the despairing
Faust plods on through another series of experiences in
his pursuit of true happiness, but only failure—or hollow
triumph that is worse—is his lot in each. Even a great
victory in battle for the Emperor proves as bitter as defeat.
Mephistopheles offers now his greatest temptations—whole
cities and even kingdoms, the most glorious of deeds, the
height of physical beauty in more women, and an earthly
immortality in fame—but Faust has sickened of all.

As before, he has reached the apex of his new life, and

almost infinite experience has failed, throughout his second youth and middle age, to bring anything other than disillusionment. In old age again, he is wearied by its cares and bankruptcy of spirit, its relentless drain of strength. There is nothing left but loneliness and bitter contemplation of the cold ashes of his youth. With the final blow of blindness, he is prepared to abandon his quest forever.

In this extremity, as he declares happiness only an illusion, he suddenly discovers happiness in envisioning a vast humanitarian project. He decides to reclaim coastal swamps and to build upon the free soil homes for millions of men who will labor to maintain their freedom. With this purpose—forgetfulness of self in service to others—the now joyous Faust realizes his ultimate moment, the very peak of human happiness.

But at this very moment, Faust dies. Mephistopheles, it seems, has won his wager with God: Faust indeed has sinned greatly. The Devil claims the soul of the old scholar, but the angels, descending in a shower of roses, dispute him and bear Faust's soul to heaven because, through all Faust's erring, he has ever instinctively traveled toward the light.

Margaret, whose sin and death were the work of Faust, is first to greet his soul in the afterlife. It is her mission to be his guide, for "woman is the eternal saviour of man."

> "His noble spirit now is free,
> And saved from the Devil's scheming:
> Whoever aspires unweariedly
> Is not beyond redeeming."

William Tell

BY FRIEDRICH VON SCHILLER

Born at Marbach, Germany, November 10, 1759. His full name was Johann Christopher Friedrich von Schiller. He wished to be a clergyman, but was educated at a military school under the patronage of the Duke of Wurttemberg, and was appointed military surgeon to a regiment in Stuttgart. In 1781 he published his first play, "The Robbers," which idealized brigandage; it created a sensation. The play was produced in Mannheim in 1782. When Schiller was refused leave of absence to see the play, he attended it secretly. Upon his return to Stuttgart, he was arrested and imprisoned. The duke proposed that he confine his writings to medical topics. Schiller's conflicts at this time were resolved by his appointment as "theatre poet" at Mannheim. He had written two plays in a lighter vein, and he was soon to publish the tragedy, "Don Carlos" (1787). It was in 1787 that he met Goethe, and their intimate friendship dominated the remainder of his life. Most famous of Schiller's later dramas are, "Maria Stuart," "The Maid of Orléans," and his last drama, "William Tell," which has as its subject the struggle of a nation (Switzerland) to free itself from tyranny. He died at Weimar, May 9, 1805, after years of ill health.

The fateful enmity of the tyrant Gessler, Governor of the Swiss cantons, and William Tell, an obscure huntsman, begins during a tempest on Lake Lucerne when Tell braves the angry waves to row to safety a peasant who is pursued by the Governor's horsemen. "The lake may take pity on him; but the Governor, never," says Tell.

His opinion of the bloodthirsty Gessler is shared increasingly by the peasantry as the oppressor fills the old jails, builds a huge new prison at Altdorf for more victims, and sets his cap upon a pole before it, commanding that all who pass must bow to it or pay the penalty of death. Public anger is fanned into rebellion when Gessler blinds an aged man for a trifling misdemeanor. Tell, the individualist, holds aloof from the rebels' councils, but promises his aid when needed.

A friend of the peasants is the aged Baron of Attinghausen, but his nephew and heir, Ulrich of Rudenz, fascinated by the splendor of Gessler's court and love for Bertha, the Governor's ward, is allied with the tyrant. The Baron warns Ulrich that Bertha is being used only to bait him, and that the freedom-loving people will prevail in the end, but the youth goes to join Gessler. While they are together hunting, however, Bertha reveals that she will love him only if he joins in the fight to liberate his own people from Gessler's grip.

Tell prepares to pay a promised visit to his father-in-law, a leader of the rebels, and his wife, fearful that the Governor counts him as an enemy, asks him in vain to postpone the trip. Tell insists that he has nothing to fear, and sets off with his crossbow, accompanied by Walter, his son.

They pass the prison where Tell, failing to salute the Governor's cap, is seized by guardsmen. Several peasants are trying to rescue him when the Governor's hunting party rides up and Gessler demands an explanation from the huntsman. Tell declares his failure to salute was an oversight, and the Governor remarks that he has heard that Tell is a master of the bow. Walter boasts: "Yes, my lord! My father can hit an apple at a hundred yards!" Says Gessler: "Very well, you shall prove your skill now. Shoot an apple from the boy's head. If you miss, your own head shall pay the forfeit."

The spectators are horrified. Tell falls upon his knees, imploring Gessler to withdraw so barbarous a command. He bares his own breast, but the Governor laughs and says: "It is not your life I want, but the shot—the proof of your skill." The boy speaks up: "Shoot, Father! Don't be afraid. I promise to stand still." Tell removes two arrows from his quiver, puts one in his belt, takes aim and sends the other on its way. The boy remains standing. Walter runs to his father, crying: "Here's the apple, Father! I knew you'd never hit me!"

Tell falls upon his knees to embrace his son, but Gessler has not finished with him. "A word with you, Tell," he commands. "I saw you place a second arrow in your belt . . . what was the object?" Tell answers: "If the first arrow had struck my child, the second would have gone through your heart."

Gessler orders him bound and taken to the prison at Kussnacht for his threat; but a great storm comes up which proves to be the huntsman's salvation. Since he alone can take the boat through the gale, his guards release his bonds and Tell steers to a shelving ledge, leaps out, and with his foot thrusts his captors' boat back into the waves. Now, he tells a fisherman, he is planning "a deed that will be in everybody's mouth!"

Meanwhile, Bertha has been borne off by Gessler's men. Ulrich, who earlier had condemned his master for Tell's ordeal and had declared that to keep silent longer would be treason to his country and his King, has gone over wholly to the side of his people. But he returns too late to find the old Baron of Attinghausen alive; his uncle has died with this injunction to the peasants: "The day of the nobles is passing. The new day of the people is at hand . . . the flower of chivalry is cut down, but freedom waves her conquering flag on high. . . . Hold fast together, men— hold forever fast. . . . Be one—be one—be one——"

Ulrich rallies the peasants and is acclaimed their leader. He directs that they arm and wait for a fiery signal on the mountain tops, then swoop down upon the tyrant. A more ominous figure in the revolt, however, is hidden upon the brow of a hill overlooking a road—it is Tell. With his cross-bow ready in his hand, he awaits Gessler who is expected to enter the pass below. Gessler soon appears with his retinue. His way is barred by Armgart, a peasant woman, and her seven children. She cries to the Governor: "Mercy, my lord! Pardon! . . . Pardon! . . . My husband lies in prison. My children cry for bread. Pity, my lord, have pity on him!"

Gessler shouts: "Step aside or, by Heaven, I'll ride you down!" Armgart throws herself and her children before the horses, crying out: "Very well, then ride us down." Gessler shouts: "I've been too mild a ruler to these people. From now on, I must change. I will proclaim a new law throughout the land. I will——"

The sentence is never finished; an arrow pierces his body. Clutching his breast, Gessler cries: "It is William Tell's work! . . . O Lord, have mercy on my soul!" Armgart rejoices: "Dead, dead! He reels, he falls! . . . Look, children! This is how a tyrant dies!"

The shaft that killed Gessler ignites the signal fires of revolution, and at daybreak peasants and workingmen are tearing down the prisons. In one they find Bertha; they rescue her just as burning timbers are about to fall on her. The liberated peasants, with Ulrich and Bertha among them, now throng Tell's home with the cry: "Long live William Tell, our shield and savior!" Bertha, greeting the commoners as comrades, asks to be accepted into their League of Freedom. Her request is granted and she gives her hand to Ulrich. He proclaims: "And from this moment all my serfs are free!"

Nathan the Wise

BY GOTTHOLD EPHRAIM LESSING

Born at Kamenz, Saxony, Germany, January 22, 1729. He first attended the Latin school in the town, then was sent to a school at Meissen where he made amazing progress —especially in mathematics and the classics. He entered the University at Leipzig in 1746 as a theology student. He became irresistibly attracted to the theater and started writing for it, in spite of strong opposition from his father who was a minister. In Berlin, he laid the foundation for his reputation as a brilliant critic of the history of the drama, which was to find full expression in his book, "Laokoon" (1766). He traveled widely, then accepted various posts in Germany—at Leipzig, Hamburg, Berlin and Breslau, finally settling, for his remaining years, in Wolfenbuttel as librarian—a post which was offered him by the Prince of Brunswick. The range of his gifts as a dramatist is indicated by the fact that of his three most famous plays, "Minna von Barnhelm" is a comedy, "Emilia Galotti" is a tragedy, and "Nathan the Wise" is a philosophic drama. Lessing's health became affected by excessive work and anxiety over his many debts, and he died February 15, 1781.

Nathan, a Jewish merchant returning to Jerusalem after a business journey, learns that his adopted daughter, Recha, has been rescued from a fire at his home by a young German Templar of the Third Crusade, a captive whom the Saracen, Sultan Saladin, spared because he resembles Saladin's brother.

Nathan, to whom it was said God had given "the greatest gift, wisdom, and the most worthless, riches," goes to thank the Templar who wanders daily about the Saviour's tomb. The youth first scorns the thanks and the offered reward of a Jew: ". . . If you insist upon a reward, this mantle was slightly scorched in the flames when I rescued your daughter . . . When it is all in rags . . . I will come to borrow the money from you to buy another."

Nathan takes in his hand the scorched cloth and the Templar sees a tear fall upon it. He asks in surprise: "Are there good Jews in this world?" Nathan replies: "There are good men in every land. The tree of life has many branches and roots. Let not the topmost twig presume to think that it alone has sprung from mother earth. . . . We did not choose our races for ourselves. Jews, Moslems, Christians—all alike are men. Let me hope I have found in you—a man."

The Templar apologizes and takes Nathan's hand in

friendship. Names are exchanged, and Nathan appears surprised to learn that the youth's name is Curd von Stauffen. He says no more, for he is summoned by the Sultan who seeks a loan. Saladin is impressed by the gentleness and wisdom of Nathan, and impulsively asks what religion seems to him the truest and best. In answer, Nathan relates a story:

"Once upon a time there was a man who possessed a precious ring. Whoever wore the ring was endowed with the magic power to win the love of God and man. When the owner of the ring died, he left it to his favorite son; and when the son died, he left it in turn to his favorite son." Finally the ring descended to the father of three sons, all equally dear, and he was troubled to decide which should have it. He decided to have made two more rings, so exactly like the first that he was unable to distinguish among them, and gave one to each son. But the sons fought among themselves, each claiming to have the original— exactly, Nathan points out, as the Jews, the Mohammedans and the Christians are wrangling about their three faiths.

Asked for his own advice, Nathan quotes to Saladin the words of the judge to whom the sons came: "'If each of you received this ring straight from his father's hand, let each believe his own to be the true and genuine ring. Of this you may be sure: your father loved you all, and it was his ardent wish that all of you should love one another.'"

The Sultan is deeply impressed. He bids Nathan go in peace, but the merchant offers the loan of his gold, stipulating that he must withhold a part of his fortune to pay his debt to the young Templar. The Sultan recalls the youth who resembles his brother, and bids Nathan bring him to his court.

Meanwhile, Daya, the Christian companion of Recha, has told the Templar that Recha is a Christian whom Nathan had stolen as an infant and reared as a Jewess, a crime punishable by death at the stake. The Templar, who has come to love Recha, resolves to rescue her from Jewish heresies. He repeats Daya's charge to the Christian Patriarch who sends a lay brother to spy upon Nathan.

But the lay brother, arriving at Nathan's home, recognizes him as a benefactor, saying: "Do you remember how, about eighteen years ago, a certain squire confided into your hands a little Christian girl? . . . I was that squire. The babe . . . was the daughter of Wolf Von Filneck. Her mother had just died and her father was compelled to flee to Gaza. Shortly after that he was killed at Ascalon."

Nathan completes the story, revealing that just after the child was entrusted to him, the Christians massacred all the Jews in Gath, including Nathan's wife and seven sons whom he had sent to his brother's home for safety. Nathan had sworn undying hatred of Christendom, but he took the Christian child, kissed its cheek and accepted it as a gift from God to replace his own loved ones.

He asks now if the name of the child's mother was Von Stauffen. The lay brother says he believes that it was, but he will bring to Nathan a little prayer book, found in her dead father's pocket, which lists his relatives and those of his wife.

Later, Saladin, who has taken Nathan under his protection, summons him, with Recha and the Templar, to his palace. He favors a marriage of the young couple and asks Nathan's consent.

Nathan: *Don't ask me. Ask her brother.*

Saladin: *And who is her brother?*

Nathan: *This young Templar.*

Then Nathan explains that the writing in the dead father's prayer book has disclosed that the Templar's true name is Leo Von Filneck, that Von Stauffen was his mother's name, and that Leo and Recha are brother and sister, the children of Wolf Von Filneck. And Wolf Von Filneck, he discloses, is the brother of Saladin. The Mohammedan knight, in love with the Christian girl, had taken the German name of Von Filneck.

Thus the story of the three golden rings finds another parallel amid the general reconciliation at the Sultan's court: Christian, Jew and Moslem have a common bond in this reunion of the children of Christian and Mohammedan who have a Jewish guardian and a Moslem uncle.

NORWEGIAN PLAYS

Hedda Gabler

BY HENRIK IBSEN

*Born in Skien, Norway, March 20, 1828, son of a prosper-
ous merchant. His full name was Henrik Johan Ibsen.
When he was eight, his father failed in business, and the
poverty in which the family lived made a lasting impression on the boy. At fifteen, he was apprenticed to an
apothecary, an occupation which he detested and from
which he could find relief only in writing poetry. He read
widely, especially in poetry and theology, and, in 1850,
went to Christiania as a student. His first play, "Cataline,"
was produced there in 1850. The next year he was appointed "theatre poet" of the new National Theatre at
Bergen. His duties included those of manager, producer
and designer, as well as poet, and he wrote for the National
Theatre a group of plays dealing with Norwegian themes.
In 1864 he left Norway and, for nearly three decades,
resided in foreign countries, chiefly in the cities of Rome,
Dresden and Munich. "Brand" (1866) and "Peer Gynt"
(1867) are two of the greatest of his plays, the first
portraying a fanatic whose slogan is "All or nothing," the
second recording the adventures of a quixotic dreamer.
"Pillars of Society" appeared in 1877. From then until
the end of the century, Ibsen was writing the plays by
which he is best known. These include: "A Doll's House,"
"Ghosts," "An Enemy of the People," "The Wild Duck,"
"Hedda Gabler," and "The Master Builder." A radical
individualism characterizes Ibsen's later plays. They were
at first greeted with bitter hostility, but were later acclaimed. He returned to Christiania in 1891. Before his*

death on May 28, 1906, he had suffered an almost complete physical and mental collapse, and had isolated himself even from his family.

Hedda Gabler, who has been a belle of her set, returns from her honeymoon with George Tesman, a rather colorless scholar, to begin married life in the pretentious villa given them, at great sacrifice, by her aunt. Hedda's chill selfishness moves the aunt to reflect: "God love and preserve Hedda Tesman—for George's sake."

Thea Elvsted, young wife of the elderly Sheriff Elvsted, calls to ask the Tesmans to keep a friendly eye on Eilert Lovborg, an erratic genius who has just returned to the city from their town. Mrs. Elvsted has succeeded in bringing into the life of Lovborg a stability that has enabled him to write a successful book, but she fears that city temptations may be his undoing.

While Tesman is writing a note inviting Lovborg to call that evening, Hedda, who has manifested extraordinary interest in the news of Lovborg's return, extracts from Mrs. Elvsted the confession that she loves Lovborg, and that they have been "good comrades." Hedda asks: "And are you no surer of him than that?" Thea answers: "A woman's shadow stands between Eilert Lovborg and me." Hedda anxiously asks who the woman can be. Mrs. Elvsted doesn't know.

Judge Brack, a friend, coming in to invite George to a party in his honor, discloses that Lovborg is now a rival of Tesman for a professorship at the university, a post that Tesman has counted upon for the support of himself and Hedda and to repay their debts. When they are alone, Hedda taunts George, saying that she supposes she now must wait for the liveried footman and the saddle horse she has wanted. She will have one thing to play with, anyhow, she reminds him—the pistols of her father, General Gabler.

Tesman goes to visit his aunt, and Brack, calling to take him to the party, finds Hedda toying with the pistols.

She tells Brack that she is "mortally bored to be everlast-
ingly in the company of one and the same person," and,
at the suggestion that she loves George, says: "Faugh—
don't use that sickening word." It would be a relief indeed,
she adds, if a third person were to enter their lives, a
possibility suggested by Brack.

They are interrupted by the return of George and the
arrival of Lovborg. Lovborg tells them that his earlier
work will be dwarfed by one he is now writing, a book on
the civilization of the future. He offers to read from it,
but George and Brack are going to the party. Hedda
invites him to remain for supper with her and Mrs. Elvsted.
When George and Brack go for a drink, Lovborg reproaches Hedda for her marriage, and asks: "Was there
no love in your old friendship for me?"

Hedda answers: "I wonder . . ." She confesses that
there had been in it a fascinating beauty, but she had
broken with him "because our friendship threatened to
develop into something more serious. Shame upon you,
Eilert Lovborg!" She confesses that she did not shoot him,
as she had threatened, because she is "a terrible coward"
and dreaded scandal; too, she adds that this "wasn't the
worst part of my cowardice—that night." Lovborg passionately replies: "Ah, then it was your craving for
life . . ."

Mrs. Elvsted arrives, and Lovborg is tortured between
his gratitude to her and his passion for Hedda. He decides
to go to the party, returning to call for Mrs. Elvsted at
ten o'clock. When they have gone, Hedda triumphantly
predicts that Lovborg will return "with vine-leaves in his
hair—flushed and fearless." But at daylight George comes
in to report that Lovborg drank himself into a stupor after
reading a part from his amazing book. George recovered
the manuscript when Lovborg dropped it on the way
home, and Hedda induces him to give it to her "to read"
before he returns it.

Brack comes, after George has left, and reveals that
Lovborg slipped away from his companions, went to a
disreputable house and was arrested after a fight. Brack

leaves. Lovborg enters and is joyfully greeted by Mrs. Elvsted. He laments that he has arrived too late—that the manuscript which Mrs. Elvsted had made possible for him to write he has torn to bits. "I have torn my own life to pieces," he cries.

"To my dying day," Mrs. Elvsted answers, "I shall think of this as though you had killed a little child." But Hedda does not disclose that the manuscript is, in reality, safe; nor, after Thea has gone, does she return it to the distraught Lovborg. Lovborg mourns: "Thea Elvsted's pure soul was in that book!" Hedda gives him one of her pistols, saying to him: "Take it, Eilert Lovborg, and use it . . . use it beautifully . . . Promise me that!" He leaves with the pistol and she throws his manuscript into the fire. Hedda cries: "I am burning your child, Thea Elvsted! Your child and Eilert Lovborg's. I am burning—burning your child!"

Tesman returns and she tells him that she has destroyed the manuscript. "I did it for your sake, dear. I couldn't bear the idea that anyone should throw you in the shade," she insists. Tesman is regretful, yet, at the same time, happy that "lovable Hedda" should care so for him; he agrees to keep the fate of the manuscript secret. Then Thea arrives, frantic because of rumors that Lovborg has killed himself. Brack follows to tell them that Lovborg is dying in a hospital after shooting himself in the breast.

"Not in the temple?" asks Hedda. "Well, the breast is a good place, too . . . at last a deed worth daring." Thea, at Tesman's hypocritical bemoaning of Lovborg's work, discloses that she has Lovborg's notes for the book, and they go to a table to examine them. Hedda and Brack continue their conversation in low voices.

Hedda: *What a beautiful act . . . a shot in the breast!*

Brack: *I fear I must dispel your illusions . . . for poor Mrs. Elvsted's sake I thought it best to put a little luster over the facts . . . He is already dead. He was found shot in the boudoir of . . . a "professional lady."*

Hedda: *But the bullet entered his breast?*

Brack: *No—the bowels.*

Hedda: *What curse is it that makes everything I touch turn ludicrous and mean!*

Brack reminds her that the pistol was found. Hedda, in terror, asks what will happen if the owner is identified. "Then comes the scandal," Brack answers, but he points out that there can be none so long as he keeps silent. "I will not come forward to testify about the pistol," he says, "if——"

Hedda finishes: "If I put myself in your power, Judge Brack. If I become yours, to be at your beck and call from this time on . . . No, I cannot endure the thought of that! Never." She looks at her husband and Mrs. Elvsted working together over the notes. She muses: "Doesn't it seem strange to you, Thea? Here you are sitting with Tesman —just as you used to sit with Eilert Lovborg." Her husband replies that indeed Thea is inspiring, that they shall work together, and that Hedda shall amuse herself with Brack.

Hedda excuses herself and goes into the next room. She plays a mad dance on the piano, then shoots herself—in the temple—with the remaining pistol.

A Doll's House

BY HENRIK IBSEN

The Christmas season finds young Nora Helmer completely happy as she prepares gifts and a Christmas tree for her three little children and for her husband, Torvald, who is accustomed to chaffing her with amused tolerance as "my little lark," "my little squirrel" and "my little spendthrift." Indeed, Nora has continually wheedled from him such small sums of money as he can afford, but now an end to the need for scrimping is in sight: Torvald has been appointed manager of the bank, with a substantial raise in salary.

To a surprise caller, Mrs. Linde, an old friend whom

Nora has not seen in ten years, she reveals the secret of her apparent extravagances. When she and Torvald were first married, Nora tells her, Torvald had driven himself into a serious illness, and was required to live for a time in Italy. Because Torvald was too proud to borrow the money to do so, she secretly raised the needed sum by a loan secured on the signature of her father, now dead. Since that time, she has been repaying the loan with what money she has been able to tease from Torvald and to save from the household budget.

Nora means never to tell the strict Torvald—fearing that the knowledge of what she has done will humiliate him—until perhaps the time comes when she is no longer pretty, and "when my dancing and dressing-up and reciting have palled on him." Through the misery of the years of her scrimping, she has liked to imagine that some day some rich old gentleman would fall in love with her and would leave her a great estate; but now Torvald's appointment has ended the long strain.

Nora promises that Torvald shall provide a job at the bank for Mrs. Linde, now widowed and lonely. Torvald and Dr. Rank, the Helmers' closest friend, come in. While they chat, a bank employee of unsavory reputation, Nils Krogstad, calls on Torvald, much to Nora's agitation. But when she reflects that now Krogstad will be the underling of her husband at the bank, she is strangely merry. It is from Krogstad that she borrowed the money. The others leave. While Nora is romping happily with her children Krogstad slips back.

He demands to know if he is to be replaced in the bank by Mrs. Linde with whom, years ago, he had been in love. He pleads for his job, declaring that he has atoned for a single past slip and that he is determined to re-establish himself. Then he threatens that, should he be discharged, he will not only reveal Nora's borrowing to her husband, but will disclose that she, in her ignorance of the law, signed her dying father's name to the bond.

When Torvald returns, he declares Krogstad a cunning forger who is not worth redemption; Nora must not ask that he be spared. He abstractedly lectures on the influence of a guilty parent upon children, and goes into the room that is his office. Nora, now pale with terror and doubt, refuses to play again with the children. She echoes her husband's words: "Deprave my little children? Poison my home? . . . It can't possibly be true!"

The following day finds her even more depressed, avoiding her children and fearfully awaiting Krogstad's letter to her husband. She is saddened, too, when Torvald again refuses to spare Krogstad at her pleading—chiefly because the clerk, a former schoolmate of his, adopts "a familiar tone" that grates on his new importance. In her desperation, Nora resolves to ask Dr. Rank for money to redeem her note, but before she can do so, he reveals that he is soon to die of a disease now far advanced, and he tells her that he is in love with her. With his declaration, Nora feels that this escape is closed.

Krogstad comes again, secretly, to tell her that he has prepared a letter informing her husband of the loan, but he urges her not to do anything desperate—that everything can be handled quietly. She hints at suicide and Krogstad jeers: "Under the ice, perhaps? Down into the cold, coal-black water? And then, in the spring, to float up to the surface, all horrible and unrecognizable, with your hair fallen out . . ." As he goes out, he drops the letter in the letter box.

Nora then tells Mrs. Linde: "A wonderful thing is going to happen . . . but it is so terrible . . . it mustn't happen, not for all the world." Mrs. Linde promises to go to Krogstad to plead for her.

Nora, to keep Torvald from the letter box, rehearses for him a dance she is to perform at a masquerade party the next evening. Torvald at length finds out that a letter from Krogstad has come but he promises not to read it until after the party.

While the Helmers are at the party, Mrs. Linde sees Krogstad. Explanations lead to a reconciliation of the former lovers, now both widowed, lonely and needing each other. Mrs. Linde's faith in him reawakens the goodness

in Krogstad: he wants to try to recapture the letter before
Torvald can read it, but Mrs. Linde has come to feel that
the Helmers must have a complete understanding. She tells
Nora that she must tell her husband the truth.

At home after the party, at which Nora's tarantella had
been a huge success, Helmer, warmed by champagne, tells
his wife that he has been seeing her as his young bride
again, and that he could not wait longer to be alone with
her. Rank interrupts them, coming in to say good night.
He has been having a merry evening, perhaps his last, as
even now a black-crossed card, a signal to Nora that he is
definitely doomed, is lying in the Helmer letter box. Rank
jokingly remarks that, at his next masquerade, he will
wear a costume of invisibility, and Nora broodingly
answers that she may be with him then.

When Rank has gone, Torvald opens the letter box, and
goes to read his letters. Nora is preparing to leave the
house, thinking of the icy black water pictured by Krogstad,
when Torvald stops her with a bitter torrent of condemnation. He calls her a miserable creature, a liar, a hypocrite;
he mourns this blow to his pride and position. Finally, he
decides that they must continue with the pretense of married life, but that Nora must not be allowed to bring up
her children.

Nora has become ominously cold and quiet when another letter from Krogstad arrives. It says that, in remorse,
he is destroying the bond. Torvald laughs in relief: "I am
saved, Nora! . . . You, too, of course . . . I have forgiven
you everything. I know that what you did you did out of
love for me." But Nora, her face set, compels him to sit
down for their first serious talk in the eight years of their
married life.

Telling him that they have never really loved, nor has
she ever been fully happy, she says: ". . . Our home has
been nothing but a playroom. I have been your doll-wife,
just as at home I was Papa's doll-child; and here the children have been my dolls . . . I must try and educate myself—you are not the man to help me in that. I must do
that for myself, and that is why I am going to leave you

now." He protests that she talks like a child, but she declares she must learn for herself "who is right, the world
or I."

She tells him why she no longer loves him: "It was
tonight, when the wonderful thing did not happen; then
I saw you were not the man I had thought you. I have
waited so patiently for eight years . . . Then this horrible
misfortune came upon me; and I felt quite certain that
the wonderful thing was going to happen at last. . . . I
was so absolutely certain that you would say: 'Publish the
thing to the whole world' . . . and then you would come
forward and take everything upon yourself, and say: 'I am
the guilty one!' . . . It was to prevent that that I wanted
to kill myself."

Nora leaves the house, saying to Torvald that reconciliation can come only if "the most wonderful thing of all"
should happen, so that their marriage could become real
wedlock. As the door closes, Torvald is hopefully repeating
the phrase: "The most wonderful thing of all——?"

Peer Gynt

BY HENRIK IBSEN

Peer Gynt is a Norwegian farm lad who wastes his time in
lazy dreaming, boasting and brawling—a symbol of the man
who ever colors truth and fact in wishful compromises,
evasion and selfishness.

Ase, his old mother, berates him for his neglect of the
farm. He answers her: "Darling, ugly little mother, you
are right in every word . . . don't be cross . . . just be
patient . . . someday I will be a kaiser!" She reminds him
that his sloth has cost him a bride, Hegstad's daughter,
who is about to be married. Peer impetuously decides to
attend the wedding and to break it up. He sets out, after
first perching his protesting mother on the rooftop.

At the wedding Peer is scorned for his rags and his lies by all the company—except one girl, Solveig, a new-comer, and even she avoids him upon discovery of his reputation. His feelings hurt, he gets drunk, and, at the bridegroom's appeal, goes to bring the bride from a store-house where she has locked herself in. Meanwhile, his mother arrives, armed with a stick to give Peer "the dub-bing of his life." Suddenly, the guests see Peer Gynt fleeing up the mountain with the bride over his shoulder. Ase cries: "I hope you fall and break—— Take care of your footing, child!"

Now Peer Gynt embarks upon a symbolic series of fantastic adventures. Abandoning the stolen bride, he goes deep into the wilderness and there marries—and deserts—the daughter of the Elf King. In the wilderness he comes upon the Great Boyg, a monster as inexplicable and formless as the enigma of existence. Repeatedly he vainly tries to find a passage through the monster to attain the mountain top. In desperation he challenges the Boyg to battle. It replies: "The Great Boyg conquers, but does not fight," and the exhausted Peer Gynt finally falls to the ground. He is about to be devoured by a cloud of birds when women's voices and church bells are heard in the distance. The Boyg capitulates with the words: "He was too strong for me. There were women behind him to help him in the fight!"

Peer Gynt builds himself a hut in the forest, and here Solveig comes to share his outlaw's exile. She tells him: "This is where I belong . . . I hastened here on my snow-shoes, and when they asked me: 'Whither are you going?' I answered: 'I am going home.'" Soon Peer Gynt comes once again upon the daughter of the Elf King and their ugly child. The two cannot be driven away, and Peer, again taking his "roundabout" course, decides to leave. Solveig says only: "Don't go too far, my dear." He replies: "Be my way far or near, you must wait."

He goes to say farewell to his mother and finds her dying in the bed where he had slept as a little boy—where he and she once played that the bed was a sleigh and sped in fancy to "the Castle West of the Moon and the Castle East of the Sun." Peer Gynt takes his mother in his arms and begins to tell her a fairy story to calm her fears. He tells her that the King is giving a feast in the castle—that indeed she is invited; that the ringing in her ears is only the sound of the sleighbells, the rushing noise is the wind in the pines, and the light she sees from afar comes from the King's palace. He reports that they are welcomed with greatest honor, with cakes and wine, and he entrusts her to the care of St. Peter. Then he closes her dead eyes, saying, "Ay, ay, now the journey's done . . . For all my days I thank you, for your beatings and your lullabies." He presses his cheek against her mouth. "There, that was the driver's fare," he murmurs.

Now Peer is off again, to wander over the world. He sells slaves in America, idols in China, as well as rum and Bibles. He has been robbed, but has recouped his loss by setting himself up as an Arabian prophet on the rim of the African desert. He runs away with Anitra, a dancing girl. When they stop to rest, he attempts to prove "that your old Prophet can still caper like a young colt," and begins a labored dance. While he is absorbed in his antics, she grabs his moneybag and gallops off on his horse.

And so Peer Gynt struggles on with his planless life. He is crowned King of the Lunatics in an insane asylum, he becomes an archeologist before the Sphinx, and, at last, finds himself on a boat bound homeward to Norway. The ship is wrecked. Peer Gynt and the ship's cook cling to a frail spar, large enough only to save one. Peer thrusts the cook into the sea and saves himself. Eventually he reaches Norway.

Now he has had enough of adventuring and hopes for a serene old age at home. But on the heath he meets a Button-Moulder who says: "I have been sent for you . . . you are to go into my ladle . . . I must melt you up." Peer Gynt protests that to lose his soul, his identity, his self, is not fair. "I'm not really a bad soul. At worst, you may call me a bungler, but certainly not an exceptional sinner," he pleads.

That, says the Button-Moulder, is just the trouble: "You're not bad enough for the sulphur-pit, nor good enough for Paradise. And so, into the ladle you go!"

Peer Gynt insists: "But you cannot kill a soul! Haven't I been a personality? An individual? Myself?"

"You have been selfish," the Button-Moulder replies, "but not yourself."

Peer Gynt asks the answer to his riddle: "What is it, to be one's self?" The Button-Moulder answers: "To be one's self is to deny one's self." He declares that Peer Gynt can have neither the reward nor the punishment accorded an individual soul, and must go into the ladle of nonentity unless he can prove himself a sinner worthy of Hell. Choosing Hell rather than nothingness, Peer Gynt recites that he has sold slaves, cheated, deceived and saved himself at the cost of another man's life; but these, says the Button-Moulder, are but trifles.

The two have come to Peer Gynt's hut, and in the doorway stands Solveig, now a middle-aged woman, who has serenely waited through the years for Peer Gynt's return. She stands proudly, dressed for church, her prayer book in her hand. Peer Gynt throws himself at her feet and calls upon her to cry out his sins and trespasses.

Solveig: *You are here! Oh, God be praised!*

Peer Gynt: *Cry aloud my crime to you!*

Solveig: *Your crime? To me? You have made all my life as a beautiful song!*

Peer Gynt: *But who am I? And where have I been?*

Solveig: *You are my beloved. And you have been ever in my faith, in my hope, in my heart.*

From behind the hut comes the Button-Moulder's voice: "We shall meet again, Peer Gynt. And then we shall see . . ."

Solveig adds: "I will cradle thee, I will watch thee; sleep and dream now, my dear child." Peer Gynt buries his face in her lap.

SWEDISH PLAYS

The Father

*Born in Stockholm, Sweden, January 22, 1849, his full
name being Johan August Strindberg. After a short period
of study at the University of Upsala, he became a school-
teacher. Later, he was appointed librarian in the Royal
Library. His first play, "In Rome," deals with the life of
the sculptor, Thorvaldsen. Strindberg was married three
times. He expressed contradictory mental attitudes, and is
not easily classified. During one period of his life he was
on the verge of insanity. After writing the stories and
sketches of "Married" (1884–86), he was prosecuted for
assailing the dogma of the communion, but he defended
himself and was acquitted. He was a prolific writer, and is
generally regarded as Sweden's greatest modern author. In
addition to his gloomy play, "The Father," he wrote a
play entitled "Miss Julia" (sometimes called "Countess
Julia") which he described as "naturalistic." From his early
skepticism he turned to a kind of mysticism. "Swanwhite"
and "A Dream Play" are products of this mood. He died in
1912.*

A clash of wills between Captain Adolf, a scientist, and his
wife, Laura, over the destiny of their child, Bertha, has
reached a crisis. Adolf complains to Laura's brother, the
Pastor, that the women of his household—even the servants
—are usurping what he feels is his right as a father. The
Pastor recalls that Laura was adamant in her stubbornness
even as a child.

Adolf flatly tells Laura that Bertha is to live away from the home, that home "with its disruptive influences," and to learn to be a teacher. He reminds his wife that the law gives jurisdiction over the children to the father. Laura replies: "And in case it is not known who is the father of the child? . . . Suppose the wife has been unfaithful?" Adolf retorts: "There is no such case! Have you any other questions?" Laura, the seed of an idea planted in her mind, merely says: "None whatsoever."

She loses no time in her subtle campaign to destroy the faith of the community in her husband. She hastens to tell a new doctor, who is to live at their house, that Adolf's sanity is affected; that he buys boxes of books that he never reads, studies a microscope for clues to another planet, is irritable and obstinate "beyond the bounds of sanity." The Doctor, who has admired Adolf's writings, learns that Laura has been intercepting her husband's orders for books and that his microscopic studies have been wholly practical, but he cannot quite free himself from Laura's insinuations.

Laura now extends her scheming to the child. When Adolf attempts to explain to Bertha that spiritualism, an obsession of Laura's mother, is nonsense, she protests: "But Grandmother says you don't know what you are talking about. And Mother says so, too." Bertha adds that she would love to go away and study, "but Mother won't let me."

Adolf again insists to his wife that Bertha is to go, but she repeats that he may not be the father of Bertha and so is powerless to enforce his will. She taunts him to such fury with this thought that he rushes from the house, declaring that he will not return before midnight.

But, by midnight, he has not come back, and Laura again is strengthening her influence over the Doctor, insisting that Adolf is not in his right mind. "But I believe him to be quite sane," the Doctor protests. She continues: "Is it sane for him to insist that he is not the father of his own child?" The Doctor wavers; he agrees that Adolf must be watched carefully.

Laura's plot is furthered when her husband, returning, asks the Doctor if paternity can ever be proved. Disappointed when he finds that it cannot be, he declares his belief that all women are faithless. The Doctor warns that his thoughts are becoming morbid and that he must exercise greater control, but Adolf cannot rid himself of his fear. Even when Laura, in an interlude of affection, swears that he is the father of Bertha, he cannot believe her. He is suspicious now of even her tenderness, and declares to her that love between the sexes is only strife, that there is endless struggle between every husband and wife. One of the two, he says, must meet defeat, and, of course, the victor will be the stronger.

"Then I am the winner," Laura declares, "for I have the strength of the law on my side." She threatens that, with the aid of the law, she will have him committed as a madman. She says to him: "The Doctor will offer his professional testimony that you are a dangerous person to be at large. . . . You have fulfilled your function as an unfortunately necessary father and breadwinner . . . We can live comfortably on your pension . . . You are not needed any longer, and you must go." In a passion of fury, Adolf throws a lamp at her as she backs from the room.

Now everyone believes Adolf to be insane; the living room has been barricaded to restrain him, and the Doctor has sent for a strait-jacket. The Pastor comes, and Laura explains: "It began with the wild fancy that he was not Bertha's father, and it ended with his throwing the lighted lamp in my face." The Pastor asks if she is blameless, and, at her protestation of innocence, says: "Oh, well. Perhaps I had better keep still . . . After all, blood is thicker than water."

As the Doctor is instructing the housekeeper to slip the strait-jacket on Adolf when he signals, Adolf bursts into the room with his arms loaded with books, exclaiming: "The whole story is to be found here, in every book! The story about the cruelty, the unfaithfulness, the treachery of every woman!" The Pastor asks if he knows he is insane, and Adolf answers: "Yes, I know it well enough. But do you know how I became so? That is the question!"

Bertha comes into the room and reproaches her father for throwing the lamp at her mother; suppose it had hit her? He answers: "Would it have mattered much?" Bertha exclaims: "You are not my father if you can talk like that!" She runs from the room at his outburst: "Not your father? So you, too, know that? Who told you? Come now, confess!" He is in a frenzy of grief and anger. He cries: "And now the child, too! All of them, all set against me!" The Doctor motions to the housekeeper who slips the strait-jacket on him—with the apology that the child must be protected.

Adolf cries: "I wish I had killed the child! For life is a hell, and death is a heaven . . . Children belong to heaven." He is now safely bound and Laura returns. She says to him: "Adolf, look at me. Do you think that I am your enemy?" He replies: "Yes. I think that all the members of your sex are my enemies. My mother, who brought me into the world against her will. My sister, who exacted obedience from me as a child. The first woman I embraced, who repaid me for my love with ten years of illness. My daughter, who took sides with you against me. And you, my wife, who have used me up and then rejected me like a cast-off garment."

Laura protests: "Before God and my conscience, I consider myself innocent. Your existence has crushed my heart like a heavy stone, and I have tried to shake off the oppressive burden. These are the facts, and if I have struck you a fatal blow, I ask your forgiveness."

"This sounds so plausible and so tragic," he retorts. ". . . To search for God, and to find the Devil—this is the tragedy of all married life." He is cold and asks for a cover. Laura spreads a shawl over him. She says: "Give me your hand, friend."

Adolf exclaims: ". . . The hand that you have bound! . . . But I can feel your shawl against my face. It is warm and soft, like your arms, and it smells of vanilla, like your hair when I first met you. . . . We walked in the birchwoods, with the oxlips and the thrushes . . . Life was beautiful in those days. And what is it now? You did not wish this, and I didn't, and yet it happened. Who, then, rules over our destiny?"

"God alone rules," Laura answers. Adolf adds: "The god of strife."

HUNGARIAN PLAYS

The Guardsman

BY FERENC MOLNÁR

*Born January 12, 1878, in Budapest, Hungary. He was
educated at the Royal College of Science, in the Law
Faculty at Budapest, and at the University of Geneva.
During his college years he started writing short stories and
plays, and became so interested in this field that he became a reporter instead of a lawyer when he graduated.
He worked on several Budapest papers and, between 1914
and 1918, was a war correspondent. In 1907 he established
his reputation as a dramatist with his play, "The Devil."
His most original play was "Liliom," successful in its own
right and subsequently repopularized in a musical adaptation, "Carousel," by Rodgers and Hammerstein. "Liliom"
was followed by "The Guardsman" and "The Swan." For
the last-named he received the cross of the French Legion
of Honor. His later works did not maintain the high stand-
ard of these first plays, but his articles and sketches are
clever and sophisticated. He was much sought after for his
wit and personal charm. He came to America in 1940,
and died in 1952.*

In their Vienna apartment, the Actor and his lovely wife,
Marie, Viennese stage favorites, are in a temperamental
quarrel as he packs his things for a three-day guest appearance in Olmutz. The Actress is moodily playing a
Chopin nocturne as he bickers with the maid, Liesl, and
with Mama, a combination cook and fictitious mother of

Marie when occasion requires. An amiable listener is Bernhard, a critic and old friend of the couple.

The Actor declares that now, after only six months of
marriage, Marie no longer loves him. As she weeps, he
storms quietly: "Let us separate then . . . Let us confess
honestly that this is the end . . . That will be better than
this sort of thing—these everlasting lies, these hidden tears,
this—this Chopin music——" He is interrupted by Rosenzweig, a bill collector, to whom he gives theater passes. He
then resumes his reproaches—only to be interrupted again
by the delivery of roses for Marie. He demands surrender
of the message sent with the flowers, but she refuses—declaring that the sender admires, appreciates and loves her.

When she leaves the room, the Actor confides to Bernhard that he himself had been sending the roses under an
assumed name as part of a plan to test his wife. He recalls
that she had at least seven springtime romances before
marriage, each lasting only six months. He fears that he is
to be the next to be deserted now that she has taken again
to Chopin and daydreams. He discloses that he is prepared
to masquerade as the man he believes she is seeking.

Marie has told him, he says, that her current romantic
ideal is a foreign soldier, and he is sure that if he assumes
the role of a mysterious Russian Guardsman he will learn
finally if she is lost to him (as well as whether or not he
is a really good actor). He has painstakingly planned all
the details for the masquerade—costume, make-up, voice
and accent—and has hidden his uniforms in the apartment
of a friend next door.

So far, the plan has worked perfectly. He walked by
outside until she happened to see him from the window:
he saluted but, to his joy, she pulled down the window
shade. But the next time she smiled. He, using the name
Wassilly Samsonov, sent the first flowers, and Marie later
insisted to him that they came from a silly girl admirer.
Other roses he sent she left at the theater. Finally she
agreed, in a note, to meet the Guardsman, and the Actor
invented the Olmutz engagement to prepare for his call
of this evening. The Guardsman is supposed to be in the

street, waiting to appear at her signal from the window.
As the Actor and the critic watch, Marie furtively gives the
signal. The Actor bids his wife a tragic farewell; she kisses
him with ostentatious passion.

Marie succeeds in dismissing the critic, and arrays herself in her most fetching tea gown. She is playing the
Chopin nocturne again when the Guardsman, speaking
with a strong accent and wearing the imposing uniform of
a Russian prince, is ushered in. They have tea and chat
conventionally, but soon the Guardsman, after a sincere
tribute to the professional artistry of her husband, begins
to speak of love—and finds some demure encouragement.
He rises to approach her, but she hurriedly offers one of
her husband's "not very good" cigarettes. "These," he says
emphatically, "are very good cigarettes." He feels that he
had best leave at once before "my feeling may carry me
too far," but she invites him to visit her box at the opera
later that night.

He is quick to appear at the box where Marie is sitting
with Mama and, in an anteroom, loses no time in renewing
his wooing. She tells him: "I do not mind your making love
to me but you must not do it with so definite a purpose.
And you must remember . . . I love my husband." But
he persists, rather fearfully, "respecting the fact that you
are in love with your husband," and then she qualifies her
declaration: "Between loving and being in love there is a
wider gulf than between not loving and being in love." He
replies with difficulty: "Well, that makes me very—that
makes me very happy."

Of her husband's love, she only says, rather dolorously:
"God knows everything." He comments that the Actor certainly is incomparably handsome; she agrees that he is
handsome and intelligent, but hints that her married life is
somewhat dull. He suggests that she may care to deceive
her husband, and she majestically goes back to her box.
But she soon returns to him; he congratulates her for her
"very good answer" to his suggestion, and she horrifies him
by denying that she has yet answered. Then she declares

that she never could deceive her husband. Joyously, he is about to throw off his disguise when Bernhard appears.

The critic jests with the Guardsman, intimating that he has another affair elsewhere, and Marie indignantly goes back to her box. Once more the Guardsman declares that he is going to make one last violent effort: when Marie says, "Leave me forever," he will reveal himself as her husband, all his doubts dissipated. But to his dismay, and before Bernhard, she declares her admiration for the Guardsman: ". . . At last a man who has no ringing voice, a man who, thank God, is neither intelligent nor brilliant —nor melancholy, nor sentimental . . . after all these years —at last a MAN." She, "burning with a great flame," kisses the anguished Guardsman and bids him call at her home the next afternoon at five.

As she waits, next day, the Actor returns with his trunk and bags, explaining that he has been recalled to the Vienna theater. He questions her on her activities while he has been gone, telling her that the doorman had spoken of a soldier calling. No doubt Liesl's lover, answers Marie. She becomes angry at his continued inquisition and threatens to leave him, compelling him to declare that he loves and trusts her utterly.

It is nearly time for the Guardsman's call, and she urges the Actor to go out for a walk for half an hour. She denies expecting a caller, and he agrees to go as soon as he has unpacked his costumes for the night. She takes up a novel and lies back on the sofa to read. He kneels behind the open trunk and begins to change into his Guardsman's uniform, keeping up a conversation about the theater.

Promptly at five o'clock, he rises from behind the trunk in his Guardsman's uniform, and exclaims: "His majesty himself could not be more punctual." She looks at him; there is a pause. Suddenly a smile brightens her face. She takes on the tone and manner she has assumed when with the Guardsman, and speaks with artless ease: "Good afternoon, Prince." He shouts: "Are you trying out a part—are you acting?" "No," she answers, "you are doing the acting . . . I'm going on with our little comedy . . . the comedy

that I've been playing for your sake since yesterday afternoon." She declares that she has recognized him from the
start. He denies this, but Rosenzweig, the bill collector,
returns and, to the Actor's discomfiture, recognizes him at
once, although observing that the Actor's own wife might
be deceived.

Marie then tells her husband: "I wanted you to play the
comedy out to the end . . . I didn't think that you'd rob us
of that beautiful night." She says she is crying "because
you love me so—and because I am just a bit ashamed of
myself." She goes to the piano again as the critic arrives.
Bernhard blandly says, in what may be a gallant falsehood,
that Marie confided her recognition to him, and he suggests
that the Actor remove his "rather ridiculous" costume. The
husband answers: "I'd look even more ridiculous if she
hadn't recognized me." He begins to unpack, their quarreling is resumed and Marie plays again the Chopin nocturne.

Liliom

BY FERENC MOLNÁR

Liliom, an engaging blusterer who is a barker for the
Widow Muskat's merry-go-round in a Budapest amusement park, is attracted to Julie, a visitor. The jealous Mrs.
Muskat tells her to stay away, and Liliom, taking sides with
Julie, is discharged. They sit together on a park bench
under the acacia blossoms and Liliom, although warning
her that he is a "good-for-nothing fellow," asks Julie to
marry him. She accepts.

They go to live in the hovel of Mrs. Hollunder, Julie's
aunt, but Liliom has no job and soon, in his humiliation
and self-contempt, he habitually growls at his wife and
occasionally beats her. Her aunt advises Julie to divorce
him and marry a well-to-do carpenter who is attentive to
her, but Julie seems content with the unhappy Liliom.

Soon she tells him that she is to have a baby. On hearing the news, he throws himself on the sofa and buries his head in the cushion; Julie covers him with a shawl and tiptoes from the room.

With the added responsibility of fatherhood, Liliom desperately seeks some way to get the badly needed money. He agrees to attempt, with a crony, the holdup of a factory cashier. He is hoping to take Julie and their baby to America with the money, but the robbery is a failure and, in a struggle, Liliom is fatally wounded.

Brought home to die, he tells Julie: "There's something I want to tell you—like when you've finished eating in a restaurant—and it's time to pay up. . . . Well—I beat you —not because I was mad at you—no—but because I can't bear to see anyone crying. . . . Tell the baby—I wasn't much good—but—I thought that perhaps—in America . . . If the carpenter asks you—marry him. And the child—tell him he's his father. . . . Tell me, little Julie, do you think I'll see—the Lord God today? . . . Hold my hand, Julie, tight—tighter—I'm going."

Julie caresses the dead face, crying: "Sleep, Liliom, sleep. . . . Now I can tell you, you bad, rough, unhappy, wicked—dear quick-tempered boy . . . It was wicked of you to beat me . . . but sleep peacefully now . . . I love you, Liliom—I never told you this before—I was ashamed —but now I can tell you. . . ." She covers his face and leaves the room. Then two men in black enter; they are the Heavenly Police who bid Liliom to come before the Judgment Seat.

At the Judgment Seat, Liliom faces the Magistrate as defiantly as in life. Asked if he is sorry that he was a bad husband, he explains: "I couldn't get work. I couldn't bear to see her—all the time——" "Weeping?" the Magistrate finishes for him. "Why are you ashamed to say the word?" Liliom asks if he did right to steal for Julie, and the Magistrate answers: "Yes . . . but are you sorry you beat her?" Liliom shame-facedly insists that he is sorry for nothing, and denies that he died for love of Julie and their unborn child.

The Magistrate rules that Liliom shall remain in Hell for sixteen years, until the stubbornness is burnt out of him. At the end of that time, he may have a single day on earth to do "something good, something splendid" for his daughter to prove that his soul has been purified. The Policemen beckon and Liliom, pausing only to ask for and light a cigarette, walks through the door of the Crimson Pit and into a blast of flame.

Sixteen years later, Julie and her daughter, Louise, are living in a rickety cottage on the edge of town. Julie has chosen to reject the carpenter and remain a widow, even though the factory wages of herself and Louise leave them in poverty. But they are happy as they prepare to eat their meal in their little garden on a bright spring Sunday. Then Liliom appears, two Heavenly Policemen waiting near by to observe his actions.

Julie, assuming him to be a beggar, offers him soup. Liliom asks if Louise is her daughter, then inquires for her husband. He is dead, Julie answers, and Louise adds: "He went to America to work and he died there . . . Poor Father, I never knew him." She asks Liliom if he knew her father and he nods. "Was he really a very handsome man?" the girl inquires. "I wouldn't exactly say handsome," he replies. But to the girl's confident statement that her father was "an awfully good man," the incorrigible Liliom declares: "He wasn't exactly so good, either. As far as I know, he was what they call a clown, a barker in a carousel . . . something of a bully, too. He even hit your dear little mother."

Julie indignantly denies this: "No, never. He was always good to me." She orders him to go. Louise echoes her mother: "Go, in God's name, and let us be. Why are you making those ugly faces?" But Liliom, striving frantically to redeem himself, pleads: "Don't chase me away, Miss; let me come in just for a minute—just long enough to let me show you something pretty, something wonderful . . . Miss, I've got something to give you." He looks around furtively to make sure that the Policemen are not watching; then, from his pocket handkerchief he takes a glittering star that he has stolen from Heaven.

But Julie and Louise again order him off. He cries: "Miss —please, Miss—I've got to do something good . . . a good deed——" Louise repeats her order to him to leave, and the now exasperated Liliom suddenly slaps her resoundingly on the hand. She looks dazedly at him, Liliom bows his head forlornly, and Julie rises with an astonished stare at Liliom. Louise, in wonderment, tells Julie that the slap "didn't hurt—it was like a caress—as if he had just touched my hand tenderly," and Julie softly orders her into the house. She asks the beggar if that is what he came for—to strike her child. He answers: "No . . . but I did strike her —and now I'm going back."

She asks: "In the name of the Lord Jesus, who are you?" He answers: "A poor, tired beggar . . . Are you angry with me?" Julie, her hand on her heart, answers dazedly: "Jesus protect me—I don't understand it—I'm not angry— not angry at all." Liliom goes to the doorway, leans for a moment against the doorpost, then walks slowly off, followed by the Policemen who regretfully shake their heads at his failure.

Julie stares into space. Louise asks her what has happened. Says Julie: "Nothing has happened . . . A beggar came who talked of bygone days, and then I thought of your father." Louise, still pondering Liliom's slap, asks Julie if anyone ever had hit her so, and if it is possible that so sharp a blow may not hurt at all.

Julie answers: "Yes, my child. It has happened to me, too . . . It is possible, dear, that someone may beat you and beat you and beat you—and not hurt you at all——"

CZECHOSLOVAKIAN PLAYS

R.U.R.

BY KAREL CAPEK

Born in Bohemia in 1890. After studying at Prague, Berlin and Paris, he started writing—mostly short stories with his brother Joseph. Soon, he became producer at the Municipal Theatre in Prague, and wrote some of his best-known plays—"R.U.R.," "The Insect Play," "The Macropulos Secret," and "White Malady." "R.U.R." was the play which introduced the word "robot" into common usage. He also wrote travel sketches, essays and biographies—notably the two books about his good friend, Thomas G. Masaryk, entitled, "President Masaryk Tells His Story" and "Masaryk on Thought and Life." He died December 24, 1938.

Helena Glory, daughter of the president of Rossum's Universal Robots, has come to the island factory where the Robots, mechanical but human-like creatures, are manufactured. Harry Domin, manager of the plant, is telling her of the Robots' origin while around them the strange machine figures go about their tasks.

The original Rossum, a mad scientist, discovered the secret of how to create living organisms; he finally succeeded in fashioning one in the shape of a man. He quickly created others, fancying himself a god. But he died shortly thereafter, and his son, a businessman, saw the possibilities of wholesale manufacture of the Robots for commercial uses. Soon he was selling Robots all over the world.

Domin, who offers to dissect Sulla, his Robot secretary, to demonstrate the machine-like nature of Robots, points out that the creatures are manufactured in different grades, at various prices. The finer types are more efficient and brilliant and command a higher price. All Robots last for twenty years. Helena reveals that she has come to put a stop to this exploitation of these innocent beings, but Domin and his staff assure her that the Robots are incapable of human feelings; only occasionally do they refuse to work. When that happens they are sent to the stamping mill where they are turned in as material for new Robots. She suggests that their rebellion may be their souls in revolt, but Fabry, the engineer, insists that Robots haven't any. To create souls, he adds, would increase the cost of production.

Helena asks why some of the Robots are made in female form; Domin explains that they are sexless and incapable of love, but females are made to supply the need for servants, saleswomen and stenographers. He reminds her that he and she, however, can afford to be a bit mad at times—the most interesting faculty of real human beings—and he asks her to marry him. She accepts him.

Ten years later, when Domin and Helena are about to celebrate their wedding anniversary, there is reported several unexplained outbursts among the Robots. They have smashed furniture and machinery in the factory. Their rebellion is symptomatic of a Robot revolution throughout the world. This has come at a time when there has been a startling failure on the part of human beings to reproduce —the human race seems threatened with extinction. In a newspaper which her husband has neglected to conceal, Helena reads that the Robots have massacred more than seven hundred thousand people. She begs Domin to close the factory and leave before it is too late. Domin now confesses to her that the Robots have seized all their firearms and have taken over their means of communication and transport.

They have only one hope left. Domin has learned that a mail boat is on its way to the island; if it arrives, they will know that human beings have put down the revolution, and it will then be safe for them to leave (with the formula for the manufacture of the Robots) on a gunboat which he has kept in readiness for just such an emergency. The mail boat does reach port, but the Robots capture it. They seize the gunboat and begin to besiege Domin's house.

At this point, Dr. Gall, the factory physiologist, admits that it is he who has made possible this revolt: he has been secretly attempting to transform the Robots into real human beings—giving them feelings such as resentment, irritability and pain. Helena owns that she has influenced Gall to try to endow the Robots with souls, hoping for a brotherhood between Robots and humans. Busman, the advertising manager, now comes forward with a suggestion: their only chance may be to buy their safety with the formula, for without it the Robots will all die in twenty years without being able to replace themselves.

But Helena has burnt the formula. She says: "It was so awful . . . no more children being born . . . human beings supplanted by machines . . . soulless creatures coming to the top . . . I couldn't stand it any longer."

Suddenly the lights go out. There is an explosion and the Robots pour into the house. They kill all the occupants —the last humans left on earth—except Alquist, the old chemist. They spare him in the hope that he can re-discover the secret of their creation. The Robots' leader proclaims: "Robots of the world! The human race is dead! A new might has arisen—the rule of the Robots!"

Under the compulsion of the Robots, Alquist strives to duplicate Rossum's feat of creation, but he fails. Radius, the Robot leader, commands that he succeed: the Robots have accomplished miracles of labor, but they are dying fast and soon there will be none of them left. Alquist protests his helplessness, and the leader orders that he shall dissect a Robot body to learn how it is made. Finally Alquist consents to try, saying to Radius: "You will have it. Into the dissecting room with you then." He hits the leader on the chest. The Robot recoils. "Ah," notes Alquist, "you are afraid of death." "I?" protests Radius. "Why should I be chosen?" But he goes to the table and gets ready for dissection. The chemist, however, cannot bring himself to do this murder. He exclaims: "Oh, Lord, let not mankind perish from the earth." Exhausted, he falls asleep.

Helena, a radiant young Robotess, enters with Primus, a handsome Robot. They examine Alquist's test tubes and books, then Helena goes to the window and says: "The sun is rising . . . Oh, Primus, don't bother with the secret of life. What does it matter to you? Come and look quick. . . . See how beautiful the sun is rising. . . . I feel an aching in my body, in my heart, all over me."

Primus replies: ". . . Last night in my sleep I again spoke to you . . . we spoke a strange new language. . . . And when I touched you I could have died." Helena tells him that she has found a strange place, a weed-grown cottage where two humans have lived. There is a garden there, and two dogs who licked her hands. She continues: "And when I am there in the garden I feel there may be something . . . What am I for, Primus?" Primus does not know, but he tells her that she is beautiful. She places her hand wonderingly on his hair, noting that his head, his shoulders and his lips are different from hers.

Primus speaks: "Do you not sometimes feel your heart beating suddenly, Helena, and think how something must happen?" She answers: "What could happen to us, Primus?" She laughs. Alquist awakes and exclaims: "Laughter? Laughter, human beings!" But then he sees the Robots. As Helena shies away from him, he says wonderingly: "What? You are timid, shy? Let me see you, Robotess." Primus steps forward. "Sir, do not frighten her," he commands.

"What, you would protect her?" Alquist says. "Laughter—timidity—protection—I must test you further. Take the girl into the dissecting room . . . I wish to experiment upon her." Primus threatens that he will kill Alquist if he persists, then pleads that the chemist dissect him, instead; he does not wish to live without Helena. Alquist agrees to experiment upon him, but now Helena bursts into tears. The chemist says with amazement: "Child, child, you can weep —tears! What is Primus to you?"

Helena offers herself for the dissecting room, telling

Primus that if he goes she will kill herself. Primus turns to Alquist: "Man, you shall kill neither of us." To the scientist's query, "Why?" he answers haltingly: "We—we—belong to each other."

Alquist bids them go, and as they leave he adds: "Adam—Eve."

RUSSIAN PLAYS

He Who Gets Slapped

BY LEONID ANDREYEV

*Born in Orel, Russia, June 18, 1871, his full name being
Leonid Nikolayevich Andreyev. He studied law at the uni-
versities of Moscow and St. Petersburg, and then became
police court reporter for a Moscow paper. His short stories,
published in a daily paper, attracted the attention of
Maxim Gorky, and laid the foundations of his literary fame.
His stories are extremely gloomy. "The Red Laugh"
(1905) is a protest against war; "The Seven Who Were
Hanged" (1909) indicts capital punishment. In addition
to the play, "He Who Gets Slapped" (1916), produced in
Europe and America, he wrote several other plays: "The
Life of Man" (1906); "Anathema" (1909); "Samson in
Chains" (1916); and "The Waltz of the Dogs" (1922).
In the revolutionary crisis of 1918–19 he attacked the Bol-
shevik régime and fled to Finland. His last work, "S.O.S.,"
a warning against the revolution, was written shortly before his death in Finland in 1919.*

Into the anteroom of a circus in a large French city, where
the manager, "Papa" Briquet, Zinida, his wife, musicians,
clowns, and a visitor, Count Mancini, are discussing the
affairs of the day, comes a strange gentleman. He is obviously a man of brains; he looks like a society man, but he
acts so strangely that Briquet at first thinks that he is
drunk. When asked his name, the stranger replies: "I don't
quite know myself—yet." Briquet persists: "But what can
I do for you?" The stranger answers: "I want to be a

clown, if you will allow me." He admits that he has had no experience as a circus performer, yet he is quite sure that he can make good. He stands with a finger on his forehead, thinking. Then he says: "Eureka! I shall be among you *He Who Gets Slapped*."

The time is morning. In the adjoining circus hall a rehearsal is going on, and preparations are under way for an evening performance. The cracking whip and the shouts of the riding master are heard from the ring. There is music, too. From time to time, members of the circus troupe join the group in the anteroom. Jackson, the chief clown, overhears part of the conversation and comments: " 'He Who Gets Slapped'—that's not bad." The stranger responds: "I rather like it myself. It suits my talent. And, comrades, I have even found a name—you'll call me 'HE.' "

During the course of this conversation two other members of the troupe, in circus costume, have entered the room—Consuelo, "the equestrian tango queen," and Bezano, a bareback rider. Consuelo regards herself, and is regarded by her associates, as Count Mancini's daughter. The Count, it appears, not only takes a rake-off on Consuelo's earnings, but is trying to bargain her off as the bride of the fat, rich and sensual Baron Regnard, though Consuelo herself seems inclined to accept the attentions of Bezano, a youth who has been her instructor.

Consuelo, who was named after the heroine of one of George Sand's novels and who later turns out to be a girl from Corsica of unknown parentage, exerts a dominating influence by reason of her beauty and charm. Everybody loves her, and HE wants to protect her. Zinida, who is a lion tamer, asks Bezano whether he is in love with Consuelo. He gives a noncommittal answer: "Like my horses, I have no words. Who am *I* to love?" Bezano is overheard by HE, and, as the bareback rider departs, HE says: "I feel as dizzy as a young girl at her first ball. It is so nice here—slap me, I want to play my part. Perhaps it will waken love in my heart, too. Love, do you know—I feel it!"

Count Mancini and the Baron, to whom he is trying to sell his pretended daughter, are both consumed by erotic desires. They hate one another. In the anteroom in which HE realized his ambition to become a clown, the Baron confronts Consuelo. He is a tall, stout man in evening dress, with a rose in his buttonhole; he stands with feet well apart and gazes at her with convex, spider-like eyes. "Your father," he says, "is a swindler and a charlatan. He should be turned over to the police." He continues: "Consuelo, silly girl, I love you unbearably . . . unbearably, do you understand?" He falls on his knees before Consuelo, but she is only disgusted by his antics.

HE is determined to break up the match, and when he next meets Consuelo he uses his knowledge of palmistry to convey a warning. The lines in her hand, he says, predict that if she marries the Baron she will perish. HE tells her that the only one who can save her is himself. HE goes on to tell her about "an old god in disguise who came down to earth only to love you, foolish little Consuelo." Consuelo mocks him, and when he presses his suit ardently, she gives him a slap.

On the following morning, a gentleman comes into the anteroom. He is dressed in black and has an extremely well-bred appearance. His face is yellowish, like an invalid's. HE receives the gentleman with scant courtesy, and it soon becomes clear from the conversation between the two that this man is an "intellectual" who is now living with the woman who was formerly the wife of HE. The gentleman speaks of a "strange and insulting letter" that HE wrote to his wife before he left home. HE exclaims: "To the devil with my wife!" The gentleman, startled, raises his eyebrows. HE laughs. Then the gentleman says: "Such language! I confess I find difficulty in expressing my thoughts in such an atmosphere, but if you are so . . . indifferent to your wife, who, I shall allow myself to emphasize the fact, loved you and thought you a saint, then *what* brought you to such a . . . step? Or is it that you cannot forgive me my success? And when I, a more lucky rival . . ."

HE interrupts the gentleman's words at this point with a burst of laughter and the comment: "Rival! You—a rival!"

The gentleman mentions a book. HE looks at him with curiosity and mockery, and says: "You are talking to me about *your* book? To *me?*" Thereupon, the gentleman raises downcast eyes and declares: "I am a very unhappy man. You must forgive me. I am deeply, irreparably, and infinitely unhappy."

HE walks up and down. HE questions him: "But why? Explain it to me. You say yourself that your book is a tremendous success, you are famous, you have glory; there is not a yellow newspaper in which *you* and *your* thoughts are not mentioned. Who knows *me?* Who cares about my heavy abstractions, from which it was difficult for them to derive a single thought. You—you are the great vulgarizer. You have made my thought comprehensible even to horses. With the art of a great vulgarizer, a tailor of ideas, you dressed my Apollo in a barber's jacket, you handed my Venus a yellow ticket, and to my bright hero you gave the ears of an ass."

The gentleman grows more and more restive under this castigation, and says, "My wife still loves you; our favorite discussion is about your genius. She supposes you are a genius. We, I and she, love you even when we are in bed. Tss! It is I who must make faces. And when at night I go to my lonely thoughts, to my sleepless contemplations, even then I find your image in my head, in my unfortunate brain, your damned and hateful image!" The comment of HE on this is: "What a comedy! How marvelously everything is turned about in this world; the robbed proves to be a robber, and the robber is complaining of theft, and cursing!"

After this verbal duel between HE and the man who has taken his place "out there" in a world that cares very little about circuses, a second and even more tragic duel occurs between HE and Baron Regnard. The happiness—the very life—of Consuelo is at stake.

In the anteroom in which so many aspirations, hopes, heartbreaks, and disillusionments have unfolded, members of the circus troupe discuss an impending benefit performance in honor of Consuelo for which the Baron has

provided a carload of roses "to cover the entire arena."
Consuelo is to gallop on roses—"hymeneal roses"—and
champagne is to flow like water.

The performance takes place: Consuelo enters the anteroom on the arm of the Baron; on the surface all is happiness. But no one has taken into account the somber motiva-
tion of He Who Gets Slapped. HE poisons a glass of wine
which he offers to Consuelo. She innocently drinks half of
it. HE drinks the other half. Both die. The Baron shoots
himself.

The Lower Depths

BY MAXIM GORKY

*Born in Nizhni Novgorod, Russia, March 14, 1868, his real
name being Alexei Maximovitch Pyeshkov. He grew up in
poverty, ran away from home at the age of twelve, and
for several years lived the life of a drudge and a vagabond.
His first writings were short stories, published in newspapers. They dealt with the lives of tramps and humble
workers, and introduced a new note in Russian literature.
His later writings, from about 1897, are novels and plays.
The best known of his novels, largely autobiographical, is
"Foma Gordeyev." The best known of his plays is "The
Lower Depths," a vivid portrayal of the dregs of humanity
gathered in a doss-house. It has been translated into many
languages and performed in many countries. Gorky was a
friend of Lenin and of Stalin, and was an active participant
in the Russian Revolution. His birthplace was renamed
Gorky in his honor. He died in 1936.*

In a cavern-like cellar, the greedy Kostilyoff's night lodging
for the poor, are huddled a group of outcasts—murderers,
thieves, a prostitute, half-starved workers, a decadent no-

bleman, a drunken actor. They are living without hope, yet clinging to lives that they struggle to color with vodka, seduction, gambling and empty boasts.

There is Kleshtch, the locksmith, impoverished but proud that he is a workman, rasping the lodgers' nerves with his filing and his callous brutality to his wife, Anna, who, desperately afraid, is coughing out her life on a bed covered with dirty chintz. Kleshtch is waiting for his freedom, a freedom that his miserable earnings will cancel.

Anna finds some kindness in Natasha, young sister-in-law of Kostilyoff, but none from him or from his wife, the scheming Vassilisa. The latter is finding some comfort in a liaison with young Pepel, who is a thief because his father was a thief. But Pepel, who shares his loot with the others, has tired of Vassilisa, and is making advances to her sister.

The Baron, a little man attempting to be pompous with his memories of past glories (he can remember his transition only in terms of the clothes he wore, the last a convict's garb for embezzlement), is another of the group. His means of support is Nastya, the prostitute who is forever striving to delude herself with an imagined true-love affair of the past. It amuses Pepel to make the Baron bark for his drinks. The Actor, a drunken relic of former stage glories (he once played a grave digger in "Hamlet"), and Satine, a card sharper and realist, are other principals among the sad community.

Into this dead-end existence comes Luka, an old pilgrim, with a bundle at his back and a kettle and teapot slung from his belt. Shy and gentle, he takes a place among them, offering an understanding pity and holding out hope of redemption—even if the gospel he preaches may be a gospel of illusion.

To Anna he is a godsend; he helps her to die, telling her: "Just have faith! Once you're dead, you'll have peace—always. There's nothing to be afraid of—nothing. Lie quietly. Death is kindly. You die and you—and you rest . . . Where can we find rest on this earth?" Anna answers: "But—perhaps—perhaps I get well . . . ? Just to live a little

longer . . . just a little longer! Since there'll be no suffering
hereafter, I could bear it a little longer down here . . ."
But she dies, after a life of rags and blows, with hardly an
interruption in the cards and brawling; Kleshtch alone is
disturbed—at thought of the burial fee.

Luka tries to help Pepel, too. He urges him to go to
Siberia, "a fine country, a land of gold. Anyone who has
health and strength and brains can live there like a cucum-
ber in a hothouse." Pepel, moved, asks if there is a God.
Says Luka: "If you have faith, there is; if you haven't, there
isn't. . . . Whatever you believe in, exists. . . ." Vassilisa,
realizing Pepel has tired of her, offers him both money
and her hated sister, Natasha, if he will rid her of her
husband. She plays on Pepel's pity for the beaten Natasha,
and his hatred of her husband through whom he has been
twice jailed.

Kostilyoff comes, seeking his wife. He screams insults at
her and at Pepel. The thief seizes him by the collar, but
frees him when old Luka comes down. Luka tells Pepel
that he has forestalled a murder, and again urges him to
go away and start anew—with Natasha, if he loves her. But,
later, Kostilyoff and Vassilisa are again beating Natasha
who screams as boiling water from the samovar falls on her
legs. Pepel, rushing to save her, strikes Kostilyoff and kills
him. He is dragged to jail, and the maimed Natasha, believing he killed only for love of her sister, is taken to a
hospital from which she later disappears. Vassilisa, accused
by Natasha, also is taken to jail, despite the fact that she
placed the blame on Pepel alone.

Luka has offered hope to the Actor. He tells him that
there is a free hospital for drunkards—"Oh, in some town
or other . . . I'll tell you the name of it presently—only in
the meantime, get ready. Take yourself in hand—and bear
up . . . you'll begin life all over again." The Actor is elated,
but Luka has not told him the name of the town and where
they are going. Satine says to him: "The old man bilked
you from top to bottom. There's nothing—no towns—no
people—nothing at all!" Later, the Actor crawls off the stove
and asks Tartar, the porter, to pray for him. He drinks

with a shaky hand, and then almost runs to the passage leading to "the Waste," a weed-grown area in the rear of the lodging house.

Luka has now disappeared, and in the cellar Satine, the Baron and Kleshtch are discussing him over their drinks. Nastya is brooding over her misery and declaring she will leave—crawl naked if necessary. The drunken Baron asks what can be the sense of railing, and Satine tells him: "To hell with the lot! Let them yell—let them knock their damned heads off if they feel like it! Don't . . . interfere with people as that old fellow did . . . It's he—the damned old fool—he bewitched the whole gang of us." Kleshtch adds: "He persuaded them to go away—but failed to show them the road. . . . The old man didn't like truth very much—as a matter of fact—he strongly resented it—and wasn't he right, though? Just look—where is there any truth? And yet, without it, you can't breathe!"

Satine shouts: "Shut up! . . . Fools! The old man's no humbug! What's the truth? Man! Man—that's the truth. He understood man—you don't! . . . He lied—but lied out of sheer pity for you . . . God damn you! Lots of people lie out of pity for their fellow beings! . . . They lie—oh, beautifully, inspiringly, stirringly! Some lies bring comfort, and others bring peace—a lie alone can justify the burden which . . . condemns those who are starving! The weakling and the one who is a parasite through his very weakness—they both need lies—lies are their support, their shield, their armor! But the man who is strong, who is his own master, who is free and does not have to suck his neighbor's blood—he needs no lies. To lie—it's the creed of slaves and masters of slaves! Truth is the religion of the free man!"

He confesses that Luka affected him "as acid affects a dirty old silver coin," and drinks to his health. Then he quotes the pilgrim: " 'Why . . . people live in the hope of something better. For example, let's say there are carpenters in this world, and all sorts of trash . . . people . . . and they give birth to a carpenter the like of which has never been seen upon the face of the earth. . . . Everyone . . . lives in the hope of something better. That's why we must respect each and every human being!'" And Satine adds: "Man must be respected—not degraded with pity—but respected, respected!"

The Baron, his mind trying to comprehend, but knowing only that he is afraid—afraid of what is to come—goes out to look for Nastya. Other lodgers, drunk, enter with vodka, smoked fish and pretzels, and the group returns to its brawling, drinking and singing. There is a shout, and the Baron calls that the Actor has hanged himself in the Waste. Says Satine: "Damned fool—he ruined the song."

The Cherry Orchard

BY ANTON CHEKHOV

Born in Taganrog, Russia, on the Sea of Azov, January 17, 1860, his full name being Anton Pavlovich Chekhov. He was first educated in his native town, then went to the University of Moscow to study medicine. He received his degree in 1884, but practiced medicine only during the cholera epidemic of 1892. He started writing while he was still a student, but his early works were almost entirely humorous and suggest nothing of the depth and psychological scope of his later writings. His first play, "Ivanov," was produced in 1887. In 1891 his travels took him to the penal colony of Sakhalin, and the play which he wrote as a result of this visit was instrumental in having the penal laws of the day revised. When "The Sea Gull" was first produced in St. Petersburg (Leningrad), it was a complete failure, but two years later, it was revived by the Moscow Art Theatre and proved a great success; from that time on, Chekhov's connection with the stage was very close. "Uncle Vanya," "Three Sisters," and "The Cherry Orchard" were all produced at the Moscow Art Theatre. In 1900, he was elected an honorary fellow of the Academy of Science, but when the election of Maxim Gorky to the same society was canceled by the Government, Chekhov resigned. He died July 2, 1904.

Lyubov Andreyevna, owner of an ancestral estate in Russia, returns from a self-imposed exile in Paris to seek peace in her girlhood home. She is accompanied by her daughter, Anya, seventeen, who had gone to Paris to make the return trip with her mother, and her brother, Gaev, an ineffectual aristocrat whose chief interests are billiards and caramels.

The estate, with its famous cherry orchard, heavily mortgaged, is about to be foreclosed, leaving the family virtually penniless. Lyubov, absent since the death of her husband seven years ago, laments: "Oh, my sins! I've always thrown my money away recklessly like a lunatic. I married a man who made nothing but debts. My husband died of champagne—he drank dreadfully. To my misery I loved another man, and immediately—it was my first punishment—the blow fell upon me, here, in the river . . . my boy was drowned and I went abroad—went away forever . . . not to see that river again. . . . I shut my eyes, and fled, distracted, and he after me . . . pitilessly, brutally. I bought a villa at Mentone, for he fell ill there, and for three years I had no rest day or night. . . . Last year, when my villa was sold to pay my debts, I went to Paris and there he robbed me of everything and abandoned me for another woman. I tried to poison myself . . . and suddenly I felt a yearning for Russia. . . . Lord, Lord . . . do not chastise me more."

Among those who have come to greet her is Lopahin, a merchant who recalls Lyubov as a splendid, kind-hearted woman who befriended him when he was a peasant child. He reflects: "My father was a peasant, it's true, but here am I in a white waistcoat and brown shoes, like a pig in a bun shop. Yes, I'm a rich man, but for all my money, come to think, a peasant I was and a peasant I am. I've been reading this book and I can't make head or tail of it."

Anya tells Varya, Lyubov's adopted daughter, that her

mother simply cannot understand the change in their fortunes. Although they had only enough money for the trip from Paris, she brought with her her mincing young valet, Yasha, and insisted upon the most expensive meals for the party, which included Charlotta, Anya's governess. Varya tells Anya that Lopahin still has failed to propose to her, despite a neighborhood assumption that they are to marry. "There's really nothing in it—it's all like a dream," she says to Anya.

Lopahin tells Lyubov that he loves her more than his own kin for her kindness to him when his father and grandfather were serfs of her family. He suggests that she can avert the forced sale of the estate, set for August, if she will raze the house and cherry orchard and develop the land for summer villas. He offers a loan to help, but to Lyubov and Gaev the thought of razing the beautiful old orchard is incredible.

Later, Lopahin persists: "One tells you in plain Russian that your estate is going to be sold, and you seem not to understand it. Every day I say the same thing." Lyubov answers: "Villas and summer visitors—forgive me saying so—it's so vulgar." She chatters of a telegram from her lover, demanding her return to Paris; of summoning an orchestra for a dance some evening, and of the drabness of the peasants' lives. She promptly discourages Gaev's plan to work in a bank. "You must stay as you are," she tells him. Although the servants and the family have only soup to eat, she gives a beggar a gold piece, and calls for another loan from Lopahin.

On the very evening of the sale of the estate in town, Lyubov engages an orchestra for a dance, although she reflects: "It's the wrong time . . . Well, never mind." Varya comforts her with the assurance that Gaev, who has attended the sale, probably has bought in the home with authorization sent by a wealthy great-aunt, but Lyubov knows that the sum is not enough even for the arrears, and cries: "My fate is being sealed today, my fate . . ."

She tells Trofimov, a penniless student who has won the heart of Anya, that she cannot conceive of life without tho house and orchard. She tells him that now she is drawn back to her worthless lover in Paris who again is ill and alone. She says: "I love him! He's a millstone about my neck, I'm going to the bottom with him, but I love that stone and can't live without it."

Gaev and Lopahin, the latter giddy with joy, return. Lyubov demands to know at once if the home is lost. Lopahin cries: "I have bought it! . . . Now the cherry orchard's mine! Mine! . . . Tell me that I'm drunk, that I'm out of my mind, that it's all a dream! If my father and grandfather could rise from their graves and see all that has happened! How their Yermolay, ignorant, beaten Yermolay . . . has bought the finest estate in the world! I have bought the estate where my father and grandfather were slaves, where they weren't even admitted into the kitchen. . . . It is all fancy . . . Hey, musicians! Play. . . . Come, all of you, and look how Yermolay Lopahin will take the ax to the cherry orchards. . . . We will build houses on it and our grandsons and great-grandsons will see a new life springing up there."

Lyubov sits down, crushed and weeping, and to her Lopahin says: "Why, why didn't you listen to me? My poor friend! Dear lady, there's no turning back now." He is led away, calling for the musicians to play. "All must be as I wish it," he exults; and, ironically, "Here comes the new master of the cherry orchard!"

Soon the leave-taking comes in the house now stripped bare. Lyubov, her face pale and quivering, has given her purse to the peasants. Gaev is to work in a bank; Lyubov is going to Paris to live as long as possible on the money sent by the great-aunt; Varya, still waiting in vain for Lopahin's proposal, is to be a housekeeper in a distant town; Anya is to remain in school while Trofimov, her betrothed, completes his studies in Moscow.

Lopahin has brought a bottle of champagne, but only Yasha drinks. An ax is heard in the distance, and Anya brings her mother's plea that the workers wait until she has gone. Lyubov, gallantly courageous now, says her farewells and speaks of only two cares: the health of old Firs, the butler, and Varya. She is assured that Firs has been sent to the hospital, and is promised by Lopahin that he will marry Varya; but again, and finally, he fails to propose to the weeping girl.

Lyubov and Gaev, the last to go, wait until they are alone, then fall into each other's arms in smothered sobbing, afraid of being overheard. Lyubov weeps: "Oh, my orchard!—my sweet, beautiful orchard! My life, my youth, my happiness, goodbye! Goodbye!"

They leave, and there is only the sound of doors being locked, the carriages driving away, and in the distance the sound of the ax. The ancient Firs, deathly ill, totters in, tries the door and sits on a sofa. He cries: "Locked! They have gone. They have forgotten me . . . Never mind." He lies down, is motionless, and a sound like that of a breaking harp string is heard, dying away mournfully. Then there is only the sound of the ax.

The Three Sisters

BY ANTON CHEKHOV

A year after the death of their father, an army officer, the Moscow-bred sisters Prosorov—Olga, Masha and Irina— are finding life drab and increasingly hopeless in a Russian provincial town. Only the proximity of a near-by artillery post and the company of its officers make their existence bearable.

Olga, the eldest, twenty-eight, is a teacher at the high school; she finds her work hateful, and herself already aging and tired, her dream of a happy marriage fading; she is sustained solely by the hope of selling the house and returning to Moscow. Masha, little more than twenty, is married to Kuligin, a teacher of far more years who has failed of the stature her school-girl mind had given him. For her there is no hope of Moscow; she only whistles softly to herself as her sisters make their plans. Irina, at twenty, dreams of finding happiness and love in Moscow. A brother, Andrey, a scholar, is in love with Natasha, twenty-eight, an over-dressed villager who affects shyness and humility; his sisters find it hard to believe that he will marry her.

On Irina's birthday, the callers include Chebutikin, sixty, an army doctor who once loved the sisters' mother; Baron Tuzenbach, thirty, a lieutenant in love with Irina; brooding Captain Soleni, and a newcomer, Vershinin, forty-two, commander of the post. Vershinin has two daughters and a second wife who frequently threatens suicide to annoy him. A birthday cake is sent by Protopopov, head of the District Council. The sisters hope Protopopov will marry Natasha, but Andrey proposes to her and she accepts him.

With the marriage of Natasha and Andrey and the birth of a child, Bobby, the lot of the sisters becomes even more unhappy. Natasha, dropping her humility, dominates the sisters, her husband and the servants. She takes the room of Irina, who now works at the telegraph office, for the child; Irina must share Olga's room.

Vershinin, whose wife is endlessly quarrelsome, and the unhappy Masha, bored by her husband and his colleagues, are drawn together. One day Vershinin tells her of his love for her. She at first protests, then in resignation answers: "Go on, it's all the same to me." They are interrupted by Tuzenbach and Irina. The Baron has resigned his post to seek some satisfying work in civil life, and Irina, finding the telegraph office dull, is still obsessed with her hope of discovering happiness in Moscow. She is worried, too, because Andrey, frustrated in his plans for distinguished scholarship and now disappointed in Natasha, is gambling and losing heavily.

A gay evening with guests and entertainers has been planned, but Natasha compels Andrey to cancel the invitations on the pretext that little Bobby is ill. Soleni returns to confess his love to Irina. Rebuffed, he swears that he will kill any rival. Natasha receives a message from Protopopov inviting her to take a drive with him in his troika, and she laughingly accepts. "How funny these men are," she says.

At two o'clock in the morning, the household is awakened by a fire in the village. Refugees come to the Prosorov home for shelter. Natasha, abusing old Anfisa, the nurse, declares that she is now mistress of the household: Anfisa must go, and Olga and Irina must move downstairs. Old Chebutikin is drunk; by his fault a woman patient has died. Soleni enters, resentful at Irina's friendship with the Baron, and Vershinin brings a rumor that the battery is to be moved from the village.

Masha, quarreling with Kuligin, discloses that Andrey has mortgaged the house—in which the sisters share ownership—to pay his gambling debts, and that Natasha has the remainder of the money he has borrowed. Irina weeps—in disappointment at the failure of the brother from whom so much had been expected, and at her own frustration. She is now working in the town council offices, but she is no happier; she realizes at last that she will never return to Moscow. She cries: "I've grown thinner, plainer, older . . . and time goes and it seems all the while as if I am going away from the real, the beautiful life, further and further away down some precipice." Olga urges that she compromise and accept the plain Baron.

Masha confesses that she is in love with Vershinin: "It is all awful. . . . How are we going to live through our lives, what is to become of us? . . . My dear ones, my sisters . . . I've confessed, now I shall keep silence . . . Like the lunatics in Gogol's story, I'm going to be silent . . . silent . . ."

Andrey, finding his sisters together, sulkily confesses to the mortgage of the house. He berates them for their disapproval of his wife, "a beautiful and honest creature, straight and honorable." He insists that they respect her, even in spite of her affair with Protopopov, and declares he is proud in his place as a mere member of the District Council. Then he weeps: "My dear, dear sisters, don't believe me, don't believe me . . ."

The night ends with Irina's decision revealed to Olga: "I

esteem, I highly value the Baron, he's a splendid man! I'll marry him . . . only let's go to Moscow! I implore you, let's go! There's nothing better than Moscow on earth! Let's go, Olga, let's go!"

Soon the rumor that the battery is to be removed is confirmed—it has been ordered to Poland. Farewells are being said at the Prosorov home. Irina is to be married to-morrow to the Baron; he has work and she is happy in having been accepted for a teacher's position. She tells Kuligin: "If I can't live in Moscow, then it must come to this. . . . It's all the will of God." Olga is now head-mistress of her school and is living there with old Anfisa. Vershinin kisses the sobbing Masha farewell, leaving her to the dull Kuligin.

Old Chebutikin comes to tell Irina that the Baron has been killed in the duel with Soleni, and the three sisters huddle together in grief. Says Masha: "They are leaving us . . . we remain alone, to begin our life over again. We must live . . . we must live . . ."

Irina, her head on Olga's bosom, cries: "There will come a time when everybody will know why, for what purpose, there is all this suffering. But now we must live . . . we must work, just work! Tomorrow, I'll go away alone, and I'll teach and give my whole life to those who, perhaps, need it."

Olga reflects, as the military bands are heard playing in farewell: "The bands are playing so gaily, so bravely, and one does so want to live! . . . Time will pass on, and we shall depart forever . . . but our sufferings will turn into joy for those who shall live after us . . . Oh, dear sister, our life is not yet at an end. Let us live . . . It seems that in a little while we shall know why we are living, why we are suffering . . ."

The music fades, the smiling Kuligin brings out Masha's coat, and Andrey wheels out Bobby in a perambulator. Old Chebutikin sings softly: "Tara . . . ra-boom-deay." Reading his paper, he reflects: "It's all the same! It's all the same!"

The Power of Darkness

BY LEO TOLSTOY

*Born in the Tula region of Russia, September 9, 1828, the
son of a wealthy landowner. His full name was Lyov
Nicholayevich Tolstoy. He studied law and languages at
the University of Kazan, and, after his education, joined
the army, fighting in the Caucasus and at Sevastopol. Some
of his early writings deal with his army life. He resigned
from the army, and, after a year of travel, when he became
disgusted with the artificiality and materialism of the life
of his time, he settled down at his family estate in Mas-
naya Polyana. In 1862 he married. The next fifteen years
were absorbed in the management of his estate, in domestic
life, and in the writing of his two fictional masterpieces,
"War and Peace" and "Anna Karenina." In 1881 he experienced a religious crisis which gave his energies new
direction, and led to the writing of books dominated by a
religious and humanitarian spirit. To this period belong not
only such works as "What I Believe" and "The Kingdom
of God Is Within You," but also "The Kreutzer Sonata"
and "Resurrection." To this same period belong also his
dramas, "The Power of Darkness" and "The Living Corpse."
In 1901 he was excommunicated by the Russian Orthodox
Church. He spent the last years of his life as a peasant,
having renounced his titles and lands. He died November
20, 1910.*

Depravity and deceit have been among the crops on the
farm of the well-to-do but sickly old Peter. His second wife,
the young and restless Anisya, is secretly consorting with
Peter's young farmhand, Nikita, who loves girls and drinking but not his work. Now Nikita has compounded his sin
by seducing Marina, an orphan, and his simple but honor-

able old father, Akim, has insisted that he marry the girl.

Anisya is reproaching Nikita, demanding that he refuse to wed Marina. She declares she will kill herself if he deserts her. Nikita promises that he won't, although he would prefer to go on with the ceremony and only return to Anisya as his mood dictates. Anisya is embracing him in gratitude when Nikita's mother, Matryona, enters.

Matryona is a stranger to the scruples of Akim; she merely crosses herself before the icon . . . if Nikita has won the wife of a rich man, so much the better. Sending her son out, she suggests to Anisya a simple way to forward her romance: old Peter is going to die soon anyhow, and she has a powder that, administered in seven small doses in his tea, will soon free Anisya. Anisya pays well for the powders and agrees to the plan.

Old Akim takes Nikita to task for wronging Marina. "I want to start—what d'you call it?—to start you honest . . . If my son has offended against her—I mean, if he now refuses—and she, what d'you call it?—an orphan—I mean it's all wrong. You can hide it from men, but not from God, Nikita . . . Don't lie. Did anything happen?" he asks him. Nikita swears that he has not seduced the girl. Old Akim, deceived also by his wife, subsides. Nikita, however, begins to feel uneasy. Says he: "I'm sweet as honey on the girls, but when you've sinned against 'em and then have to swear to a lie, it ain't so good . . ."

Six months later, Anisya has given Peter two of the powders. He is near death, but neither she nor Matryona can find his money and he has sent for his sister. They are discussing the possibility that the old man will turn over his money to her when he appears in the doorway, moaning: "I'm burning inside. It's so hard to die!" Matryona helps him back to bed, and as she does so, feels his money-bag around his neck. She tells Anisya where his treasure is. She urges that he be wholly poisoned at once, before his sister comes.

Nikita comes in from the fields. His mother directs him to seize the money—and to let Anisya keep none, since "women are such bad managers." He is reluctant, but agrees as Anisya rushes from the house, wailing: "My dear, lovely, darling husband is gone!" Matryona, rolling up her sleeves, goes to prepare the body for burial.

Nine months later, Nikita has married Anisya but has continued his affairs with other women, notably Akoulina, Peter's daughter by his first wife. This is no secret from Anisya, but she fears to appeal to the law to strip him of her money. Akim learns the tragic history of the match when he comes for money to buy the horse that Nikita promised him. His son, drunk, returns from town, gives Akim the promised sum and then displays presents he has bought for Akoulina.

Anisya berates him for buying the presents with her money, and Akoulina, who has accompanied Nikita, retorts: "Your money indeed! You wanted to steal it, but couldn't get away with it! . . . You're a bitch who murdered her own husband!" Anisya threatens to murder her, too, and Nikita tells his wife to be silent or he will throw her out of the house. Old Akim tosses his gift on the table, leaving with this warning to Nikita: "Take your money back. It's filthy! . . . You're stuck fast, Nikita—stuck fast in sin. . . . Come to your senses . . . It's the soul that God wants."

Nikita's new affair continues until the following autumn, when a neighboring peasant courts Akoulina. The girl, however, keeps to her house with "pains in the stomach," and gossip moves the prospective bridegroom's father to ask Matryona if there is "something wrong." Matryona heartily assures him that Akoulina is sound as a bell; that she is a lovely and virtuous bride with a generous dowry. The father is won over, and Matryona reminds him not to forget her after the wedding—that she has been to much trouble in making the match.

But as the wedding plans are made, Akoulina is furtively delivered of a child. Nikita pleads with Anisya to take it to a foundling hospital to avoid a scandal. His wife refuses: "It's your dirt and it's up to you to clean it up. . . . You take that child down cellar and dig a hole." She is seconded by Matryona who offers to hold a light, cautioning her son not to forget to baptize the infant before it is buried.

The wedding day comes, but now Nikita, tortured by his sins, avoids the party. He is trying to hang himself in the barn when Anisya and Matryona come upon him. He cries: "Mother, what have you done to me? I'm a lost soul . . . I hear it whimpering—whimpering—all the time!" They talk reassuringly to him, and he agrees to follow them back to the wedding party. But when he enters alone he is barefooted, and calls out: "Father Akim, are you here? Men of the village, are you here? Well, here am I, a sinner!"

Anisya and Matryona frantically try to silence him, but, sinking to his knees, he continues his confession: "I have sinned against you, Akoulina! Your father died no natural death! He was poisoned . . . I poisoned him!" Akoulina cries: "He's telling lies! I know who did it!" Nikita goes on: "I poisoned him, Akoulina. And I seduced you. Forgive me in Christ's name!"

Old Akim urges him on: "Speak, my son! Tell everything, make your soul—what d'you call it?—clean! Don't be afraid of men; God—God—He's the one to talk to!"

Nikita rushes on: "I poisoned the father, dog that I am, and I ruined the daughter . . . Her and her baby . . . I crushed out the baby's life with a board . . . I sat on it and I heard the bones crunch . . . and then I buried it. I did it, all alone . . ." He begs the forgiveness of Akoulina and old Akim. His father answers joyfully: "God will forgive you, my own son! You didn't have mercy on yourself; God will have mercy on you. God, God, He is the One to trust!"

Akoulina, protesting that it was she who asked Nikita to dispose of the baby, exclaims: "I will tell the truth! Ask me!"

But Nikita concludes: "No need to ask . . . I planned it all, and I did it all, myself. I am ready for my punishment . . . There is nothing more to say . . ."

The Dybbuk

BY S. ANSKY

*Born in Russia in 1859, his real name being S. Rappaport.
He was brought up as an Orthodox Jew, but accepted
assimilation as an answer to the Jewish problem, and
attacked Jewish orthodoxy. As a political refugee in Paris
in the early 1890's, he shunned his fellow Jews and studied
French folklore. Later, however, excitement over the Drey-
fus case aroused his Jewish consciousness. He went to
Berne, Switzerland, for a while, and identified himself with
the Russian Social Revolutionary movement. Previous to
the outbreak of the first World War, he visited Jewish
cities and towns, collecting a mass of folklore material and
anything of ethnological, cultural or historic interest. He
started dramatizing much of this material, and two of the
folk stories are included in his best-known play, "The
Dybbuk" ("Between Two Worlds," 1913). Because of the
war and the Bolshevist revolution, "The Dybbuk" could
not be played in Russia, but had its première in the Jewish
Theatre in Warsaw a month after Ansky's sudden death.
Later, it had a successful run in New York.*

Channon, a mysterious and brooding youth, is the most
brilliant of scholars at the Synagogue of Brainitz, center of
a Chassidic community where life is on a plane midway
between reality and a faith-created world of the supernatural. In Lithuania he had won the degree of rabbi, but
then he had vanished for a year, and it is rumored that he
has since been studying the forbidden Kabala.

Channon is greatly interested when the other students
hold a discussion concerning miracle-working rabbis—in
particular, Rabbi Elchannon of Krasny, who is reputed to
be able to evoke evil spirits, even Satan himself. He marks

the name in astonishment and says, as if to himself: "Elchannon? . . . Elchannon!—that means the God of Channon!" He walks reflectively to the Ark, where are kept the scrolls of the Law, and notes that in them, as in virtually everything he encounters, there faces him the number thirty-six. He meditates: "Thirty-six is Leah. Three times thirty-six is Channon . . . Le-ah: that makes Le-ha, which means not God . . . not through God . . . a terrible thought, and yet it draws me nearer and nearer."

There is a knock, and there comes to visit the Ark the beautiful Leah, daughter of Sender, the rich merchant, her companion, Gittel, and Leah's nurse, Frade. Channon's unwavering gaze upon Leah moves her to explain to Gittel that he, a poor student, for a time was a guest at her home. It is apparent that she returns his love. Later, he hints of his passion to another student and threatens that if he cannot attain the wealth he needs to fulfill it, he will resort to unholy powers.

Then comes word that Sender, after rejecting three suitors, has at last bethrothed Leah. Channon cries: "How can that be? So it was of no avail—neither the fasts nor the absolutions, nor the spells! . . . What is there to do . . . by what means . . ." Then his face is illuminated in ecstasy. He cries: "Ah, the secret of the double name is revealed to me! I see him! I—I—have won!" He falls—never to be awakened.

Before her wedding, Leah observes the custom of dancing with the old women in the courtyard. When she returns she appears to be in a trance. She murmurs: "They seized me . . . and clutched me to them with their cold, withered hands . . . my head swam. . . . Then someone came and carried me far, far away. . . . If the bride is left alone before the wedding, spirits come and carry her off." There is dirt upon her dress.

Continuing her reflection on spirits, she tells her nurse that she cannot believe Channon's life can be so wholly snuffed out. One called the Messenger, an arbiter at the Synagogue, tells her that some vagrant souls, finding

neither rest nor harbor, pass as Dybbuks into the bodies of
the living until they have attained purity.

Leah asks Frade if, on her ceremonial visit to the graveyard to ask her dead mother to her wedding, she may
invite Channon. She has located his grave, she says, in a
dream in which Channon "told her his trouble" and
begged her to invite him. Frade goes with her to the graveyard, and when they return Frade reports that Leah had
fainted. She hints at other strange happenings there.

When Leah is approached by her bridegroom, she
springs up and thrusts him away, saying: "No! You are
not my bridegroom!" She falls upon a churchyard grave
which bears the inscription: "Here lies a pure and holy
bridegroom and bride, murdered to the glory of God in
the year 5048." She cries out: "Holy bridegroom and bride,
save me!"

The guests lift her, she looks wildly about, then declares
—but in the voice of a man: "Ah! Ah! You buried me, but
I have come back to my destined bride. I will leave her
no more!" Says the Messenger: "Into the bride has entered
a Dybbuk."

Sender takes Leah to the venerable Rabbi Azrael of
Mirapol, who commands the Dybbuk to leave her body.
She shrieks in the voice of Channon: "Mirapol Rabbi . . .
I know that angels and archangels obey your word, but
me you cannot command. I have nowhere to go. On every
side the forces of evil lie in wait to seize me. Have mercy!"
Azrael expresses his pity, offering his power to defeat the
evil spirits, but he orders that the Dybbuk must leave.

The voice of Channon refuses, and Azrael commands
the Dybbuk to leave or undergo malediction and anathema.
But Channon, with no faith in Azrael's promise of help
against evil, again refuses. "The loftiest height of the world
cannot compare with this resting place that I have found,"
he answers. Azrael then adjures him for the last time,
threatening to deliver him to the fiends of destruction.

But before the anathema can be pronounced, the permission of the City Rabbi is required. The City Rabbi
brings a new factor into the proceeding: three times on the

previous night, the dead Nissin ben Rifke appeared to him in his dreams, asking that Sender be tried for a mortal injury—he has not kept a pact with the apparition's son, now the Dybbuk. Azrael summons Sender, as well as Nissin ben Rifke, to court.

A sheet is hung to screen the dead man from the living, and Azrael draws with his staff a holy circle beyond which he must not pass. A messenger is sent to proclaim the summons in the graveyard, and soon it is announced that Nissin ben Rifke is present. The City Rabbi, as his spokesman, cites the dead man's charge that Sender pledged his daughter to Channon before the children were born, but that Sender rejected the youth because of his poverty. Now the dark powers have torn him from the world.

Sender denies malice in his sin, contending that over the years he had forgotten the pact. The judges rule that he shall give half his fortune to the poor and pray for Nissin ben Rifke and Channon as though they were his own kin. They ask also that the father command his boy to leave Leah's body. The trial is ended, and Leah is called again before Azrael, who commands the Dybbuk to go. Channon, deaf to his dead father's pleas, reiterates his refusal.

Now Azrael and his aids, with shrouds, horns and black candles, call upon the Higher Spirits to pull the Dybbuk from Leah by force; but in spite of her contortions, it remains. The Spirits of the Middle Plane, too, are powerless. Only when Azrael employs the ultimate command, with excommunication, does the Dybbuk promise to leave. Azrael then lifts the ban of anathema, imploring peace for the soul of Channon. Leah, with the Dybbuk's voice, cries: "Say Kadish for me! The hour of my going was predestined —and it has come!" She swoons, and Azrael, leaving to lead the procession for her postponed wedding, draws around her with his staff the protective circle.

As a wedding march is heard in the distance, Leah awakens and speaks. "Who sighed so deeply?" The voice of Channon replies: "I." He explains that he cannot be seen because she is within the magic circle. Leah pleads:

"They are coming to take me to a stranger . . . come to me, my true bridegroom."

"I have left your body—I will come to your soul," answers the voice of Channon, as his white-robed figure appears against the wall. Now Leah happily sobs that she can see him. As the music draws nearer, she goes toward Channon; their two forms merge in the gathering darkness.

Azrael, heading the wedding party, enters—only to bow his head and say: "Too late!"

GREEK PLAYS

Lysistrata

BY ARISTOPHANES

Born about the year 448 B.C., an Athenian citizen, the son of an Athenian landowner. Little is known of his life beyond what we learn from his dramas. He came as the last in succession of the brilliant group which included Aeschylus, Sophocles and Euripides, and he was the comic dramatist of the group. He is believed to have written about fifty comedies, but only eleven survive, chief among them being, "The Birds," "The Frogs," "The Clouds," "The Knights," and "Lysistrata." "Lysistrata," first given in 411 B.C. and often revived, has been produced in the United States during recent years with great success. Aristophanes died about 388 B.C.

The Peloponnesian War has been dragging on for eighteen long years, and the beautiful Lysistrata, in common with the other wives of Athens, is heartily tired of the intermittent absence of their warrior husbands. She decides that it is time to bring an end to this situation. The only solution, she concludes, is a boycott to deprive the husbands of their wives' love.

Lysistrata sets out to enlist the other women in the plan, but finds them somewhat reluctant. One thinks that to so punish their husbands would be punishing themselves; others offer similar excuses. Lysistrata tells them that they are cowards and that the poets' jibes about woman's frailty are well deserved.

But she perseveres in her determination, and convinces

the women at last that peace surely will come if they all dress, powder and perfume themselves irresistibly, then withhold their favors from their men unless they promise to take steps to end the war forthwith. The wives agree to try the scheme, and, for a start, seize the public funds. The old men of Athens try to burn them out of the treasury, but the embattled women retaliate with pitchers of water upon their heads. The President of the Senate arrives at this juncture, ordering the arrest of "that traitress," Lysistrata.

The women win the scuffle that follows, the President admitting defeat; but he asks an explanation for the feminine onslaught upon the treasury. Lysistrata blandly explains their purpose: to save the public money so that the men won't fight any wars over it. The President protests the absurdity of their fancy that the war is being fought over mere money. Lysistrata assures him that of course it is; that every war is for the sake of money—else why are politicians always manufacturing wars? Merely as an occasion to steal, she says.

Then Lysistrata announces that, from now on, things are going to be different: the men won't be able to get any money for fighting because the women are going to take over the treasury. And why not? They manage the household finances. But household finances, the President tolerantly explains, are quite different; the public money is necessary for the fighting. To this Lysistrata readily agrees, but adds that the fighting itself is hardly necessary.

The listening women, weary of the argument by this time, seize the President, unclothe him and dress him as a woman. They tell him that they are going to take the state into their own hands, rescue it from the muddling of men, unravel the knots of war just as they straighten out a skein of wool, and unite all nations into a single thread of peace and good will.

But the President persists: war, after all, is the business of men, he says. Nothing of the kind, Lysistrata replies, it is the business of women—for who suffers most in the loss on the battlefields of sons and husbands? To end the debate, the women again seize the official and garb him as a corpse. He retreats in terror.

After a time, the wives of the enemy city of Sparta join in the boycott. The plan is a success: the husbands of both cities surrender to their wives, and, to recapture their love, agree to end the war. Here a male chorus observes that it was a wise philosopher who called women the paradoxical sex: you cannot live with them and you cannot live without them. A female chorus replies that, say what you will and do what you will, the women always have the last word, for theirs is the unanswerable argument. Together the choruses agree that there has been enough of idle quarrels: they urge that the discord cease.

Lysistrata is chosen as intermediary between the Athenian and Spartan envoys for formal termination of the conflict, and she lectures them soundly at the start of their conference. She is a woman, she says, but hopes that she is not without some sense; she reminds them that they are all of the same blood, the same gods and the same language. Why, then, do they kill each other? Why should they not come to terms? She agrees that it may be necessary for animals to fight, but certainly not for men—particularly for Greek men—to fight among themselves while barbarians are looking on.

A Spartan delegate announces that his side is ready to make peace if it gets what it wants, and an Athenian observes that what both the Spartans and Athenians want is to get their wives back again. Lysistrata sees some feasibility in this, but orders that first the former enemies must go off to a feast to repair their friendship. After that, she says, each warrior may take his woman home.

A Spartan seconds this idea, proposing, further, that they all get drunk—a suggestion not unpleasant to one Athenian who notes that people are surliest when most sober. If there were more drinking bouts among diplomats, he thinks, there would be no war; they would drown their quarrels in wine, have some singing together, and decide that, after all, an enemy could still be a good fellow.

The warriors try Lysistrata's program, and at length re-

turn as bosom friends. This accomplished, she bids them
each take his woman, and all join in a dance of peace as
the chorus pleads:

> "O let us pray
>   To the gods today
>   That every field
>   May its harvest yield,
>   While in peace we eat
>   Our bread and our meat.
>   O Venus, arrayed in love, restore
>   The hopes and joys we have lost in the war . . .
>   Let the sword be forgotten for evermore."

Electra

BY EURIPIDES

*Born in 480 B.C., on the island of Salamis, near Athens. He
was of humble birth, but received a good education and
began his dramatic writing in youth. Euripides belongs to
the great dramatic period of ancient Greece. Aeschylus was
a generation older; Sophocles was Euripides' contemporary
and his active rival in dramatic contests. Euripides is believed to have written more than ninety plays. Only eighteen (or nineteen) of these are extant. He was more appreciated in later times than in his own age, because he
was an innovator and something of a radical. During his
lifetime public opinion was changing; popular religion, the
foundation of tragedies at that time, had been undermined,
and a growing skepticism had become apparent in connection with the legends upon which that religion was
founded. Gods and heroes no longer commanded the un-
questioning faith which they had previously inspired, and
theatrical audiences had less and less of the musical and
poetic training which had prepared them to appreciate*

classical tragedy. Euripides, noting these subtle changes,
modified his drama to meet the new tastes and interests.
His plays include: "Alcestis," "Medea," "Iphigenia in
Tauris," "Iphigenia in Aulis," "The Trojan Women," and
"Electra." It is believed that "Electra" was a product of
his later years—possibly around 413 B.C. The date of his
death was approximately 406 B.C.

At early dawn, before a desolate mountain hut, a peasant
is hailing the new day and bemoaning the plight of his
young wife, Electra, banished daughter of the dead warrior, King Agamemnon, and his Queen, Clytemnestra.

In his reverie he recalls the triumphant return of Agamemnon after the conquest of Priam, only to be murdered
by his wife and her lover, Aegisthus, who now rule Argos
and Mycenae. Orestes, Agamemnon's son, was saved from
a like death by an old friend of the slain King, and was
given into the care of King Strophio in Phocis; but Electra
suffered a harsher fate: because Aegisthus feared she might
have a child, sired by some powerful house, to avenge her
father if she were allowed to wed in her own class, he
sought first to kill her, too, but was dissuaded by Clytemnestra. He decreed, however, that she must marry this poor
peasant and thus remain powerless to menace his rule.
The peasant has left Electra virgin, since he feels himself
unworthy of a princess.

Electra, appearing, herself cries out in bitterness at her
lot, calling curses upon her mother. The peasant then
chides her for toiling, but she voices her thanks to him for
his kindness and tells him of her determination to make his
home bright. As he goes to his work and she to the spring
for water, two armed men enter—Orestes, her brother, and
his friend, Pylades, son of Strophio.

Orestes tells Pylades that, come to avenge his father, he
has just offered sacrifice of his tears and tresses and a black
lamb upon his father's grave. He plans to lurk in the mountains to await his chance for revenge, meanwhile searching
for his sister, of whose humiliation he has heard. As they

speak, Electra approaches; Orestes, deeming her only a farm maid, plans to question her. She cries out her grief as Agamemnon's daughter, and her brother remains silent as a chorus of women of Argos appear in festal dress to ask her to lead in the morrow's rites. She replies that she cannot while her mother lies in the usurper's arms "and blood is about her bed."

Orestes now comes from concealment. Electra does not recognize him as he cautiously tells her that he brings word of her brother—that Orestes seeks word of her. She tells him of her life with the peasant and he, to test her, asks if she would be willing to aid her brother in the slaying of their mother for revenge. Yes, she replies—with the same ax that slew her father.

The peasant returns and is bidden by Electra to hasten to the old friend of her father, now in exile as a herdsman, that he may come to hear the news of Orestes whom he rescued. She bids him bring meat to help make the strangers welcome. The peasant soon returns with the old man who, having noted the sacrifice upon Agamemnon's grave, has suspected the return of Orestes. He recognizes the grown Prince by a scar upon his brow. Her brother is made known to Electra and they embrace.

The talk is now of revenge, and the old man, demanding that Orestes strike down both Aegisthus and his mother, tells the Prince that Aegisthus is, at that very moment, in a near-by pasture preparing a wreathed ox for sacrifice, guarded only by a few of his servants. Orestes asks how he may lure his mother forth as well, but Electra demands the doing of this deed. She bids the old man tell Clytemnestra that she has borne a son, news which will bring the Queen to the hut. Orestes sets forth, and Electra waits with a sword—ready to kill herself should her brother fail.

Soon a messenger appears with word that Aegisthus is dead. The usurper hailed Orestes and his men as they approached, and, unaware of their errand, invited them to share in the sacrificial rite. Orestes stripped the limbs of the ox, but omens of doom at Orestes' hands startled the King. While Aegisthus studied the animal, Orestes brought his sword down upon his foe and Aegisthus fell dead. The young Prince then identified himself to the servants and was hailed as a deliverer.

Orestes and his men arrive with the body of Aegisthus. Electra curses the body and it is then hidden in the hut to await the coming of Clytemnestra whose chariot is approaching. Orestes shrinks from the thought of killing his own mother, but, scorned by Electra as a coward who fears to avenge his father, he agrees to strike the same stealthy blow that killed Agamemnon. He goes to hide himself in the hut.

Clytemnestra arrives, accompanied by her handmaidens. When Electra reproaches her for her exile, she lays the blame for her misdeeds on Agamemnon. Clytemnestra goes into the hut, followed by Electra, to bless her grandchild. Her death cry is heard: "O children, children: in the name of God, slay not your mother!" Then her body and that of Aegisthus are borne from the house. Orestes comes forth, lamenting the sin of having killed his mother, but Electra declares hers the blame.

In their surpassing grief, they tell of the tragedy they have just caused. Orestes cries out at the memory of his mother, her raiment bloodied, baring her bosom and falling to her knees. Electra tells that her mother touched her cheek and moaned, "Mercy, my child, my own!" Electra, in pity, dropped the sword, but Orestes, blinding his eyes with his mantle, struck the death blow, the sword finding his mother's throat. But Electra says, "I gave thee the sign and the word, I touched with mine hand thy sword." The two kneel together and cover their mother's body with raiment.

In the sky there appears a vision of Castor and Polydeuces. They declare the Queen's doom a righteous one, but not the deed itself. They ordain that Electra shall become the wife of Pylades in exile, and say that Orestes must flee from Argos to Athens where, at length, Phoebus shall take the stain of murder upon his own head, allowing the Prince to at last find happiness after penance. The brother and sister, so briefly reunited, say farewell to each other and to Argos.

The Trojan Women

BY EURIPIDES

Before the ruined walls of ancient Troy, a few days after the battle in which King Menelaus of Sparta, and Agamemnon, general of the Greeks, had taken the city, there appears dimly in the early dawn the mourning figure of the god, Poseidon. Bodies of dead warriors lie before the huts of the captive women who await disposition among the Greek leaders, and a tall, white-haired woman is sleeping on the ground—it is Hecuba, Queen of Troy, the wife of Priam and mother of Hector and Paris.

Poseidon laments the destruction of the Trojan wall which he and Apollo had built, and cries that Priam lies unburied by his own hearth while the captive women wail and the victors await the winds that will take them to their homes. He reflects that Helen, the wife of Menelaus whom Paris had brought to Troy, also awaits in a hut, a prize of war; that Hecuba's child, Polyxena, has been secretly slain and Priam and his sons are gone, while her daughter Cassandra, the virgin seeress beloved of Apollo, has been marked as the prize of Agamemnon.

The goddess, Pallas Athena, appears, and with Poseidon conspires to destroy the home-going Greek ships in revenge. Poseidon cries to the conquerors: "How are ye blind, ye treaders down of cities, ye that cast temples to desolation, and lay waste tombs, the untrodden sanctuaries where lie the ancient dead; yourselves so soon to die!" The dawn comes, and Hecuba awakens to mourn her tragic fate and curse Helen as the cause. The other captive women rise to echo her cries.

But even more crushing news is unwillingly brought by

the Greek herald, Talthybius. He informs Hecuba that
Cassandra is to be the bride of Agamemnon, hints that
Polyxena is dead, and reveals that Andromache, the wife
of Hector, is to be the prize of Pyrrhus, Achilles' son; Hecuba herself is fated to be the slave of the despised Odysseus, King of Ithaca.

Cassandra appears, bearing a torch and walking as in a
dream in her bridal garlands. She chants dire prophecies of
the Greeks' empty victory, with death for Agamemnon
and "the dark wanderings" of mother-murder that shall
destroy the House of Atreus. She becomes conscious of
the awed Talthybius, and, tearing off her garlands, goes to
"the house of Death to lie beside my bridegroom," with
a final word of comfort for her city and for Hecuba, who
collapses to the ground, broken in grief.

A chariot approaches from the town, laden with spoils
and bearing a mourning woman who holds a child in her
arms—Andromache, the widow of Hector, and her baby,
Astyanax. Andromache, crying her grief to Hecuba, calls
down God's wrath on Paris "who sold for his evil love
Troy and the towers thereof." She confirms to the agonized
Hecuba that Polyxena has been slain at Achilles' tomb.

Andromache asks how she can become the wife of
Achilles' son without shame to herself and her beloved
Hector, but Hecuba counsels that she honor her new lord
and thus, perhaps, be permitted to rear Astyanax as a
future savior of Ilion. But the gentle Talthybius returns
with news that Odysseus has prevailed in council, and
ordered that the child is to be dashed to death from the
wall; if Andromache casts a curse upon the Greek ships,
the baby is to have no burial. The stricken mother, calling a curse upon Helen, addresses her baby:

"Go, die, my best-beloved, my cherished one,
   In fierce men's hands, leaving me here alone. . . .
      Weepest thou?
Nay, why, my little one? Thou canst not know.
And father will not come; he will not come. . . .
How shall it be? One horrible spring . . . deep, deep

Down. And thy neck . . . Ah, God, so cometh
   sleep! . . .
And none to pity thee! . . . Thou little thing
That curlest in my arms, what sweet scents cling
All around thy neck! . . . Kiss me. This one time;
Not ever again. Put up thine arms, and climb
About my neck; now, kiss me, lips to lips. . . .
Quick! Take him: drag him: cast him from the
   wall. . . .
To the bridal . . . I have lost my child, my own!"

Andromache, half swooning, is driven to the ships, and
a soldier bears the child to his death.

Then enters King Menelaus, a prey to violent and con-
flicting emotions, with his rich arms and his bodyguard.
He declares that he came not for the accursed Helen but
for "the thief" Paris "who stole away my bride." He discloses that Helen is his prize of war, to be killed or led
home, and shall be cast out to angry death at the hands of
his slain soldiers' families. He orders: "Up into the chambers where she croucheth! Grip the long, blood-reeking
hair, and drag her to mine eyes!"

Hecuba is pleading that he slay her forthwith, else she
will ensnare him again, when Helen passes through the
ranks of soldiers, gentle and unafraid, her raiment carefully ordered. She asks to prove her innocence, and at the
plea of Hecuba, who is prepared to answer her, is allowed
to speak. She says that she was bewitched by the goddess,
Cypris, to flee with Paris and, once the spell was broken,
had repeatedly striven to escape to Menelaus; she begs her
husband's harbor and comfort.

Hecuba derides her story of enchantment and capture
by force, declares she spurred Paris to his doom through
her own vain ambitions, and challenges the claim that she
has attempted escape. She and the other captives appeal
for Helen's death, and Menelaus turns fiercely upon his
wife; but when she kneels and wreathes her arms about his
knees, he merely orders her put aboard a ship other than
his own, swearing that she shall die upon the return to
Sparta. She goes, followed by the prayers of the captive

women that she, "with mirror of gold, decking her face so fair, girl-like," shall die at sea.

Talthybius returns, bearing the body of Astyanax; he tells Hecuba that Andromache has asked that the babe be buried upon the great bronze shield of his father. He goes to prepare a grave, and Hecuba cries out her sorrow anew over the broken body of her grandson. She wraps him in burial raiment, and the wailing women bear the body off on Hector's shield as flames rise in the city's ruins. Hecuba tries to die in the fire, but is restrained by soldiers.

Hecuba, with the other captive women, laments their plight to the dead:

"O Earth, Earth of my children; hearken! and O mine
    own,
Ye have hearts and forget not, ye in the darkness lying!
Surely my knees are weary, but I kneel above your
    head;
Hearken, O ye so silent! My hands beat your bed!
Even as the beasts they drive, even as the loads they
    bear,
We go to the house of bondage. Hear, ye dead, O
    hear!"

A great crash is heard, and the city wall is lost in smoke and darkness. A trumpet sounds, and the captive women go "forth to the long Greek ships and the sea's foaming."

Oedipus the King

BY SOPHOCLES

Born at Colonus, near Athens, probably in 495 B.C. In his plays he departed from the traditional form by introducing three actors on the stage, by writing his plays with certain actors in mind, and by being the first to employ Phrygian music. Only seven of over a hundred dramas of Sophocles

*remain today—his minor poems, elegies, and satiric dramas
have all perished. His works are outstanding for their skill-
ful construction, their profound interpretation of human
nature, and their tragic intensity. "Oedipus the King"
(known also by its Greek title, "Oedipus Tyrannos," and
in the Latin form, "Oedipus Rex") is the first of a trilogy
which includes the two other plays, "Oedipus at Colonus"
and "Antigone." Another great play by Sophocles is "Electra." It is interesting to note that Sophocles and Euripides
both wrote masterly plays with Electra as a heroine. The
date of Sophocles' death is said to be about the year
406 B.C.*

A throng of suppliants is gathered at the palace of King
Oedipus, at Thebes, to implore his aid against a mysterious
pestilence. They hope that again he will save them as
when, some ten years ago, he solved the riddle of the monstrous Sphinx. Laius, then King, had gone to consult the
oracle of Delphi but had been mysteriously slain on the
journey, and the vacant throne—with the hand of Laius'
Queen, Jocasta—had been given in gratitude to Oedipus,
a wandering young prince of Corinth.

Oedipus tells the suppliants that he already has sent
Creon, Jocasta's brother, to Delphi to learn what may be
done to save the city. As he speaks, Creon returns with
the oracle's counsel that Thebes will be cleansed of the
pestilence only when its people cast out the slayers of
Laius. Oedipus, who had heard little of the circumstances
of Laius' death, is told that he was killed by a band of
robbers; only one man of Laius' party returned, so shaken
that he remembered virtually nothing of the tragedy.
Oedipus pledges to avenge the murder and proclaims his
curse of exile upon the slayer, or slayers: ". . . let his days
be foul and life unfriended grind him till he die."

Oedipus, at Creon's urging, sends for the aged and blind
seer, Tiresias, to seek some clue to the slayer. The seer first
refuses to speak, telling Oedipus only: "With thee, with
thee there lies, I warrant, what thou ne'er has seen nor

guessed." But, aroused by the infuriated Oedipus' charge that Tiresias himself planned the murder, he declares: "Thou art thyself the unclean thing."

Oedipus answers that Creon must have influenced the seer to utter so incredible a charge, but Tiresias, his blindness mocked, declares that Oedipus is indeed the slayer, that he shall be revealed not as a stranger but as a Theban, and that, finally beggared and blinded himself, he shall crawl in exile, "the brother-father of his own children, the seed, the sower and the sown, shame to his mother's blood, and to his sire son, murderer, incest-worker." Oedipus orders the death of Creon, but the people are divided in their loyalty, and a threatened struggle is only averted by the intercession of Jocasta.

Jocasta, alone with Oedipus, attempts to comfort him by deriding the power of seers. To illustrate, she recalls another foretelling: an oracle once warned Laius that, should he have a son, he would be slain by the son's hand. She points out that Laius was really slain by robbers "at the crossing of three ways"; besides, his son, when three days old, was cast out to die on a desert mountain, his feet pierced to the rock by a blade of iron, so that he could not have fulfilled the prophecy.

But, at mention of the crossings, Oedipus' memory is stirred; he questions Jocasta further, then miserably tells her the following: he was reared by Polybus, King of Corinth, and his Queen, Merope, but, shaken because a drunken banqueter once questioned his birth, he had consulted an oracle which predicted that he would slay his father and wed his own mother. Anguished, Oedipus had fled Corinth to avoid such horror, and, coming to a crossing like the one described by Jocasta, had been crowded by a chariot. Angered, he struck a servant, then killed the master who attacked him, finally killing others of the party—just as the Queen had recounted.

The miserable Oedipus has left one single hope that he is not the slayer of his wife's husband: he sends for the lone living witness of the fight, now a herdsman, who had reported that a band of robbers, not one man alone, had

killed Laius. But, meanwhile, there comes from Corinth a
stranger to report that Polybus has died, and Oedipus and
Jocasta again are encouraged to believe the oracle false.
Oedipus voices his lingering fear, however, that he still
may defile his mother, Merope, and the stranger reveals
that Polybus and Merope are not his parents.

The stranger says that he himself had brought the child
to Polybus from a high glen of Kithairon, where he had
been a shepherd. Jocasta stands riveted in horror as he
goes on to say that the baby was found with a spike
through both his feet; thus Oedipus was named "Who
walks in pain." A shepherd, one of Laius' men, had given
the child to the stranger. Oedipus asks his name, and a
citizen believes the shepherd the same man who had escaped from Laius' slayer.

The citizen suggests that Jocasta is able to name him,
but the tortured Queen pleads with Oedipus to listen to
no vain tales and to abandon his quest for the truth: "For
God's love, no! Not if thou car'st at all for thine own life
. . . my anguish is enough. O child of woe, I pray God,
I pray God, thou never know!" Oedipus, nevertheless,
sends for the herdsman. Jocasta cries a farewell and rushes
into the palace. Oedipus scornfully declares that Jocasta
fears that revelation of his birth and name will mar her
pride, and there is hope that he may be of divine birth.

But now a terrified old man, the shepherd, is led in.
He is identified by the stranger as he who brought the
child. Oedipus is pointed out as the baby, now grown, and
the shepherd, realizing the monstrous tragedy, tries in vain
to silence the stranger. Then, under threat of torture, he
reveals that Oedipus is indeed the son of Laius, and had
been given to him by Jocasta to destroy—pity had forced
him to betray the trust.

Oedipus rushes insanely into the palace. Presently a messenger emerges to tell that Jocasta had fled into her old
bridal room, crying the name of Laius and the horror of
"husband from husband born and child from child." The
tormented Oedipus, sword in hand, had broken into the
room, to find her hanged. He had loosed the knot, then

tore from her breast a golden pin, plunging it into his eyes
and crying: "Out! Out! Ye never more shall see me nor the
anguish nor the sins of me!"

The blind and bleeding Oedipus is led forth from the
palace before the weeping throng, cursing Apollo and the
shepherd who had failed to give him death, pleading that
he be cast out of Thebes, as he had pledged, to wander
alone as a thing of unutterable evil.

Creon comes, and to him Oedipus begs care for his two
daughters. Creon brings them for the King's farewell, then
bids the blind Oedipus to return to his house while he
seeks the guidance of Apollo as to whether he shall banish
him. Oedipus pleads that his daughters remain with him,
but Creon removes them, with the final word to Oedipus:
"Seek not to be master more. Did not thy masteries of old
forsake thee when the end was near?"

Oedipus is led into the house, and the doors close behind
him.

Prometheus

BY AESCHYLUS

*Born at Eleusis in 525 B.C., he was the first of the three
great Greek tragedians (the other two being Sophocles and
Euripides). In his youth he was a soldier, fighting against
the Persians at Marathon and Salamis. In 499 B.C., when
he was twenty-six, his plays were first given at Athens; his
dramatic career continued for almost forty years. He is
supposed to have written about ninety plays, but only seven
are extant. These include the three plays constituting the
"Orestes" trilogy—"Agamemnon," "Choephoroe," and "The
Eumenides"—and "Seven against Thebes" and "Prometheus." Aeschylus traveled widely. In the development
of the drama he was a decisive innovator, introducing dia-
logue as an integral part of the play, and using costumes*

*and scenic decorations. His poetic works were lofty and
vigorous, with a strong sense of tragedy underlying them
all, and he was a master of contrasts and suspense. He died
in 456 B.C., and was buried at Gela.*

At the rim of the world of the gods, the demigod, Prometheus, is being punished for offending Zeus, the father
and ruler, because, in pity for weak mortals, he stole fire
from heaven to begin the civilization of mankind. Violence
and Force, ministers of Zeus, chain the silent Prometheus
to a rock which juts from the towering mountains at the
coast of a sea unknown to men. Only after they have
bound his limbs and departed does Prometheus lament his
lot to the Sea Nymphs, sent by the pitying Ocean to comfort him.

After reciting his earlier help to Zeus in overthrowing
rival gods and demigods, Prometheus explains:

"And by my counsel helped, the king of gods
 Hath recompensed me with these bitter pangs.
 For kingship wears a cancer at the heart—
 Distrust in friendship. Do ye also ask
 What crime it is for which he tortures me?
 That shall be clear before you. When at first
 He come upon the throne, he instantly
 Made various gifts of glory to the gods
 And dealt the empire out. Alone of men,
 Of miserable men, he took no count,
 But yearned to sweep their track off from the world
 And plant a newer race there. Not a god
 Resisted such desire except myself.
 I dared it! I drew mortals back to light!
 For this I am enchained upon the crag,
 The prey of winds and the beaks of ravenous birds.
 Behold me now, a god who pitied men,
 Himself denied the pity of the gods . . ."

Father Ocean also comes to comfort him, but offends
Prometheus with the rebuke: "You have no business to

befriend mankind in defiance of the gods." The chained demigod retorts: "And you have no business to come to me with unwelcome counsel." But he relents, and Father Ocean returns to his caverns at Prometheus' warning that he, too, may incur Zeus' wrath by his visit. The Sea Nymphs then bewail the plight of Prometheus: "All the mortal nations join me in my song of woe; and with them sings the pitying land, and with them sings the sea, and the rivers and springs and all growing things murmur afar their sympathy for thee."

Prometheus, saying, "I sent blind hopes into the hearts of men; I gave them fire, the seed of all the arts," then tells the Sea Nymphs how his gift "raised men from the brutish state and gave them the joys of life." He adds: "Eyes had they, and they saw not; ears, and they heard not; but, like shapes in dreams, they stumbled in wild confusion down the days and the years that they could not count. Houses they had not, but lived like ants in sunless caves underneath the earth. And I showed unto them how the stars rise in their mystery and plant flowers of fire in the night. And I gave them numbers, the foundation of wisdom; and memory, the mother of song; and language, the minister of thought . . ."

The Sea Nymphs suggest that perhaps Zeus may be right, that light cannot serve a race that is spiritually blind; that the beauty of men is unbeautiful, their strength little, and their hopes futile; their life is only a brief day, and death comes at its fairest hour. Prometheus makes no answer to this, but declares himself content, "for I know a secret which Zeus would fain wrest out of my heart. It is the secret that will overthrow him in the end. The Fates have so decreed. The reign of Zeus shall be ended in Time. For Time is stronger than Tyranny, and in the end both man and god must bow under the yoke of grief. The time has not yet arrived for me to disclose the plans of Destiny."

This secret he finally tells to the maiden Io, who comes, banished by the jealous Hera, queen goddess, when Zeus fell in love with her. By means of a relentless gadfly and the myriad following eyes of Argus, the spy god, Hera has hounded Io to this end of the earth, and Io asks Prometheus if she had not best throw herself into the sea.

He tells her that it is not appointed for her to die and that she should not grieve, for he knows the secret ways of Destiny whereby Zeus shall be destroyed. He explains, prophetically: "He shall in time beget a son more mighty than himself. . . . After many years of restless wanderings over the earth, thou shalt find peace at last. God shall make thee glad with the gentle touch of his hand. And thou shalt bear him a son; and from this son, in generations to come, there shall spring the mighty Heracles, deliverer of myself and all mankind."

But Prometheus, further enraged by Io's plight, challenges Zeus, declaring: "Yea, by his own son shall he be thrust down from his throne unless he learns from me how he can best save himself. For I alone know the secret; and I alone can foretell the means of his escape." Zeus sends Hermes to learn the secret, and the messenger arrogantly demands: "Answer me, thou sinner against god, thou champion of the despised human race, thou filcher of the divine fire—Zeus demands the answer at once. What son of Zeus shall cause him to be hurled from his throne in time to come?"

"Begone with thy speech that is fit for a servant instead of a god!" Prometheus retorts, in fury. "I had rather stand here, chained to the rocks, than grovel as a slave in the halls of Zeus. Retread thy steps in haste, and tell thy master that to all his commands I answer—nothing!"

Hermes tells the Sea Nymphs that Prometheus is mad, and warns them to return to their caverns and escape the fate that Zeus shall inflict upon him. Won by his courage and compassion, however, the sea maidens choose to suffer the fate of Prometheus, and in a chaotic explosion of the elements, with the mountains crumbling and storms raging, they and Prometheus sink into the abyss. Above the tumult is heard his voice:

"Aye, not in mere word but in real deed now the earth rocks through the air, and the thunders crash down with roar upon roar, and the eddying lightning splashes fire in my face, and the whirlwinds are driving the dust around about me, and the blasts of the tempests pile clouds over cloud, and the sky and the ocean are rolled into one in a passion of sound! O Beautiful Mother, O Earth, I call upon thee. And thee, too, I beseech, O world-encircling light, behold the injustice of my god-sent woes!"

Prometheus is overwhelmed, and with him his secret.

LATIN PLAYS

The Menaechmi

BY PLAUTUS

Born about 254 B.C., his full name being Titus Maccius Plautus. Very little is known about his early life. The only record we have states that he left his native town at an early age, settling in Rome where he was employed in a theater. He must have written many plays during his lifetime, but there are only twenty extant today, one of which is "The Menaechmi." All his plays were based on Greek originals, and, in many cases, were hardly more than translations; but Plautus was a masterly translator and his characters stand out so vividly that they have served ever since to remind us of the lives and social mannerisms of people of ancient times. He was a general favorite in republican Rome, and was especially admired by Cicero. Died in 184 B.C.

Almost identical twins were born to a merchant of Syracuse, in Sicily, and were named Menaechmus and Sosicles. Several years later, Menaechmus was stolen and carried off to the city of Epidamnus. The grieving grandfather, in his affection for the lost boy, gave his name to Sosicles. When the twins are grown to manhood, Menaechmus of Syracuse sets out in search of his brother. He arrives in Epidamnus, unaware that his twin brother is there also.

Here, the brother is first shown to be, with good cause, the despair of his jealous wife. He is seen leaving his house, berating his spouse as a shrew and a harpy, promising that she shall have good cause for her jealousy. He confides to

Whiskbroom, a professional parasite, that he has stolen his wife's mantle and is going to give it to his friend, Erotium, a trollop who lives next door.

The two go to Erotium's door, and the husband presents the mantle with many blandishments. He suggests that a fitting return would include a dinner for himself and Whiskbroom. Erotium agrees, and the two men go to the Forum for preliminary drinks while the meal is being prepared.

Meanwhile, the twin from Syracuse has arrived with Messenio, his slave. The latter warns him of the depravity of Epidamnus, urging an end to the search for the missing brother since their money is nearly gone. His master gives his purse for safekeeping to the slave who continues his warning against the cunning people of Epidamnus "who think nothing of accosting a stranger" and bilking him of his money, when Erotium steps out of her house and endearingly accosts the Syracuse Menaechmus, thinking him to be his brother.

She asks why he hesitates to enter when dinner is ready, and the confused twin asks her, quite formally, what business he has with her. Why, the business of Venus, Erotium replies coyly. Messenio whispers to his master that the lady undoubtedly is a schemer for his money, and asks her if she knows his master. He is Menaechmus, of course, replies Erotium. This amazes the twin, but Messenio explains that spies of the city's thieves probably have learned his name.

Erotium, tiring of what she considers foolery, tells Menaechmus to come in to dinner and bring Whiskbroom. Whiskbroom, he answers, is in his baggage—and what dinner is she talking about? The dinner he ordered when he presented his wife's mantle, she replies. He first protests vainly that he hasn't any wife and has just arrived in the city, then begins to realize the possibilities of a dinner and a pretty girl. He sends Messenio to the inn, giving him orders to return for his master at sunset.

After the meal, he leaves the house with a garland on his head and the mantle over his arm; Erotium has told him to have it retrimmed. He is chuckling over his luck—dinner, kisses and an expensive mantle—all for nothing, when the irate Whiskbroom, who has lost the Epidamnus twin in the Forum crowd, meets him and berates him for dining before he could arrive. Quite naturally treated as a stranger, Whiskbroom angrily rushes to tell the other twin's wife of the stolen mantle.

The Syracuse brother, further baffled because the unknown Whiskbroom addressed him by his name, is pinching his ear to make sure that he is awake when Erotium's maid comes out and hands him a bracelet to be taken to a goldsmith for repair. He suspects that something is amiss, and hurries off to the inn to tell Messenio of the happy shower of valuables that has been raining upon him.

Now the furious wife, told by Whiskbroom of her man's trick, rushes out of her house just in time to meet her husband returning from the Forum, expecting Erotium's banquet. She tells him to return the mantle or stay out of her house, and the husband goes to Erotium to get it, resolving to buy his sweetheart a better one. He is stupefied when she declares him a liar and a cheat, and tells him that already she has given him both the mantle and her bracelet. So the Epidamnus twin finds the doors of both his wife and mistress slammed in his puzzled face, and goes off to get the counsel of his friends.

The Syracuse Menaechmus returns, the mantle still over his arm, in search of Messenio, who has left the inn. His brother's wife sees him, and, assuming him to be her husband, demands that he confess his shame. He asks her of what he should be ashamed—and, furthermore, why she should address a total stranger so. He adds that he didn't steal her mantle, that a lady gave it to him. This is too much for the wife, who calls her father from the house. The father, also assuming that he is the husband, tells him that he must be crazy. This idea seems an excellent means of escape for Menaechmus: he feigns insanity so violently that the father rushes off for a physician, the wife seeks safety in the house, and Menaechmus goes off to resume his hunt for Messenio.

As the father comes back with a doctor, the real husband returns. He flies into a rage when his wife and father-in-law add to his troubles by implying that he is quite mad. His anger convinces the doctor of his insanity, and he summons slaves to bind him and take him to an asylum. Just then, Messenio appears, and, thinking the struggling husband his master, overpowers the slave. As a reward he asks for his own freedom. The husband tells Messenio that he doesn't know him, but by all means to consider himself freed; then he begins to suspect he may really be a bit crazy when Messenio tells him that he will return shortly to give him the money he has been safeguarding. Husband Menaechmus is not too addled, however, to profess ownership of the purse.

The husband goes to Erotium's house in further search of the mantle. The Syracuse twin returns, in his quest of Messenio, at the moment when the servant hurries back with his purse. His master upbraids him for having been gone so long, but the slave protests that he has just saved his owner from ruffians and has been set free. The master is pondering this new muddle when his twin appears from Erotium's house.

The two brothers rub their eyes in bewilderment on seeing each other, but explanations quickly bring recognition. They embrace. The happy master truly sets the slave free, and the brothers decide that the first Menaechmus shall go to live with his twin in Syracuse. Messenio announces an auction in the morning of the husband's goods, everything to go to the block—even the wife, if there be a buyer.